I0124909

Peasants and Revolution in Rural China

This book explores rural political change in China from 1850 to 1949 to help us to understand China's transformation from a weak, decaying agrarian empire to a unified, strong nation–state during this period. Based on local gazetteers, contemporary field studies, government archives, personal memoirs and other primary sources, it systematically compares two key macro-regions of rural China—the North China plain and the Yangzi delta—to demonstrate the ways in which the forces of political change, shaped by different local conditions, operated to transform the country. It shows that on the North China plain, the village community composed mainly of owner-cultivators was the focal point for political mobilization, while in the Yangzi delta absentee landlordism was exploited by the state for local control and tax extraction. However, these both set the stage, in different ways, for the Communist mobilization in the first half of the twentieth century. It argues that although landlordism was much less developed in North China than in the Yangzi delta, the North China plain was more hospitable to the Communist revolution, because the village community on the North China Plain, once fully mobilized and organized, enabled the Communists to secure sustained long-term support in human and material resources. It was based on the North China villages, and supported by the human and material resources generated from them, the Communists eventually grew into a formidable power able to defeat their adversaries and win the victory of 1949. Overall, this book is an important addition to the literature on the history of the Chinese Revolution, and will be of interest to anyone seeking to understand the course of Chinese social and political development.

Chang Liu is Senior Research Fellow at the Center for New Political Economy, Fudan University, Shanghai, China.

Routledge studies on the Chinese economy

Series Editor
Peter Nolan
University of Cambridge

Founding Series Editors
Peter Nolan, University of Cambridge and
Dong Fureng, Beijing University

The aim of this series is to publish original, high-quality, research-level work by both new and established scholars in the West and the East, on all aspects of the Chinese economy, including studies of business and economic history.

Peasants and Revolution in Rural China

Rural political change in the
North China plain and the
Yangzi delta, 1850–1949

Chang Liu

Routledge
Taylor & Francis Group

LONDON AND NEW YORK

First published 2007
by Routledge
2 Park Square, Milton Park, Abingdon, Oxon OX14 4RN

Simultaneously published in the USA and Canada
by Routledge
270 Madison Ave, New York, NY 10016

*Routledge is an imprint of the Taylor & Francis Group,
an informa business*

Transferred to Digital Printing 2009

© 2007 Chang Liu

Typeset in Times New Roman
by Graphicraft Limited, Hong Kong

All rights reserved. No part of this book may be reprinted or
reproduced or utilised in any form or by any electronic,
mechanical, or other means, now known or hereafter
invented, including photocopying and recording, or in any
information storage or retrieval system, without permission in
writing from the publishers.

British Library Cataloguing in Publication Data
A catalogue record for this book is available
from the British Library

Library of Congress Cataloging in Publication Data
A catalog record for this book is available

ISBN10: 0-415-42176-4 (hbk)
ISBN10: 0-415-54422-X (pbk)
ISBN10: 0-203-96241-9 (ebk)

ISBN13: 978-0-415-42176-8 (hbk)
ISBN13: 978-0-415-54422-1 (pbk)
ISBN13: 978-0-203-96241-1 (ebk)

To my wife and my son and in memory of my father

Contents

List of illustrations

Acknowledgments

I have been indebted to many individuals and institutions in the long course of completing this study, from its dissertation stage to the final completion. First, I would like to thank the History Department, the Center for Chinese Studies, and the Graduate School of University of California at Los Angeles (UCLA) for providing me with financial support over years which enabled me to finish my graduate study at UCLA. Advice and comments from the professors of my dissertation committee, Michael Mann, Richard von Glahn, and Scott Waugh, made my dissertation writing encouraging and rewarding. I owe a great debt to my dissertation advisors, Professor Kathryn Bernhardt and Professor Philip Huang, who have read every draft of my dissertation and also advised and encouraged me at various stages of the book. Their critical and constructive comments greatly sharpened my arguments and have improved the presentation of the book.

My sincere thanks also go to Bai Nansheng, Cao Jinqing, Chen Jianhua, Chen Ping, Chen Xiwen, Cheng Hong, Cheng Nianqi, Cui Zhiyuan, Clayton Dube, Patrick Dowdey, Du Ying, Richard Gunde, Christopher Isett, Bruce Jensen, Jin Guantao, Jin Zhongren, Stephen Lesser, Li Huaiyin, Li Peidong, Liu Qingfeng, Lu Hanchao, Pan Ming-te, Pu Guoqun, Qin Hui, Bradly Reed, Jonathan Shao, Pamela Siska, Matthew Sommer, David Wakefield, Wang Qingjia, Wei Chengsi, Michael Wilson, Xu Xiaoqun, Zhang Letian, Zhang Rongming, Zhou Guangyuan, Zhou Qiren, Zhou Yuming, and Zhu Hong for their comments, help, and encouragement at different stages of this study.

Professors Jian Chen, Joseph Esherick, Elizabeth Perry, Peter Purdue, Keith Schoppa, and Mark Selden have read all or part of the manuscript. Their comments and encouragement deserve my special thanks.

Most parts of Chapter 8 were published in *Modern China* (2003: 3–37), I thank the journal for allowing me to reuse them in this book. I also thank Stanford University Press and Routledge for allowing me to reproduce materials from their previous publications in Table 1.9 and Map A.1 of this book.

I am deeply grateful for the generous support I received from the Center for New Political Economy at Fudan University and its director, Professor

Shi Zhengfu, during the last stages of my work. Also to Dr. Wang Xiaoqiang for recommending my book to Professor Peter Nolan and his book series. In addition, I want to thank Professor Peter Nolan, Peter Sowden, the editors at Routledge, and the editorial committee of Routledge, for their acceptance and publication of this book.

Finally, I wish to express my deepest gratitude to my parents and especially to my wife Shanshan and my son Jinshi. Without their wholehearted support it would have been simply impossible for me to complete this study.

Introduction

Toward a multi-regional comparative study of rural China

This study deals with two aspects of rural political change in China during the second half of the nineteenth century and the first half of the twentieth century—the changes at the local and communal levels as well as the changes in state-rural society relations. The areas under its inquiry are the North China plain and the Yangzi delta (Map I.1). It is a comparative study of the two macro-regions as well as of rural political changes experienced by the two regions under different political regimes, including the Communist forces.

With few exceptions, the study of rural society in modern China usually focuses on a particular area. This tradition of local study has dominated the field of social and economic history and has also restricted scholars for many years. Up to now, the two most studied rural areas have been the North China plain and the Yangzi delta.[1] One obvious reason for this is the availability of source materials: these two areas happen to be the richest in this regard. A more substantial reason is the importance of these two areas in modern Chinese history. The North China plain was the major base of the Communist forces during the War of Resistance against Japan (1937–1945) and the Civil War (1946–1949). The Yangzi delta, on the other hand, was the core area of Nationalist control before and after the War of Resistance, and also the core of Japanese occupation during the war. In addition, these two areas exemplified two different rural economies: the North China plain possessed a relatively self-sufficient agrarian economy, whereas the Yangzi delta had a highly commercialized one. Scholars have also been interested in exploring the political implications of these two very different rural economies.

Although the Communist revolution was the most significant event that swept rural China during the period covered by this book, the revolution is usually treated as a subject matter of its own, independent of the study of rural society. To be sure, for many scholars, the study of the latter is to provide a better understanding of the former, and this is especially true for the study of rural North China.[2] But, in general, the revolution is perceived as a radical departure from traditional society, and this perception encourages people to focus on the differences between the revolution and existing rural

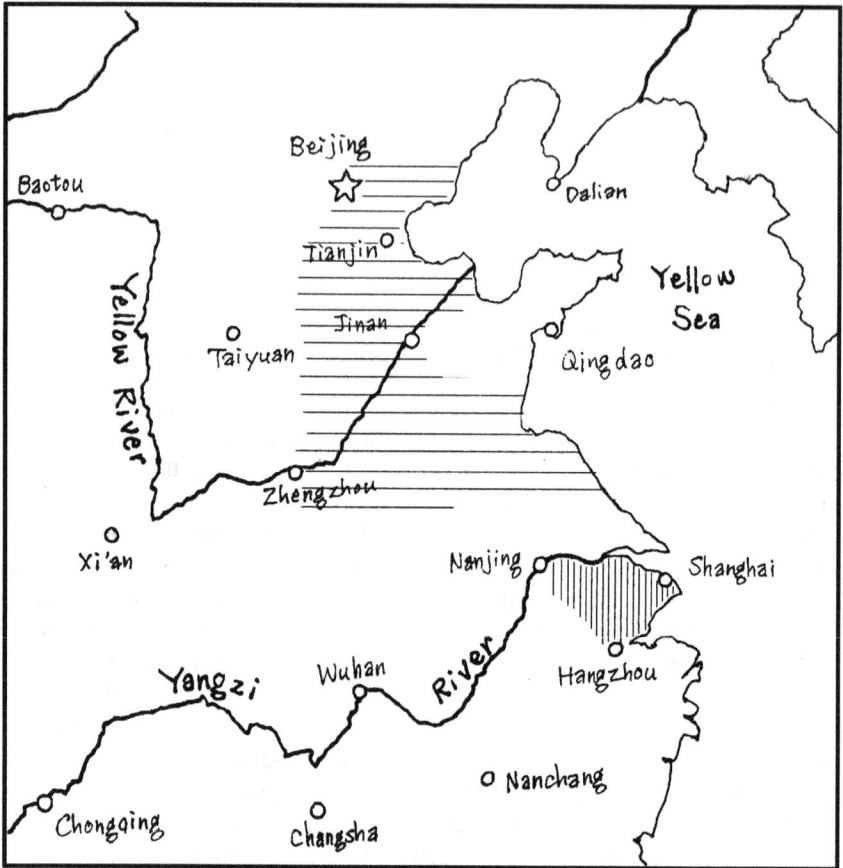

	North China plain
	Yangzi delta

Map I.1 The North China plain and the Yangzi delta.

conditions rather than exploring connections and linkages between this historical conjuncture and the long-term changes of rural society.[3]

Similar to the study of rural society, the study of the Communist revolution is also locally oriented, focusing on South China (Jiangxi and Hunan provinces in particular) during the Nanjing period (1927–1937) and North China (mainly the North China plain) during the War of Resistance. The reason for this shift of geographical focus can be attributed to the fact that during these respective periods the revolution was most sweeping and successful in these areas.

The advantage of concentrating on a single area, while distinguishing between long-term changes and the revolution is obvious: narrowing down our focus can help us to piece together a more detailed and accurate picture. Past scholarship has already produced many important works on both areas (the North China plain and the Yangzi delta) and in both subjects (the study of rural society and of the revolution).[4]

These achievements should not blind us, however, to the disadvantages of such an approach: narrowing down our focus may also lead us to lose sight of the bigger picture. For example, without a systematic comparison between the North China plain and the Yangzi delta, we cannot satisfactorily answer why the former became the hotbed of peasant collective resistance and the latter the core of government control. Similarly, if we do not relate the Communist movement in rural North China to the previous long-term changes, we cannot correctly assess to what extent the revolution departed from these changes and in what sense, if any, it benefited from and championed them. As for the revolution itself, if we focus only on the areas where it succeeded while neglecting the areas where it failed, we cannot adequately explain why it succeeded in some areas but failed in others.

Thus, a comparative study that covers different macro-regions and relates the revolution to long-term changes is indispensable. The ambition of this book is to pioneer a study of this sort. The reasons the North China plain and the Yangzi delta were chosen for a comparison are the same as those that have previously interested many scholars: the rich source materials (and also the rich scholarship) of the two areas and their close relevance to the major trend of modern macro-history. One further reason is that the Yangzi delta had *never* played a significant role in the Communist revolution. Though the Communists also made great efforts to launch and sustain revolution there before and during the War of Resistance, their efforts yielded nothing consequential. Largely because of this, the Communists' efforts in this area have long been ignored. However, the futility of the Communists' efforts in the Yangzi delta can be a perfect foil to their very success in North China. By comparing the two we can certainly shed new light on the Communist revolution.

On the whole, therefore, this study intends to answer the following questions: What differences were there in long-term political changes between the North China plain and the Yangzi delta?; What differences were there in political mobilization between the Communists and other political forces in these two areas?; And what differences were there in the Communist revolution in the two areas?

Before starting the empirical study, some theoretical issues about the state and the revolution need to be addressed. For peasants and rural society, both the state and the revolution were outside factors; nonetheless, both exerted great influence on rural China. Compared to peasant society, which was the *thing-in-itself*, they were highly organized and purposeful forces and hence the *things-for-themselves*. In local studies, they are usually treated as self-regulated agents and autonomous outsiders rarely subject to local conditions. However, in comparative studies, this assumption has to be cast aside first.

Redefining the state

The state occupies the center of scholarly attention in the study of rural political change in modern China. It is generally agreed that modern state-making, or state strengthening, is the driving force behind the changes in state–society relations and rural politics.[5] In the literature of social sciences, state-making refers to the rise of the modern nation-state. This process is characterized by the rapid expansion and penetration of state power into local society and the strengthening of state control over the local populace and resources (Tilly 1975a). All these phenomena were observed, to be sure, in modern China and they had a great impact on rural society. They thus certainly deserve serious scholarly attention.

However, the theory of state-making tends to define an autonomous state power and a one-way relationship between state and society, especially when it is applied to local studies. Once we engage in a comparative study of different regions, we find the notion of an autonomous state of little help in answering questions raised by geographical comparisons. For example, on the North China plain since the late Qing, the state continuously had exploited village communities as an institutional means to mobilize rural resources and to carry out various modernization projects, but this did not happen in the Yangzi delta. Why did the state behave so differently? To find the answer, we should examine the concrete state–society relations in these two areas, rather than resort to the notion of an autonomous state. In other words, we have to redefine the state.

On the North China plain, the natural village was a large, nucleated community, composed of mainly owner-cultivators. This type of community organized its residents into an insular group and marked out the primary boundaries of their social intercourse. In the Yangzi delta there was no rural community of this type. Rural society was torn by the profound stratification between absentee landlords and tenant-peasants and rural community was shaped by the scattered pattern of residence but integrated more tightly by absentee landlordism and market forces into a larger market network. This basic difference in communal structure and class formation determined the different strategies of state-making and also the different patterns of rural political change in the two regions. On the North China plain, the village was the focal point of political control and mobilization, whereas in the Yangzi delta, absentee landlordism and class structure were exploited by the state for social control and tax extraction. This comparison shows clearly that before the state could exert its influence on local society, it was first subject to the conditions of local society. In this sense, the state is not an autonomous power immune to local influences; rather, it is always *locally* defined. This is especially true in a large and geographically diverse country like China.

To redefine the state, we therefore must consider a two-way relationship and the continuous interaction between the state and society. Through this interaction, the state not only impacted local society, it was also conditioned *by* local society. In different areas, the state, in response to particular local conditions, behaved differently and the state–society relationship thus varied. To study state–society relations and rural political change in a particular area, we should first examine local conditions such as communal structure and social formation, for these factors defined the local political arena and pre-conditioned state–society relations.

Rethinking the revolution

The Communist revolution is generally considered to have been a radical departure from old society, old conditions and old practices. The separate study of the revolution and long-term rural changes has reaffirmed this perception. It is true that the Communists introduced many radical changes into rural China. However, once the Communists had established their political rule in an area (no matter how small this area was), it actually functioned as a state. Their relations with local society were therefore governed by the logic that governs state–society relations universally; and their policies and strategies for mobilizing, organizing and controlling local society were also conditioned by local society. Because of this, a certain dimension of continuity should be found between the revolution and the old society. This continuity, however, can be seen clearly only through a comparison of the revolution with the long-term changes.

For example, during the War of Resistance against Japan, the Communists established their resistance bases on the North China plain and vigorously enlisted peasants' support for the revolution. With regard to its basic strategy, Communist mobilization did not differ fundamentally from that of previous states and political forces. The Communists also exploited the village as an institutional means to organize peasants and mobilize resources. They actually moved even further. By organizing everyone tightly into his/her village community and making all taxes the village's collective responsibility, they changed multi-layered state–society relations into a bilateral state–village relation. The village community, thus effectively organized and mobilized, became the real base that empowered the Communists to finally win the 1949 revolution. Similar continuity can also be found in the Yangzi delta. Here, once the Communists had established their guerrilla regime during the war, they too, as this study will show, made use of absentee landlordism to mediate landlord–tenant conflicts and to ensure tax collection.

These interesting phenomena drawn from an interregional comparison prompt us to rethink the revolution in terms of *continuity*. The revolution pursued by the Communists was not just a radical departure from the past, it also maintained a dimension of continuity with the past. By combining the two, i.e., adapting itself to the existing situation and exploiting certain crucial and well-established institutions and practices, on the one hand, and introducing new changes, on the other, the Communists often gained an edge on their opponents and competitors. Without this, their revolution could scarcely have survived the bitter struggle with its adversaries, let alone succeeded.

Even so, the revolution did not succeed everywhere. The real base from which the Communists steered their revolution to its final success is rural North China. To find out why the revolution succeeded here, we should ask why it failed elsewhere, such as in the Yangzi delta.

Past scholarship on the revolution has emphasized either structural factors, such as class structure and socio-economic conditions, or the efforts made by human agents, i.e., Communist maneuvering (Huang 1991: 324). Neither approach can sufficiently explain why the revolution succeeded in North China while failing in the Yangzi delta. According to past scholarship, it seems that conditions in the latter were more, or at least no less, conducive to a successful revolution, because here landlordism was more developed and the conflicts between landlords and peasants were much more intense and widespread than in North China; also, there was no lack of Communist maneuvering. However, the Communists scored no real success despite these favorable objective conditions and the great efforts they made here.

To seek the real answer, we have to understand that the revolution is a long-term struggle, rather than a simple function of socio-economic structure or an immediate creation of agents' activities and maneuvers such as transitory insurrections. It needs to be built up step by step through continuous interaction and exchange between the structure and agents. For this cause to grow and succeed, the real crucial factor was *long-term support* in human and material resources. From the practical angle, the capacity of this support of a local society was more important than other socio-economic factors (such as class structure) in determining the outcome of a revolution; and without this support, no human efforts alone can make a successful revolution. The point can be made most strikingly by comparing the revolution in the Yangzi delta with that on the North China plain. In the Yangzi delta, though the Communists could easily stir up peasant resistance against landlords, they could not, as we will see, obtain long-term support in resources from the countryside. In North China, the fully-mobilized and well-organized villages enabled the Communists to secure this support. It is this major difference that determined, to a great extent, the success of the revolution in North China, and its failure in the Yangzi delta.

1 Comparison of rural communities in the North China plain and the Yangzi delta

A Chinese rural community is a human settlement that occupies a finite physical space and also provides a tangible social space and source of identity. Numerous rural communities constitute the building blocks and organic cells of rural China. However, rural communities vary from each other significantly with different regions due to different geographical, ecological, social, and historical factors. This chapter surveys and compares rural communities on the North China plain and in the Yangzi delta in the late Qing period.[1] Although both regions have long been under a common sovereignty, the geographical and social settings of the two regions differ substantially, thus two distinct types of rural communities have emerged.

Villages on the North China plain

On the North China plain,[2] the basic rural community was a natural village. Generally speaking, a natural village there was a compact and nucleated rural settlement with an average size of a hundred or more households. To a great extent, this was a self-contained world to its residents, of whom the majority were owner-cultivators. The villagers' major social activities were carried on within this world, and various networks and groupings were set up for these activities. The most important of these that organized the whole village as a collectivity was the village-wide religious association. Before the twentieth century, this village-wide association took care of all public affairs, and its councilors provided *de facto* leadership for the village. Thus, before the twentieth century, the social landscape of the North China plain was made up, to a large extent, of a multitude of such self-governed, autonomous village communities.

The formation and composition of North China villages

On the North China plain, a natural village was physically characterized by a relatively large (in comparison with its counterparts elsewhere in China), compact and nucleated settlement. In the village, all the households lived close to each other. Their houses were built closely together to form a

Table 1.1 Village size in six North China counties, *c.* 1800s

County[a]	No. villages	Total households	Average size
Tengxian	1,647	91,456	56
Guanxian	333	22,160	67
Engxian	508	30,544	60
Liangxiang	117	7,624	65
Fengren	845	50,749	60
Luanzhou	1,347	75,697	56
Total/Average	4,797	278,230	58

Sources: *Tengxian xuzhigao*, 1968 [1911]: 7–38; *Guanxian xian zhi* 1968 [1843]: 172, 324–5; *Engxian zhi* 1968 [1909]: 30, 62; *Liangxiang xianzhi* 1968 [1924[b]]: 54–9, 125; *Fengren xianzhi* 1968 [1892]: 162–187; *Luanzhou zhi* 1969 [1898]: 323.

[a] Of these six counties, the first three are in Shandong Province, the last three in Zhili (Hebei) Province.
[b] The number of villages and population figure of Liangxiang are from 1889 and 1888 respectively.

compact whole, separated only by streets or lanes (Fukutake [1950] 1976: 380–381; Hsiao 1960: 14; Gamble 1963: 11; Huang 1985: 65). This residential pattern, along with the large size of the village, formed the two morphological characteristics of North China villages.

On average, a North China village contained about 100–150 households. A foreign observer in 1899 wrote that in a district of Linqing County, Shandong Province, 64 villages were to be found. Among them, the smallest had 30 households and the largest had more than 1,000. The average number of households was 188 (Smith 1899: 19). However, judging from contemporary local gazetteers, the village size was much smaller than this figure. Table 1.1 shows the average village size in six North China counties cited in late-Qing local gazetteers.

The substantial gap in size between these villages, as cited in local gazetteers and found from field observations, can be attributed to the fact that the figures drawn from county gazetteers were derived from official household registrations, which usually under-reported population size. Since there are few first-hand sources shedding light on village size during the Qing, we must reconstruct the late-Qing picture by referring to data collected during the Republican period (1912–1949). Most of these data are drawn from field studies by modern social scientists, they are certainly more reliable. For example, field studies done in the 1920s and 1930s show that in Dingxian, the average village size was 146 households, while in Tangxian and Luancheng county, the figures were 170 and 140 households respectively (Li Jinghan 1933: 25–26; Fukutake [1950] 1976: 378–379). These three counties were all in Hebei Province. Another investigation, based on a survey of 2,740 Hebei villages, reports the average village size was 103 households (Fukutake 1976). According to an estimate made by the Mantetsu Investigation Department,

Table 1.2 Size of 33 North China villages,[a] 1930s

Village group	No. village (%)		No. household (%)		Average size
< 50	1	3.03	29	0.61	29
50–100	10	30.30	855	18.06	86
101–150	11	33.33	1,324	27.97	120
151–200	5	15.15	924	19.52	185
> 200	6	18.18	1,602	33.84	267
Total/Average	33	100.00	4,734	100.00	143

Source: Philip Huang (1985: 314–320).

[a] These 33 villages were located in 26 counties: of these, 21 were in Hebei and 5 in Shandong.

the average Shandong village had 137 households (see also Fukutake 1976). During the late 1930s and early 1940s, the Mantetsu ethnographers carried out detailed investigations of 33 North China villages (Table 1.2). Of these villages, the smallest had 29 households and the largest had 331. The total number of households in these 33 villages was 4,734, giving an average village size of 143 households.

One can argue that these data drawn from the Republican period cannot represent the situation during the late Qing due to demographic change. To be sure, we should take population growth into consideration. According to the population data available, between 1850 and 1933 the population of Hebei and Shandong increased about 39 percent, from 56,528,000 to 78,700,000 (Huang 1985: 322).[3] Suppose, during this period, the household number in these two provinces also increased at the same rate while the number of villages remained the same. At this rate of growth, the average size of North China villages in 1850 would still have been above 100 households. This figure is still obviously much larger than that drawn from the local gazetteers.

Along with the large size, another characteristic of North China villages was the compact and nucleated residential pattern. Both characteristics were the product of a particular combination of ecological, social, and historical conditions. Fukutake Tadashi maintains that these characteristics were closely related to village collective defense, and had little to do with the agricultural production (Fukutake 1976: 380–381).[4] In contrast, Philip Huang holds that the threat of floods and waterlogging dictated the residential pattern of North China villages: villagers built their homes in a cluster on high ground to guard against and also to cope collectively with flooding (Huang 1985: 64–65). Obviously, the two factors presented here were complementary. The formation of North China villages was attributable to both factors. Map 1.1 can give us a basic idea what a North China village looked like in the 1930s. The village is located in northern Henan.

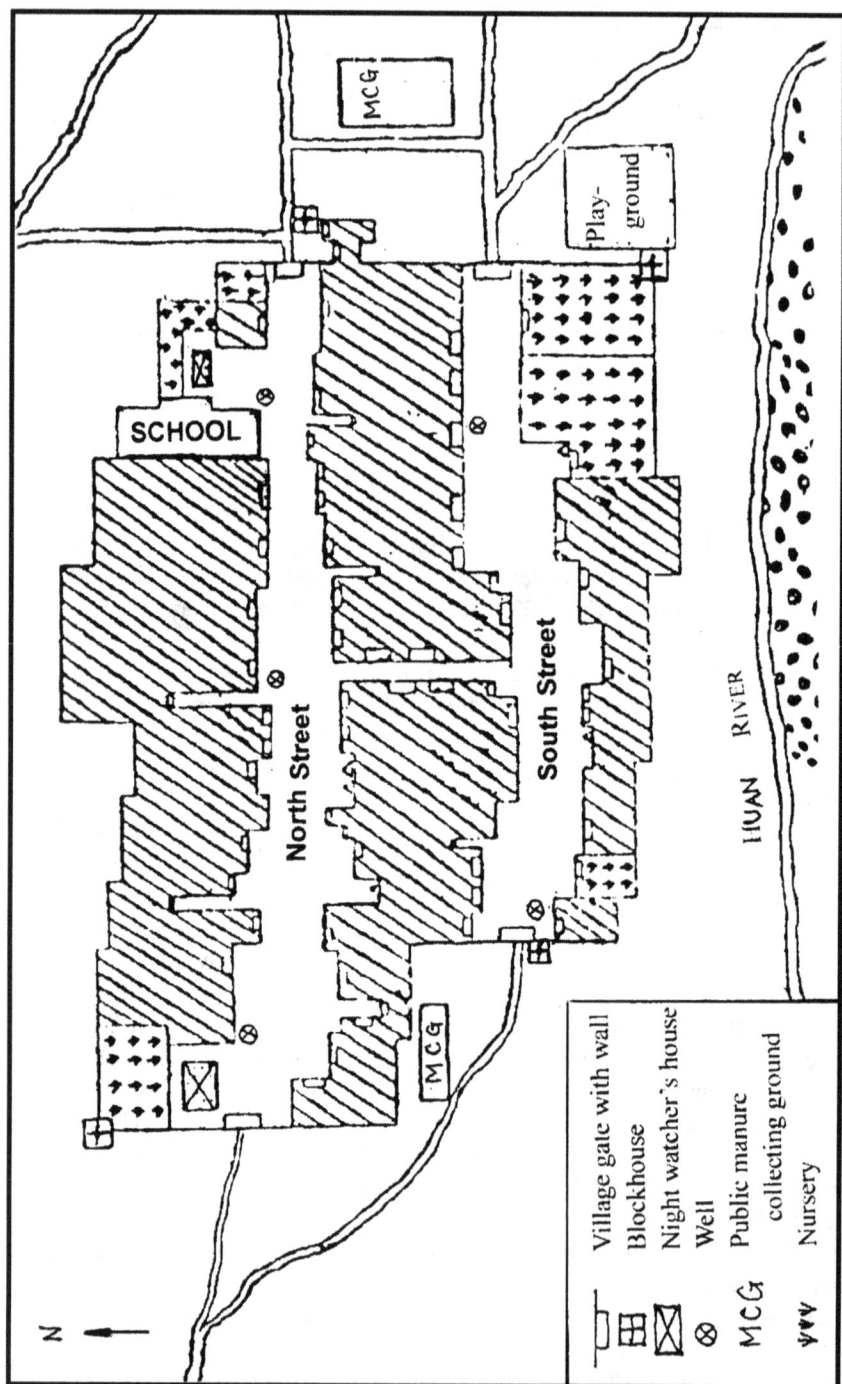

Map 1.1 Zhongshan village, Anyang, Henan, 1930s

Source: Sun Jiyuan and Sun Jiayou (1933: 3).

Note: In 1933, 115 households and 628 people lived in the village.

Legend:

Symbol	Description
	Village gate with wall
	Blockhouse
	Night watcher's house
⊗	Well
MCG	Public manure collecting ground
⋎⋎⋎	Nursery

SCHOOL

North Street

South Street

HUAN RIVER

Play-ground

MCG

N

Table 1.3 Land distribution in six villages, Dingxian, Hebei, 1928

Farmer category	Number of households (%)		Total land cultivated (mu) (%)		Average mu/hshd
Owner-cultivator	599	70.8	14,662.4	72.0	26.2
Part owner and part tenant	220	27.8	5,563.5[a]	27.3	25.3
Tenant	11	1.4	141.0	0.7	12.8
Total	799	100.0	20,366.9	100.0	25.8

Source: Li Jinghan 1933: 629.

[a] Of this land, 3,468.3 *mu* were owned, and 2,095.2 *mu* were rented. On average, a part owner and part tenant household owned 15.77 *mu*.

Table 1.4 Proportion of owner-cultivators in 25 North China villages[a]

Village group[b]	No. village	No. of households	No. of owner-cultivators (%)	
Type I	3	516	415	80.42
Type II	10	1,542	891	57.78
Type III	7	897	363	40.47
Type IV	5	804	624	77.61
Total	25	3,759	2,293	61.00

Source: Philip Huang (1985: 314–318).

[a] These 25 villages are located in 19 counties, of which 15 were in Hebei, and 4 in Shandong.
[b] Type I: Relatively uncommercialized;
Type II: Moderately commercialized;
Type III: Highly commercialized;
Type IV: Villages with developed rural industries.

Owner-cultivators made up the vast majority of the village population. This was true even in the 1930s. According to a nation-wide survey carried out by the Land Committee of the Nationalist Government in 1934–1935, the percentage of owner-cultivators in Hebei, Shandong and Henan provinces were 71.35 percent, 74.73 percent and 64.75 percent respectively. These figures were much higher than the national average of 47.61 percent (Tudi weiyuanhui 1937: 34).[5] Tables 1.3 and 1.4 provide village-level information about land distribution and the proportion of owner-cultivators in rural North China.

This pattern of landownership was clearly reflected in the local customs regarding the qualifications for village membership. Being asked how a person from Village A could qualify as a member of Village B, Hao Guoliang, the head of Sibeichai Village (Luancheng, Hebei), said that he must own both land and a house in Village B, and three generations of his ancestors must be buried in Village B (KC 1952: 3: 39). Similarly, a villager from Houxiazhai, Enxian County, Shandong, said that an immigrant who did not own land in the village could not be regarded as a village member even if he lived here (KC 1952: 4: 40).

Constrained by their economic activities, owner-cultivators were, as Huang's study demonstrates, the most insular stratum in the village. Their landholdings were located within the village and their production activities seldom brought them into contact with the outside world (Huang 1985: 220–223). A village composed mainly of owner-cultivators thus evinced a high degree of insularity and solidarity. Since most North China villages were dominated by owner-cultivators, this kind of community constituted the social landscape of rural North China. It formed a self-contained world for its residents, and not only provided them with an indispensable locus for their various social activities but also significantly defined their social intercourse.

The village as an organized community

The North China village was not only a residential area, it was also a community organized by various social activities. These activities included economic activities, cultural and religious activities, and activities related to public management, local defense, and collective dealings with the outside world.

Production and consumption were basic economic activities. Though in a pre-industrialized agrarian society these activities were basically conducted at the level of the individual household, people still needed cooperation and exchange beyond household scale on many occasions. In rural North China most of these cooperation and exchange, however, were confined within the village's boundaries. For instance, there were various kinds of mutual aid groupings in North China villages, such as famine relief associations, credit associations, mutual aid groups for weddings or funerals, and saving groups, etc.[6]

Besides organized mutual aid groups, villagers also assisted each other through various factor exchanges for production. Labor–labor and labor–draft animal exchanges (called *biangong* and *datao* locally) were two very common types of factor exchanges among villagers. These factor exchanges were usually conducted during the busy seasons and between those who had and those who did not have draft animals. House-building was another kind of labor exchange among villagers. The building of a new house usually involved village-wide cooperation. Villagers who gave help could expect reciprocity (Huang 1985: 220); however, these exchanges emphasized reciprocity rather than commercial calculation.

Of course, factor exchanges among villagers were not all limited just to this narrow range, remaining at a reciprocal level. As a matter of fact, they were conducted more extensively and intensively than one might expect, often taking the form of pure market transactions. Zhou Qiren's study of factor exchanges in Dabeiguan Village (Pinggu, Hebei) shows that even in this not highly commercialized village, the major factors, i.e. land, labor, and credit, were exchanged with an astonishingly high frequency and among a surprisingly wide range of villagers. For example, from 1927 to 1936, 97 of 98 total village households had been involved at least once in land transaction. In 1936, about 17 percent of the village's 158 labor units hired out. In the same year, villagers borrowed a total of 13,263 *yuan* from their fellow villagers, equaling 184.4 percent of the annual gross cash income of the village. All these transactions took place within the village rather than between the village and the local market town or between villages (Zhou 1992).

Religious activities were another major category of the village's social activities. Many organizations were set up in the village for this purpose. From field studies conducted by Japanese scholars in the 1930s and 1940s and the published results of these studies (*Chugoku noson Kanko chosa* [Investigation of customary practices in rural China]), we can find a full range of religious organizations and activities.[7] Of these religious organizations, it was the village-wide ascriptive religious association that organized the village as a whole. It was ascriptive because all members of the village were automatically included in the association. Before the twentieth century, this association was usually the only village-wide organization found in North China villages.

Organizing village-wide religious activities—such as collective prayers, maintenance of village temples, temple fairs and opera performances, and so forth—was of course the main function of the village-wide religious association. But it was never limited solely to this aspect.[8] Since it was the only village-wide organization, it also served as an *ad hoc* body to handle secular public affairs of the village. Because of this, it actually took on the role of the village's governing organ (Gamble 1963: 35; Duara 1988: 119). Village public affairs involved the villagers' common interests. These affairs might be generated by matters within or without the village community. Regardless of the source, they had one thing in common: they aroused public concern and necessitated collective choices and responses. Managing these public affairs was therefore a typical political process, carried out within the arena of the village and handled by villagers themselves.

In talking about the village religious association and its activities, we cannot ignore the role of village temples. In North China, every village had at least one temple of its own and most had several. For example, in Dongting *qu* (ward) (Dingxian Hebei), before 1900, there were more than 400 temples in 62 villages. Even after the radical secularization movement of 1914, there were still 104 temples in 1928.[9] Considering these 62 villages had a total of 10,445 households, the number of village temples before 1900 was astonishing. On average, each village had six or seven temples, or one for every 25 families (Li Jinghan 1933: 422–426).[10]

Temples were a very important institution in the village. The village-wide religious association always headquartered in a major village temple. Village meetings and gatherings were also held there.[11] These occasions were not just for religious events, they were also used to manage the village's secular public affairs as well. The following passage tells us exactly how religious and secular activities that were focused on the village temple were carried out:

> [E]ach village had its own temple, the deity of which had his/her date of birth . . . Sometimes the village gave an opera performance on this date and held a fair. This occasion was used also to make known village regulations, such as [prohibition against] permitting chickens, lambs, and oxen to harm the green crops, or the pilfering of crops by women and children. These prohibitions were written in large characters [on the temple wall]. Any who violated them were liable for punishment. This was true for the majority of wealthy and populous villages. But the festivals were not necessarily performed every year. Occasionally, when prayers were said in a temple on account of drought, excessive rain, or the presence of locusts, and no calamity ensued, opera performances were given as an expression of thanksgiving.
>
> (*Luanzhou zhi* [1898] 1969: 141–2)

As an organized community, the village served at the same time as an *arena* for communal activities, as an *intersection* between the village and the outside world, particularly the state, and as a *primary unit* for tradition creating and culture bearing. The importance of the village community in the organization of rural society was well recognized by the state. Though the imperial state repeatedly tried to organize rural society to fit into its sub-county administrative system, the natural village was always respected by the state and was usually taken as an independent unit. Before the twentieth century, changes in sub-county administration usually took place at the supra-village level, that is, in the realm between the county and the village.[12]

Village leadership and village autonomy

In rural North China, village-wide religious associations were usually managed by a group of village elders who bore titles such as *huishou*, *shoushi*, *xiangtou* or *dongshi* (literally, these titles mean association head, initiator, incense head, or director respectively; in reality, they were all village councilors, i.e. village leaders). Before the twentieth century these people constituted the informal village governance in the village which was responsible for both managing village public affairs and representing the village community to the outside world, especially the state. Smith, in an observation made in the closing year of the nineteenth century, classified the duties and functions of village leaders into three categories:

> The duties and functions of the headmen are numerous.[13] They may be classified as those which have relation to the government of the District,

those which relate to the village as such, and those which concern private individuals, and are brought to the notice of the headmen as being the persons best able to manage them.

(Smith 1899: 227)

All these duties and functions were performed by village leaders in a self-regulated manner with very little outside interference. In his study of North China villages, Huang gives us some concrete examples of this. In 1879, for example, a group of village *shoushi* brought a complaint before the county *yamen* in Baodi, Zhili (Hebei). The complaint arose from the attempted imposition of the *paijia* organization on the village by the *xiangbao* (the supra-village quasi official in this area). The complaint argued, "the business [in our community] of aiding the *xiangbao* in various tax chores had always been carried out by us, without error or failure." The *yamen* ruled in favor of the village leaders, noting that the old practice should be continued (Huang 1985: 225). This case clearly shows that the village *shoushi* actually handled village public affairs and represented the village in dealing with the state and its underlings. In the late Qing, this situation was well known to the local government, no serious attempt had been made to correct or change the situation (ibid.: 226).

Village leaders were not nominated or appointed by the state, they were endogenous leaders from their communities. This village leadership was by no means a formal and integrated part of the imperial administrative system. Rather, it was the product of village self-government. Gamble gives a lengthy account about how these village leaders emerged from village society. From his account, it appears that village leaders attained their posts through ability, family influence, and commitment to serving the community. These village leaders worked for the communal interests of their own village rather than for those of outside forces (Gamble 1963: 45–68).

In short, villages on the North China plain were nucleated settlements averaging 100–150 households, and before the twentieth century, they were autonomous communities governed by endogenous village leadership. These self-governed communities organized the rural populace, defined the local society, and dictated social activities of villagers. Political changes on the North China plain since the late Qing should be understood against this background.

Rural communities in the Yangzi delta

In the Yangzi delta there were few villages of the North China type.[14] The dominant pattern of rural settlement in the Yangzi delta was a small hamlet composed of about twenty households. Several hamlets typically formed a *compound* village. This multi-layered structure differed substantially from the compact and nucleated structure of North China villages. Furthermore, because of centuries of commercialization, rural communities in the delta were integrated into the market system. Commercialization also aggravated and accelerated social and economic differentiation. It reduced the majority of peasants to tenants or part-tenants, on the one hand, and drew most landlords into towns and cities, on the other. These differences in communal structure and social formation therefore shaped a different type of rural society.

The small hamlet as the dominant pattern of rural residence

Hamlets in the Yangzi delta were small, yet numerous. Possibly because of this, most Jiangnan county gazetteers did not bother to record them. From the few that did we find that a hamlet usually contained approximately twenty households.[15] For example, the average size of hamlets in Jiading County was only about 16 households (see Table 1.5).

Of course, one county is not necessarily representative of the whole delta. Since Qing local gazetteers seldom provide information about hamlet size, we have to refer to field investigations conducted in the twentieth century. Tables 1.6 and 1.7 show the average size of more than 500 hamlets located in different counties of the delta. Though the scattered information provided here is sparse, it gives us a picture that is not likely very far from the truth.

Table 1.5 Size of hamlets in Jiading county, *c.* 1911

No. of towns	No. of hamlets	Total households	Total pop.	Households per hamlet	Population per hamlet
30	2,964	46,964	220,632	16[a]	74[a]

Source: *Jiading xian xuzhi* (1930: 461–467).

[a] Both figures include towns (*zhen*). A town, of course, housed more people and households than did a hamlet. If we exclude towns from these statistics, the hamlet size would be even smaller.

Table 1.6 The size of 106 delta hamlets, 1940s

Location (County)	No. of hamlets	Total households	Total pop.	Hshd. per hamlet	Pop. per hamlet
Taipingxiang (Kunshan)	24	524	2,540	21	106
Baoanxiang (Wu)	68	1,575	7,004	23	103
Hejincun (Wu)	3	168	764	56	255
Xietangzhen (Wu)	11	524	2,426	48	221
Total/Average	106	2,791	12,734	26	120

Source: Huadong junzheng weiyuanhui tudi gaige weiyuanhui (1952), Part 2.

Table 1.7 The size of 400-odd delta hamlets, 1930s

Location (County)	No. of hamlets	Total household	Total pop.	Hshd. per hamlet	Pop. per hamlet
Beixia (Wuxi)	346[a]	5,982	27,164	17	79
Huibei (Wuxi)	32	1,560	10000-odd	49	–
Xugongqiao (Kunshan)	40-odd	(786)[b]	3,536	(19)[c]	–
Gaoyingxiang[d] (Changshu)	7	154	–	22	–
Weitingshan[e] (Wu)	19	303	1,444	16	76
Total/Average	423	8,482	–	20	–

Source: Kong Xuexiong (1934: 134, 139, 145); Nongfuhui (1934a); Shi Zhongyi (1933: 124).

[a] This figure includes four towns (*zhen*).
[b] This figure is obtained by dividing the total population by the estimated number of persons per household (4.5). This figure (4.5) is extrapolated from the data on the Jiading hamlets and the sample of 106 delta hamlets given above, which show an average of 4.7 and 4.56 persons per household respectively. I think it is reasonable to take 4.5 as the average number of persons per household.
[c] The source does not tell us the exact number of hamlets, though it does state 40 odd. I take 42 as the number and use this figure to divide total households, i.e. 786, and the figure in parentheses is the quotient.
[d] The data for Gaoyingxiang, Changshu, are drawn from an investigation made by the Rural Rehabilitation Committee (Nongfuhui 1934a: 21).
[e] Weitingshan's data are drawn from Shi Zhongyi (1933).

If we combine the two sets of data listed in Tables 1.6 and 1.7, the average size of the 522 hamlets was 21 households. We should note that the information on hamlet size discussed here is all drawn from twentieth-century sources. This means that the hamlet size in the late Qing due to the factor of population change would have been smaller, or at least similar to hamlet size in the first half of the twentieth century.

Small but numerous, hamlets in the Yangzi delta were scattered in the vast countryside, but were clustered along waterways. Map 1.2 can give us a basic idea of the topographical characteristics of the delta's hamlets. Two major factors contributed to the small size of the delta's hamlets and their scattered and waterfront pattern. The first was the delta's geographical setting and agricultural patterns; and the second, the long stability of the delta's rural society. For easy access to water (which was the chief means of transportation in this area), people built their houses along waterways. Furthermore, rice growing required closer tending than wheat, sorghum, and maize, and thus cultivators tended to live closer to their paddy plots. These two considerations imposed crucial limits on the size of delta hamlets; while a peaceful and stable society made these scattered and small sized hamlets viable.[16]

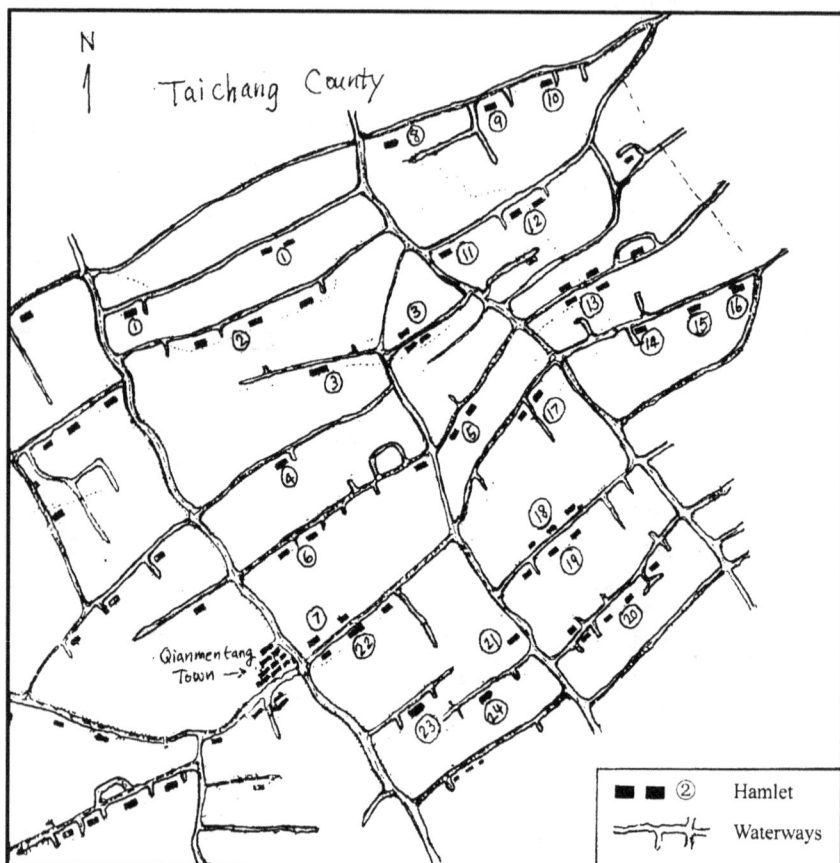

Map 1.2 Rural settlement in Qianmentang, Jiading, *c.* 1911

Source: Tong Shigao (1962 [1921]) *Qianmentang xiang zhi.*

Notes:
This is a part of the Qianmentang township (located in the northwest of Jiading County) which includes 6 *tu* (*tu* was also called *li*, a supra-hamlet unit imposed by the Qing state for administrative and taxation purposes. Detailed discussion of this Qing device should be found in Ch. 2). In 1911, 1,801 human souls inhabited here. Following are names of these *tu* and numbers of hamlets located in each *tu.*
Shibei 1 *tu*, Hamlets 1–3, 315 people (about 24 households in each hamlet);
Shibei 2 *tu*, Hamlet 4, 122 people (about 28 households in this hamlet);
Shibei 3 *tu*, Hamlets 5–7, 278 people (about 21 households in each hamlet);
Shibei 4 *tu*, Hamlets 8–16, 573 people (about 14 to 15 households in each hamlet);
Shinan 2 *tu*, Hamlets 17–20, 307 people (about 17 to 18 households in each hamlet);
Shinan 3 *tu*, Hamlets 21–24, 203 people (about 11 to 12 households in each hamlet).

According to *Jiading xian xuzhi* (1930), the average household size was 4,41 people. I used this figure to reconstruct household numbers in hamlets of different *tu* and put the results in parentheses. The total households in these four *tu* were about 408.

Compound village and multi-layered communal structure

The small hamlet in the Yangzi delta rarely constituted an independent community. Instead, hamlets are usually clustered to form what can be called a *compound* village. To understand the inner structure of this compound village, it is necessary to analyze concrete cases.

Huayangqiao is a small rural community in Songjiang County. In 1940, it had a total of 63 households clustered into four groups, each with its own name: Xuejiada (Xue Family Bank) with 9 households,[17] Hejiada (He Family Bank) with 7, Xubushanqiao (The Bridge at Xubushan) with 15, and Xilihangbang (the Western Lihang River) with 32. Xilihangbang was still further divided into three hamlets: Gaojiada (Gao Family Bank) with 13 households, Lujiada (Lu Family Bank) with 9, and Nanda (South Bank) with 10. These small groups were actually separate hamlets mainly composed of agnatic groups. Hejiada was made up exclusively of Hes of the same patrilineal line, while Gaojiada was made up by the Gaos, and Lujiada by the Lus. Xuejiada was originally comprised exclusively of five households of the Xues in 1940. Another four households in this hamlet had the surname Zhang; their grandfather had come there and settled as a beggar (Huang 1990: 147; see also MT, Shanghai 1940).

The six hamlets of Huayangqiao constituted a multi-layered community. Within this community, people distinguished themselves by their hamlet identity. To the outside world, however, they identified themselves with the community as a whole. A common communal identity was shared by all Huayangqiao residents and a fictive kinship network (this could only be found within a community, and usually did not apply to outsiders) encompassed all six Huayangqiao hamlets (Huang 1990: 145–148). This kind of multi-layered communal structure was obviously absent on the North China plain. Actually, it was quite unique, and there was no special term for this multi-layered community. Philip Huang thus uses the term "a cluster of villages [i.e. hamlets]" to refer to this Huayangqiao type of community in the Yangzi delta (Huang 1990: 148).

The type of rural community represented by Huayangqiao was common to the Yangzi delta.[18] Of the eight rural communities studied by Huang, all were larger than the hamlet size discussed above, with 52, 53, 55, 63, 80, 94, 209, and 360 households respectively.[19] However, as far as we know, at least some of these were compound villages. For instance, Sunjiaxiang, located in Wu County, had a total of 209 households. This large community was actually comprised of 29 separate and distinct hamlets, each with its own name (Hayashi Megumi 1943; cf. Huang 1990: 151). Similarly, Xiaodingxiang of Wuxi County actually was composed of three hamlets; namely, Xiaodingxiang (Small Ding [Family] Lane), Zhengxiang (Zheng [Family] Lane) and Yangmuqiao (Poplar Bridge), with 14, 45, and 21 households respectively (MT, Shanghai 1941: 18–19).

Of the eight communities studied by Huang, Kaixiangong (Kaihsienkung) was remarkable for its apparently large size. Fei Xiaotong (Hsiao-tung), who did a field study in this community during the 1930s, tells us that Kaixiangong was a natural village composed of the incredible number of 360 households. However, by examining the structure and history of this community, we find that it was a compound village similar to Huayangqiao. The local gazetteers show that 50 years before Fei's research, Kaixiangong was not a single "village." Rather, it was comprised of at least three distinct hamlets (see Appendix 1). These three hamlets belonged to different supra-hamlet administrative units; a situation that could be traced back even further to the mid-eighteenth century. The three hamlets became a single "village," i.e. under a common community name, Kaixiangong, only recently. Most probably, this occurred after the fall of the Qing and resulted from the collapse of the Qing rural administrative order. Since Fei did not refer to local histories in his study, he did not realize that Kaixiangong was originally not a single "village," but several distinct hamlets.

This history obviously had a profound impact on the internal structure of Kaixiangong. Fei shows that all of the households in Kaixiangong were clustered into four separate *yu*, forming four residential areas, one of which had its own name, Tanjiadun (Tan Family Mound). This situation was quite similar to that of Huayangqiao, and suggests that Kaixiangong was not a "natural village," but "a cluster of villages (hamlets)," i.e. a compound village.[20]

Communal activities at different levels of rural community

The multi-layered community performed different functions at its different layers. At the lower level, the hamlet was generally an agnatic group. On the one hand, as suggested by Fei, this group was a unit for social ceremony (Fei 1939: 85). On the other hand, as suggested by Huang, it was a unit for defining peasant social referents (Huang 1990: 148–149). The hamlet thus constituted the first circle of social intercourse. Participation in weddings and funerals was confined to the descent group, or hamlet, and seldom extended outside this group. Huang's investigation of Huayangqiao provides detailed insight into these matters (Huang 1990: 148–149). However, because of its small size, many social activities went beyond the hamlet's boundaries and exceeded the hamlet's abilities, demanding multi-hamlet cooperation. The compound village was thus called in to organize and handle diverse collective activities.

In the Yangzi delta, because of the region's topography, the water control system was very complex, and was made up of many levels. Huang points to three specific levels: the village level, the county level, and the level between the two (Huang 1990: 35–38). At the village level, however, water control very often required the cooperation of several hamlets. This situation resulted from a combination of the small-sized hamlet and *yu* lay-out. In many localities in the delta area, land was divided into *yu*, the size of which varied greatly. A *yu* could enclose as much as a 1,000 *mu* of land or as little as 10 *mu*.[21] According to Fei's description, water control under this *yu* system required a well-organized and concerted effort from those engaged in work there. Fei gives us a very detailed description of how people who worked in the same *jin* (large *yu* were usually further divided into several pieces of land which were called *jin* [*cien* locally]) organized the collective drainage.

For example, according to Fei, the North *jin* of the Xichang *yu* in Kaixiangong consisted of 336 *mu* of land. A common trench opened into a stream at the northern margin. Fifteen pumps could be installed at the opening, and each pump required three workers. The amount of labor contributed by each member of the *jin*, taking the household as a unit, was proportionate to the size of his land-holdings. The members of the *jin* were organized into 15 teams corresponding to the 15 pumps. The members of each team took turns annually to manage the pump. The position of chief manager, who had authority to determine when drainage should begin and stop, was also rotated among the teams. At the beginning of the year, the chief manager called the 14 other managers to a meeting. A feast was prepared as a formal inauguration. Whenever drainage was needed, the chief manager would give orders to the managers, who, early in the morning, would inform the workers on duty by beating a bronze brace. If anyone on duty did not show at the pump within half an hour, the other two charged to work on the same pump would stop their work, take the pivot of the pump to the nearest grocery and bring back cakes, fruits, and 53 pounds of wine. The cost of this meal was charged to the absent team member as a fine. If, however, the manager had failed to inform the absentee, he himself bore the responsibility (Fei 1939: 172–174).

This kind of elaborate water control system had a long history, and was very common in the delta. The following passage, quoted from a Qing source, tells the same story:

> After planting, if excessive rainfall causes flooding, the people must assemble paddle wheels to drain the water. These are called water carts [*dapengche*]. Each time there must be hundreds of them. People are distributed according to the amount of land, carts according to the number of people, and the amount of water drained depends on the number of carts. A marker is placed in the water and the level is checked constantly. The people take turns paddling the wheels, day and night without rest. There is a schedule by which the people assemble and disperse, and rules by which everything is regulated.
>
> (*Wujiang shuikao zengji*, cited in Bernhardt 1992: 35)[22]

If the people working in the same *yu* also belonged to the same hamlet, water control was the responsibility of a single hamlet. However, since hamlets were small, it was very common for the land in one *yu* to belong to and be cultivated by people from several hamlets.[23] Under these circumstances, water control became a multi-hamlet endeavor. As Bernhardt writes:

> Neighboring villages were in any event tied together by their common interest in maintaining the irrigation and drainage system and regulating the water level of their polders. Inter-village cooperation was especially critical, . . . when a polder needed to be drained during the summer rainy season.
>
> (1992: 35)

Through this frequent cooperation it was very easy to develop a close relationship and sense of community among those hamlets and their residents involved in the work.

Another factor linking neighboring hamlets was the religious activities in which several hamlets cooperated. Fei Xiaotong tells us that ten years before his investigation, there was a community-wide religious association in Kaixiangong which held an annual ceremony:

> [The meeting] would be held in the autumn after the harvest. It served as a thanksgiving to the gods responsible for the harvest and at the same time as a request for blessing for the coming year. The images of local gods would be seated among the people and an opera company would be invited to play on the stage constructed specially for the purpose. The village was divided into five groups, called *degi* [*taiji*], meaning "the foundation of the stage." Each group was responsible for the management and expenses of this gathering in turn.
>
> (Fei 1939: 103–104)

This collective religious activity was also a very important factor that linked neighboring hamlets, and gave the residents of these hamlets a sense of common identity. Kaixiangong itself was a good example of this.[24] Because of the importance of water control and religious activities in organizing the compound village, we can say that in a certain sense the compound village was a water control community and a religious community.[25]

Some important differences can be noted between the compound village of the Yangzi delta and the North China village. Though the compound village did undertake many collective endeavors which extended beyond hamlet limits, its functions were more limited than those of North China villages, in particular, its religious and political functions appear to have been far more circumscribed. This is evident in the ordering of public space. For instance, in both Kaixiangong and Huayangqiao, there were no special places for public gatherings (Fei 1939: 19; Huang 1990: 144–148). Temples in Kaixiangong did not function as a social and political center as they usually did in the North China villages. In Kaixiangong, there were two temples, located on the outskirts of the residential area, which were kept separate from everyday community life (Fei 1939: 20–21, 104–106).

Social formation and the town–country relationship

The rural community in the Yangzi delta was further differentiated from the North China village by its social formation, or class composition. In contrast to the situation in North China villages, in the Yangzi delta, the majority of rural residents were tenants or part-tenants. In many counties, tenants and part-tenants made up to 70 percent or more of farming population. Table 1.8 shows the tenant rate in ten Jiangnan counties, and Table 1.9 gives more detailed picture of the social formation in eight rural communities.

High tenancy rates indicate a high degree of social and economic differentiation within the rural population. In the Yangzi delta, it is very significant that this differentiation was also *spatially* displayed. Vigorous commercial and urban development during the Ming and the Qing period had led the majority of landlords to leave the countryside and move into the towns and cities where they could pursue commercial opportunities and enjoy the amenities of urban life. They left behind in the delta countryside an increasingly homogeneous tenant society. The 1883 edition of the Suzhou gazetteer described the situation as follows: "In Jiangnan, many 'smoking households (*yanhu*)' own great amounts of land. Of them, four to five-tenths live in cities, three to four-tenths inhabit the towns, and only one to two-tenths reside dispersed in the countryside" (Zhao Xixiao, "*Yaoyi yi* [On labor services]," quoted in *Suzhou fu zhi* 1883: 13:29b).[26] These developments are also evident in other sources: for instance, Table 1.9 shows that, of 966 households in eight rural communities, there were only five resident landlords (and not a single managerial farmer).

Table 1.8 Tenancy rate in ten Jiangnan counties, 1930s (%)

County	Tenant	Part-tenant	Agricultural laborer
Taicang	20	57	3
Fengxian	45	30	5
Qingpu	60	30	6
Wujiang	34	32	17
Kunshan	20	50	0
Jiading	30	40	0
Changshu	50	30	5
Yixing	31	48	8
Jiaxing	27	41	6
Pinghu	64	28	0

Source: Ministry of Industry (1933: 31–33); Feng Zigang (1936: 340); Zhu Xiaolong (1936: 38204–5).

Table 1.9 Social formation in eight Yangzi delta rural communities, 1930s

Category	Touzongmiao (Nantong)	Xiaodingxiang (Wuxi)	Yanjiashang (Changshu)	Yaojing (Taicang)	Dingjiacun (Jiading)	Sunjiaxiang (Wu)	Kaixiangong (Wujiang)	Huayangqiao (Songjiang)
No. household	94	80	55	52	53	209	360	63
Total cultivated *mu*	284	190	201	399	512	1,556	3,000+	550
No. resident landlords	3	0	0	0	0	2	?	0
No. managerial farmers	0	0	0	0	0	0	?	0
Cultivated land rented (%)	33.5	32.4	82.4	93.2	40.3	83.8	66	87.5
Composition of farm households (%)								
Owners	46.4	68.9	8.1	4.3	14.3	0	?	0
Tenants	50.0	31.1	91.9	93.6	85.7	97.3	?	100
Two-layered landownership	no	no	yes	yes	no	yes	yes	yes

Source: Adapted from Philip C.C. Huang *The Peasant Family and Rural Development in the Yangzi Delta, 1350–1988* (pp. 338–339). Copyright © 1990 by the Board of Trustees of the Leland Stanford Jr. university.

The spatial differentiation between landlords and tenant-peasants, how-ever, as we can understand, promoted closer economic integration of towns and the countryside. A good example was factor exchanges. While in rural North China factor exchanges were largely confined to the village, in the Yangzi delta, factor exchanges, such as land leasing and credit transactions, were rarely restricted to either the hamlet or the compound village. Rather, it occurred between rural communities and market towns, i.e., between tenant-peasants and town-dwelling landlords and merchants. On the one hand, land was rented from absentee landlords and credit was obtained from money-lenders who were all living in towns and cities. On the other hand, rents and interests were paid by tenants and debtors who were residing in the countryside. As Fei observed:

> [T]he relation between the town people and the villagers is mainly of an economic nature. It may, for example, be the relation between landlord and tenant, which under the present system of land tenure, is impersonal . . . When the villagers need external financial help, they usually resort to the system of rice-lending and usury.
>
> (1939: 275)

Contemporary field studies supported Fei's observation. For instance, sur-veys made by Japanese investigators in the 1930s tell us that in Dingjiacun, Jiading, 95 percent of rent went to towns and cities while 91 percent of credit came from towns and cities. And in Huayangqiao, Songjiang, only 4.3 percent of rents remained in the countryside and the rest was remitted to towns and cities where landlords lived (Cao Xingshui 1989: 149–150).

Commercialization also had a direct impact on rural communities. Though commercialization was driven by different forces,[27] it nonetheless pushed the peasant economy toward market-oriented behavior. According to Cao Xingshui's estimate, in the Yangzi delta, market rate for cotton was almost 100 percent, while the average market rate for cotton in cotton growing provinces was only 55 percent. Market rate for grain was 50 percent, more than double the average market rate of neighboring provinces, which was 23.5 percent (Cao Xingshui 1989: 153–155). Commercial developments greatly transformed the character of the rural community in the Yangzi delta. The rural community here was no longer a self-sufficient world. Instead, it had become more and more integrated into a larger social system through increasingly frequent and intensified intercourse and exchanges with towns and cities.[28] In this respect, no parallel development could be found on the North China plain, where the village was a self-sufficient and relatively closed world for their residents.

The different communal structures and social formations of rural com-munities shaped different patterns of communal politics. In the Yangzi delta, the rural community, whether hamlet or compound village, seldom was a self-governed entity managed by a strong endogenous leadership as in the

North China villages. Both attributes, self-governance and strong endogenous leadership, which were essential to the North China village were absent in the rural community of the Yangzi delta, because there was simply no real necessity for these institutional arrangements here.

Conclusion

On the North China plain, the natural village was a large, compact, nucleated settlement, composed mainly of owner-cultivators. It provided its residents with a basic locus and also defined their social life. The village *per se* constituted a relatively self-contained world. In the Yangzi delta, the dominant type of rural settlement was a small hamlet composed of 20 or so households. Several neighboring hamlets linked together to form a compound village. Due to long-term commercialization and profound social differentiation, the rural community in the Yangzi delta was both reduced to a homogeneous community composed mainly of tenants and part-tenants, and also integrated into a market system. Neither the hamlet nor the compound village was a self-sufficient world for its residents.

Different communal structures and social formations shaped different patterns of rural politics. On the North China plain, the village had long been a self-governed community managed by its endogenous leadership. But in the Yangzi delta, these institutional arrangements were absent in both hamlets and compound villages. Profound differences between rural communities of the North China plain and the Yangzi delta set different historical stages. Political change in these two regions since the late Qing, and especially in the first half of the twentieth century, must be understood against this basic backdrop.

2 State and rural society in the late Qing

Since the rural communities on the North China plain and in the Yangzi delta differed so markedly, the relationship between state and rural society in these two areas would certainly not be the same. However, divergence in state and rural society relations between the two macro-regions can only be seen clearly through a concrete and systematic comparison of the two areas. Dominated by the recent tradition of local studies, past scholarship has usually focused on a particular geographical area to study state and rural society relations.[1] This approach can help us uncover specific details of state–society relations in an area, nevertheless, it has its limitations. It can tell us much about the *hows* of state and society relations in a particular area, but it can tell us little about the *whys*. To explore the *whys*, we have to go beyond this approach and undertake a multi-regional comparison.

This chapter will examine and compare state and rural society relations on the North China plain and in the Yangzi delta during the late Qing from the perspective of *taxation*. As we know, taxation is a vital arena where state and society engage in an on-going negotiation, dispute, and compromise. Sometimes this mutual engagement can spill over into violent conflicts when agreement or compromise cannot be achieved on each one's "fair" share of national wealth. Compared to other aspects of state–society relations, such as administration or jurisdiction, taxation directly touches the lives of ordinary people. Everyone, i.e. every taxpayer, has to deal with the state through taxation. On the other hand, it is through taxation, that the state reaches down to grass-roots society and enters into direct contact with individual taxpayers. Taxation is therefore a very crucial and dynamic aspect of the state–society relations through which the relationship between state and rural society can be observed and studied. We will focus in particular on the differences of how the tax system played out in the North China plain and the Yangzi delta.

The characteristics of Qing taxation

Regular taxation

In the long history of imperial China, the Qing taxation system may be the simplest in both content and procedure. In Qing times, after the tax reforms of the Yongzheng period (1723–35), the labor service tax was commuted and levied on owned land. This was called *tanding rudi* (lit. amalgamating the labor service tax [*ding*] and the land tax [*di*]) in Qing terminology.[2] Thereafter, the land tax became the only regular tax landowners had to pay to the state.[3]

Along with this reform, the tax-collecting procedure was also greatly simplified. The new procedure, called *lishou guanjie* and *zifeng tougui*, required individual taxpayers to deliver their tax money (*diding*) and tax grain (*caoliang*) directly to government coffers (called *gui* or *lianggui*). Theoretically, no intermediaries, neither government functionaries nor local agents, were involved in this procedure, so as to prevent any kind of abuse.[4] In many areas, the county government even set up moveable chests in the distant countryside during the tax seasons to ease the delivery chores of rural taxpayers. Under these arrangements, taxation was reduced to a simple affair between the state and the individual taxpayer (landowner). The rural community bore no collective responsibility for governmental taxation. This formed a sharp contrast to the situation of the previous dynasty, the Ming dynasty.[5]

However, the simplicity and easiness of Qing taxation seemed to benefit only the taxpayers. For the government it was not simple and easy at all, because under this arrangement, the government had to deal with numerous taxpayers directly. This was no doubt a formidable task for the local magistrate, who was the administrator responsible for collecting taxes from myriads of taxpayers residing in the countryside. Especially if we take into consideration the limited human and material resources he commanded and the nature of the technology at that time. For these reasons, the revenue department was always the busiest one in any county *yamen*. Although the two tax collecting seasons ran for only four to six months each year,[6] the revenue department worked all year round and maintained a large working staff to ensure government taxation.[7]

The regular taxation system of the Qing was designed to meet the regular financial needs of the Qing state during peaceful times within the context of a relatively stable agrarian economy. During the first two hundred years of the dynasty, this taxation system worked fairly well without any substantial changes because of general social stability (He Lie 1972: 11; Wang Yeh-chien 1973: 27). However, this situation was not always true in different regions because the tax rate, even for regular taxation, differed greatly in different areas. While some areas enjoyed a light land tax, other areas suffered from a heavy land tax. This translated into substantial regional variation in taxation. Various taxation practices thus emerged in different localities to cope with local conditions. Moreover, since the late Qing, differentiation in local taxation practices had been furthered by irregular taxation.

Irregular taxation

From the mid-nineteenth century both the domestic and foreign situations dramatically changed. Late-Qing China witnessed large-scale domestic rebellions, increasing foreign encroachments, and a series of economic and political crises. The revenue derived from regular taxation could no longer meet the government's rapidly expanding expenditures.[8] Many irregular taxes thus came into being to meet these new needs. They had a significant impact on the Qing taxation, and a series of substantial changes followed accordingly.

The irregular tax differed from the regular tax in two ways: first, it was unpredictable, therefore, it was not possible to budget the irregular tax in the beginning of each tax year, as was done for the regular tax. Second, and more importantly, it was usually levied with urgency, and thus was little helped by the slow-moving procedures of regular taxation. In his essay "On Labor Services," Zhang Jie, a district magistrate of late Qing Zhili (Hebei) Province, described the situation in these words: "these kinds of miscellaneous labor services did not have a fixed quota, nor regular schedule. They could be very small or very big in sum, and were very urgent when summoned" (JSTB 1980: 2590). Therefore, at times of fiscal crisis,[9] the government at the different levels had to devise alternative methods to meet their needs. Unlike regular taxation, which was regulated by detailed rules spelled out by the central government, levying irregular taxes was, in most cases, in the hands of the local government. This situation resulted in a differentiation between regular taxation and irregular taxation in both methods and procedures. It also resulted in a geographical differentiation in irregular taxation itself, because the way in which the local government collected irregular taxes was greatly shaped and dictated by the local conditions.

As a matter of fact, irregular taxation was not a new phenomenon in the late Qing. It was found in various places before the mid-nineteenth century, and was especially exploited as a source of supplementary revenue by the local governments.[10] Fortunately, it was neither common nor heavy at that time, and constituted a relatively minor part of the governmental revenue structure. Since it was neither a widespread nor a serious problem before the mid-nineteenth century, it did not have a substantial impact on the overall taxation system. The dramatic political and socio-economic changes in the late Qing caused a surge of irregular taxes, which had exerted a great impact on the Qing taxation system and pushed a rapid and profound diversification of taxation patterns in different regions. A variety of tax patterns emerged which reshaped state and society relations in different regions and also powered divergent local political development. A comparison of taxation patterns between the North China plain and the Yangzi delta can give us more insight into these changes.

Taxation in the North China plain

In the first two hundred years of the Qing, the rural North China plain enjoyed comparatively simple and peaceful tax relations with the state. This can be verified by the fact that there were very few social disturbances related to tax resistance. For example, in Shandong Province, according to Chang Yu-fa's studies on social disturbances during the Qing, there were a total of 38 incidents before 1842, none of them related to tax resistance (Zhang Yu-fa 1982: 102–113).

This long-term peaceful tax relationship indicates that the existing taxation system was generally satisfactory or at least tolerated by both state and society. This peaceful relationship necessitated no substantial changes in taxation. Because of this, the Qing local gazetteers seldom mentioned any change and development in taxation during the first two centuries of the dynasty. What were talked about in local gazetteers were tax items, tax rates, and tax quotas, etc. This was not due to the negligence of the gazetteer compilers. Rather, it was not necessary.

However, this situation does not mean that the state could count on regular taxation to meet all its financial needs. Extra and irregular taxes would occasionally be levied in different localities, which the local people had to satisfy with local resources. Before the mid-nineteenth century, in North China, especially in Zhili Province, the cart service (*cheyao*) was a common irregular labor service. This service required the villages located along the imperial highway to provide carts and labor for transporting soldiers, court retainers, and supplies, whenever an imperial army passed by, or when the corteges of the imperial house went through. Sometimes the villages were even asked to provide board for the passing troops. This kind of tax was by nature irregular, but it could be very burdensome when it came. Though under normal arrangements there was a special fund allocated for this expenditure, it was far from sufficient. Therefore, the real burden in the last resort fell on local people living in the counties located along the vital communication lines. The following passage is from the Liangxiang gazetteer:

> Liangxiang County is the gateway of the Imperial Capital and the main thoroughfare of the Eighteen Provinces. [Therefore] the need for cart services is frequent and strenuous. Since the regular budget for hiring carts is small and could not meet expenses, both the local government and local people suffered a lot and have no good solution to improve it . . . People who have served in this county have all said that, since there is such a heavy burden for cart services there can hardly be benevolent magistrates.

> (*Liangxiang xian zhi* [1924] 1968: 481–482)

In order to ease the burden of the local people, the Qing authorities instigated some special arrangements. Tu Zhisheng, the Financial Commissioner of Zhili Province, wrote in one of his 1822 memoirs that:

Zhili Province was a strategic area in which the imperial capital was located. Because of this, the labor services were very heavy. Due to this reason, when tax regulations were first formulated, the authorities made the land tax in this province lighter than that in all other provinces.

(JSTB 1980, vol. 66: 11)[11]

This arrangement might have helped to ease the burden on the local people in the early period, but by the time of Commissioner Tu's memoirs, its role had already degenerated. Therefore, Tu described the situation as having been "corrupted in the course of time (*rijiu shengbi*)" (ibid.).

The outbreak of the Taiping Rebellion (1851) made the situation much worse. The abuse of cart services quickly spread across North China. As Zhou Hengqi said in his memoirs:

Henan, Zhili and Shandong provinces bore very heavy burdens of labor service . . . Because of the long enduring war [the Taiping War] cart services for the armies passing by are numerous and heavy. The local government cannot but depend on the resources of local people.

(JSWB 1972, vol. 22)

In one of his 1869 memoirs, Zeng Guofan, then the Governor General of Zhili, also said:

because of long-lasting war the labor services were very heavy in Zhili Province. The rich households [*dahu*] were forced to provide carts and horses and the poor households [*xiaohu*] money and labor . . . the carts were seen going out but never seen coming back. Nine houses out of ten were deserted.

(Zeng 1967, 27: 4525–4526)

Theoretically, cart services, like other labor services, should have followed the principles of Qing taxation, and should have been levied on owned land, and collected directly from individual landowners. However, this was not the case in practice, since this kind of tax was irregular and urgent. It was impossible for the local government to follow the principles and procedures of regular taxation. New methods had to be found to meet these irregular tax needs. These new methods had to be suitable to, and hence workable under, local circumstances. On the North China plain, the natural village was large, composed mainly of owner-cultivators, and had a long tradition of self-governance. Thus it was very easy and natural for the local government to take the village as a ready-made institutional means and ask the village to take collective responsibility for these irregular taxes.

The common means of enlisting village's efforts to meet the government demands for irregular taxes was to allocate those taxes among villages through a sub-county administrative system. Whenever there was a need for irregular taxation in a county, the village heads were summoned by the magistrate to the county seat or the headquarters of a sub-county administrative unit, such as *xiang*, *bao*, or *she*, usually located at a local market town. A tax quota was assigned to each village, and each village was required to collect this quota and deliver it to the county or sub-county administration. Though this tax quota was ultimately collected from individual households, under this arrangement, it was the village community, rather than individual households, which had to deal with the government directly and was responsible for collecting these irregular taxes and all related business.

Another important feature of this irregular taxation was that, since it was imposed on the village community collectively, the government did not care how it was allocated among the villagers. It was up to the village itself to choose the method of allocation. In most cases villages followed time-honored tradition and allocated the quota among the villagers according to land ownership. Under this arrangement, however, villages were given an autonomous power to tax. The following is a concrete example from Luanzhou, Zhili.

Luanzhou District was located along the vital communication line between Central China and Manchuria. After the outbreak of the Taiping War, the troops dispatched from Manchuria often passed through it. All of the provisions and transportation for the troops depended on local resources. The local government had to provide carts for transporting troops and their provisions. Originally there were no fixed quotas and written regulations for the cart service. It was imposed on 62 *she* by the district government.[12] The *yamen* clerks and runners could extort from villages at will. In Tongzhi 11 (1872), the magistrates You and Zhu implemented reforms of the cart service. They laid down written regulations and set up a fixed quota. The regulations were sent forth to every village to be kept and followed. The quota provided that for the transportation of every thousand soldiers, 120 carts would be requisitioned. This quota was shared by 62 *she* according to the size of each *she*. This reform put an end to the corrupt practices of *yamen* clerks and runners, and was warmly welcomed by the people of the whole district, and a stone tablet was erected to commemorate the two honest magistrates and their benevolent reforms (*Luanzhou zhi* [1898] 1969: 324–347, 344).[13]

The new method of taxation quickly got its notorious name, *tanpai*, and the tax money thus imposed and collected was called *tankuan*.[14] Regardless of its bad reputation, this method had great advantages for the state. It greatly reduced the number of the taxpayers and simplified and shortened the taxation procedure significantly. Thus, it was an efficient way for the state (the local government) to handle irregular taxation. The surge of irregular taxes since the late Qing therefore made this method a widely exploited strategy.

This strategy of enlisting village communities was also gradually employed by the local government to undertake other government projects. For example, during the period of the late Qing reforms, villagers in North China were asked to open public schools in their villages and provide funds to establish modern police in their counties.[15] Sometimes, even the recruitment of soldiers also became a mandate imposed on the village community. The following is an example of this kind found in Changzhou, Zhili, 1905:

> Because last time the amount required for soldier recruits was fairly large and the deadline was near, the village headmen [*cundong*] had no time to choose carefully, so they recruited people haphazardly. Since Magistrate Zhu did not give villages fixed quota, villages had no guidelines to follow so they sent more people than needed. If there were unqualified recruits, replacement had to be made. The expense for sending people back and forth was high and the village headmen could not afford this, so they asked villagers to bear [the expenses]. Some villages could not find a qualified person, so they collected money [from villagers] to hire one . . . Some shameless village headmen took advantage of this situation and made money from it.
>
> (Beiyang vol. 4: 39–40)

Enlisting village communities to meet the demands of the state on local resources was not totally new in rural North China, but the breadth of its employment and weight of its burden were unprecedented. This strategy was adopted not only for its convenience, but also for a lack of alternatives. The state, nevertheless, had to pay a price for the "convenience" of this strategy. Under this arrangement, the village community was mobilized to "tax" itself for the state. It therefore strained the relationship between state and village community and provoked frequent collective resistance to the state and its extractions. North China in the late Qing witnessed a series of collective tax resistance. This was the outcome of the dramatic change in state and rural society relations in this area, which contrasted sharply with the situation of the previous period. For example, in Shandong, the first collective tax resistance broke out in 1842. In the following years collective tax resistance broke out frequently and plagued almost every county of the province. Again, according to Chang Yu-fa's study, from 1842 to 1916, there were a total of 127 social disturbances in Shandong. Among them more than one-fifth were due to tax resistance (Chang Yu-fa 1982: 102–112). A well-known instance of collective tax resistance, from late Qing Guangzong, Zhili, shows clearly how the new taxation provoked the villagers' collective resistance.

The incident took place in 1902 shortly after the Boxer Rebellion. During the Boxer War the local people of Guangzong had burned churches and robbed Christian converts. After the war, the county was forced to pay 20,000 strings (*chuan*) of cash to those Christian victims. Wei, the newly arrived magistrate, ordered the villages to collect money at a rate of 40 cash per *mu* of (owned) land. Jing Tingbin, a militia *juren* from Dongzhao Village, backed by villagers from neighboring villages, refused to pay that amount. He led the villagers in a demonstration outside the county seat. Rusong, the Prefect of Shunde Prefecture (Guangzong was under the jurisdiction of Shunde Prefecture), happened to come to check the official documents in the county. He was acquainted with the previous arrangements for meeting indemnity payments in this county which set the rate of 14 cash per mu. He instructed the villagers to pay at this rate. Jing Tingbin complied and quickly paid his village's quota at this rate. Other villages also paid their quotas one after another. However, Magistrate Wei insisted on his original plan and did not carry out the Prefect's instruction. The conflict finally led to a clash between the pacifying army and protesting villagers and resulted in thousands of casualties (*Guangzong* 1969 [1933]: 50–58; see also DYDA 1985: 12–33).

The dramatic change in late Qing taxation had a lasting impact on the relationship between state and society in rural North China. On the one hand, it changed taxation from an affair between the state and individual taxpayers to the one between the state and village communities. On the other hand, it changed tax collection from a regular routine to an unusual process of political mobilization. Of course, both these changes were by no means thorough and complete at this time, but they did inaugurate a new course of development.[16] The core of these changes is that the state became more and more dependent on the mobilization of the village community to fulfill its various financial needs as well as political tasks in rural society. This strategy was, as we will see, followed and further elaborated by the successors to the Qing state in rural North China.

Prasenjit Duara uses the dual-brokerage model to analyze state and rural society relations in late imperial China. He argues that there were two types of brokerage in rural society: protective brokerage and entrepreneurial brokerage. Protective brokerage was undertaken by the rural communal leadership who tended to protect the interests of the village community in the pursuit of honor, prestige, and symbolic capital. Entrepreneurial brokerage refers to the intermediary between the state and society. A broker of this sort concerned himself with nothing but his own profits. Duara holds that the former was gradually replaced by the latter in the course of modern state-making, as the state placed a progressively heavier fiscal burden on the rural community. This situation left no room for protective brokers, and the vacuum left by the withdrawal of protective brokers was quickly filled by entrepreneurial brokers. The state tolerated this change, because only these entrepreneurial brokers were willing to cooperate with the state to enforce extractions from the village (Duara 1988: Chapter 2 and Conclusion).

In Duara's model, the protective broker represented the community, while the entrepreneurial broker was a self-serving intermediary between the state and society. Duara thus suggests that in the period of China's "modern state making and nation building," to use his words, there was a shift in state–society relations from community sheltering to individual tax farming.

However, what we found in the change of taxation pattern in rural North China during this period also suggests a shift in the opposite direction, i.e. the objective of state taxation began to shift from the individual payer to the community. This shift seems to have been ignored by Duara. Without a full awareness of the significance of this shift, our understanding of political change in rural North China is incomplete.

In my view, the two shifts represent the two sides of one process of political development in rural North China since the late Qing and throughout the Republican period. Duara's model addressed the apparent aspect of political deterioration in rural North China resulting from increasing state intrusion. My observation emphasizes another aspect of political change driven by various political forces in their mobilization of rural North China. The goal of their mobilization was to enlist the village community to meet their increasing demands on local resources. This change would be finally completed, as we will see, under Communist mobilization. To comprehend the political changes in rural North China since the late Qing we cannot afford to lose sight of this important aspect.

Taxation in the Yangzi delta

In the rural Yangzi Delta the situation was very different. Here irregular taxation in the form of labor services was a rare story for local people after the early-Qing labor service reform. Even in the late Qing, irregular labor service was not common. The general policy of Qing taxation, which reflected the general distribution of the nationwide tax sources, was that the South bore heavy land taxes but enjoyed light labor services, while the North enjoyed light land taxes but bore heavy labor services (JSXB, 1972: vol. 38). This situation was best described by a Qing aphorism which said: "The South suffers from land taxes; the North suffers from labor services (*nan kun yu fu, bei kun yu yi*)" (Tang, quoted from JSXB, 1972: vol. 34). Many delta gazetteers simply state that there was no *yi* (labor services) required of local people after the early Qing's tax reform. The 1883 edition of the Suzhou prefectural gazetteer put the situation in these words:

> The labor services in the Ming times were the most ruthless [throughout history]. Since the founding of the Qing, the new system of *juntian junyi* was installed, and people have taken advantage of this system and no longer even know the burden of labor services.
>
> (*Suzhou fu zhi* [1883] 1970: 360)[17]

The *juntian junyi* was a labor service reform carried out in the Yangzi delta during the early Kangxi period (Kangxi reign 1662–1722). The principle of this reform was the same as that of *tanding rudi*, i.e. commuting all labor services into silver and levying on land owned. The Songjiang prefectural gazetteer stated that, under this new arrangement, "there is no grade for household, all labor services are imposed on land. Money is collected from land and used to hire people for labor services. So it is land, not people, that bears the burden of labor services" (*Songjiang fu xuzhi* [1883] 1975: 1487).[18] This reform, considered the most benevolent and convenient policy of the Qing, was followed throughout the Qing times (JSTB, 1980: 66: 2585).[19]

However, land tax in the Yangzi delta area was the heaviest in the whole country. With only 5 percent of the country's registered acreage, the delta area had to contribute 10 percent of the national *diding* quota and 40 percent of the national tribute quota. According to Kathryn Bernhardt's estimate, in 1753, the average statutory tax quota for one *mu* of land (*diding* and tribute tax combined) in the delta was about three and half times the national average (1992: 44). Collecting taxes on time was thus an overriding task for the local government.

Aside from the *juntian junyi*, in the Yangzi delta, at the very beginning of the Qing, a celebrated tax reform was instituted, which abolished Ming practices in taxation and implemented a system of direct collection and delivery of taxes by the government. The Suzhou prefectural gazetteer says: "In the second year of the Shunzhi Reign (1645), Tu Guobao, the governor of Jiangsu, appealed to abolish and prohibit (Ming's) *guishou* and to institute *lishou guanjie*" (*Suzhou fu zhi* 1970 [1883]: 358). The so-called *guishou* was a remnant of the Ming *lijia* system in which landowners had to collect taxes for the government. It spelled out that for every hundred *mu* of land, landowner(s) should provide one tax collector (called *zuogui shoutou*), who was responsible for the taxes of this hundred *mu*. Anyone who assumed this position would become an immediate target of extortion by *yamen* functionaries. On the other hand, if a local bully took this position, then all the landowners would be victimized. The abolition of this practice was of immediate benefit to the local people. The new system of *lishou guanjie* (i.e., collecting and delivering taxes by officials) made the collection and delivery of taxes a government responsibility (ibid.).

Shortly thereafter, another reform followed, called *zifeng tougui*. This reform was intended to release taxpayers further from the extortion of *yamen* functionaries by asking them to pay taxes to the government chest by themselves. Under the arrangement of governmental collection and delivery, taxpayers were still subject to a customary fee extorted by *yamen* clerks and runners, since they came down to the countryside to collect taxes from each landowner (ibid.; *Jiading xian zhi*, 1880: 4: 42a). The *zifeng tougui* reform tried to reduce the interference of *yamen* functionaries in taxation to a minimum, and to simplify land taxation to a simple affair between the state and the individual taxpayer. It finally laid down, as it did in elsewhere in the country, the basic pattern of tax collection in the delta area.[20]

In order to carry out its heavy taxation responsibilities, the local government, which was handicapped by the shortage of funds and personnel, could only ask local people to provide assistance in tax collection. In the Yangzi delta, since the hamlets were small in size and numerous,[21] the local government usually overlooked this natural settlement and imposed its official business on the supra-hamlet quasi-administrative unit, the *tu*. Theoretically, the average size of a *tu* was about one hundred households. It thus contained several small hamlets. This was especially true in low-lying rice growing areas (see Map 1.2).[22] The major tax responsibility of the *tu* was tax prompting, which included sending out tax notices to landowners and assisting *yamen* runners in prompting payment. Of course, these duties varied from county to county, and over time as well. In some counties, in the early Qing, *tu* functionaries were asked to prepare tax collection books for the whole *tu* (*Suzhou fu zhi* [1883] 1970: 359; *Changshu xian zhi* [1904] 1979: 107; *Zhenze xian zhi* [1746] 1970: 1089–1094; *Jiading xian xuzhi* [1930] 1970: 219). The *tu* thus became a crucial level where state power met the rural populace.

Baozheng and the kundian malpractice

In the early Qing there were several posts in each *tu*, each of which was responsible for a different governmental duty: taxation, police, or water control. However, after the early Qing's tax and labor service reforms, in most counties, only one post was left. Though the name of the post varied in different localities, the most common one was *baozheng*.[23] The following passage is from the 1930 edition of the Jiading gazetteer, which clearly tells us about this general change:

> [In the early Qing] there were some miscellaneous labor services [*zafan chaiyao*] which had to be imposed on local people. The first one was the *liangzhang*, which was rotated among five *jia* and responsible for tax prompting. The second was the *tangzhang*, who was the leader [of his *li*] for river dredging. The third was the *lizhang*, who was responsible for local policing. The fourth was the *laoren*, who could discuss local affairs [with the magistrate]. During the Yongzheng period (1723–35), there were three left. One was the *ceshu*, whose duty was to prepare tax books and urge tax payment. One was the *xiangdi*, who took charge of river dredging. The last one was the *baozheng*, who was responsible for local policing. The *ceshu* and *xiangdi* were both abolished shortly thereafter. From that time on, the only labor service [*yi*] has been *baozheng*.
> (*Jiading xian xuzhi* [1930] 1970: 219)[24]

A *baozheng* was not a community leader, and he exercised no political authority over the *tu* in which he served. The government regulation stipulated that the person who filled this post be an honest and well-to-do landowner who owned the most land in the *tu* in which he lived and served. However, this regulation was not always complied with. To be a *baozheng* meant frequent dealings with *yamen* functionaries, which made him a target of their abuse. Therefore people were hesitant to take up this post. In reality, therefore, hiring someone to fill the post was a very common practice (*Suzhou fu zhi* [1883] 1970: 360). The person thus hired was very often a vagrant or a local bully. As the 1880 edition of the Jiading gazetteer revealed: "Since the honest people are afraid of dealing with the county *yamen*, vagrants like to take advantage of this situation, and some of them assume the *baozheng* posts for their entire lives" (*Jiading xian zhi* 1880: 4: 46b). "Half of the *baozheng*, . . . are vagrants. These people dominate rural communities and very often make trouble out of nothing" (ibid.: 1880: 8: 6a). Sometimes the person hired was not even a native of the *tu* for which he served.[25]

Theoretically, a *baozheng* was only responsible for local policing. He had nothing to do with taxation. However, since the *baozheng* served as the only liaison between the county *yamen* and the local populace, he was often pressed into handling all government affairs for the *tu* he served, especially those related to taxation.[26] This abuse produced a notorious form of malpractice in some Yangzi delta counties known as *kundian*.

In Chinese, *kun* means to tie up, and *dian* means cushion, or to cushion, hence to pay in advance. So *kundian* means to tie a *baozheng* up with his *tu*'s taxes, asking him to take complete responsibility for his *tu*'s taxes and pay in advance for any possible tax deficit. The practitioners of *kundian* were *yamen* functionaries. A stone tablet erected in 1801 in Qingpu county tells us this about *kundian*:

> According to the regulations, those who have land may become a *baozheng*, who leads the *yamen* functionary in prompting tax payment. This is to ensure that prompting can proceed peacefully and without alarm. However, there is the practice of *kunbao*,[27] which, on a rotation basis, requires (an individual) to pay for the service and to make up for any payment in arrears. There are also payments to be made for transport and other fees. There are thus many abuses.
> (*Songjiang fu xuzhi* [1884] 1975: 14: 14b; Faure 1976: 56)

In reality, there were different versions of *kundian*, and the victim of *kundian* was not necessarily the *baozheng*. Since sometimes a *baozheng* was a local bully, it was pointless or difficult to press him for personal gain. So in quite a few cases, the victims of *kundian* were the people who hired or nominated the *baozheng*. As Xiong Qiying, a *linsheng* (a stipend student in the government school, the lowest degree holder) from Qingpu County, wrote in a petition in 1866:

> [in Qingpu] for a long time, tax notices have been issued by the *yamen* runners and payments made by the *baozheng*. When the *baozheng* embezzle (tax funds), the *yamen* runners put the blame on the wealthy households, and want them to make up the difference. Nowadays, the *baozheng* who are in office are in fact actually nominated by the *yamen* runners and then said to be nominated by land-holding households

(*yuye*). Hence, innocent commoners are being punished for the misdeeds of the *baozheng*.

(*Songjiang fu xuzhi* 1975 [1884]: 14: 15b–16a)

In Jiading, this victimized figure sometimes was a *futou* (the person of the *tu* responsible for water dredging and water control). The position of *futou* was assumed by landowners of the *tu*. But local practice also dictated that they annually take turns to nominate a *baozheng* for their *tu*. If they could not find a suitable person to fill *baozheng*'s post, they themselves had to shoulder the *baozheng*'s responsibility to assist in tax prompting. They thus became the victims of extortion by *yamen* functionaries. Because of this, *kundian* in this county was called *fushu* (meaning: to tie *futou* up) (*Jiading xian xuzhi* [1930] 1970: 220–221).

The *kundian* malpractice was most serious in those localities with a relatively high percentage of owner-cultivators, such as Songjiang Prefecture. The local people suffered greatly from this malpractice and repeatedly petitioned the local government to put an end to it.[28] This situation also aroused great concern within the Songjiang government. Many orders were issued and many stone tablets were erected by different levels of government to prohibit the practice. The first one of these stone tablets was erected in 1799 by the Prefect Zhao Yixi:

Since there is *kunbao* malpractice, local people are asked to be responsible for the tax defaults of their *bao* (*tu*) and to pay service charges to *yamen* runners. This malpractice leads to innumerable abuses of power . . . Now this stone tablet is erected to make all officials, *yamen* clerks, scholars and commoners aware that . . . the malpractice of *kundian* should be eliminated forever.

(*Songjiang fu xuzhi* [1883] 1975: 1488)

However, the effectiveness of the governmental ban was quite doubtful. The recurrences of government prohibition suggested that the prohibition had only limited effect. In the 1883 Songjiang gazetteer, we find that the prohibitions were issued repeatedly by county, prefectural and even provincial governments in the following years: 1788, 1799, 1812, 1841, 1854, 1866, 1867, 1869, 1870, 1871 (ibid.: 1487–1501). The tenacity of this malpractice is undoubtedly attributed to the heavy taxation. And the severity of this malpractice was also directly related to the range of fiscal pressures on the government. The increased frequency of government prohibitions after the mid-nineteenth century indicates the escalation of the malpractice, which was due to, as we can imagine, the deterioration of the general situation resulting from domestic and foreign crises.

Because of the need to generate tax revenues, the magistrates were reluctant to stop the *kundian* malpractice for they were afraid of a tax deficit and of the ruination of their careers. As Xiong Qiying said: "the *kundian* malpractice is a long-standing one. Even those good local officials who want to stop it are very often afraid that doing so will lead to a tax deficit and thus downgrade their official dossier" (*Songjiang fu xuzhi* 14: 15a). Consequently, the *kundian* continued in many localities throughout the nineteenth century. In some places, for instance, in Jiading, it lasted until the fall of the Qing (*Jiading xian xuzhi* [1930] 1975: 221).

The *kundian* in the Yangzi delta and the *tanpai* on the North China plain shared one thing in common, i.e., they both resorted to collective responsibility (though in different degree and context) for taxation. However, we should not lose sight of many significant differences between the two. As we saw in Chapter 1 and the previous discussion of this chapter, both the communal structure and social formation of the North China village differed greatly from those of the *tu*, a supra-hamlet, quasi-administrative unit in the Yangzi delta. Zhao Xixiao, a Qing scholar from the Yangzi delta, made this very clear when he compared the communal structure and landownership between North China and the Yangzi delta:

> [A settlement where] people lived closely together in houses is called the village [*zhuang*]. To organize taxation and labor services according to this pattern of settlement is called *shunzhuang* [lit. in accordance with the village]. The areas north of the [Yangzi] River all adopted this *shunzhuang* method to collect taxes [*shunzhuang gongfu*].[29] However, this method could not be adopted in the south of the River [Jiangnan] because the geographical situations between the North and the South [of the Yangzi River] are totally different. . . . The Jiangnan area is a land that abounds in rivers and lakes. It is convenient for water transportation and communication. Therefore, people who live in this *tu* very often own land in that *tu*; and those who live in towns very often own land in several different *tu*; even for a small landholding with only several dozen *mu*, it is usually scattered in several *tu*.
>
> (*Suzhou fu zhi* [1883] 1970: 359)

These physical and social differences of rural communities determined different tax practices: *tanpai* on the North China plain and *kundian* in the Yangzi delta. They were operating within different context and also having different impact on local society.

First, on the North China plain, enlisting the village community to take collective responsibility for government irregular and extra taxes, i.e. *tanpai*, was generally considered a normal or acceptable, though not a statutory, practice. Moreover, it was employed by the local government itself (also, as we will see later, by villagers themselves). In the Yangzi delta, tying people together to ensure the collection of land tax (the regular tax) was considered to be a corrupt practice and was prohibited (no matter how ineffective the prohibition was) by the local government. This malpractice was manipulated mainly by the *yamen* functionaries, not by the local government.

Second, in the case of *tanpai*, the irregular tax imposed on the village community was a collective quota and it was up to the village itself to determine the method of allocation,[30] whereas in the case of *kundian*, the targeted tax was land tax, an individual tax, and was uncompromisingly imposed on land owned.

Third, *tanpai* was imposed on the natural village collectively, while *kundian* targeted the *tu* functionaries such as *baozheng* individually. Since the communal structure and social formation between the two were substantially different, the impact of these practices on rural communities and rural politics were certainly different. On the North China plain, the new taxation easily pitted the village against the state. Whereas in the Yangzi delta, the malpractice more often caused suffering to the individual involved, or aroused local people to protest the abuse of *yamen* functionaries, rather than provoking the community to confront the state.

Fourth, the *tanpai* was widely employed on the North China plain, while the *kundian* was not a universal phenomenon in the Yangzi delta. It was only found in some localities where the rate of owner-cultivators was relatively high.

The final and maybe the most important difference between the two, however, was timing. On the North China plain, the *tanpai* began to be widely employed in the late nineteenth century as the overall situation deteriorated. And its employment continued and intensified in the first half of the twentieth century. But in the Yangzi delta, the *kundian* was an old malpractice exploited by *yamen* functionaries throughout the eighteenth and nineteenth centuries. This malpractice did exacerbate in the mid-nineteenth century, but faded out in the twentieth century. To understand this, we should look at some important developments in taxation and state–society relations in the Yangzi delta since the late Qing.

Zuzhan: a coalition between rent and tax

From the mid-nineteenth century, the overall situation of the Yangzi delta deteriorated due to domestic and foreign crises. The area was further devastated by the Taiping War during the third quarter of the century. Under these circumstances, the tax relations were strained even further. This not only resulted in an escalation of the *kundian* malpractice as we saw above, but also an escalation of popular tax resistance (Bernhardt 1992: 236–241). This was not surprising. The same turbulence also plagued other parts of the empire. However, in the Yangzi delta, we do not find the same pattern of development in taxation and in state and society relations as that on the North China plain. For example, in the Yangzi delta, rarely were the irregular levies known as *tankuan* imposed on the rural community as a collective tax. Also we have found few cases of the local government enlisting the rural community to undertake various modernization projects, such as the establishment of modern public schools. Nevertheless, significant and unique taxation innovations were created in the Yangzi delta. One of them was the exploitation of the delta's highly developed absentee landlordism for the purpose of taxation.

In the Yangzi delta, continuous economic change and vigorous commercialization during the Ming and Qing period greatly reshaped rent relations between landlords and tenants. More and more landlords moved into cities and towns and became absentee landlords, leaving the delta's countryside an overwhelmingly tenant-dominated society. The spatial segregation between landlords and tenants made rent collection increasingly contentious. In order to collect rent effectively, in the mid-Qing the delta's landlords developed the rent bursary (*zuzhan*).[31] The rent bursary was run by hired professionals who took charge of the rent collection for several to a dozen or more absentee landlords (Tao Xu 1884: 10b; Muramatsu 1970; Bernhardt 1992: 140).[32] This institutional innovation later proved to be of great significance to the state.

For the Qing state, it seems that the development of absentee landlordism had nothing to do with taxation, since taxes had long been levied on owned land and had become an affair between the state and individual landowners. However, the profound differentiation and spatial segregation between landed and landless classes fostered intense confrontations between the two and these confrontations posed a direct threat to taxation, for in the delta, for a long time, "taxes come out of the rent (*liang cong zu chu*)." In order to ensure its taxes, the local government became more and more involved in rent collection. On the one hand, the state began to lend coercive support to the collection of rent. On the other, it also engaged in mediating rent disputes (Bernhardt 1992: 118). This involvement thus inaugurated a significant role change for the state. The state began to play the role of an arbitrator between the two antagonistic classes, not merely as an expropriator of taxes from society.

The Taiping War marked the watershed in the development of government taxation and the relationship between state and rural society in the Yangzi delta. After the Taiping War, the state, which was now eager to ensure the collection of taxes from a devastated and also a more antagonistic rural society, stepped directly into the process of rent collection. Moreover, the landlords, who were greatly weakened by the war, also surrendered more of their property rights to the state in order to secure more official backing for rent collection. This led to a coalition between the state and the landlords, and between taxes and rents. This coalition was made possible via an important institutional arrangement, the rent bursary. Tao Xu, a contemporary scholar, provides us with a short account of the origin of this coalition in his well-known book: *Zuhe* (The investigation of rents):

> In the second year of Tongzhi (1863), Suzhou city was recovering [from the Taipings]. At that time, the army and restoration [of local society] needed funds urgently. In this situation, the gentry and rich people of

the city suggested that the governor establish a rent-dunning bureau (*shouzuju*). [They were willing to] reduce the rent to 50 percent, and then divide the rent [thus collected] into three parts: one for army provisions, one for the needs of restoration, and one for their own as rent income. They also asked that officials be appointed to the bureau to enforce the rent collection . . . Since then rent collection always involved coercive government forces.

(Tao Xu 1884: 12a)

Tao's account went on to condemn the many abuses of tenants brought about by this coalition. From his account we know that the coalition originated in Suzhou, a city where absentee landlords were highly concentrated, and also a place where the rent bursary was very likely first invented. Obviously, the rent-dunning bureau proposed by the Suzhou gentry and rich people was nothing but a special version of the rent bursary (*zuzhan*). As already mentioned, the rent bursary was an innovation of absentee landlords. Its purpose was to collect rent. Now landlords invited the government to join in the bursary system and to use it for taxation. This idea was immediately capitalized upon by the local government. Since that time, the rent bursary has become an important vehicle for government taxation in the Yangzi delta.

By exploiting the rent bursary the state could meet its taxation needs rather easily during this turbulent period, while avoiding having the rural community shoulder collective responsibility for government taxation. Once again, this was not the free choice of the state, rather, it was an adaptation by the state to local conditions. Because tenants constituted the majority of the rural populace in the Yangzi delta, they were not liable for taxation. Land taxes were derived mainly from the rent income of urban absentee landlords. In many localities, taxation was an affair between the government and those urban absentee landlords. Under these circumstances, it was unreasonable to ask those tenant-composed rural communities to take any collective responsibility for governmental taxation, whether regular or irregular. This situation not only can help us to understand why there was seldom a collective *tanpai* imposed on the rural community in the Yangzi delta, it can also explain why the local government was so willing to exploit the rent bursary as an institutional means of taxation.

The convenience of employing the rent bursary to collect tax is obvious. For under this arrangement, the state only needed to deal with the rent bursary, rather than individual landlords. Since the rent bursary was a joint venture of landlords, each bursary worked for a group of landlords, the number of actual taxpayers was greatly reduced. On the other hand, this arrangement could also help the state to secure its tax, because the state was now directly involved in rent collection. Once the rent had been successfully collected, the tax was certainly there. The state could guarantee its tax by withholding its share before the rent was turned over to individual landlords.

Because of its obvious benefits to the state, this method was also adopted and gradually institutionalized by, as we will see later, various political forces and regimes which ruled this area during the Republican times.

It might seem that the coalition between the state and landlords and the conjunction of rent and tax would strengthen the landlords as a class. However, this was only true on the surface. Fundamentally speaking, landlords as a class were severely weakened by this development, because the state's involvement in rent collection (a hereditary power domain of the landlord class) gave it powerful leverage to intervene in rent affairs. This, as Bernhardt argued, "placed rent relations on an entirely new footing, one that ultimately worked to the great disadvantage of landlords" (1992: 160).

Increasing state intervention in rent collection and the weakening of the landlord class in the Yangzi delta since the late Qing posed a sharp contrast to the situation on the North China plain, where increasing state intrusion into rural society since the late Qing had resulted in a great strengthening of the village community.[33] The political implications of this differentiation were obvious. A gradually weakened landlord class enabled the state to play a larger role in mediation between landlords and tenants and turn this to its advantage. It also helped reduce tensions between the state and rural society.[34] But a strengthened and hence more combative village community on the North China plain would lead to a more intense confrontation between the state and the rural society.

Due to the highly developed absentee landlordism and class differentiation, the rural community in the Yangzi delta escaped the fate of being subjected to collective *tanpai*, which the North China village had had to endure since the late Qing and throughout the Republican times. Also thanks to this, the state in the Yangzi delta avoided provoking intense resistance from rural communities. This situation allowed a much less contentious relationship between the state and rural society in the Yangzi delta in modern times.

Lijin: a new taxation

Another significant development in taxation as well as in state and society relations was the *lijin* tax. The *lijin* tax once again shows how the state adapted itself to the local conditions of the Yangzi delta to meet its fiscal demands. As mentioned above, since the outbreak of the Taiping War, the North China village had suffered more and more from irregular taxation. Since the lower Yangzi area was the major battlefield in the war, the fiscal needs here should have been much greater than they were in North China. However, these needs seemed not to be imposed on the rural populace directly. Putting aside consideration of the devastating war situation and the high tenancy rate among rural population, the highly commercialized economy of the lower Yangzi area actually provided an alternative solution, i.e. the *lijin* tax, to meet the state's fiscal needs.

The *lijin* was basically a commercial tax. It originated in the lower Yangzi area during the early stages of the Taiping War and was used to finance the anti-Taiping campaign.[35] The *lijin* was quickly adopted in many other provinces, and it played a vital role in financing the anti-Taiping campaign. After the war it was continued and became one of the major sources of government revenue. The amount of *lijin* tax collected from Jiangsu was always the largest of all Eighteen Provinces within China Proper, accounting for more than 20 percent of the nation's total *lijin* revenue from 1869 to 1908 (Luo 1936: 464–467). To a large extent, because of *lijin*, the rural populace of the Yangzi delta were spared the irregular *tanpai* that plagued North China villagers.

To be sure, the *lijin* was also adopted in North China, but it never achieved the same success as it did in the highly commercialized Yangzi delta. As Guan Wen, the Governor-General of Huguang Provinces, argued in a debate after the Taiping War over the abolition of the *lijin*, the *lijin* tax could be abolished in the provinces of Zhili, Shandong, Shanxi, Henan, Shaanxi, Gansu, Yunan, Guizhou and Guangxi, since these provinces were not convenient for commerce and transportation, land productivity there was low, and the *lijin* income there was low and of no avail. However, Guan strongly opposed abolishing the *lijin* in Jiangsu, Zhejiang, Anhui, Fujian, Hunan, Hubei and Guandong. His suggestion was appreciated by the Qing court (Luo 1936: 21–24).

The *lijin* tax and the rent-tax coalition discussed above helped to shape a unique taxation pattern and hence a unique state–society relation in the Yangzi delta.[36] They contrasted sharply with those in the North China. Obviously, the *lijin* benefited greatly from the development of the market system in the Lower Yangzi area, which made this institutional innovation workable and successful. The state's capacity for tax extraction expanded greatly by exploiting the infrastructural development of the market system. The advantage of using market networks to collect tax is apparent, because now the state did not need to deal with numerous individual taxpayers who lived in the scattered countryside. Instead, it dealt with merchants. The number of merchants was much smaller and their commercial activities were also much easier to control, since they were concentrated in cities and towns and moved along easily controlled trading routes.

Conclusion

The relationship between state and rural society in imperial China is usually observed from the point of view of state control. This approach takes for granted that the state was the dominant force in shaping this relationship. Preoccupied by this assumption, past scholarship has paid little attention to how the behavior and policies of the state were conditioned by local societies. The approach of focusing on a single area reinforced this inclination, because it confined and narrowed our scope of observation. Only a comparison of state and society relations between different areas can help us overcome this narrow and one-sided view. From a comparison between the North China plain and the Yangzi delta we have found some noticeable phenomena, both general and particular, about state and rural society relations.

In general, we have seen clearly that, first, the state behaved differently in different areas. For a large and highly diverse country like China, we should envision many local governments operating in different areas, rather than a single state confronting the whole society. Second, the state (i.e. the local government if we are talking about the state and society relations in a concrete locality) was not always the dominant force in shaping the pattern of and changes in state–society relations. Before it could exert its influence on a local society, first of all, it had to adapt itself to the local conditions. Third, therefore, any governmental policy and strategies for control and mobilization of local society were shaped, to a great extent, by the local conditions. This situation led to a differentiation of concrete state and society relations in different areas.

In particular, this comparison brought to light a conspicuous divergence of state and rural society relations between the North China plain and the Yangzi delta. It also tells us the basic reasons for this divergence. This study has thus advanced our current understanding about state and rural society relations in these two macro-regions. In his comparative study of the two regions, Philip Huang has demonstrated how different social formation in the North China village and the Yangzi delta's rural community had brought about different degrees of state presence and also resulted in different degrees of communal consolidation (Huang 1990: 152–156). My comparison shows further how different taxation patterns and mobilization strategies of the state in these two areas were shaped by the communal structure and social formation of rural communities.

On the North China plain, the relatively large, owner-cultivator-based natural village was a ready-made institutional means for the state to mobilize rural society. Since the late Qing, the villages had been asked to shoulder more and more collective responsibilities for taxation as well as other governmental requisitions. This mobilization strategy inevitably strained the relationship between the state and rural society, and resulted in the dramatic change of village politics. However, the Yangzi delta experienced no parallel development during the same period. Here, the tenant-based small hamlets were overlooked by the state. Instead, the state benefited greatly from the highly developed absentee landlordism and market relations, and could now exploit these infrastructures to ensure its tax revenue and to avoid provoking confrontation with rural society.

Michael Mann has distinguished two types of state power: *despotic* power and *infrastructural* power. Despotic power refers to the state power imposed on the society that takes actions "without routine, institutionalized negotiation with civil society groups." Infrastructural power refers to the "capacity of the state to actually penetrate civil society," and "centrally co-ordinate the activities of civil society through its own infrastructure" (Mann 1984: 188–190). This analysis can help us to understand better the differentiation of the state's behavior on the North China plain and in the Yangzi delta. This differentiation actually reflected two different types of state power operating in these two areas. In the Yangzi delta highly developed absentee landlordism and market relations gave the state, i.e. the local government, a sort of infrastructural power, enabling it to penetrate local society, and to coordinate the activities of different social groups and classes for its own purposes, without employing a despotic, coercive force. It thus avoided direct confrontation with society. On the North China plain, the situation was just the opposite. Due to a lack of infrastructural development (both of absentee landlordism and market networks), the state could only wield coercive power upon the village and thus inevitably provoked strong resentment and resistance from rural communities.

This divergence in state and society relations between the North China plain and the Yangzi delta played a crucial part in determining the different courses of rural political change in these two macro-regions in the first half of the twentieth century. It proved to be of great significance, as we will see later, to the fate of twentieth-century China.

3 Mobilization and reorganization of village communities in North China

Prior to the twentieth century, North China villages were, to a great extent, autonomous communities governed by their own people following local customs and traditions (Gamble 1963). The state was satisfied with this situation as long as taxes were paid and order was maintained. Similarly, villages enjoyed substantial autonomy with little direct state interference (Kuhn 1975: 258).

Of course, the picture was not a static one, it changed with the fluctuations of the prevailing social conditions. As G.W. Skinner suggested, in imperial times, village communities opened and closed according to the rise and decline of dynasties. In the heyday of a dynasty, villages were open for social exchange with the outside world. As the dynasty wore out, villages closed their doors to protect themselves from outside upheaval and intrusion (Skinner 1971: 270–281). Nevertheless, this shift did not fundamentally alter the internal structure of village communities and the relationship between state and village communities. Once peace and order were restored, villages returned to their former normal and peaceful life.

However, since the outbreak of the Taiping Rebellion, this picture changed dramatically. The old social and political order began to fall apart, and a new equilibrium was yet to be established. From this point on, rural North China entered an uncertain and transitional period. The villages were now under constant pressure from the state and other political forces to mobilize the rural populace and enlist local resources. As a result, the formal village government was established in each village and the village community was reorganized into a more tightly controlled, ascriptive body corporate. This chapter will examine the political changes on the North China plain until the outbreak of the War of Resistance against Japan in 1937. The political changes during this period are very crucial for us to understand the Communist revolution in North China during the War of Resistance.

Mobilization of rural North China

Vigorous and continuous political mobilizations dominated the social and political scene in rural North China during the late nineteenth century and the first half of the twentieth century. These human endeavors were responses and reactions to the changing situation. During this period, under the pressure of both domestic unrest and foreign invasion, the state power greatly weakened and the state could no longer maintain peace and order in the local society. On the other hand, during the same period, many modern programs were forced upon villages by the state, and the state presence and penetration in local society greatly strengthened. To cope with this new situation, villagers had to organize self-defense, on the one hand, and to follow the state orders to build modern projects, on the other. These new demands thus set in motion a political process called mobilization. Though the purposes and contents of different mobilizations could be different, the practical goal of all mobilizations was always the same, i.e., to increase a social group's collective control over resources.[1]

State weakening and state strengthening

In China, the arrival of the twentieth century was accompanied by a series of crises. The Qing government faced fatal challenges both at home and abroad. Domestically, social disturbances and upheavals became extremely serious and beyond the government's control. Internationally, Western powers became more and more aggressive in their claims on China's sovereignty and resources. The situation even worsened after the founding of the Republic. In both domestic and foreign crises the state could no longer maintain peace and order effectively. *State weakening* refers precisely this situation.

Because of state weakening, North China villagers could hardly expect the state to protect them effectively. Instead, they had to depend on their own resources to maintain peace and order locally. Mobilization for self-defense was a direct response to state weakening. As Liang Shuming, a prominent scholar and social reformer of this period, angrily pointed out: "The essential role of the state is to keep peace and order, and not allow people to solve their disputes and conflicts themselves with weapons rather than by law." However, armed self-defense became common and indispensable in rural China, "because the state simply cannot do what it is supposed to do" (Liang Shuming 1990: 153–156). In cases like this, what the villagers tried to do was to maintain existing order rather than create a new one. This kind of mobilization had no dimension of modernization.[2]

In order to escape from this predicament due to its weakening, the state vigorously pursued various programs of modernization, hoping to rebuild state power and reestablish its control over society. Though people's understanding of modernization differed significantly, those who pursued it shared one belief in common: modernization meant building a powerful nation based on an advanced economy and strong national defense. To achieve this ambitious goal, the state initiated various modernization programs and also quickly expanded its governmental apparatus in order to secure whole-hearted support and compliance from society. In Western scholarship, this process is called "modern state-making" (Tilly 1975a). In contrast to the process of state weakening, I would like to call this process *state strengthening*.

State strengthening was another major cause of the political mobilization of North China villages. Obviously, under pressure from the state, villagers had to mobilize themselves and enlist local resources to implement various modernization projects initiated and forced by the state. Though in this case villagers were mobilized by the state for modernization, the political impact it had on villages was similar to that of mobilization for self-defense.

In analyzing the political development of rural North China, past scholarship has usually focused on the process of modern state-making and attributed rural political change mainly to this process.[3] By distinguishing between two different types of mobilizations resulting from both state strengthening and state weakening, this one-sided viewpoint can be avoided. As we will see in this chapter, although modern state-making was a very important factor contributing to political change in rural North China, the state was by no means the only driving force in this historical drama. Mobilization for self-defense initiated by villagers within the context of state weakening also contributed significantly to this political development.

Mobilization for self-defense

To cope with the continuously deteriorating situation, North China villagers devised various self-defense programs for their own protection. In the early twentieth century, the most popular self-defense system was the crop-watching organization. The main function of this organization was to protect crops in fields during growing and ripening seasons. In Hebei these associations were usually called *Qingmiaohui* (Green Sprouts Association), while in Shandong, *Yipohui* (Public Ground Association) was a popular name (Gamble 1963: 32–33).

According to the recollections of Shajing villagers, before the twentieth century people usually watched their crops individually. This practice was called *sankan*, which means watch separately and individually (KC, 1:174, 180). At the turn of the century, however, a new way of crop-watching conducted collectively under the direction of the *Qingmiaohui* gradually replaced *sankan*. This change was closely related to the social disturbances and economic deterioration of the time (Zhang Zhongtang 1932: 6: 231; Huang 1985: 304). Here, Arthur Smith's personal observation about rural Shandong in the last decade of the nineteenth century is especially illustrative:

> It must be borne in mind that the reason for the organization of such a society [crop-watching society] as this is the fact that so many poor people everywhere exist, whose only resources is to steal. In the consultations preliminary to the organization of a crop-protecting league, the poor people of the various villages concerned have no voice, but they

must be considered, for they will contrive to make themselves felt in many disagreeable ways.

(Smith 1899: 164–165)

While no one can trace the exact origin of organized crop-watching, it is clear that after the turn of the twentieth century organized crop-watching spread rapidly, and became a major organization in North China villages. This general trend is illustrated in the following cases.

The villagers of Lengshuigou and Houxiazhai recalled that before the twentieth century, crops in the fields were voluntarily watched by villagers. Whoever had the time to watch crops had to take care of all of the village's crops. If nobody had time to do so, the crops were left alone in the fields. This traditional method of crop watching was called *gongkan yipo* (watch public grounds voluntarily). These characters were usually whitewashed on the walls of village temples. However, this practice was given up in the twentieth century because it could no longer protect crops effectively due to increasing crop theft. Villages had to be organized and people were hired to watch the crops (KC, 4: 28–29, 35–36, 422). Lengshuigou and Houxiazhai's cases reflected the general situation in northwest Shandong.

In Shajing, the *sankan* method was replaced by the organized *Qingmiaohui* in the early twentieth century (KC, 1: 151, 154, 156, 160, 171, 187, 204). Huang Di's field investigation in northern Hebei also shows that only after the twentieth century did the *Qingmiaohui* become very active and evolve into a tightly organized village association. He observed:

> because of the Boxer Rebellion, the county government and its functions were greatly weakened. The overall situation deteriorated and became turbulent, which activated political organizations at grassroots levels in rural society, and prompted the *Qingmiaohui* to become tightly organized.

(Huang Di 1936: 10: 407–408)

Compared to crop theft, a more serious threat to local security came from bandits and disbanded soldiers. To guard against this evil, ever vigilant self-defense programs were organized. The *dageng* (night watch) was a very common self-defense program found in North China villages (Gamble 1963: 109–110). Villagers either took turns or hired people to patrol village streets during the night to guard against thieves and bandits. Although night watch had a very long history in North China villages (Spence 1978: 132), due to serious social chaos this activity became more tightly organized in the early twentieth century. Unarmed night watches were quickly replaced by armed guards in many bandit-ridden areas (Huang Di 1936: 10: 412; Gamble 1963: 112).

In areas with rampant banditry, village self-defense was highly militarized. Village walls and fortifications were built and militias were organized.

Villages were thus turned from peaceful settlements into military fortresses. For instance, in Taitou, an eastern Shandong village, during the 1920s villagers organized an armed defense program with two defensive lines guarding the village. The outer line was mined, and the inner line was composed of armed young men, fortifications, gates and gun emplacements. The village was not attacked by bandits after the organization of this defense system (Yang 1945: 143–144).

In order to protect themselves more effectively, very often neighboring villages organized united militia corps, such as *Lianzhuanghui* (the linked-village militia association), or joined the *Hongqianghui* (the Red Spears), a village-based secret society which was active in North China during the first three decades of the twentieth century. These multi-village defense organizations were designed to guard against large groups of bandits and unruly soldiers. The power of these multi-village defense programs is illustrated in the following story.

In 1926, a bandit union of 600 bodies was planning to attack Dabaiyu, a Red Spears village in west Shandong. The plot was discovered and the village gathered 2,000 members from neighboring Red Spears villages to counter-attack. The bandits were severely defeated and the remaining bandits ran into mountains and dared not offend the village again (Zhang Zhongtang 1932: 6/244–245; see also Gamble 1963: 302–303).

Organization of different self-defense programs in villages was reactive in nature, with no aim of changing the existing order and structure of rural society. Nevertheless, villagers were mobilized and new institutional arrangements were made so as to undertake these self-defense activities. Village politics under this situation was bound to change.

Mobilization for modernization

It is a real paradox that although the state was too weak to ensure peace and order in rural society, it was strong enough to impose its modernization plan upon villages. Of course, modernization was also pursued by other social and political forces such as urban intellectuals. To carry out various modernization projects, support and compliance from rural society were indispensable, especially for the modernization projects which targeted villages directly. A typical example of this can be found in the establishment of public schools in villages.

Beginning in 1901, the Qing government issued many edicts on education reform, this was an important part of late Qing's modernization efforts. The 1903 National Education Regulations outlined a modern education system for the entire country, calling for the establishment of modern western-style four-year primary schools in villages. Various governments followed this outline during the Republican period (Mao Lirui and Shen Guanqun 1988: 4: 226). The abolition of the imperial examination system in 1906 triggered a nation-wide boom in school-building.[4] The Nationalist government pushed villages even harder in this direction. In 1928, the Nationalist government made four-year primary education compulsory for all children (Gamble 1963: 104).

On the North China plain, modern western-style schools were established in some villages as early as 1894 (Gamble 1963: 5). These pioneering schools were usually privately sponsored and financed. Soon after 1900 a handful of county governments also became involved in this school-building endeavor. However, in general, no government funds were provided to finance this project. Villagers were supposed to undertake educational reforms themselves using their own resources (ibid.: 104). This ambitious plan of educational modernization was, of course, a new concept to most North China villagers. Regardless of whether villagers were willing to cooperate, sooner or later, modern schools were established in many North China villages.

Since school-building was not initiated by villagers, the development of modern education in rural areas was determined, to a great extent, by the effort and enthusiasm of local governments. A good example of this can be found in Dingxian, Hebei. As a model county, Dingxian's modern education system scored very high in early Republican times. This achievement is attributed to strong county leadership. In 1914, after Sun Faxu became the county magistrate, he conducted an inspection tour of each village and took great pains to persuade villagers to transform their village temples into village schools. According to villagers' recollections, that year in Dongting *qu* (ward) more than 200 village temples (which account for more than half of the total temples in this *qu*) were transformed into village schools (Li Jinghan 1933: 422). So effective was Sun's leadership that 44 percent of schools in operation in 1928 were actually opened during his tenure as county magistrate (Gamble 1963: 6). By 1925, in Dingxian, almost every village had a public school (Li Jinghan 1933: 128, 177).

For villagers, the campaign to modernize education translated into greater political and economic pressure. To open a public school in a village was not just a one-time endeavor. Once a school was established, it required daily management and all-year round financial support. To support this daily routine, villagers not only had to make certain institutional arrangements such as organizing the board of trustees of the village school, appointing the principal and hiring teachers, they also had to allocate resources and coordinate various interests within the village. Though this modernization campaign was initiated by the state, the actual impact it had on village politics was similar to that of organizing village self-defense. In both cases, villages had to make new institutional arrangements and allocate resources to support these endeavors.

In fact, state strengthening also meant a rapid downward expansion of the state apparatus. This downward expansion was intended to control rural society and enlist its resources in a more direct and efficient fashion. Rural North China thus saw an increasing and more aggressive state presence. Under this situation, villagers not only had to deal with the state and its functionaries more often, they also had to meet its increasing financial demands. The introduction of a modern police force in rural areas was a good example of state expansion. Though this project was carried out by local governments, villagers had to allocate their resources to finance it.

A modern police force was first instituted in Zhili (Hebei) in 1904 when Yuan Shikai was the governor. That year, Yuan ordered five counties to abolish their existing *baojia* system and establish a modern police force (Mackinnon 1980: 155–156). The aim was to strengthen state control over local society. Following Yuan's example, rural police systems were established soon afterwards in all North China counties.

Because the government had no funds to finance this project, villagers were asked to pay for the newly established police force and also to provide recruits. In some counties, a surcharge was levied on land, which was called *jingkuan fujia* (the surcharge for police fee). In other counties, this financial burden was left to the village, which as a collective was asked to pay the police fee (ibid.: 158–159). For example, according to Gamble, five of eleven sample villages reported that the police fee was a standing item in the village's annual expenditures. The actual amount paid by these villages varied significantly; and fluctuated in different years (Gamble 1963: 114–115). In Shunyi County, the police fee was called *cuntan jingkuan* (the police fee imposed on the village), and was regularly levied on villages. According to Shajing villagers, the police fee was instituted in early Republican times and, together with *xuekuan* (the school expenses), were the two major village expenditures (KC 1952: 1: 174, 180; 2: 325, 334). In Changli County, the police fee was first levied in 1914 and was imposed on the village collectively. After 1917, this fee became a land surcharge (KC 1952: 5: 361, 363, 402).

During this period, North China villages were not only the objects of state mobilization, they were also the target of various social reforms. These social reforms were initiated and directed by urban intellectuals (this also includes Western missionaries). Since the late 1920s, urban intellectuals often had brought reform programs into villages aimed at raising literacy among villagers, educating them in modern scientific knowledge, and organizing them into various political and economic organizations that reformers thought were essential for the modernization of rural society.

Due to the enthusiastic support and encouragement from the Nationalist Government, after 1928 rural reform became a major issue nationwide that attracted great national attention (Hayford 1990: 158). The reform was known as Rural Reconstruction (*xiangcun jianshe*). The two major battlefields of Rural Reconstruction were in the North China plain and the Yangzi delta. On the North China plain, the most influential experiments in Rural Reconstruction were the Zouping experiment, led by the Shandong Institute of Rural Reconstruction (*Shandong xiangcun jianshe yanjiuyuan*), and the Dingxian experiment, led by the Association for Mass Education Movement (*Pingmin jiaoyu cujinghui*). Though these experiments affected only a small portion of North China villages, they offered a special window for us to have a closer look of village political changes under their reforms aimed to rejuvenate and modernize rural China.

Village communities under mobilization

Continuous and vigorous political mobilization had a profound impact on village politics. It was a major driving force that powered political change in North China villages during the first half of the twentieth century.[5] To distinguish mobilization for self-defense from that for modernization not only suggests that both the state and the village played important roles in this historical drama, but more importantly, it enables us to examine the actual impact various types of mobilization had on village politics. No matter how great the differences were between various types of political mobilization, people had to adapt their mobilization strategies to local conditions. Since the natural village on the North China plain was a ready-made institution for organizing rural society, all political forces exploited this institution heavily. The impact that different mobilizations had on village politics was therefore virtually identical: they all led to the formalization of village governance and the reorganization of the village community.

Formalization of village governance

The first substantial change in village politics brought about by various types of mobilization was the formalization of village governance, the establishment of a formal and secular village government. In rural North China, prior to the twentieth century, village public affairs were managed by the council of the village-wide religious association. The character of this association was, as Gamble observed, fundamentally social rather than political, and it operated in a very loose fashion (1963: 33–34). Once the historical context changed, this institutional arrangement and its working style were forced to change.

Entering the twentieth century, the formal and secular government gradually took the place of the old religious council in most North China villages. The driving force behind this political change was no doubt the various types of political mobilization either for self-defense or for modernization. The establishment and evolution of the *Qingmiaohui* can exemplify how mobilization for self-defense fueled this change.

The *Qingmiaohui* was a self-defense organization established in many villages in the first half of the twentieth century. Setting up and running a *Qingmiaohui* involved various collective activities related to organization, management, and decision-making. For instance, villagers had to decide whether to watch crops by themselves or by hire watchmen; codify regulations to manage this activity; and allocate resources to finance this project.[6] Carrying out these matters was beyond the capacity of the old religious councils. Villagers therefore added new functions to this old organ and changed its name, so as to reflect its newly acquired functions. This, however, did not necessarily mean a reshuffling of the old council. In many cases, the same personnel now assumed more responsibilities and wielded greater power. The following case illustrates this.

Zhongshancun was a northern Henan village located near the county seat of Anyang (Map 1.1). Before the Republican era, there was a *Qiubaoshe* (Harvest Protection Association) in the village. The main function of this association was to collect money from villagers after the autumn harvest to pay for an opera for the entertainment of the gods (*yanxi choushen*). Entering the Republican era, the villagers renamed the *Qiubaoshe* as *Qingmiaoshe* (Green Sprouts Association) and gave it more public responsibilities. During the busy seasons, the *Qingmiaoshe* selected people to watch the village's crops. In wintertime, it assigned people to night watch duties. The *Qingmiaoshe* also collected various *tankuan* levies for the government (Sun Jiyuan and Sun Jiayou 1933: 3: 32–33).

At first glance there appeared to be no radical changes to the old religious council in terms of its organization and personnel. The leaders of the *Qingmiaoshe* were usually addressed in the same manner as before as either *huishou* or *shoushi*. Nonetheless, the change of functions led to changes in the nature of the council itself. Previously the main function of the religious council was to organize various religious activities, which were not necessarily conducted on a regular basis. A poor harvest could prompt the suspension of a temple fair or an opera performance. But this was not the case for the organization of self-defense activities such as collective crop-watching. Self-defense was a year-round activity, requiring a standing fund for financial backing, and an authoritative organ for management and regulation enforcement. This situation forced the religious council to change its old way of operation and transform itself into an authoritative governing organ.

Because now the *Qingmiaohui* became the most powerful organization in the village, it gradually became the village's governing body, assuming the role of village government. As Huang Di observed:

> [the] *Qingmiaohui* is not only responsible for crop-watching for the village, it is also responsible for the safety and security of all villagers' lives and property. In addition, it organizes and manages all other public activities in the village.
>
> In regard to a village's external affairs, the *Qingmiaohui* takes responsibility for protecting the village's interests. Whenever there are levies demanded by armies or governments, they are always handled by the *Qingmiaohui*. . . . [on such an occasion] if there is no *Qingmiaohui* to bargain with outside forces, and to allocate [levies] among villagers, the village's loss will be greater. Conflicts and cooperation between villages are also handled by the *Qingmiaohui*.

As far as the village's internal affairs are concerned, the *Qingmiaohui* is responsible for taking care of public properties such as temples and temple land, and other public land and trees. It is also responsible for maintaining and building village public works. It also manages village religious and educational activities . . . Even disputes between families, relatives and neighborhoods very often went to the councilors of the association for judgement.

(Huang Di 1936: 409, 413–414)

The evolution of the *Qingmiaohui* shows how mobilization for self-defense gave a strong impetus to the establishment of more formal and authoritative governance in the village. Since North China villages were also mobilized to undertake some modernization projects, mobilization for modernization also had a significant impact on the formalization of village governance. The establishment of modern public schools in the village is a good example of this. No one will deny that opening a village public school differed substantially from organizing a village self-defense program in content and meaning to a village community. However, the actual impact they had on political life in a village was very much the same.

To open a school in a village meant the village also had to manage and finance it. Financially, village schools were supported by village public funds. The tuition paid by students made up a small portion of the school's income. Huang Di estimated that the average annual expenditure for a village primary school in north Hebei during early 1930s was about 200 *yuan*. The tuition charged per student was usually one *yuan* per year (Huang Di 1936: 10: 402).[7] The average size of the student body in a village school was between 20 and 30, and tuition fees thus only accounted for 10 percent to 15 percent of school funding.[8] More than 85 percent of school funds came from villages' public income. In his sample villages, Gamble found that school funds came from the rent of villages' temple lands, the commission from the sale of lands or some special products, and the profits from village granaries and other village-owned properties (1963: 107). Li Jinghan's field study of Dingxian also shows that rent from village public land constituted about 41 percent of school income (Li Jinghan 1933: 207). However, if a village was without these sources or these sources were insufficient, the land owned or cultivated by villagers would be the major source of school funding. This was very common in most North China villages (Huang Di 1936: 10: 401–402).

Since the establishment of a village public school involved a great deal of public management and demanded continuous financial support, an authoritative governing body was needed to carry out these tasks. In some villages, the school was run by the village head, but in most villages the school management was assigned to a special committee called the *xiaodonghui* (the board of trustees for the village school). The members of the committee were usually village councilors (Zhang Zhongtang 1932: 6:

256; Li Jinghan. 1933: 174; Huang Di 1936: 10: 402; Gamble 1963: 105). Thus opening village schools again gave old village leaders more authority and called for daily management and financial support; this further helped to formalize and strengthen the village governance.

As discussed previously, mobilization for modernization was usually stimulated by political forces outside the village, primarily by the state. In its pursuit of modernization, the state was eager to mobilize the rural popu- lace and enlist local energies. On the one hand, the state introduced modern projects such as schools to villages; on the other, it also pressed villages increasingly harder for local resources. Noticeably, the two parties involved in this game were the state and the village community, not the state and the individual villagers. It was the village community as a collective that bore the direct responsibilities to the state. In order to make villages more compliant and work more efficiently, the state vigorously urged the village to organize a formal government in accordance with its design and requirements.

The state's efforts to formalize village governance can be traced back to as early as the last decade of the Qing, and continued and intensified in the Republican era.[9] Starting in Zhili (Hebei) Province in about 1900, North China villages were asked by the local government to set up two new offices, the village head and the assistant head (*cunzheng* and *cunfu*), which were intended to substitute for the *difang* or the *dibao* (Gamble 1963: 3, 39).[10] These village officers were to be elected by their fellow villagers and were responsible for all village public affairs. But from the state's point of view, they should serve also as government agents in the village, not just the autonomous leaders of the village. They were required to follow govern- ment orders and to fulfill government tasks in the countryside. In many counties, the county magistrates asked villagers to organize the *Qingmiaohui* and asked the *Qingmiaohui* to take the role of *de facto* village government (KC 1952: 1: 180, 204, 4: 29; Myers 1970: 60, 100; Duara 1988: 198).

After 1928, the Nationalist Government took more radical steps to fur- ther this political process. On June 5, 1929, the government promulgated the County Organization Act (*Xian zuzhi fa*). The aim of this Act was to organize rural society into the unified *xiangzhen linlü* (townships, villages and neighborhoods) system so as to strengthen political integration in rural areas and also to strengthen government control over rural society. Under this system, a *xiang* (an administrative village) needed to comprise a min- imum of 100 households (FGDQ 1936: 1: 535).[11] Since most villages in North China had more than 100 households, the natural village was generally respected by this law, and was equivalent to, in most cases, the administr- ative village.[12] This Act also spelled out in detail how the *xiang* government was to be organized, what officers and committees it should have, and how these were to be elected and composed (ibid.: 1: 537).[13]

Under the continuous pressure of various political mobilizations and state efforts to formalize village governance, village politics changed rapidly. By the 1930s, in most villages on the North China plain, the formal government and standing finance became the norm. However, this formal village government possessed a dual character: it was both a self-governing organ of the village and an agent of the state. This created tensions between community and state interests and presented a dilemma to the village governments. Along with increasing state intrusion, state interests frequently outweighed community interests. This would, as we will see in the next chapter, lead to intense conflicts between the two and a rapid deterioration of village politics.

Reorganization of the village community

Continuous political mobilization not only led to the formalization of village governance, it also called for the reorganization of the village community thus to strengthen the village's control over both its people and resources. Accordingly, the reorganization of the village community focused on two aspects: (1) the enforcement of compulsory village affiliation, and (2) the definition of village territory. Again, these changes can be examined in the case of the *Qingmiaohui*.

The enforcement of compulsory affiliation

As previously mentioned, the *Qingmiaohui* was a self-defense association organized in the village and supported by the community as a whole. Since the main function of the *Qingmiaohui* was to protect crops, every villager who owned or cultivated land was automatically a member. This ascriptive nature means that no one could withdraw from it at his or her will.[14] Upon being asked under what circumstances a member could quit the association, some *Qingmiaohui* members in Suxian, Anhui, answered: (1) when one does not own land; (2) when one's land is not located within the association's watching sphere; and (3) when one is no longer farming. In fact, they added that no one had ever quit the association (Qiao Qiming and Yao Yong 1934: 15). This principle of compulsary affiliation was designed to consolidate the *Qingmiaohui*. And since the *Qingmiaohui* was a village-wide association, this measure actually served to strengthen the village's control over its people.

The *Qingmiaohui* was not only responsible for crop-watching, very often it also took care of the whole village's security. For this reason villagers who did not own or cultivate land were also members of the association. For instance, in northern Hebei, besides crop-watching, the *Qingmiaohui* was also responsible for the safety and security of the village. Therefore even non-farming households, such as village shopkeepers, were also under the rule of *Qingmiaohui* and were thus members of the association. They enjoyed the same rights as farming households, and also shouldered the same responsibility to the association (Huang Di 1936: 409).

As a matter of fact, all of the village self-defense programs were organized in ways similar to the *Qingmiaohui*. They were based on the village community as a whole and demanded mandatory affiliation. For example, in Taitou every family was required to take part in the village's defense program. Wealthy families equipped themselves with weapons; and all able-bodied men in the village were organized into teams. Each family was responsible for supplying night-watching crew (Yang 1945: 143). Qiao Qiming's investigation of two branches of the *Lianzhuanghui* in Suxian tells us that the association required all adult males living within its sphere to be members; each household was required to provide at least one member. Only families living outside of the sphere of the association could quit the association (Qiao Qiming and Yao Yong 1934: 7).

Why did villagers adhere so firmly to compulsory affiliation? The chief reason was that villagers wanted to eliminate "free riders," to ensure the mobilization of everyone in the community, and hence to maximize the strength of these self-defense programs.[15] According to interviews with *Qingmiaohui* members conducted by Qiao Qiming, non-members could not have the same rights as members unless they paid their shares of crop money. If a non-member was unwilling to pay the money, then the crop-watcher would not provide any protection even if his crops were being stolen under the watcher's nose (ibid.). In fact, Qiao's informants told him that all villagers were compelled to join the crop-watching association, no one remained outside.

A similar account is found in Zhang Zhongtang's field study of the early 1930s. In west Shandong many villages had joined the Red Spears. According to the rules governing the Red Spears, when a member village was attacked by bandits or disbanded soldiers, the neighboring member villages were required to provide immediate assistance. If a member village failed to do so, it would be punished by the other member villages (Zhang Zhongtang 1932: 243). Though the Red Spears was a supra-village organization, it usually recruited the whole village as its member, not individual villagers (Dai 1973: 83; Perry 1980: 197–205). Once a village joined the society, all of its residents became members. If someone in the village did not want to be included, he would repeatedly be forced to "donate" substantial sums of money to the society or he would be forced to pay high financial charges until he joined it (Zhang Zhongtang 1932; Perry 1980: 198).

It is clear that in order to guard against bandits a self-defense organization had to protect the whole village, otherwise it could not protect even its own members in the village. No one can imagine that a self-defense organization could effectively protect its members in a village while allowing bandits to enter the village to attack non-members. The only way to effectively protect the village was to keep bandits out of the village entirely. This meant that non-members, if there were any, could enjoy the same protection of a self-defense organization. This was not only unfair to members, but would jeopardize the organization itself. If "free riders" were tolerated, then a strong and effective self-defense program could not be enforced. In order to protect themselves effectively, the only solution for villagers was to enforce compulsory affiliation and rule out any free-riding. Only a fully mobilized village was best able to maximize its strength, enlist every bit of its resources, and effectively protect its members.[16]

The definition of village territory

To organize and maintain village collective programs such as self-defense, financial support was very crucial. In rural North China, the major source of village revenue was the land owned and cultivated by villagers. Villages usually collected money from villagers to support various public projects. The rate of collection was based on the amount of land villagers owned or (in some villages) cultivated. Though this land was by no means a village's public property, it was controlled and assessed by the village. Huang Di's field study estimates that in north Hebei, the money collected from land accounted for between 70 percent to 80 percent of a village's income (Huang Di 1936: 10: 415–416). It was therefore no wonder that villages showed great concern for their land. In the first half of the twentieth century, under the increasing financial pressure due to continuous mobilization and increasing state taxation, assessments on land quickly became jealously guarded by villages. This situation brought about another important change to villages, the definition of village territory.

Before the twentieth century, there was no clearly defined territory in North China villages.[17] Entering the twentieth century, however, the village territory was gradually demarcated as a village was mobilized. The first push toward this change came from the establishment of the *Qingmiaohui*. As a crop-watching system, the *Qingmiaohui* delimited clear boundaries within which the land was to be watched and protected. In many places, these boundaries were called *qingquan* (the green circle). The *qingquan* refers to the circle that demarcated the areas watched and protected by a village's *Qingmiaohui* (KC 1952: 1: 59, 174, 205, 5: 49; Gamble 1963: 18–19; see also Duara 1988: 198). The land falling within this circle was the territory of a specific village, from which the village collected its revenue. Due to frequent land transactions between villages, the *qingquan* was not originally fixed. In local parlance, this unfixed green circle was called *huoquan*, which means a living circle and hence an unfixed circle (KC 1952: 1: 174, 180, 185, 206).

To a village, a living circle meant that its revenue base was not stable. Because under this arrangement, once a villager sold his land within the circle to an outsider, the village lost its assessment on that piece of land. Without a stable revenue base, a village would not be able to meet its rapidly expanding fiscal demands such as financing the school and self-defense projects, and paying various government *tankuan* dues.[18] To stabilize a village's revenue base, the only solution was to clearly define its territory. As a result, in most villages, the *qingquan* gradually transformed from a *huoquan* to a *siquan* (meaning: dead and hence fixed circle), or from "living" and flexible boundaries to "dead" and fixed boundaries (KC 1952: 1: 180, 185). Once a village's *qingquan* was defined as a "dead" circle, all of the land within this circle became this village's uncompromising territory. This arrangement was not designed to prohibit land transactions across village boundaries, rather, it was aimed at safeguarding a village's revenue base. Though villagers could sell their land to outsiders, this did not constitute a transfer of the village's territory. Thus the assessment of the land sold to outsiders remained within the circle, i.e. the village. The outside buyers had to pay various dues for the land to the village that owned the territory in which the land was located. In Hebei, the practice was called "*màidi bu màiquan*" (lit. land can be sold, but the circle cannot) (Huang Di 1936: 10: 415).[19]

The definition of village territory involved reorganizing the village community in a fashion similar to what had occurred in compulsory affiliation for self-defense. By fixing boundaries, a village could ensure its revenue base in spite of a fluid land market; and with this fixed territory, a village could control and mobilize its resources more effectively.

State efforts for the reorganization of the village

As discussed earlier, North China villagers not only mobilized themselves for self-defense, they were also mobilized by the state for its modernization programs. The state was also very eager to reorganize villages in a similar fashion to what the villagers had done to protect their own interests. Therefore, the state warmly embraced the villages' practice of fixing boundaries. During the Nanjing period, special regulations were issued by both central and local governments requiring villages to define their territories.[20]

In 1929, the Nationalist Government published "The Implementation Act of Xiangzhen Self-Government" (*Xiangzhen zizhi shishifa*), following the promulgation of the County Organization Act. The Act required administrative villages and townships (*xiangzhen*) all over the country to define their territories. Articles 3, 4 and 5 of the Act stated that

> According to Article 8 of the County Organization Act, the definition of *xiangzhen* territories should be conducted under the direction of the ward head [*quzhang*] together with representatives from the county government. Each *xiang* and *zhen* should define their territories according to their original boundaries . . . If the boundaries of a *xiang* or *zhen* are not clear or if there are border disputes between villages, the ward head should consult with the concerned *xiang* or *zhen* heads and then report the case to the county government for resolution.
>
> (Wu Shuzi and Zhao Hanjun 1930: 150)

In Hebei, the regulations for defining village territory were published in March 1929. The purpose of the regulations was, as the first sentence of the first article stated, to "define village boundaries so as to facilitate villages in administering their territories." Interestingly enough, the regulations emphasized that village territoriality was distinct from land ownership. Immediately after the first sentence of the first article, the regulations state: "However, it [the definition of village boundaries] has no implications for landownership" (HBFG 1929: 7: 26–27).[21] Obviously, this principle was identical to the practice of *màidi bu màiquan* discussed above. This principle underscored the village's jurisdiction over its territory but not the land ownership within the territory. This was a practical solution for securing the village's territory and hence, the village's revenue base, against frequent land transactions between residents of different villages.

In the eyes of local governments, the definition of village territory had even more direct advantages. It provided a solution for securing a village's *tankuan* base and solving border disputes between villages, a local headache which had been magnified under the increasing pressure of *tankuan* levies. Therefore, many local governments urged villages to define their territories. For example, in 1936, both Luancheng and Shunyi county governments ordered villages to fix their boundaries and retain all taxes paid on the land within these boundaries (KC 1952: 3: 515; 6: 380; see also Duara 1988: 201–203). The county magistrate of Shunyi stated in his order:

> In view of the fact that we seek to bring village administration under a single law, we have determined the "principle of land belonging to a village" [or village territoriality, *shudi zhuyi*]. This is what the villagers call the dead sphere. Even if Village X's land has been sold to [a resident of] Village Y, all the *tankuan*, including crop-watching, education, police, and all other dues, are to be paid to Village X. . . . This rule will be implemented from the day of the announcement. The villages whose finances have not yet been ordered according to this principle can now avoid disputes; those who have already implemented it naturally do not need to do so again.
>
> (cited in Duara 1988: 203)

Of course, the state's attempts to reorganize village communities were not limited to the definition of village territory. Rather, since the late Qing, the state had vigorously urged reorganization of village communities so as push villages to carry out various governmental tasks more rigorously and efficiently. This was especially true during the Nanjing period. For this purpose, the state issued many detailed laws and regulations aimed at reorganizing rural communities. In Hebei, for instance, the provincial government published 17 separate Acts in March, 1929, concerning the reorganization of the village community. These Acts were:

1 The general outline
2 Organization of the neighborhood (*linlü*)

3 The village assembly
4 Election of the village head, deputy head, and neighborhood head
5 The village office (*cungongsuo*)
6 The village supervision committee
7 The village mediation committee (*xisonghui*)
8 Definition of village boundaries
9 Village rules and regulations
10 Village finance
11 Village granary
12 Road construction
13 Ditch dredging
14 Village sanitation
15 Village education
16 Customs improvement
17 Evaluation of village officers.

(HBFG 1929: 7: 4–41)

They covered every aspect of a village's public life, from politics to economy, from public construction to social security, from education to customs and morality. These Acts demonstrated clearly that the state was very eager to improve village governance and strengthen village community through reorganization of every aspect of village's public life. The ultimate goal behind the state's efforts was of course to mobilize and enlist rural populace and resources in a more effective and efficient way, and thus achieve state's objectives in rural society.

Rural Reconstruction in North China villages

As mentioned previously, in the 1920s and 1930s rural China also witnessed a new development, i.e., a reform movement under the name of Rural Reconstruction. Rural Reconstruction was initiated by social reformers and was supported and encouraged by the Nationalist state. Though the commonly shared goal of the movement was to reform and rejuvenate rural China, reformers working in different areas had to adapt their reforms to local conditions. Concrete reform approaches and objectives therefore varied significantly from region to region. On the North China plain, reformers also took the village as an institutional means to mobilize peasants and reform rural society. Their reforms therefore had the same impact as the various types of political mobilization did on the village community. In this section, two cases of Rural Reconstruction, Zhaicheng's village reform and Zouping's experiment, will be examined.

Zhaicheng Village was located 9 miles east of the county seat of Dingxian, Hebei, a rural community of 330 households with 19 surnames.[22] As early as the 1890s, Mi Jiansan, a native of Zhaicheng, after failing the imperial examination at the provincial level, began to occupy himself with educational reform in the village. In 1902, he established several schools in the village, including a junior primary school, a senior primary school, a girls school, and a citizens school. All schools were open to the villagers and their children free of charge. At that time, Mi Jiansan's son, Mi Digang, returned from studying in Japan. Inspired by the achievements of Japan's rural reconstruction and transformation, he went further to launch an ambitious reform aimed at transforming all aspects of village life which he called *cunzhi*.[23]

To undertake such a massive reform, the village, first of all, had to mobilize all of its resources. In 1904, in order to finance village schools and other public projects, the village decided to centralize public funds and manage them under a single authority. Originally, these funds were collected from different sources, expended for different purposes and managed by different organizations. For example, the *Gongchaiju* (the public service bureau) was responsible for collecting the rent on 405 *mu* from village public land to subsidize the households that provided cart services.[24] There were also 13 religious and entertainment societies in the village, which owned a total of 183 *mu* of public land and possessed 600-odd *cuan* of cash. Now all land and funds were pooled together, managed by the village government, and used for financing public activities, especially reform projects (Yin Zhongcai and Mi Digang 1925: 44–46). Furthermore, in 1917, a thorough land survey to assess villagers' tax liabilities was completed. Afterwards, the village's *tankuan* dues were imposed equally on privately owned land (ibid.: 26–27).

The reformers urged everyone in the village to take an active part in various projects. For this purpose, the village was completely reorganized and a new village government was established. According to *The Outline of Organization of Village Self-Government* laid down in 1915, all villagers were organized into eight self-regulated neighborhoods (*zizhiqu*). Each neighborhood had a head who was elected by its residents. The eight neighborhood heads plus the three village headmen and seven clerks constituted the village assembly which was responsible for both legislation and administration. The village administration was handled by the village government (ibid.: 30–32, 38–44).

The village government was responsible for all aspects of village life. Various special committees and associations were set up to undertake different tasks. For example, financial and economic activities were carried out by an organization called the *Yinli xieshe* (the cooperative for promoting public interests). All villagers were members of this cooperative, the main functions of which included managing public funds, handling savings and loans, organizing consumer cooperatives and cooperatives for selling and buying, and so forth (ibid.: 49–54). According to regulations, the purpose of this organization was to promote a cooperative spirit among villagers, and to increase the common interests of the community (ibid.: 49–54).

The village government also organized various societies such as the Good Deeds Society (*Deye shijianhui*), the Custom Improvement Society (*Gailiang fengsuhui*), the Village Harmony Society (*Jimuhui*), and many projects for rural reconstruction, including agricultural improvement, road construction, well digging, sanitation, forest protection, self-defense, and so forth (ibid.: 116–164). Most strikingly, the village government even organized a cooperative called *Nashui zuhe* (the tax payment cooperative) for tax collection. The purpose of this cooperative was to make tax payment convenient for the villagers and tax collection easier for the government. The cooperative bound villagers together with the collective responsibility for collecting land tax (not *tankuan* levies). Under this arrangement, each year, villagers paid their taxes to their neighborhood heads. The village government then collected taxes from the neighborhood heads and delivered them to the county treasurer (ibid.: 54–56). In this way villagers could avoid dealing with tax collectors directly and thus kept themselves from being taken advantage of by those predators.

Zhaicheng's reforms were highly praised and enthusiastically supported by the government at various levels and by various social reformers.[25] It served as a model for village reform in North China. In the early Republican period, both county and provincial authorities issued decrees requiring villages to adopt the Zhaicheng model. Zhaicheng's reform also exerted great influence on Shanxi's village reform. Shanxi later became the model province for village reform (*cunzhi*) and its reforms in turn greatly influenced other provinces in North China (Li Jinghan 1933: 117–119).

The Zhaicheng reform highlighted some of the essential features of Rural Reconstruction on the North China plain that followed the Zhaicheng.[26] In the Zhaicheng reform, the village was the institutional means exploited by the reformers and it was also the primary target of the reform. The reform created an authoritative and omnipotent village government, and reorganized the village community along the lines of ascriptive affiliation. All these features were identical to the political changes experienced by North China villages under the pressure of various political mobilizations discussed in previous sections. Zhaicheng inspired many reformers and more ambitious reforms were launched in the 1920s and 1930s, among them the most acclaimed one was probably the Rural Reconstruction in Zouping County, known as Zouping's experiment.

Zouping's experiment was led by the Shandong Institute of Rural Reconstruction (SIRR hereafter) during the 1930s. In order to carry out rural reconstruction projects, the designers and organizers of the experiment established a new organization called the *Xiangnong xuexiao* (the villager-peasant school). Later the name of the school was changed to *cunxue xiangxue* (the village school and the *xiang* school, here *xiang* refers to ward rather than administrative village. In Zouping there were a total of 14 *xiang*) (Xu Yinglian *et al.* 1936: 204, 233).[27] In the minds of its designers, the villager-peasant school was simultaneously an educational, political and economic organization (Kong 1934: 27). The primary purpose of this school was "to advance society and organize the countryside" (*tuidong shehui, zuzhi xiangcun*) (Xu Yinglian *et al.* 1936: 193).

The village school was based on the natural village. All villagers were automatically its students (*xuezong*), and they were divided into several departments according to age and gender (Liang 1989: 672). Liang Shuming, the famous advocate and practitioner of Rural Reconstruction and also the chief architect and director of the Zouping experiment, said: "Our aim is to use the *xiangxue cunxue* to organize rural society, use education to release the internal energies (*neili*) of rural society, and to improve and promote rural society through the efforts of the peasants themselves." For this purpose, it was necessary "that every person in the village actively and vigorously participate in village public affairs" (Liang 1989: 676, 720). In other words, the reformers gave the village school the task of mobilizing everyone in the village. Only when a village community was fully mobilized and well organized could it, Liang asserted, successfully pursue social reform and progress (ibid.: 678, 720). Liang firmly believed that this was the best and only way for rural reconstruction to build an ideal society in China (ibid.: 395–433).[28]

The village school was designed to take charge of all village public affairs, such as administration, defense, public construction, political and cultural campaigns, entertainment, and so forth (Xu Yinglian *et al.* 1936: 171–248; Kong 1934: 30–45). The school, in effect, was an authoritative village government (Liang 1989: 675, 677; Xu Yinglian *et al.* 1936: 212, 221, 230–232).

It is worth noting that in order to undertake these activities the school also organized many special groups in the village, such as women's associations, youth leagues, moral improvement societies, and various economic cooperatives. These groups were affiliated to and also under the guidance of the school (Xu Yinglian *et al.* 1936; Liang 1990: 429–430). For example, the cotton cooperative, the most successful cooperative in the Zouping experiment, had more activities that revolved around the school than any other cooperative (Alitto 1979: 256–257). In North China villages, these groups were usually voluntary organizations and functioned independently of village administrations. But now they were organized by and under the guidance of the village school, i.e. the village government. The aim of controlling these groups was, as the reformers stressed, to "establish an economic system in which capital is controlled, enjoyed, and owned in common" (ibid.: 253) and therefore to avoid social and economic stratification among villagers, and the exploitation and oppression of the poor by the rich (Liang 1990: 429–432).

The Zouping experiment echoed to a large extent the Zhaicheng reform, but on a larger scale.[29] Both reforms had many things in common: they both exploited the natural village as an institutional means to mobilize rural populace and reorganize rural society. Both made the village government more authoritative and the village community more tightly knit and controlled. Though the reformers were able to exert greater impact on village communities than the local governments did in their efforts to improve village governance and strengthen village community, the reformers still fell short of their goals. On the one hand, their reforms affected only a small number of villages. On the other hand, the success of the reforms even in these chosen villages was quite limited, because the reformers did not have solutions to the many political and socioeconomic problems they faced. As Liang Shuming confessed, besides the emotional and psychological mistrust between urban intellectuals and village peasants, the major problem the reformers encountered was that peasants suffered from exorbitant taxes and levies but the reformers could do nothing to help; the peasants wanted land but the reformers had no land to distribute. As a result, the "so-called rural movement caused no real rural movement (*haocheng xiangcun yundong er xiangcun budong*)" (Liang 1990: 581). Many criticisms of Rural Reconstruction, especially those from left-wing intellectuals and the Communists, also discounted the reform from this point of view, arguing that the movements merely alleviated the symptoms of rural crises and failed to provide a permanent cure to the crises.[30] The criticisms of Rural Reconstruction by both its proponents and opponents underscored socioeconomic factors in political mobilization. And it was the Communists, as we will see in Chapter 5, who capitalized on these criticisms and turned the reformers' dilemma to their advantage in their wartime mobilization.

4 The state and North China villages in a changing world

Although continuous political mobilizations powered major changes in village politics, political changes in rural North China were not caused by this factor alone. During this period, villages on the North China plain were also subject to the influences of other factors and forces, especially increasing state intrusion and accelerating socioeconomic stratification. Unlike political mobilizations, these factors impacted villages from an opposite direction and tended to weaken and disintegrate the village community. This in turn, led to the deterioration of village politics. As a result, conflicts within the village and confrontations between villages and the state became epidemic in rural North China.

Village politics under state intrusion

The formal village government was the product of continuous political mobilization. From the very beginning, this government played a dual character. On the one hand, it was self-government working for the public interests of the community. On the other, it was also a state agent responsible for implementing various orders of the state. Since community interests and state interests were often in conflict, village leaders had a hard time pleasing both parties at the same time. They were thus confronted by a dilemma: No matter what they did, they could not avoid offending one of the two parties. However, this situation also provided them with an opportunity to exploit their positions for their own benefit.

Even so, village power holders could not do as they pleased. Their choice in this political game was ultimately determined by the intensity of state intrusion and also by the solidarity of a village community. In the first half of the twentieth century, state intrusion grew in frequency and intensity. As a result, the administrative power held by the village government expanded rapidly and became increasingly alienated from its constituency. Since the expansion of this power was the result of state intrusion, and the power itself was often backed by the state, it became increasingly unrestrained and unchecked within the village. This inevitably opened the door to the abuse of power and led to the deterioration of village politics.

However, these consequences were not the intention of the state. As we have seen from the last chapter, the state, for its own interests, wanted to improve village politics. For only a strong and healthy village government could work effectively and efficiently for the state. In order to improve village politics, different regimes, especially the Nationalist Government, vigorously brought in many new institutions to the village. Following its reunification of China in 1928, the Nationalist Government had introduced an electoral system, a village assembly, a supervisory committee, and many concrete regulations into the village, with the hope of reformation of village politics and the rejuvenation of the village community.

No matter how well these institutions and regulations were intended and designed, they did not work well in practice. This is not to deny the sincerity of the state's efforts to improve village politics, or to ignore the positive effects (no matter how insignificant) brought about by these efforts. The fact is that these effects could not offset the negative consequences brought about by state intrusion. Before analyzing the impact of state intrusion, let us first examine how these new institutions worked in the villages.

Efforts to improve village politics

The electoral system

The electoral system was introduced into villages in the late Qing (see Chapter 3), but it was not put into practice until the promulgation of the County Organization Act (*Xian zuzhi fa*) in 1929 by the Nationalist Government. This Act stated that the village head and assistant head were to be elected by their fellow villagers through a formal vote (FGDQ 1936: 537). Its aim was to enlarge political participation in the village, and to change the current situation whereby a small group of village councilors dominated village offices (Gamble 1963: 142, 150).

In some isolated cases, this electoral system altered the monopoly of village offices by traditional village councilors. For example, Gamble's survey tells us that in one Hebei village the electoral system gave the poor villagers an opportunity to change their situation in village politics. The first election was held soon after the promulgation of the new law. The men chosen as village head and assistant head both came from the "front street," the poor residential section of the village. The election thus toppled the old order of wealthy villagers dominating village government (ibid.: 167).

However, this case was by no means common. In most villages the old practice of selecting village heads from and by the village councilors persisted tenaciously (Myers 1970: 259). In many localities, property-ownership was still an essential qualification for serving as village head or assistant head. This qualification was even written in local regulations and sanctioned by local governments. For example, in Luancheng County, owning a prescribed amount of property was one of the qualifications for village head (KC 1952: 3: 29). This requirement made it impossible for poor villagers to enter village politics.

The practical reason for this property requirement, from the standpoint of both local governments and villages, was that this arrangement was necessary to fulfill the *tankuan* dues that were frequently imposed on the village. Since most villagers did not have cash until after the harvest, very often the village heads had to make payments in advance and collect the money later. Under these circumstances, the ability to make pre-payments of the *tankuan* and other urgent needs was crucial for a person to serve as village heads (JLY 1985: 1: 92–93). As long as this property requirement existed, the situation of a small group of powerful and wealthy villagers dominating village government would not change. Therefore, in most villages, the electoral system was adopted merely in form. It brought about no substantial change to the existing power structure within the village.[1]

The village assembly

The establishment of village assemblies (*cunmin dahui* or *cunmin huiyi*) was intended to expand villagers' participation in public affairs, democratize the procedure of decision-making, and alter the old pattern of village politics. This institutional framework was also introduced by the Nationalist Government. *The Implementation Regulations of Xiangzhen Self-Government* stated that the village assembly was the legislative and decision-making organ. Its duties included selection and recall of village officers, initiatives and referendums, and the examination and approval of all important public affairs of the village (Wu Shuzi and Zhao Hanjun 1930: 153–154). Despite the Act, this framework took root in few villages. In the best case, the village assembly gave villagers a chance to express their opinions on important public issues, but the final decisions were seldom made by the assembly.

For example, in Lengshuigou (Licheng, Shandong), the village assembly was rather effective. The most important village financial affairs were discussed at the assembly, and villagers expressed their opinions freely during the assembly meeting. But the final decisions were made by the village heads rather than by a vote of the villagers (KC 1952: 4: 8–9). In Sibeichai (Luancheng, Hebei) and Houjiaying (Changli, Hebei), the situation was quite similar. The main function of the assembly was for villagers to express their opinions about important public affairs such as financial issues and self-defense programs. However, the assembly did not make any major decisions (KC 1952: 3: 46–48; 5: 11). Compared to villages without assemblies, the situation in these villages was no doubt a step forward, because now common villagers' voices could be heard.[2] But this too fell far short of preventing village councilors from dominating village affairs.

Village finance

A village fund handled by the village heads was very often a temptation to abuse power. To supervise the management of village finances, villages were asked to establish supervisory committees (*Jiancha weiyuanhui*). According to Article 44 of the County Organization Act, the duty of this committee was to supervise village finances and inform on village heads who transgressed laws and neglected duties (FGDQ 1936: 1: 537). To implement this article, local governments worked out detailed regulations for the operation of the committee. For example, in the fourth *qu* of Wanping County (Hebei), the regulations stated that the purpose of the supervisory committee was to approve village budgets and audit the income and expense accounts of the crop-money. It required that the village budget be sealed by the committee before it was put into effect; all expenditures above the budget allowances had to be properly explained, if not, the village heads and assistant heads were required to refund the money (Gamble 1963: 142–143).[3]

However, very little evidence suggests that this institutional design worked effectively.[4] It seems that of all the new institutional designs, this one performed most poorly. As Gamble commented, based on his observation:

> So far as we could find, the effort was futile and the committee existed only on paper. None of the village account books that we saw bore the imprint of the *hsien* seal as required by the proposed regulations, and we know from personal experience how loath the leaders of many villages would be to have outsiders examine and audit their accounts and thereby be in a position to question their handling of the village finances.
>
> (1963: 143)

Interference in the organization of the village government

Contrary to the situation discussed above, the negative effects that state intrusion had on village politics were very strong, they entirely offset the state's efforts to improve village politics. Increasing state intrusion forced village governments to be subordinate even more to the state until they finally became simple agents of the state. This development alienated the village government from its constituency, and made it increasingly uncontrollable by villagers.

One important aspect of state intrusion was the state interference in the organization of village government. Though the state acknowledged in theory that the village government was the self-government of the village, it reserved the right of arbitrary interference in village affairs, especially in the organization of village government. To secure this right, special rules and regulations were worked out by the government. These rules and regulations provided that the election of village officers must be supervised by representatives from the county or ward (*qu*) government. Otherwise, the election would be invalid (HBFG 1929: 11–12; Gamble 1963: 298).[5] To complete a valid election, the county government would issue a certificate of official appointment to the elected village head (HBFG 1929; KC 1952: 1: 97, 3: 59, 61, 4: 24; Gamble 1963: 4, 41).

This whole procedure underscored the state's power to interfere in village government rather than emphasizing the self-governing nature of the village government. Through this procedure, village officers were not only regarded as community leaders elected by their fellow villagers but also considered, to some degree, to be government officers appointed by the state. Although this appointment was usually served as a subsequent acknowledgment, it reminded people that the power of the state was over the village government.

Some local governments exercised even greater power in interfering in the organization of village government. For example, in Henan Province, the magistrates and the *qu* heads had the right to change any village officer whom they thought to be unqualified even though the officer was legally elected by his fellow villagers (Nongfuhui 1934b: 73–74). This not only gave local governments substantial power to interfere in village politics, it also became an important source of conflict between government and village communities. The following story recorded by Liang Shuming illustrates this situation. Liang recalled an election held in a village in which the county magistrate informed villagers that the incumbent village head could not be reelected. Nevertheless, the incumbent was reelected, so the magistrate asked villagers to hold a new election. This time the incumbent's son was elected. When the supervisor declared the election invalid, the villagers dispersed in an uproar. The magistrate persuaded the villagers to vote once again, and this time the most notorious person in the village was elected (Liang Shuming 1990: 328).

State interference in the organization of village government was not necessarily negative. Since village elections could easily be manipulated by village elites, state interference could prevent this type of abuse and impose an outside check on village politics. However, this interference also changed the basis of legitimacy in village government because under this arrangement, community support was no longer the only power source for village government. Instead state support became even more important. Judging both by its motivation and effects, this interference forced the village government, supposedly a self-governing body, to comply with the state, even when state interests conflicted with the village community.

The tanpai in rural North China

Increasing state intrusion aimed at more effective control of rural society and extraction of more resources from it. More state extraction not only meant more taxes and levies, it also meant that villagers had to use their own resources to fulfill a wide range of official duties. During the Republican period, more and more government duties were imposed on villages.

Besides drafting laborers and soldiers, a popular practice in the late Qing (see Chapter 2), villages were also required to take collective responsibility for purchasing government bonds (*gongzhai tanpai*), prohibiting opium-smoking, consuming licensed salt (*dayan tanpai*, for combating salt smuggling which was rampant in North China), and so forth (Sun Xiaocun 1934: 18; Li Zuozhou 1936: 72–74; Chen Tisi 1936: 92–95; HBGM 1980: 1: 4–6).[6] However, no matter how onerous these official duties were, they paled when compared to the notorious *tankuan* or *tanpai*.

Heavy *tanpai* was the inevitable result of state expansion. In Chapter 2, we saw that this new form of tax was instituted and exploited to meet the state's urgent financial needs after the outbreak of the Taiping War. Thereafter, and especially since the beginning of the twentieth century, the financial demands of the state skyrocketed as did the *tankuan* levies imposed on the village. By the 1920s and 1930s in North China, the *tankuan* levies had already greatly surpassed land taxes and land surcharges and became the heaviest burden imposed on the rural populace. A 1934 survey by the Rural Reconstruction Committee of the Nanjing Government reported that:

> In the northern provinces of China, the tax that is similar to a land surcharge or even heavier than that, and which has now become the awful burden of peasants, is temporary levies [*lingshi tanpai*].[7] Though land surcharges are heavy, they have restrictions, but these temporary levies are imposed without restrictions. Because of this, the *tanpai* is heavier than the land surcharges for North China peasants. . . .
>
> As far as the provinces are concerned, *tanpai* is levied in Henan, Hebei, Shandong, Shanxi, Shanxi, Ganshu, Suiyuan, and Chahaer provinces. It is even found in some Southern provinces, such as Hunan, Hubei, Jiangxi. In a word, in areas that are lacking good transportation facilities, under wicked political conditions, with unenlightened peasants, and during wartime, there are *tanpai* levies.
>
> (Sun Xiaocun 1934: 148, 13)

Although the *tankuan* levies were paid by individual villagers based mainly on their landholdings, they differed fundamentally from regular land taxes and surcharges in that they were imposed on the village community as a collective. The party ultimately responsible for them was the village community, not individual villagers as was the case with land taxes. Moreover, the *tankuan* levies were collected via rural administrative systems, and directly by wards, and especially village heads, not by state tax bureaus and collectors.[8] As we have seen, compared to regular land taxes, this method of taxation was a convenient and efficient way for local governments to meet their rapidly expanding financial needs. It must be emphasized that it was the communal structure and social formation of North China villages that made this method feasible. Since the late Qing this method had been seriously exploited by the state. As a result, in rural North China it was the *tanpai* rather than land surcharges that became the main revenue source for local governments and the major tax burden imposed on peasants.

For example, in Henan, the *tankuan* levies amounted to ten times the regular taxes in 1932 (Sun Xiaocun 1934: 152). And in Hebei, an official from the provincial land survey committee reported that land taxes and surcharges were 0.1 *yuan* per *mu* of land, and the *tanpai* was three or four times this amount (Zhang Youyi 1957: 84). Similarly, in Suiyuan, the chairman of the provincial government, Fu Zuoyi, reported in 1935 that

> of the total tax burden on a peasant during one year, the provincial taxes amount to 10 percent, the county taxes amount to between 15 and 20 percent, while the *tankuan* levied by ward and village governments amounts to between 75 and 80 percent. From this, we can see that peasants suffered most from ward and village *tankuan*, rather than from regular provincial and county taxes.
>
> (Zhang Youyi 1957: 87)[9]

These provincial surveys were substantiated by much county and village level data (Nongfuhui 1934b: 79–82; Amano Motonosuke 1936: 13–15, 32–35; Huang 1985: 279, 285).

Village politics under the tanpai

Though the *tanpai* provided the state with a very convenient means of satisfying its financial needs, for the village government it was an onerous burden. In the process of *tankuan* collection, the village government bore full responsibility for this arduous duty. However, to fulfill this task, the village government needed the cooperation of the villagers. Therefore, within the community, the cooperation of the villagers was essential to the successful collection of the *tankuan*. Under the heavy burden of rapidly increasing *tankuan* levies, it was impossible to expect this cooperation from villagers. Many contemporary sources tell us that villagers hated to pay their *tankuan* dues, therefore the collection of *tankuan* was a serious headache for village heads (KC 1952: 3: 59; 4: 25).

To collect *tankuan* from an uncooperative community, the village government could only expect support from the state. The state was fully aware of this situation and was willing to back *tankuan* collection with the coercive forces it commanded. The newly established police force and military guards were engaged in this endeavor and were responsive to village heads' requests for enforcing *tankuan* payments (Huang 1985: 287–288). As Yang Yuan, the village head of Shajing said, any time a villager refused to pay his *tankuan* dues, the village head could file a charge to the police and this villager would be punished (KC 1952: 2: 344–345). Sometimes, village heads simply asked policemen to collect *tankuan* dues from those defaulters (Gamble 1963: 76).

Support from the state greatly enhanced the power wielded by village heads. Moreover, since the powerful support was from outside, it profoundly altered village politics. Now the village administration became very hard to control from within the community. Village heads could easily request policemen to punish villagers for defaulting *tankuan* payments, whereas villagers could not easily accuse village heads of abusing their posts. A villager from Shajing complained that if villagers were dissatisfied with their village head, they could not accuse him before the county government directly and individually. To be effective, a bill of complaint had to be signed by a majority of villagers and sent by a chosen representative, prefer- ably an educated and able person, to the county government. Otherwise, the county government would ignore the complaint (KC 1: 127). The cases thus brought to county or ward authorities were very often arbitrated in favor of village heads, especially when the disputes were over *tankuan* levies (Duara 1988: 220). The collection of *tankuan* therefore introduced coercive forces of the state into the village and resulted in a rapid expansion of village government.

The expansion of village government did not result in the more efficient management of village affairs; instead, it merely alienated village power holders from their constituencies, causing them to behave more like state agents. State intrusion and extraction thus transformed village administra- tion from a self-government to a subordinating branch of the state. This alien- ated village government had to carry out various onerous official duties, but could not expect real support and cooperation from the community. These official duties made continued service extremely difficult for village heads, who were caught between conflicting state and community interests. The office of village head became a thankless job: "instead of being sought after, it was being avoided and refused" (Gamble 1963: 2). Many village heads complained about their hardships and wanted to resign from their offices (KC 1952: 3: 54, 4: 25). Some even committed suicide under the pressure of collecting the *tanpai* (Zheng Shijun 1977: 6700). A vivid description of their feelings and dilemmas is found in a short report from a village head of a Shandong village:

> Ba has been village head for more than ten years. He knows that one cannot ignore the orders of his superiors. However, if he is just a "yes"- man, he will displease his fellow villagers, and also his conscience will not allow him to do so. He is going to resign but he knows that his superior will not agree. And he wants to stop working but he is afraid of being punished. It was really a predicament for him.
>
> (Mao Dun 1936: 11.32)

However, those who wanted to exploit this office for their own interests were now given a rare opportunity. Consequently, the power vacuum left by honest people was quickly filled by those whom Duara (1988) refers to as "entrepreneurial brokers." These profit-seekers openly competed for village offices. As a field report stated: "ordinary peasants looked upon the position of village head as being as vicious as a viper, while landlords and local bullies considered it a ready source of profit. During elections, they practice bribery openly, acting like buffoons" (Zhang Youyi 1957: 384).[10] The only concern of these entrepreneurial brokers was how to exploit their power to reap material gains for themselves. Under their rule the abuse of power prevailed and village politics rapidly deteriorated.

Over time, extortion and misappropriation of *tankuan* levies were common phenomena. Since *tanpai* levies were frequent and irregular, and their collection controlled by village heads who usually did not inform villagers about allocations, it was very difficult for villagers to know clearly the exact amount of *tanpai* collected (HBGM 1980: 1: 7–8). This gave village heads an opportunity to make a profit for themselves. For instance, in Zhangjiatun, a small village with about 100 households located in Xintai, Hebei, a levy of 540.36 *yuan* was collected by the village head for a ward fee for security guards. Villagers filed a lawsuit against the village head over this levy. When the village head was brought to court, it was revealed that the regular quota for this village was only 120 *yuan*. The money above this amount was used to entertain ward policemen and to fill the coffers of the village head (NFH 1934: 5: 164). Similar cases were found everywhere in North China as documented by many contemporary surveys (Nongfuhui 1934b: 96; Amano Motonosuke 1936: 50–52; KC 1952: 2: 345, 3: 47–48, 512–513; Zhang Youyi 1957: 91; Gamble 1963: 199–200).

Besides the embezzlement of *tankuan* levies, many village heads also used their positions to avoid taxes and levies. As a contemporary newspaper reported:

> It is common practice for the wealthy people in the village to pay fewer levies than poor people. Because those wealthy people are usually village officers, they can exploit what passes through their hands and shift levy burdens to the poor and powerless.
>
> (Zhang Youyi 1957: 74)

This corruption definitely deepened and widened socioeconomic differences among villagers and intensified conflicts between wealthy power holders and common villagers. In the villagers' eyes, therefore, the unfair allocation of *tankuan* was a more vicious thing than the *tankuan* itself. As Duara points out, with regard to the role of the tax burden in provoking peasant protests against the state, important factors were not only the absolute size or the burden of the *tankuan per se*, but also how the burden was perceived (1988: 253, note 10).[11]

To make matters even worse, the local government usually tolerated or sometimes intentionally ignored the abuse of power by these predatory village heads because only they were willing to cooperate with the government to squeeze villagers, even though the benefits of this practice to the state were questionable. The state yielded, as the Crooks noted, a maximum of unpopularity and a minimum of revenues (Crook and Crook 1959: 16). Most of the revenues that were extracted from villagers went into these predators' stomachs and their purses. While the government could hardly realize a significant increase in revenues, the villagers suffered from an increasingly heavy burden of taxes and levies (Sun Xiaocun 1934: 12: 1, 3).

The deterioration of village politics under the heavy burden of the *tanpai* was a conspicuous crisis in rural North China during the 1920s and the 1930s. As many studies have pointed out, this was the outcome of state intrusion into and extraction from rural society (Kuhn 1975; Huang 1985; Duara 1988). However, state intrusion and extraction were not the sole reason for the deterioration of village politics. If the *tanpai* had not been a collective levy imposed on the village community, even though it was heavy, very likely, its impact on village politics would have been different. Only by being levied on the village collectively could the *tanpai* exert such a substantial negative impact on village politics, which resulted in the corruption of village power and the deterioration of village politics.

The conflicts between the state and the village

The *tanpai* transformed taxation from an affair between the state and individuals to an affair between the state and village communities, and from a tax procedure to an administrative procedure. This change not only led to the deterioration of village politics but also strained state–village relations and intensified conflicts between the two. In the villagers' eyes, the state was losing its legitimacy not only because its *tanpai* was intolerable but also because it tolerated, even co-conspired in, the abuse of power by predatory village heads. During the Republican period, intense conflicts between the state and villages over increasing *tanpai* became a major political issue in rural North China.

In their protests and resistance against the state, villagers were not a disorderly band, but, rather, they were well organized by their respective villages. The village community provided them with a ready-made organization in their struggle. In North China, especially along the border between Hebei, Henan and Shandong, many instances of tax resistance were organized by the Red Spears or other secret societies such as the Heavenly Gate (*Tianmenhui*), the Big Swords (*Dadaohui*), and the Yellow Gauze (*Huangshahui*), to name only a few (Dai Xuanzhi 1973; Tanaka 1930; Perry 1980). Though the Red Spears was an supra-village organization, it was based on the village community. Instead of drawing followers individually, it recruited villages as collective members. This organizational base enabled the Red Spears to mobilize large masses, sometimes hundreds of thousands, very quickly and efficiently. Tax resistance organized in this fashion was usually large in scale and violent by nature. Protestors very often occupied the county *yamen*, drove away the magistrate, destroyed the tax and police bureaus, killed evil officials and functionaries, and even fought with government armies (Tanaka 1930: 252–274; Dai Xuanzhi 1973: Chapter 6).

The conflicts between the state and villages were also extended into the village communities. Since the corruption of village power was the product of state intrusion, the struggle against this oppressive and corrupt power thus indirectly targeted the state. Since all of the struggles directly or indirectly targeted the state, they could be very easily channeled into anti-state political insurrections. This was exactly what the Communists tried to do in pre-war North China. From 1925 to 1935, the Communists were very active on the North China plain in organizing peasant protests. Their slogan for mobilizing the peasants was: "resisting taxes and levies, opposing the wealthy and bullying village heads (*Kangjuan kangshui, fandui haoshen cunzhang*)." As a matter of fact, instances of major tax resistance and peasant insurrection on the North China plain during the late 1920s and the early 1930s were often organized by the Communists (HBGM 1980, vol. 1; JLY 1985, Part I).

Although state intrusion offset the state's efforts to strengthen village communities and improve village politics, and resulted in intensified conflicts between the state and villages, not all villages displayed the same degree of solidarity. The solidarity of a village was determined by the class structure of that particular village, which in turn was determined by the socioeconomic conditions within the village. As Philip Huang's study demonstrated, villages responded to state intrusion differently according to their internal structure. While solid communities composed mainly of owner-cultivators tended to present a united front in resisting outside intrusion, highly stratified villages were at the mercy of opportunists working for outside powers (Huang 1985: 304–306). To understand these differences, we have to turn our attention to the socioeconomic changes within North China villages.

Village communities in a changing society

Rural North China in the first half of the twentieth century not only underwent profound political changes but also witnessed accelerating socioeconomic differentiation. This socioeconomic change also had a profound impact on village politics. Because of differentiation, villagers were increasingly divided along lines of social and economic status. This social division cut through kinship ties and neighborhood bonds and assumed an increasingly important role in village social and political life. This development in turn weakened village communities, paralyzed village public opinion, the only effective check on village administrations, and overturned the power balance within the village. In this sense, the socioeconomic change counteracted human efforts at strengthening village communities. It was thus the antithesis of political mobilization.

Class division and confrontation within the village

Before the twentieth century, the North China village was composed mainly of owner-cultivators who owned the land they cultivated and earned their living from their own means of production. Owing to the partible inheritance system and an active land market, land transactions occurred frequently among villagers. Thus, few households could maintain the size of their landholding over generations. It was even less likely that an equitable distribution of land among village households would persist. However, fluctuations at the individual household level did not necessarily change the general pattern of landownership in a village. Entering the twentieth century owner-cultivators still constituted the majority of the population in most North China villages.

This economic situation had no doubt shaped villagers' mentality for generations and was embodied in local customs and practices. Martin Yang tells us, for example, that although the families in Taitou were continuously rising and falling, since this cycle of change was common, no family regarded another as significantly different from itself, and each family took pride in its own possessions. Inequality of income did not seriously threaten the sense of village solidarity (Yang 1945: 132). On the other hand, landownership was the primary requirement for village membership. People who owned no land were not regarded as qualified members of a village even though they physically resided in the village (Chapter 1).

In a village composed mainly of owner-cultivators, lineage was the most important intra-village ascriptive network for organizing villagers and articulating their interests. Most North China villages were multi-lineage villages (Li Jinghan 1933; Gamble 1963). The lineage performed various functions in village society (Yang 1945: 241; Duara 1988: 92–95). Village politics were actually organized according to the principle of lineage representation; village councilors came from the different lineages (Huang 1985: 238; Duara 1988: 115–116). If the lineage organization in a village was weak, the neighborhood took on the role played by lineages elsewhere (Gamble 1963: 36). Both lineage and neighborhood were intra-village ascriptive networks because they embraced everyone who met their qualifications as a member. These networks organized villagers vertically, rather than horizontally, through kinship ties or residential bonds. Obviously, only in villages with little socioeconomic differentiation could these intra-village ascriptive networks play a dominant role in village politics.

However, rural North China in the first half of the twentieth century experienced accelerating socioeconomic differentiation fueled by population pressure and commercialization. A direct consequence of socioeconomic differentiation was that, in some villages, class divisions gradually replaced lineage and neighborhood to play a significant role in grouping villagers. Martin Yang outlined this development in Taitou, showing that, aside from clan and neighborhood, families of similar social and economic status tended to separate into special groups. He observed:

Two or three Liu families, for example, lived in the neighborhood where most of the Yang families live. The Lius are very poor and do not have much to do with the Yangs because they feel inferior to them, and the Yangs do not make overtures to them, either. But another Liu family, which has recently become prosperous, has gradually become intimate with the Yangs. Their children were asked to attend the Christian school.

(Yang 1945: 157)

Class divisions grouped villagers along social and economic lines. It thus introduced a new type of intra-village network and also created new social tensions within the village.[12] A typical case is found in Gamble's study of Village B, located in Wanping, Hebei. A total of 307 families lived in the village and were split into two groups: the poor from the "Front Streets" of the village, and the wealthy from the "Back Streets." Though the village government was controlled by the Back Street, the Front Street managed to control the Fair Association, which was responsible for organizing the annual village fair and plays. It collected the funds needed for these activities by imposing arbitrary assessments on the wealthy families. The wealthy families resented these assessments and forced the government to discontinue the fairs. Led by the Fair Association, the village poor then demanded a separate school for their children. After the founding of the new school, they again demanded a separate fund. The struggle continued, and the village was "on its way to splitting into two separate units" (Gamble 1963: 164–169).

Due to accelerating socioeconomic differentiation, in more and more villages the village leadership was increasingly concentrated in the hands of a certain group of people who formed to some degree a self-perpetuating group: an exclusive club within the village. This group dominated village power and their positions were very often hereditary (Gamble 1963: 39, 150; Huang 1985: 237; Duara 1988: 107). The people from this group were well recognized. For them, it was very reasonable to choose a person from among their peers to fill any vacancy in village leadership.

For example, in both Shajing and Houjiaying, when a village councilor retired or died, the remaining councilors would select a villager from among their peers to fill the vacancy. The successor's descent group was informed afterwards (KC 1952: 1: 133–134, 5: 9). Though these councilors were nominally still the representatives of their own lineages, their power was no longer rooted in lineage representation alone. Instead, more and more their power came from their personal influence in the village. This shift of power base enabled village leaders to be increasingly independent of their lineages, and to form an exclusive political group in the village.

In highly stratified villages, this situation would become extreme. In such villages, differentiation between the village elites and commoners evolved into open confrontation. Though people belonging to the same social group might come from different lineages or neighborhoods, they were organized according to their common social and economic interests rather than interests derived from their lineages. The latter were now overshadowed by the former. As a result, class rather than lineage dominated village, and village politics was characterized by open class competition and confrontation. The Crooks' on-site observation of the events at Ten Mile Inn provides a good example of this.

Ten Mile Inn, located in Wu'an County, Hebei Province, in the foothills of the Taihang Mountains, had about 400 households during the 1930s. It was a highly stratified village with sharp contrast between the rich and the poor. The 20 richest families possessed nearly 2.5 times as much land per capita as the middle peasant families, and had a per capita income 7 times higher than the families of poor peasants and hired laborers. These 20 families had, in addition, two draft animals each, while the remaining families had only "one leg each," which meant that on average, every four families shared only one donkey. Poor peasants constituted five-eighths of the total village population. Since they did not have land or capital, they depended on rented land and usurious loans. They thus were at the mercy of landlords and usurers.

Though there were three major lineages in the village, the Wangs, Fus and Lis, which accounted for 95 percent of the total village population, these ascriptive groups were overwhelmed by the confrontation between the rich and the poor. In order to maintain a favorable bargaining position, the landlords organized their own association which determined the price of agricultural labor on a very rigid "take it or leave it" basis. "To leave it" meant "added suffering for those without enough land of their own." Every morning the association sent down a representative to hire labor for all those who needed it at the previously determined price (Crook and Crook 1959: 3, 51).

In this highly stratified village, poor villagers were excluded from village governance. Class overshadowed lineage in village politics. Before the Nationalists took over North China, all village affairs, such as the collection of taxes, protection of crops, prayer for rain, and the organization of opera performances, were handled by the village temple association. Though this association was a village-wide organization, members were required to own 40 *mu* of land or more. The head of the temple association was rotated exclusively among the ten wealthiest villagers.

In the early 1930s, the *baojia* system was introduced into the village by the National Government. But this was of little consequence to the village government because the same people held office in both the old and the new organizations. To be sure, lineage still played a role in organizing village politics. For example, after the establishment of the *baojia* system, the three *bao* heads were from the three major descent groups of the village (Crook and Crook 1959: 1–17).[13] But on the whole, property qualification obviously outweighed lineage representation, and village governance was characterized by the exclusive dominance of the wealthy people of the village.

Changes in the allocation of tankuan

The shift of village power from lineage to class inevitably brought some substantial changes to village politics. In particular, village government increasingly became the representative of special interest groups while its decisions showed favoritism to the wealthy. The change in the methods of *tankuan* allocation in severely stratified villages clearly illustrates this situation.

We know that in most North China villages, land was the single most important source for various *tankuan* levies and the main basis for its assessment (Huang Di 1936: 10: 414–415; Nagamura 1951: 96–97). For example, of the six KC villages, three, Houjiaying, Lengshuigou, and Houxiazhai, imposed *tankuan* on landowners. In Lengshuigou and Houxiazhai, two villages composed predominantly of owner-cultivators, the principle of levying *tankuan* on landowners was strictly adhered to and all levies were imposed according to the amount of land owned. Tenants paid nothing if they owned no land. Even labor services were provided by landowners, tenants had no obligations (KC 1952: 4: 13, 51–52, 307, 420).

The case in Houjiaying was slightly different. Here, though landowners shouldered the burden of the various levies, the land was divided into three grades with different assessment rates. According to this rate scale, one *mu* of first-grade land equaled two *mu* of second-grade land and three *mu* of third-grade land (KC 1952: 5: 317). The purpose of this arrangement was apparently to make the *tanpai* more equal among villagers. Obviously, only when owner-cultivators constituted an overwhelming majority in a village could the practice of imposing *tankuan* on owned land be feasible.

However, continuous differentiation in the first half of the twentieth century made land distribution increasingly uneven in many villages. People who owned more land in the village were usually more powerful and influential; they were certainly not happy to shoulder major *tankuan* burdens by themselves. The village government now had to make new arrangements to satisfy this interest group.[14] Gradually, in those seriously differentiated villages, *tankuan* assessment was shifted from the amount of land owned to the amount of land cultivated, and even levied on households rather than on land. All these arrangements were obviously in favor of landowners. From six KC surveyed villages we find changes in Shajing, Sibeichai and Wudian. Socioeconomic stratification in these three villages was particularly serious.[15]

In Shajing, *tankuan* levies were imposed entirely on cultivated land, but labor service was still provided by villagers according to the amount of land owned (KC 1952: 2: 346). In Sibeichai, both owned-land and cultivated-land were subject to *tankuan* levies, but at different rates. Zhang Yueqing, a former village head, tells us that five *mu* of rented land equaled one *mu* of owned land for assessment purposes. If the land was rented out by a resident landlord, two-thirds of the assessment went to the landlord and the rest was paid by the tenant. However, if the land was owned by an absentee landlord, the tenant alone was responsible for the assessment (KC 1952: 3: 32).

The situation in Wudian was more complicated. Here, *tankuan* levies were imposed on both the land and the households. Villagers who cultivated land paid levies based on the amount of land cultivated, and those who leased out their land paid levies based on the number of household members. Since payments assessed on land were higher than payments assessed on households, this arrangement favored landlords. Moreover, according to this arrangement absentee landlords paid nothing (KC 1952: 5: 409). Though there were some differences, the new arrangements in these three villages were obviously beneficial to landowners, and especially to landlords at the expense of tenants, who had long been entitled to tax exemption.

Community disintegration and its political consequence

A more serious consequence of socioeconomic stratification was the disintegration of the village community itself. On the one hand, it gave rise to influential interest groups in the village. On the other hand, it resulted in, as Philip Huang pointed out, the formation of a poor peasant economy in many villages. Poor peasants were "part-peasant, part-workers tied at once to family farming and to wage labor" (Huang 1985: 294–295). Since their economic status in the community was low, they were very often excluded from village public affairs and were not considered to be fully qualified village members.[16] The thanksgiving celebration (*xiehui*, village public celebrations held after harvests) in Shajing illustrate this point.

In Shajing, as in many North China villages, after every fall harvest, there was a big celebration in the village. Villagers had to pay their *tankuan* dues at this time, and afterward, a dinner party was served. However, not all villagers could attend this party. Before the thanksgiving celebration, villagers would receive one of two kinds of invitation. One invitation had the word *qingchahou* (meaning: pure tea only). Villagers with this invitation could only have tea during the celebration gathering. The other notice read *cuchahou* (meaning: coarse tea [food] will be served). Those who received this invitation could attend the dinner party. The basis for this division was the amount of land the villagers owned. A minimum of eight *mu* of land was required for a dinner invitation. If a villager owned less than this amount of land, for example, if he owned only five *mu* of land, he could share a full dinner with another villager who owned three *mu* of land. Those who did not pay *tankuan* could not attend the dinner party (KC 1952: 1: 113–114).[17] In Shajing, of the 64 households, 19 (30 percent) could not attend the thanksgiving meal (ibid.). Hence they were not honored in the same way as qualified villagers (who owned eight *mu* or more of land). The impact of this discrimination must have been greatly felt by these villagers.

Shajing's case was by no means exceptional; the same situation was found in many villages. In Houxiazhai, for example, owning land was required in order to participate in the village assembly and elect village officials; those who owned no land had no right to elect village officials (KC 1952: 4: 404).

The exclusion of poor peasants from village public affairs was of course a form of discrimination, but it also reflected the fact that poor peasants had little interest in village public affairs since most of those affairs were *tankuan* related. Du Fuxin, a poor peasant of Shajing, expressed this explicitly by saying that he had no interest in village's official business, and he also had no time or money to take part in village religious activities (KC 1952: 1: 135).[18] Since poor peasants were excluded from village public affairs and had also lost interest in these affairs, they thus became marginal or semi-marginal elements of the community. The expansion of this stratum in the village contributed to the disintegration of the village community.

The expansion of the poor peasant stratum in the village came at the expense of the owner-cultivator stratum; the growth of the former meant the decline of the latter. Though in rural North China owner-cultivators constituted the bulk of village households, this stratum was shrinking steadily in many villages due to the accelerating socioeconomic differentiation in the first half of the twentieth century. Philip Huang's study of the peasant economy of North China convincingly demonstrates that from the early Qing until the 1930s, rural North China changed from a basically unstratified society composed of owner-cultivators to a partly stratified society composed of landlords and tenants, employers and wage workers (Huang 1985: 293). The percentage of owner-cultivators dropped continuously *vis-à-vis* the gradual rise of the other social and economic strata, especially the poor peasant stratum. Tables 4.1 to 4.4 show this change in rural North China from various angles during the 1920s and 1930s. The impact of this socioeconomic change was deep and far-reaching.

In rural North China, as Philip Huang points out, owner-cultivators were the most stalwart members of the village community, and the mainstay of community activities. In contrast to poor peasants, their economic activities took place on their own holdings. Landownership gave them not only respectability in the community, but also a vital stake in village public affairs (Huang 1985: 256, 305). A village community composed mainly of

Table 4.1 Social differentiation in three Henan counties, 1928–1933

County	Landlords		Rich peasants		Middle peasants		Poor peasants and wage laborers		Rest	
	'28	'33	'28	'33	'28	'33	'28	'33	'28	'33
Xuchang	1.1	1.1	4.7	5.0	21.2	17.0	64.2	68.1	8.8	8.7
Huixian	4.1	4.4	9.7	8.1	24.6	24.7	55.2	58.0	6.4	4.8
Zhenping	6.9	6.4	5.7	6.7	15.4	14.6	59.9	60.8	12.1	11.5

Source: Nongfuhui (1934b: 23–25).

Note: Total households = 100%.

Table 4.2 Social stratification in three northern Anhui counties[a]

County	Landlords		Owner-cultivators		Part Tenants		Tenants	
	1931	1935	1931	1935	1931	1935	1931	1935
Fengyang								
No. of households	5	9	208	216	57	72	5	9
(%)	1.82	1.98	75.63	71.29	20.73	23.76	1.82	2.97
Shouxian								
No. of households	2	2	126	148	17	25	5	8
(%)	1.33	1.09	84.00	80.88	11.33	13.66	3.34	4.37
Wuhe								
No. of households	6	10	143	133	26	27	17	27
(%)	3.13	4.83	74.48	64.25	13.54	17.88	8.85	13.04

Source: Zhang Youyi (1957: 734–735).

Notes: Total households = 100%.
[a] The numbers in this table are drawn from 12 villages in these three counties.

Table 4.3 Land concentration in 10 Hebei villages

Year	Land owned by poor peasants and wage laborers	Land bought or mortgaged from	Land sold or mortgaged to
1927	6,862.89	–	–
1930	6,348.11	164.29	679.07

Source: Chen Hanshen (1936: 239).

Note: Unit = *mu*.

Table 4.4 The long-term trend in farm size, 1890–1933

Region	1890	1910	1933	1933/1890
Wheat region	26.55	19.80	16.50	62.15
Rice region	12.15	11.55	10.80	88.89
Average	20.25	15.90	13.80	68.15

Source: Yan Zhongping (1955: 286); Buck ([1937] 1968: 270).

Note: Unit = *mu*.

owner-cultivators fostered a high degree of insularity and solidarity. In a village such as this, the owner-cultivator group as a whole held a powerful check on the village government. The chief means of this check was public opinion, which was shaped and maintained by the majority of villagers, primarily the owner-cultivator group. In this sense, the owner-cultivator group was the definer of village politics.

In North China villages, public opinion was the most effective check on village power. Public opinion reflected conventional morality and the values system.[19] It functioned in two ways as a moral check. On the one hand, it set up a standard of behavior for power holders and guided them to pursue what was universally honored. On the other hand, it prevented them from abusing their power. Because of this, public opinion was an essential factor in village politics.

The effectiveness of public opinion as a moral check was determined by two factors, the deference of village power holders to public opinion and the strength of public opinion itself. Obviously, the second factor is more important than the first. Because if a power holder was a profit-seeker, he would ignore the moral guidance of public opinion as much as he could. This was the situation found in many villages during this period. But as long as public opinion was consolidated and strong, it could effectively prevent abuses of power.

For example, Houxiazhai was a relatively unstratified village composed mainly of owner-cultivators. In 1938, the villagers were dissatisfied with the conduct of their village head, Wang Qinglong, and they were able to force him to resign without taking the matter to county authorities (Huang 1985: 262–263). On the other hand, Gamble's field study offered a very good example of how a unified public opinion can balance the power held by village heads.

Village D, located 7 miles northwest of Peiping (Beijing), in 1933 there were 142 households. Of 114 village farming families, only ten had more than 30 *mu* of land and only five had more than 60 *mu*. The three largest family holdings were 196 *mu*, 90 *mu* and 80 *mu* respectively. Though we do not have concrete statistics on land distribution among the rest of the villagers, we can infer this was a village composed of owner-cultivators by the fact that the village had a high literacy rate.[20] For those 13 years old and older, the literacy rate was 41 percent; almost 80 percent for the males and 3.5 percent for the females (Gamble 1963: 192–196). Though a self-perpetuating group of village leaders controlled village administration, their power was largely checked and balanced by their fellow villagers. The following interesting stories can illustrate this point.

In 1928, the old village accountant left, and the assistant village head offered to do the job for the same pay of $2 a month. However, his offer was rejected by villagers on the grounds that no village head or assistant head should receive money for his services. As a result the assistant head resigned and his successor did the accounting work concurrently without pay (ibid.: 201). In 1929, the village head proposed a special assessment of 10 cents per *mu* of land to offset the village's deficit resulting from his extravagant expenses earlier in the year. Villagers refused his proposal and filed suit with the county government. The village head, along with his two sons, was forced to resign from the village council. Both sons had been appointed by their father in 1926 (when he was appointed village head) in an attempt to monopolize village affairs (ibid.: 199–200). The same situation occurred again in 1932 when village leaders tried to furious the village *tankuan* to 50 cents per *mu*. The villagers were so incensed that they hurled abuse at the village leaders and refused to accept the rate. The village leaders, anticipating trouble if they continued to insist on the proposed rate, compromised and decreased the rate to 40 cents per *mu*. Gamble summarizes the case thus: "It was definitely a case where the group was able to exert enough pressure to force the village leaders, who usually were quite independent in making their decisions, to listen and accede to the force of public opinion" (1963: 206).

As a matter of fact, public opinion did not function to guide and restrict village leaders exclusively, everyone in the village was under its control (Yang 1945: 150; Gamble 1963: 135). Similarly, everyone could use public opinion to protect himself or herself against any kind of abuse. What made it important was that, for the majority of villagers, it was their chief means of power *vis-à-vis* village leaders. Nevertheless, this power was different from the power held by village leaders. It was an "extensive" and "diffused," to use Michael Mann's terms (Mann 1986: 7–8), power that no individual or small group could control. Its strength was determined by the solidarity of the community that held it, which in turn was determined by the strength of the owner-cultivator stratum in the village. Obviously, if a village was severely stratified, strong public opinion would be a rarity. In this situation, a moral check on the village government would be very weak or nonexistent. This would certainly open the door for the abuse of power. Huang's study, based on contemporary Japanese scholars' surveys, convincingly demonstrated the close relationship between community dissolution and political deterioration.

Huang categorized the six villages surveyed by the Japanese scholars (the results of the survey were published in 1952 in six volumes, under the title of *Chugoku noson kanko shosa* [Investigation of customary practices in rural China] with the chief editor Niida Noboru) into three groups, according to the degree of socioeconomic differentiation. Houxiazhai and Lengshuigou were solid villages composed mainly of owner-cultivators. Shajing and Sibeichai were villages that underwent a high degree of partial proletarianization. Wudian and Houjiaying were highly stratified villages. Villagers from the first two and the latter four villages displayed remarkably different political behavior. In Houxiazhai and Lengshuigou, villagers tended to present a united front in resisting outside intrusion as well as guarding against the abuse of power by village power holders. In the other four villages, villagers were plagued by community dissolution and were at the mercy of local bullies who relied on outside forces to squeeze profits out of the villages (Huang 1985: 259–274).

The decline of public opinion as a moral check also caught the attention of local governments. Xu Shuren, who served as the magistrate of Zouping County during the Rural Reconstruction experiment, said that due to economic crises in the countryside, people were motivated solely by material gain. As long as there were material gains to be made, people ignored morality. Therefore the criteria for right and wrong and good and evil disappeared. As a result, the number of bullies, thieves and bandits increased. Because of this, and the frequent military demands of the time, few qualified people were willing to be village heads. This provided opportunities for local bullies. Whenever there was a village election, local bullies tried their best to be elected. Sometimes villagers even recommended them because they were more capable of dealing with armies and government authorities. Though this phenomenon was not common in the countryside, it spread gradually among villages. Once conditions in a village deteriorated, there were few ways to reverse the trend (*Cunzhi*, vol. 3, no. 4).

We must keep in mind that all of the changes resulting from social and economic evolution took place concurrently with increasing state intrusion into rural society. These two forces greatly weakened the village community and led to the deterioration in village politics. State intrusion resulted in the expansion and alienation of village administration, while the social and economic changes stratified village communities and led to the decline of the owner-cultivator stratum. In this situation the power balance within the village was toppled, and village government became an unrestricted power, thus opening the door for more abuse.

Conclusion

Increasing state intrusion and accelerating socioeconomic stratification in the first half of the twentieth century brought about substantial changes in North China villages. These two factors, however, impacted different realms of village life. State intrusion not only increasingly alienated village government from its constituency, but also, by imposing increasing *tankuan* levies on the village as a collective, pushed the village into opposition against the state. However, different villages responded to outside pressures differently. In some villages, state intrusion aroused strong resistance, while other villages simply surrendered to state pressure. This difference is due to the specific social and political structures of different villages, which in turn were determined by the degree of socioeconomic stratification. In the first half of the twentieth century, accelerating socioeconomic stratification greatly weakened many villages. As a result, in these villages, public opinion, the only powerful check against the village government, dissolved. This opened the door for more abuses of power. Only in villages where socioeconomic stratification had not taken a heavy toll, could villagers impose a powerful check on village government through a strong public opinion. Resistance to outside intrusion was also found to be most aggressive in these villages.

State intrusion and socioeconomic stratification created great tension between the state and the village and also wreaked havoc within the village. This tension was the major source of widespread anti-state resistance and struggle against corrupt village governments in rural North China during this period. All these political dramas were of course based on the village or set in the village. Only the Communists were able to offer practical measures to harness this tension and turn it to their advantage in their revolution in wartime circumstances. The following chapter will examine the efforts of the Communist revolution in rural North China.

5 The Communists and North China villages

The outbreak of the War of Resistance against Japan in July 1937 ushered in a new stage of political drama in rural North China. The Japanese occupation of the North China plain gave the Chinese Communists a rare opportunity to test their wartime mobilization tactics.[1] Prewar political and socioeconomic changes provided the crucial prerequisites for the success of Communist mobilization. However, Communist mobilization did not differ fundamentally from the various types of political mobilization we have seen in previous chapters with regard to its basic strategy: it also took the natural village as the institutional means to mobilize, reorganize, and control rural society.

Two dimensions of the Communist mobilization differed from previous political mobilization. On the one hand, the Communists exploited the strategy more thoroughly and completely. They thus transformed the multi-layered relationship between state and rural society into a bilateral relationship between the state and the village. On the other hand, they provided effective solutions for the rural political and socioeconomic crises discussed in previous chapters. These crises had stratified and weakened village communities and therefore plagued previous efforts to mobilize villages by various political forces. The Communists introduced essential economic and political reforms into North China villages which enabled them to successfully mobilize and transform the villages into the strongholds of their revolutionary cause.

Taxation and state–village relations

The Japanese occupation of the North China plain after the Lugouqiao Incident (July 7, 1937) left a huge political vacuum in the countryside. With their limited forces, the Japanese could only consolidate their power in large cities, in strategic towns, and along vital transportation routes. The political vacuum they left gave the Communists great opportunities to establish base areas, expand their forces, and conduct guerrilla warfare behind enemy lines.[2] In their base areas the Communists assumed the role of the state and ruled the vast countryside on the North China plain. The relationship between the Communists and local society was therefore subject to the same logic that governed state–village relations on the North China plain before. This relationship can be seen clearly in the realm of taxation.[3]

The Jin-Cha-Ji Border Region

The first Communist base area established in North China after the outbreak of the war was the Jin-Cha-Ji (Shanxi-Chahaer-Hebei) Border Region (Map 5.1). On January 11, 1938, the Jin-Cha-Ji Border Region Government was established in Fuping county (Hebei), with jurisdiction over 40 counties in Shanxi, Chahaer and Hebei provinces. The Jin-Cha-Ji base later included almost two-thirds of Hebei, an area which formed the major part of the base. By the end of 1944, it controlled a total of 110 counties and more than 19 million people (JCJ 1984: 1: 227). The Jin-Cha-Ji base was always a "model anti-Japanese base" and had received lavish praise from both the central committee and the North China Bureau of the CCP (JCJ 1984: 1: 281). Because of its location and its model status we will take the Jin-Cha-Ji base as an example to discuss Communist mobilization on the wartime North China plain.

Communist mobilization on the wartime North China plain is a very broad topic which alone deserves a lengthy and detailed study. My discussion in this chapter will not cover the whole range of the issues involved. Rather, I will again approach it from the angle of taxation. The time period of my main concern is from 1938 to 1941, a crucial period for the establishment and consolidation of the Jin-Cha-Ji base. During this period, tax reforms played a dominant role among the various Communist social, economic, and political programs. It had a major impact on both state-society relations and village politics.

The Communists were simultaneously undertaking three mutually supportive and dependent tasks in the base area during the war: (1) mobilizing the rural populace; (2) maintaining and expanding their political and military forces; and finally, (3) conducting guerrilla warfare against the Japanese. Of these tasks, the mobilization of the rural populace was of primary and paramount concern, because without a well-mobilized mass base it was impossible to sustain such an arduous and protracted guerrilla war. As Peng Zhen, the secretary of the Jin-Cha-Ji CCP committee, said in May 1938, early in the base's establishment:

> During the war for national self-defense and liberation, the financial mobilization [*caizheng dongyuan*] of the broad masses is of the utmost relevance to military development along the frontline. It is of equal importance as military operations . . . However, the majority of party branches and members at various levels of our regime have never tried their best to deal with this vital issue, i.e. to mobilize people from various social classes and strata to provide financial support. Some people have simply banished it from their minds. This is the most serious defect in our work.
>
> (JCJ 1984: 4: 1)

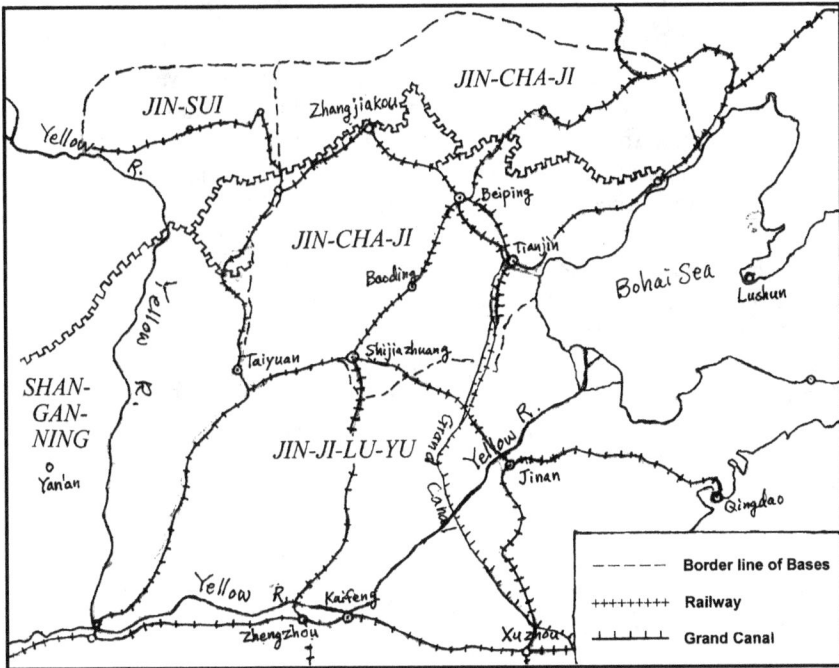

Map 5.1 Jin-Cha-Ji and neighboring bases, 1941.

Though mobilizing people financially and materially was by no means the sole concern of the Communist wartime effort, it was indeed one of most urgent tasks on the Communist agenda. For the Communists, financial mobilization meant the mobilization of material resources and manpower to support their regime, their armies and the war. Since the Border Region government functioned essentially as a state, financial mobilization thus meant taxation. Nevertheless, the emphasis on the mobilization of people for taxation indicated that the Communists were searching for an efficient way to collect taxes.

As we have already seen, taxation is a crucial meeting point between state and society. It is defined and conditioned by both parties, and neither can act at its own discretion. This was also true for Communist taxation. The Communists had to take local conditions into consideration in order to make their taxation system workable in local areas. As we will see, more so than those of its predecessors, Communist taxation in their North China bases relied heavily upon the village community as the basic unit for allocation, accounting and collection. The financial and tax history of the Jin-Cha-Ji base is a very illuminating case in this regard.

Three stages of tax reforms and two principles of new taxation

The taxation system in the Jin-Cha-Ji base experienced three stages of evolution judging from the methods and procedures employed in taxation. The first stage was a short period of anarchy in finance and taxation before and shortly after the founding of the base. During this period, there was no unified regime or army; different armed forces did what they wanted in the name of resistance against Japan. Anyone could claim that his was a resistance force and ask people for provisions. It was said that sometimes there were even eight or nine commanders with different troops staying in a village on the same night. This situation was described as: "Commanders are enough to match the hairs on an ox, chairmen are to be found everywhere under the Heaven (*Siling sainiumao, zhuren biantianxia*)." Various military demands were handled by the mobilization committee of the war zone (*Zhandi dongyuan weiyuanhui*, or simply *Dongweihui*) which was established in local areas after the withdrawal of the Nationalist regime. The first was therefore called "the stage of the mobilization committee" (*Dongweihui jieduan*) by Peng Zhen in his September 1941 report (JCJ 1984: 4: 53).

The mobilization committee functioned as a quasi-local government, it allocated various military levies following the principle of "reasonable burden" (*heli fudan*). This principle was based on a September 1937 agreement between Zhou Enlai and Yan Xishan, who represented the Eighth Route Army led by the CCP and the Second War Zone of the KMT respectively (Feng Tianfu 1987: 172). The so-called "reasonable burden" was often explained as "those who have money should contribute money, those who have more should contribute more, and those who have less should contribute less" (*youqian chuqian, qianduo duochu, qianshao shaochu*) (JCJ 1984: 1: 694). Once the new levy based on reasonable burden was put into practice, most old taxes and levies, the land tax included, were abolished.[4] However, since there was no unified system or regulations nor any unified standard for allocation, this levy of reasonable burden did not work very well. On the one hand, it could not meet the rapidly increasing demands of the war, and on the other, people resented the anarchic approach.

The Communists quickly realized that if there was no constant and reliable tax base, the government's fiscal needs could not be met and both the Communist-led base regime and the resistance war would soon collapse. Thus, on March 6, 1938, two months after the founding of the base, the base government promulgated "The Implementing Regulations for the Village Reasonable Burden Tax in the Jin-Cha-Ji Border Region (*Jin-Cha-Ji bianqu cun heli fudan shishi fangfa*)." The regulations sought to terminate the anarchic situation in finance and taxation, and establish a unified finance and tax system in the base area. In this new system the village was designated as the basic unit for government taxation.[5] It was therefore called the reasonable burden on the village (*cun heli fudan*) (JCJ 1984: 4: 145). The new fiscal policy ushered in the second stage in the development of the tax system of the Jin-Cha-Ji base, which we can properly call the stage of reasonable burden on the village.

During the second stage, the village was designated as the basic unit of allocation, accounting, and collection for various taxes. As the first article of the regulations clearly states: "the reasonable burden tax takes the village as the basic unit (*cun wei benwei*)" (JCJ 1984: 4: 152).[6] This immediately became the cardinal principle of Communist taxation as well as of Communist mobilization in rural North China during wartime, which we may call the principle of *taking the village as the basic unit*. Through this realignment in taxation, the village became the only entity which dealt with the state in the realm of taxation.

Obviously, the strategy embodied in the principle of taking the village as the basic unit in taxation was not new. From previous chapters we have already seen that the strategy of enlisting the village for the purpose of taxation was exploited repeatedly by the various political regimes that ruled North China. However, none of these regimes had made this strategy the governing principle of the whole tax system. In this regard, Communist taxation in the North China base area was a radical departure from its Qing and Republican predecessors.

For the Communists, the ultimate goal of tax reform in the base was to build a unified fiscal system based on a solid ground through which taxation could be a simple process of allocation and collection of assigned quotas via administration. To achieve this, the Communists believed that the reasonable burden on village should be further expanded to that on the county level. Song Shaowen, the Chair of the Border Administration Committee and the head of the Department of Finance of the Border government, stated in his February 1940 work report that the "reasonable burden on village" was the base for the "reasonable burden on the county" (*xian heli fudan*). The goal of finance and taxation reform in the base area was finally to build the reasonable burden tax at the country level (JCJ 1984: 4: 35). Song remarked:

> Our task is ... to raise the village reasonable burden to the county reasonable burden. What we want to do is to make our financial work from county to township, and from township to village *a simple process of allocation* [of tax quota], and from village to township then to county *a simple process of collection* of tax money. Only when we have established a unified system such as this, can we succeed in our financial mobilization.
>
> (JCJ 1984: 4: 32)

The "reasonable burden on the village" was meant to equalize the tax burden of a village among its villagers, but it could not equalize tax burdens of different villages because even within the same county, economic conditions of different villages varied significantly. Only if the tax burden was shared by villages within the same county in accordance with their actual economic conditions could the tax burden be reasonable and fair to these villages. This is why the Communists hoped to raise the village reasonable burden to the higher level, the county level. However, there were insurmountable difficulties for any such attempt, because the economic information of a village was a jealously guarded secret of the village, inaccessible by outsiders.[7] Without this knowledge, it was impossible for the Communists to achieve the goal of reasonable burden for the county. As a matter of fact, no evidence even shows that the Communists ever made real efforts to achieve this goal.[8] The Communists were actually satisfied with the reasonable burden at the village level and exploited the village fully for their mobilization purposes.

Within the village, the reasonable burden tax system allocated taxes among households according to their economic conditions. The Implementing Regulations of March 1938 stipulated that for every household, the part of its income that exceeded subsistence needs was taxable at a progressive rate (JCJ 1984: 4: 152–154). This measure embraced another major principle of Communist taxation (as well as of Communist mobilization): *the class line*. The principle of the class line gave Communist taxation a new dimension which distinguished it from the previous practice of collective taxation, such as the *tanpai*.

In the case of the *tanpai*, the village community was also taxed as a collective. The difference between Communist taxation and the *tanpai* was that in the case of *tanpai*, the village could choose its own method for allocating the *tanpai* among its villagers, and most villages actually followed the time-honored method to collect *taipai* from the land owned by villagers. Under Communist taxation, though the village was also collectively taxed, it was deprived of this power. The Communists spelled out universal regulations for allocating the village tax quota among villagers. These regulations were governed by the principle of the class line and stipulated that village households be taxed at a progressive rate according to the real income of each household. Within the Communists' scheme of taxation, the class line was an indispensable supplement to the village-based taxation. By imposing the tax burden mainly on the wealthy households of the village, it not only made tax burden more equitable thus to win the support of the majority of villagers but also led to the demise of the old power structure within the village.

For example, in the Central Hebei base area (*Jizhong gengjudi*), the tax regulations provided that villager households were graded mainly by the land they owned. A *mu* of land capable of producing one *picul* (150 *catties*) of coarse grain was defined as a standard *mu*, and each standard *mu* was in turn classified as a "unit of wealth (*fuli*)." The first 1.5 units of wealth per person were tax-exempt. Above this level, every five *mu* of land per person was counted as one grade. Thus a family with five *mu* of land or less per member was graded as Grade One household, while one with more than five *mu* but less than 10 *mu* per member was graded as Grade Two, and so on up to Grade Six. For Grade One household, the tax rate was 1 unit of tax for each *mu* of land, for Grade Two, 1.2 units per *mu*, Grade Three, 1.4 units, and for Grade Six, 2 units (JCJ 1984: 4: 157–159; see also Friedman *et al.* 1991: 41). Under this system, the major tax burden in the base area fell on the shoulders of landlords and rich peasants (Guo Zhenshou and Li Shifang 1985: 239; Feng Tianfu 1987: 174). The principle of the class line embodied in the reasonable burden tax had, as we may expect, a very strong and profound impact on village property relations and class structure, and hence on village politics. I will discuss the political implications of this tax system to the village community later.

Song Shaowen's February 1940 report indicated that according to the Communists' plan, the reasonable burden on village was only the first step for building their ambitious finance and taxation system. As it finally turned out, this system was the unified progressive tax (*Tongyi leijing shui*).[9] On August 13, 1940, the CCP North China Bureau published "The Political Program of the Jin-Cha-Ji Border Region (*Jin-Cha-Ji bianqu muqian shizheng gangling*)," which was later widely known as the "Double-Ten Program (*Shuangshi gangling*)," because it contained 20 articles. In this program, the CCP North China Bureau announced that the Border government would implement the unified progressive tax in the base area (JCJ 1984: 1: 85). Shortly thereafter, the Border government published "The Provisional Measures for the Implementation of the Unified Progressive Tax in the Jin-Cha-Ji Border Region (*Jin-Cha-Ji bianqu tongyi leijingshui zanxing banfa*)" and "The Implementation Details of the Provisional Measures (*Jin-Cha-Ji bianqu tongyi leijingshui zanxing banfa shishi xize*)" on November 10. At this point the finance and taxation system of the base area entered its third stage: the stage of the unified progressive tax.

The unified progressive tax merged all taxes into a single progressive tax. As the Article 8 of the "Double-Ten Program" states:

> Institute the unified progressive tax in grain, fodder and money, with an exemption threshold and the highest progressive rate. Improve import-export taxes, and abolish the land tax and all other taxes and levies. The Government will not increase any taxes or levies without the permission of the Border Political Council [*Bianqu canyihui*]. Improve village finance, stipulate strict rules and regulations for [village] finance, and eliminate corruption and waste.
>
> (JCJ 1984: 1: 85)[10]

Though many important changes were made in the unified progressive tax, there was no deviation from the Communists' commitment to follow the principles of taking the village as the basic unit and of the class line in building a tax system and levying taxes. These two principles were important not only in taxation, but also significant for Communist mobilization during the war and afterwards. They enabled the Communists to mobilize rural society and to consolidate their power successfully in the base areas. The Communist success in rural North China should be largely attributed to the implementation of these two principles.

In spite of the fact that these two principles were mutually supportive and complementary in the whole scheme of Communist mobilization, they were not on an equal footing. For Communists, the principle of the class line was subordinate to the principle of taking the village as the basic unit. The class line was always *applied within* the village community and *confined by* village boundaries. It was employed to level down the differences between the rich and the poor, and between the powerful and the powerless within the village, and to revitalize an egalitarian and hence more solidary village community. In the North China base areas, the class line had never been used to forge a united trans-village class front. This is a key point for us to understand wartime Communist mobilization in North China.

State and rural society relations under the new tax system

The tax reforms in the Jin-Cha-Ji base area were accomplished by the institution of the unified progressive tax. Under this new tax system, the relationship between the state and rural society was fundamentally altered. The new tax system abolished the land tax, the single most important tax collected in rural China for thousands of years, once and for all in the base area. The land tax had always been collected by the state from individual landowners, and, especially in the Qing, very little collective responsibility was involved in this tax. The relationship between the state and rural society embodied in traditional land taxation was therefore a relationship between the state and individual landowners. Abolishing the land tax and imposing all taxes on the village community as a collective thus dramatically changed the relationship between the state and rural society in the base area.

Actually, in the first stage of tax reform, the land tax had already been abolished together with most other taxes and levies for pragmatic reasons, because, during this period, the transition of regimes and the subsequent chaos curtailed the Communists' ability to collect taxes (JCJ 1984: 4: 53–54). Land taxation was then temporarily resumed in the second stage, the stage of village reasonable burden, due to urgent financial needs (JCJ 1984: 4: 2, 5). However, the abolition of the land tax was the ultimate goal of the Communists. Both Song Shaowen and Peng Zhen, the leading figures of the Border Region government and the party committee, had made this very clear. Though they held that the land tax was comparatively less pernicious than other taxes, it was still unfair because merchants and capitalists had no obligations to pay this tax. Moreover, among landowners, it was unfair to small holders, because it was collected indiscriminately from acreage without consideration of the quality of the land or the landowner's economic situation, and because there was neither an exemption threshold nor a progressive rate (JCJ 1984: 4: 28–29, 54–55). For these reasons, the Communists were determined to abolish the land tax, provided conditions allowed that to be done (ibid.).

In the stage of the unified progressive tax system, the role of the village community was emphasized by the Communist state more than it had been during the previous second stage, because in the second stage, the land tax was resumed and was collected from individual landowners rather than the village as a collectivity. The abolition of land tax under the unified progressive tax system, however, made the village community the sole taxpayer. Though the unified progressive tax was finally shouldered by individual villager households, it was the village that was responsible for grading its households according to their economic conditions (JCJ 1984: 4: 359, the fifth chapter of the Provisional Measures). It was also the village that bore the responsibility for allocating the assigned village tax quota among its villagers as well as for collecting it from them (JCJ 1984: 4: 335–339, 477–478). The success or failure of the unified progressive tax was thus entirely dependent on the compliance of the village community.

Liu Lantao, the secretary of the Beiyue District Party committee (the Beiyue District was the largest sub-base in the Jin-Cha-Ji base, located in the northwest of the base and included northeast Shanxi and northwest Hebei), emphasized in one of his 1941 party work reports that the village was the basis for the institution of the unified progressive tax. All the works related to the investigation and evaluation of household grades, and to the raising or lowering of the exemption threshold should take the village as a unit (JCJ 1984: 4: 298). *The Border Administration Herald* (*Bianzheng daobao*), the official newspaper of the Border government, stressed on March 16, 1941, that: "The village is the basis for all our works in the base area. The successful implementation of the unified progressive tax should also depend on the government of each village" (JCJ 1984: 4: 402). The same emphasis was repeated again and again by the Party and government in official documents, work reports, as well as newspapers published in the base area.

The institution of the unified progressive tax in the base area brought an end to the transformation of taxation from a mainly state–individual affair to the one of entirely state–village intercourse. Though this new tax system was the creation of the Communists, the evolution was inaugurated, as we saw in Chapter 2, by the late Qing state and was continued by the various regimes in North China during the Republican period. Having completed the process, the Communists, however, became the full beneficiaries of this institutional change.

Thus, the Communist state was freed from dealing directly with a great multitude of individual taxpayers, a formidable chore that no government in a pre-modern agrarian society could undertake without compromising its efficiency.[11] This change also greatly simplified the procedures of taxation, making it a simple process of allocating the tax quota among villages. It was then the village's responsibility to undertake all the tedious work of taxation such as assessing village households, allocating village tax quota among villagers, collecting money, grain and fodder (the three forms of tax in the base area during the war) from villagers, and finally remitting tax money to the government and preserving tax grain and fodder for the government.[12]

The success in tax reforms received high praise from the CCP's central leadership. *The Liberation Daily* (*Jiefang ribao*), the official newspaper of the CCP's Central Committee, published a signed article on September 7, 1941, which stated:

> The unified progressive tax [system] was a great revolution to the old taxation system in China. It cleared away the confusions and disorders in the old taxation system, rooted out the old, corrupt taxation apparatus that embezzled at every level of taxation and provoked resentment everywhere . . .
>
> The institution of the unified progressive tax is a great achievement of the Jin-Cha-Ji Border Region Government in their financial reconstruction. It is also a right step for the implementation of New Democratic financial policy. This tax system together with the regulations for implementing it are a model for showing how the Chinese Communist Party carries out the policies of the united front in its financial field. This tax system safeguards the vital interests of the various classes within the resistance front. It thus strengthened and developed the united front.
>
> (JCJ 1984: 4: 343–344, 347)

Although the unified progressive tax was created and implemented in the Jin-Cha-Ji base, its principles were also adopted by other Communist base areas in North China.[13] It actually represented the general pattern of Communist taxation in the North China bases. This taxation system not only resulted in a profound change in overall state and rural society relations, it also brought about a dramatic change in property relations and class structure within the village community. Both changes had a profound and far-reaching impact on village politics.

Changes in the village under Communist mobilization

Under Communist mobilization, village society changed greatly. This change was characterized by two aspects which corresponded to the two dimensions of Communist mobilization. On the one hand, the class structure within the village was changed: the old rural elite declined, the middle peasantry thrived, the village community became more homogenous hence more solidarity. These changes greatly helped the Communists to strengthen their control over the village. On the other hand, the village community was further integrated into the Communist political system and became the lowest administrative unit of the Communist state.

Change of class structure within the village

From the very beginning, the Communists had pursued a tax policy which sought to distribute the tax burden in favor of the poor and discriminate against the rich. The new tax system based on this principle of class line taxed villager households progressively according to their income above subsistence needs. Under this system, especially during the first two stages of tax reforms, the major tax burden fell mainly on landlords and rich peasants, while poor peasants and the majority of middle peasants enjoyed tax exemptions or very light taxes. As a result, this tax system narrowed the economic gaps among villagers substantially while reinforcing and rejuvenating the owner-cultivator stratum within the village. This social stratum had been in decline due to socioeconomic stratification, population pressure, heavy taxation, political corruption, and social disturbances. But now this downward trend was reversed by the Communists.

The tax burden in the base area prior to the implementation of the unified progressive tax was shouldered by wealthy villagers—mainly landlords and rich peasants (Guo Zhenshou and Li Shifang 1985: 239; Feng Tianfu 1987: 174). For example, in Wugong, a central Hebei village, after the implementation of the reasonable burden tax, during the second stage of tax reform, 40 percent of the households, including virtually all the owner-tenants and about 20 percent of the owner-cultivators, were exempt from taxes. The village tax burden was borne by the top 25 households in the village, particularly the five households that hired long-term labor or rented out significant amounts of land (Friedman, Pickwicz, Selden 1991: 42). Because of this, we are told, "the gap decreased between them and the poorest households, yet the basic structure of an independent tiller economy remained intact" (ibid.).

Since land was the major form of property in the countryside, the "reasonable burden tax" graded village households mainly according to the amount of land they owned. Under this tax system therefore land was no longer so keenly sought after. Instead, it now became a burden to those wealthy households in possession of large amounts of land. They were eager to dispose of their land that was above a certain amount and was thus progressively taxed. Some immediately divided their land among their family members, some quickly sold their land without much concern as to the price, some simply gave away their surplus land. This situation led to a dramatic change of landownership in the base area. It reversed the long-term trend toward land concentration and socioeconomic stratification, and initiated a process of land equalization among villagers: what we may call a process of *destratification*. Here, the example of Ten Mile Inn is illustrative.

In this southern Hebei village, the system of reasonable burden tax freed 70 percent of village households from any tax burden, and only the richest 30 percent of households were called upon to pay the tax (Crook and Crook 1959: 46–47). Those upon whom the burden of tax fell tried any and all means to avoid tax payment, or at least lower their grade on the progressive tax scale. Wang Pan-yen, the second biggest landlord of the village, sent one of his four sons to join the Eighth Route Army. As a soldier's family, he was thus entitled to special consideration in taxation and also received special help in farm work. Wang Feng-ch'i, a rich peasant, divided his 100 *mu* of land among his five sons just before the new tax took effect. For those who for various reasons could not divide family property, the only solution was to sell the land. Fu Hsin, the chief landlord of the Fu clan, quickly sold 30 *mu* of land. The land thus sold was purchased by middle peasants or newly rising poor peasants (ibid.: 48–49).

The experiences of Ten Mile Inn were by no means unique, but were to be found everywhere in the Jin-Cha-Ji base area.[14] As Liu Lantao stated on July 30, 1941:

> Because of the institution of the New Democratic political system and the establishment of the revolutionary organization for the resistance, now in the base area the feudal exploitation by landlords has diminished, and has been exterminated. Land is in the process of being divided up . . . In the base area, the situation that landlords own the means of production is changing rapidly.
>
> (JCJ 1984: 2: 199)

Table 5.1 is a set of land transaction statistics in the Beiyue District since the outbreak of the war. It can give us a general idea of how the tax reforms changed landownership in the base area.

From Table 5.1 we can see that in the 24 villages in the consolidated areas (*gonggu qu*) the landlords and rich peasants had sold and mortgaged out a

Table 5.1 Land transactions in the Beiyue district during the war (July 1937–May 1943)

Area	Category	Landlord	Rich P	Middle P	Poor P	Wage L
Consolidated area[a]	Sold	1,320.61	1,061.30	765.00	492.45	7.30
	Bought	35.25	113.77	1,192.18	669.89	102.15
	Mortgaged to	423.10	175.94	118.53	44.00	3.00
	Mortgaged from	4.85	85.35	496.00	401.23	16.24
Guerrilla area[b]	Sold	1,410.20	1,354.68	1,173.89	818.00	19.13
	Bought	106.22	514.30	2,232.64	1,215.87	68.84
	Mortgaged to	1,375.72	1,844.42	1,374.95	654.78	18.00
	Mortgaged from	–	232.30	2,469.65	1,742.50	62.87

Source: JCJ (1984: 2: 226).

Notes: Unit = *mu*.
[a] Based on a survey of 24 villages in the consolidated areas.
[b] Based on a survey of 31 villages in the guerrilla areas.

total of 2,980.95 *mu* of land, and had bought and mortgaged only 239.22 *mu* during the first six years of the war. Their net loss was 2,741.73 *mu*. During the same period, the middle peasants, poor peasants and wage laborers had bought or mortgaged a total of 2,877.69 *mu*, and had sold and mortgaged out 1,430.28 *mu*, and thus had gained a total of 1,447.41 *mu* of land. While in 31 villages in the guerilla areas, the landlords had sold and mortgaged out a total of 5,985.02 *mu*, and had bought and mortgaged only 852.82 *mu*. Their net loss was 5,132.2 *mu*. The middle and poor peasants and wage laborers had bought and mortgaged a total of 7,792.37 *mu*, and had sold and mortgaged out 4,058.75 *mu*. The net gain was 3,733.62 *mu*.

The main reason for this massive turnover in landownership in these villages was that the landlords and rich peasants wanted to avoid the heavy tax burden, and the poor and middle peasants took advantage of this situation to increase their landholdings and improve their economic situation (JCJ 1984: 2: 227). Table 5.2 shows other statistics based on a survey of 35 villages in consolidated areas and 42 villages in guerrilla areas which tells the same story.

Table 5.2 shows that the land owned by the landlords and rich peasants in the 35 villages in the consolidated areas had decreased from 38.36 percent to 29.73 percent in total acreage during the period from 1937 to 1942, for a net loss of 8.63 percent. The land owned by the middle and poor peasants had increased from 59.61 percent to 68.51 percent during the same period, for a net gain of 8.9 percent. In the 42 villages in the guerrilla areas the situation was almost the same. The landholdings of landlords and rich peasants had dropped from 37.42 percent to 28.76 percent of total acreage during

Table 5.2 The change of landownership in Beiyue district during the war

Class	Consolidated areas[a]			Guerrilla areas[b]		
	1937	*1941*	*1942*	*1937*	*1941*	*1942*
Landlord	16.43	11.28	10.17	10.47	8.41	7.61
Rich peasant	21.93	19.15	19.56	26.95	22.02	21.15
Middle peasant	41.69	48.36	49.14	40.65	46.08	47.6
Poor peasant	17.92	19.13	19.37	20.00	20.81	21.33
Wage laborer	1.18	0.67	0.75	0.81	0.55	0.55
Other[c]	0.85	0.81	1.01	0.87	1.47	1.96
Total	100.00	100.00	100.00	100.00	100.00	100.00

Source: JCJ (1984: 2: 224).

Notes: Unit = % of total acreage.
[a] Based on a survey of 35 villages in consolidated areas of Beiyue district.
[b] Based on a survey of 42 villages in guerrilla areas of Beiyue district.
[c] This category includes households of workers, peddlers, merchants, vagabonds, etc. The numbers given for this category often do not match the gap between the whole and the sum of other categories. However, the differences are very small.

this period, for a net loss of 8.66 percent. The middle and poor peasants had gained 8.28 percent, their landholdings increasing from 60.65 percent to 68.93 percent of total acreage.

Along with the decline of the landlord economy, the base area also witnessed the rising prosperity and expansion of a middle peasant economy. Liu continued: "The peasant petty commodity economy has developed and risen rapidly in the last four years, especially in 1940.[15] Now it is the dominant economy in many areas." "The number of middle peasants increased greatly, and the middle peasant economy rose significantly. The areas where the class relationship changed most radically are those consolidated core areas of the base" (JCJ 1984: 2: 200–201, 210). Liu Lantao used the phrase "squeezing into the middle from the two ends (*liangbian xiang zhongjian ji*)," and "small at the two ends and big in the middle (*liangtouxiao zhongjianda*)" to describe the change of class structure in the base area (JCJ 1984: 2: 203). This picture is in sharp contrast to that of the general rural conditions found in North China prior to the war. The change in class structure in the Beiyue District of the base area is reflected in Table 5.3.

Tables 5.2 and 5.3 are taken from the same survey and reflect different angles of a same picture. Table 5.3 shows clearly what the phrase "squeezing into the middle from two ends" really meant. During the period from 1937 to 1942, in the 35 villages in the consolidated areas the percentage of middle peasant households had increased 8.89 percent, from 35.42 percent to 44.31

Table 5.3 The change of class structure in Beiyue district

Class		Consolidated area[a]			Guerrilla area[b]		
		1937	1941	1942	1937	1941	1942
Landlord	H%	2.42	2.05	1.91	1.69	1.58	1.50
	P%	3.61	2.85	2.51	1.81	1.14	1.29
Rich p	H%	5.91	6.02	5.8	7.95	6.97	6.81
	P%	8.45	7.87	7.88	12.23	10.25	10.13
Middle p	H%	35.42	42.65	44.31	36.14	41.01	41.93
	P%	40.57	43.04	47.47	39.03	43.75	44.40
Poor p	H%	40.47	38.59	37.72	43.05	41.65	41.78
	P%	35.71	35.00	33.94	39.02	38.81[c]	39.08
Laborer	H%	7.06	3.06	3.23	4.74	3.24	3.25
	P%	4.82	2.55	2.41	3.21	2.13	2.22
Other[d]	H%	8.72	7.16	6.9	6.25	5.55	4.09
	P%	6.25	5.78	5.28	4.29	3.72	2.91

Source: JCJ (1984: 2: 222–223).

Notes: H% = the percentage of household; P% = the percentage of population.
[a] Same as Table 5.2 [a].
[b] Same as Table 5.2 [b].
[c] The original number from the source book is 28.81; it does not match the total sum in this column. I think this number should be 38.81. If so the deviation in this column would be 0.2.
[d] See Table 5.2 [c].

percent. Their share of the population had increased 6.9 percent, from 40.57 percent to 47.47 percent. The landlord and rich peasant households and population had decreased 0.69 percent and 1.67 percent respectively. And the poor peasant and wage laborer households and population had decreased 6.58 percent and 4.18 percent respectively.

In the 42 villages in the guerrilla areas, the middle peasant households and population had increased 5.79 percent and 5.37 percent respectively. The landlord and rich peasant households and population had decreased 1.33 percent and 2.62 percent, the poor peasant and wage laborer households and population had decreased 2.76 percent and 0.98 percent. Differences in the extent of change between consolidated areas and guerrilla areas were, we are told, due to the variations in the war situations in these areas (JCJ 1984: 2: 214–219).

Another survey of 27 villages in central Hebei in the summer of 1941 also tells the same story. In these 27 villages, 36 percent of the hired laborers had acquired sufficient land to become independent tillers. Another 20 percent had achieved what the party called middle-peasant status, and 1.8 percent had become rich peasants. Among those previously designated as poor peasants, 28 percent had risen to middle-peasant status, 0.4 percent to rich peasant. On the other hand, 34.9 percent of rich peasants had declined to middle peasant, and 8.1 percent to poor peasant (Friedman, Pickwicz, Selden 1991: 42–43). A similar story is also found in Ten Mile Inn. The Crooks tell us that as a result of the tax reforms, the village had become a community of middle peasants with roughly equal holdings. Landlords and rich peasants, tenants and long-term laborers had practically disappeared (1959: 161).[16]

As stated earlier, in late 1941, the Border government implemented the unified progressive tax in the base area. This new tax targeted 80 percent of the households and population in the base area, and granted tax exemption only to the poorest villagers—who amounted to no more than 20 percent of the total households and population. This change was an adaptation to changed property relations and also an indicator of changed class structure in the base area.[17] To be sure, this tax was still the "reasonable burden" progressive-rate tax.[18] It was not designed to stop or alter the socioeconomic transformation started by the early stages of tax reforms. However, it did slow down the speed of the transformation. As Liu Lantao explained in one of his 1941 Party work reports:

> After the institution of the unified progressive tax and the Double-Ten Program, the [rate of] decline of the landlord economy will be slowed down. However, the landlord economy and the feudal exploitation it represented will never thrive again. This fact is beyond any doubt.
>
> (JCJ 1984: 2: 199–201)

Therefore, on the whole, the Communist tax reforms brought about a profound transformation in the base area. This transformation was "gradual in process, but revolutionary in consequence": a revolution that was identical to, as Friedman, Pickwicz, Selden observed, a *restoration*, because "it reversed the long-term downward trend in the countryside, repaired much that seemed damaged in the village, revived the rural economy, and healed social divisions" (1991: 43–44).

Past scholarship of the Chinese Communist revolution has mainly focused on the period of the War of Resistance against Japan and has already produced a large body of literature (see Introduction). However, little attention has been paid to the tax reform in the anti-Japanese base areas and their impact on both state–society relations and village property relations or class structure. In discussing Communist socioeconomic reforms in the base areas, scholars have usually concentrated on the rent and interest reduction campaign and attributed socioeconomic changes in the anti-Japanese base areas mainly to this campaign. However, we should note that the tax reform took chronological precedence over the rent and interest reduction campaign. The tax reform was put into practice at the outset of the base area, while the rent and interest reduction campaign was not implemented on a mass scale in the North China base areas until 1942 (Baba 1984: 48–50; Wei Hongyun and Zuo Zhiyuan 1990: 135; Zhao Xiaomin 1990: Chapters 8–11).[19] Suzanne Pepper's study demonstrated that until late 1943, rent reduction had not been "thoroughly" implemented in most villages of the (Jin-Cha-Ji) base area (Pepper 1978: 251–252). One reason for the delay in implementation of the rent and interest reduction was that the Communists were afraid that it might arouse class confrontations in the village, and hence jeopardize the united front.[20] Because of this, the Communists were willing to wait until they thought the base areas were consolidated and secure enough. As Liu Shaoqi emphasized in the winter of 1942, only when basic military and political security had been achieved could the rent and interest reduction be implemented on a large scale (Dorris 1976: 68: 709).

Another and more important reason for the delay in the implementation of the rent and interest reduction was that in rural North China, landlordism was not a dominant phenomenon. The rent reduction was thus not so urgent nor appealing as tax reforms to the broad mass of the rural populace. For example, Pepper's study on the Communist Shandong base area shows that in local grievances rent and interest was usually after other issues, such as taxation, local bullies and corruption, and hence also in the program of Communist mobilization (Pepper 1978: 260–274). On the other hand, heavy taxation was always among the most serious of local grievances and was thus the most important and urgent target of Communist mobilization and reform (ibid.). Pepper tells us that: "Indeed, some cadres had found that alleviating the tax burden was the most pressing demand of the masses" (ibid.: 1978: 262).

Based on these facts, Pepper holds that: "With respect to rent and interest reduction alone, however, the policy apparently played a very subordinate role in the initial development of the Communists' anti-Japanese base areas because it had not been widely implemented at that time" (1978: 276). The question that Pepper leaves unanswered is: what was the major force that led to changes in village class structure before the large-scale implementation of the rent and interest reduction? As the above discussion tells us, it was the tax reform.

To re-evaluate the role of rent and interest double reduction in the Communist mobilization of rural North China is by no means to deny the significance of the class line in mass mobilization. On the contrary, I would like to argue that the class line had always played a vital role in Communist mobilization. However, it had done so mainly through the tax reform. By integrating the class line, the Communist tax reform was more than a simple fiscal measure, but also a social and economic reform. It gave the Communists a very powerful means to transform property relations and class structure within the village community, and to reverse the long-term socio-economic decline in the countryside. This dimension of socio-economic reform had never been a part of previous tax systems. In this sense, the Communist taxation was truly revolutionary.

The political implications of the change of property relations and class structure within the village community were conspicuous. On the one hand, they undermined the old rural elite by depriving them of their properties through progressive taxation. On the other hand, they restored the middle peasantry. This newly revived social stratum once again dominated the village community. These changes greatly benefited the Communists by allowing them to have a more effective and rigid control over the village, because now there no longer was an independent social and political force based on property ownership in the village to challenge the absolute authority of the Communist state, also because the newly revived middle peasantry was grateful to the Communist regime and willing to comply with the regime so as to safeguard their own gains.

New middle peasants

Among the middle peasants, except for a small portion who had recently dropped from rich peasant or landlord status, most benefited greatly from the Communist regime and the tax reforms that it introduced. They, especially the previously poor peasants, experienced substantial improvement in their economic situations and social status, so they supported the new regime and were willing to fight for it. As Yang Shangkun, a top leader of the CCP, said in 1944:

The middle peasants in North China are large in number. Because of the achievements of democracy and freedom, their economic burdens have been lightened and their living conditions have been improved. They thus support the anti-Japanese democratic regime. They are the important [zhongyao] social base of this regime.

> The poor peasants are exploited by others, they are the semiproletariat in the countryside. With the correct financial and economic policies, they can improve themselves economically. This improvement is beneficial to the base area. They are the principal [*zhuyao*] social base of the anti-Japanese democratic regime.
>
> (JCJ 1984: 1: 117)

Within the village, middle peasants, especially those new middle peasants, played an increasingly significant role in village public life, and became the dominant group in village politics. The so-called new middle peasants were those "who had risen from the ranks of the once debt-burdened poor to become owners of land and a force in the village" (Crook and Crook 1959: 73).

A contemporary field survey conducted by a research team headed by Zhang Wentian in northern Shaanxi tells us the following story. The survey was taken in 1942, and it shows that the middle peasants were an expanding stratum in the village as the circumstances of the once poor peasants continuously improved. This social stratum was politically more active, and also worked more energetically and vigorously for the Communist regime. Both in the party and the government, the majority of people had a middle peasant background. Middle peasants possessed considerably greater prestige than other strata in villages and villagers tended to elect people from middle peasant or wealthy middle peasant backgrounds to be village officers. This was because they believed that these people could represent their interests better, were capable of handling village affairs, and were good at dealing with superior officers. Besides, they thought these people could afford to lose time in farm work (*wudeqi gong*). On the other hand, middle peasants and wealthy middle peasants were the staunchest supporters of the Border Region government, the Eighth Route Army and the party. They were well aware that the improvement of their livelihoods was due to the Party's policies and the protection of the army and the government. Thus, they were willing to bear various burdens for the government without complaint (Zhang Wentian 1986: 61–62).

Though Zhang Wentian's survey details the situation in the Shaan-Gan-Ning (Shaanxi-Ganshu-Ningxia, located in Northwest China) Border Region, it reflects, nevertheless, the general situation of North China base areas. For example, statistics show that in 1940 in seven central Hebei counties, 87.9 percent of village committee members, 90.9 percent of village chairs, and 82.1 percent of county councilors were middle peasants or poor peasants (JCJ 1984: 2: 59). And in the Taihang Base, as Goodman's study shows, middle peasants became increasingly dominating in the local leadership of the CCP during the war and provided more than two-thirds of all village level cadres by the end of the war (Goodman 2000: 258–259). The Crooks tell us that in Ten Mile Inn, the new middle peasants were the staunchest supporters of the reforms which the Communists introduced. The Crooks remarked that:

The old middle peasants, who in the early days had played an active part in the resistance against the Japanese invaders, were now greatly strengthened by this new accession to their numbers. The result was a stiffened resistance to the enemy.

(1959: 74)

The same situation can also be found in Hinton's Long Bow village.[21] The growth of middle peasants and their dominance at local level leadership in base areas incurred doubts and suspicions from some party leaders and triggered fierce policy debates within the party. Nonetheless, numbers of middle peasants continued to grow as well as their political influence.[22]

The focal point of Communist mobilization and the building block of the Communist state

Although the class line played a very important role in Communist mobilization, in the North China base areas, it was the village community, not any specific class which was the primary object of Communist mobilization, organization and control of rural society. The village community was the very building block of the Communist regime and state. As the Communists themselves repeatedly emphasized, the village was "the basis of all our works in the base area" (JCJ 1984: 4: 402), and to build a strong village government was "the central issue in the construction of our regime" (Hebei 1983: 1: 106). Because of this, no matter how important the class line was, it could not overshadow the principle of "taking the village as the basic unit." In the whole scheme of Communist mobilization and Communist state-making, the class line was subordinate to, while also serving, the latter. This could be seen very clearly in the case of the peasant association.

The poor peasant association was created by the Communists in their North China bases, it comprised of poor and middle peasants, excluding landlords and rich peasants. This organization had played a significant role in the Communist mobilization of rural society. It was employed to wage class struggle against landlords and rich peasants. However, this organization and the class struggle it conducted were strictly confined within the village. It was established in each village, recruited members within its own village, and most interestingly, it also targeted class enemies living in the same village. Village boundaries demarcated the arena for all its activities. Though this association played a very important role in mobilizing peasants, it had never become a united class front transcending village communities and was always under the leadership of the village party branch and the village government.

For example, in Ten Mile Inn, the peasant union was organized under the leadership of the village Communist Party branch, and embraced the great majority of families other than those of the landlords and rich peasants. Rallied by the peasant union, the poor and middle peasants played a more significant part in village politics. For instance, the union led peasants to visit the homes of landlords and rich peasants in the village to force them to contribute the grain they had hidden. Gradually, the village government came to be dominated by the union activists. However, the union was never a united class front transcending village boundaries (Crook and Crook 1959: 51–54, 58–59).

Interestingly enough, the union finally became a village-wide ascriptive organization, its membership identical to the village membership itself. We are told that later in 1947, the "objects of class struggle" in the village were graded into three categories. The basic and also lightest punishment meted out to these "objects" was to be "barred from membership in the peasant union." This punishment formally deprived them of all of the political rights a villager was entitled to. For example, all the village's public affairs—such as decrees of the village government, laws and directives from superior governments, and all village affairs (including arrangements for substitute plowing, taxation, production, etc.)—were discussed at the peasant union meeting (Crook and Crook 1959: 146–148).[23] "Besides this, exclusion from the peasant union made one not only a political but a social outcast, for with the disappearance of religious observance and clan ceremonials, the peasant union had become the centre of social life" (ibid.: 148).

A similar situation could also be found in the women's association. Although women did not constitute a social class, the women's association was very similar in nature to a class organization, for neither gender nor class was territorially bounded. However, in the Communist base areas of North China, the women's association was subject to the same restrictions as was the poor peasant association. The women's association and its activities were strictly confined within the village, and under the control of the male-dominated Party branch and village government. In her study of women's issue in the Chinese Communist revolution, Kay Ann Johnson shows very clearly that the activities of the women's association in the wartime North China bases were restricted by the village Party branch and government, women's efforts for equal rights were therefore fruitless (Johnson, K. A. 1983: 63–75).

Alienation of the village government

Under Communist mobilization, the village in the North China base areas was required to perform more and more functions and assume more and more roles for the state. The village was no longer an autonomous social entity, rather, it became the lowest administrative unit of the Communist state. This situation, on the one hand, reduced the complex, multilayered relationship between the state and rural society to a simple, bilateral relationship between the state and village community. On the other hand, it reduced the individual villager to a mere ascriptive member of his or her village, and excluded him or her from direct dealings with the state. All these changes greatly facilitated the Communist state in organizing and controlling rural society.[24]

However, for the village government this situation meant nothing but heavier and greater responsibilities to the state. These responsibilities alienated the village government from its constituency and reduced it to a mere state agency. During wartime, collecting taxes became the overriding task for the village government.[25] Under the pressure from the superior government, many village governments were reduced to a simple taxation apparatus of the Communist state. Indeed, in one of its directives the Border Region government complained that many village governments had become merely perfunctory organs of taxation (*zhiying jiguan*), and many other tasks—such as, promoting the village economy; solving villagers' economic problems; and implementing other policies and regulations of the Border Region government—had been neglected (Hebei 1983: 2: 422). The same document admitted that this situation was mainly attributable to their superior governments who cared about nothing but the payment of taxes. This kind of leadership was denounced as *yaozhangshi lingdao* (meaning: tax dunning leaders) (ibid.: 423).

Caught in between state and village interests, the village government found itself once again in a dilemma as it had been under the previous regimes. In order to reduce or evade their responsibilities to the state, and to protect the village interests under their constituents' pressure, many village governments sought to turn inward. It thus led to what the Communists condemned "village compartmentalism" (*cun benwei zhuyi*). The base government launched relentless attacks on any sign of it. So-called village compartmentalism referred to the practice that put village interests first and foremost while ignoring and sacrificing the state interests. It was displayed very clearly in the realm of taxation. As we have seen, the Communist taxation made the village a collective taxpayer and allocated the tax quota according to the economic conditions of a village, this induced villages to underreport their resources and wealth in order to lower their tax quota. In the Jin-Cha-Ji base, this practice became a fairly common phenomenon. The Party and the Border Region government issued many administrative orders and launched campaigns to eliminate this phenomenon (JCJ 1984: 4: 403, 415–421). However, this "evil" could hardly be eliminated since it was deeply embedded within this state–village relationship.[26]

Intense Communist mobilization inevitably led to the rapid expansion and bureaucratization of village administration. As a result, village administration became a full-time job and village expenditures swelled tremendously. Although forbidden by government regulations, in some villages the village heads became full-time cadres (*tuochan ganbu*) who no longer engaged in farming. In reaction to this, Song Shaowen specifically pointed out in one of his 1940 work reports that village heads should not be full-time cadres (JCJ 1984: 4: 18).[27] In this same report, Song also mentioned that some villages spent village funds lavishly for entertaining officials and soldiers and for subsidizing village cadres. In central Hebei, for example, some village governments could spend 1,000 *yuan* a month. Song estimated that in the base area on average each village wasted 40 *yuan* a month. While government regulations stipulated that the monthly allowance for Grade A villages (with more than 150 household per village) be set at only 20 to 30 *yuan*, for Grade B and Grade C villages, it was only 15–20 *yuan* and 2–12 *yuan* respectively (ibid.: 4: 9–19, 645–647, 652). Song attributed this waste to "liberalism," a lack of strict regulations, and ineffective supervision. But in the final analysis, the presence of full-time village cadres and the waste of village funds were the product of the rapid expansion and bureaucratization of village administration.

Wasting village funds quickly became a rampant problem in the base area. To combat this wrongdoing, the Border Region government launched a campaign in late 1938 to rectify village finance. The Central Hebei base area reported that, after the rectification, most villages reduced their expenditures by 50–80 percent. On average, each village saved about 140 *yuan* a month (JCJ 1984: 1: 690–692). However, this deep-rooted problem was not easily wiped out. In a 1941 work report of the Ji-Re (Hebei and Rehe) sub-region government, we find that wasting village funds was still listed as one of the major deficiencies in financial management (JCJ 1984: 1: 600).[28]

Conclusion

In summary, the tax reform introduced by the Communists during the first half of the war brought about fundamental changes in the relationship between state and rural society as well as in class structure within the village. The reform substantiated the strategy and principles of Communist mobilization in rural North China.

Communist mobilization mainly focused on two dimensions and followed two principles. On the one hand, the Communists changed the relationship between state and rural society from a complex, multi-layered one to a simple, bilateral relationship between the state and the village. In the scheme of Communist mobilization, the village was taken as the basic unit: it functioned simultaneously as a rural community, a body corporate, and an administrative unit. This arrangement excluded independent dealings between individual villagers and the state. More importantly, it required the village community as a collectivity to be responsible for all government tasks. This change enabled the Communist state to mobilize rural society and enlist both human and material resources much more efficiently than any of its predecessors could.[29]

On the other hand, the Communists insisted on following the class line to solve the problem of socioeconomic stratification in rural society. Their progressive tax system decisively transformed property relations and class structure within the village. After several years of implementation of this tax system, the village communities in the base areas were once again dominated by owner-cultivators. This change strengthened not only the village community itself but also the Communist control over it, because the socioeconomic homogeneity recreated by the Communists fostered communal solidarity and the dissolution of the rich eliminated a substantial challenge to the Communist regime from the propertied classes.

Changes in the relationship between the state and rural society and in village class structure not only enabled the Communists to mobilize rural society effectively and efficiently in support of their regime, their army, and the War of Resistance, it also laid down the foundation for their 1949 victory and the future development of the Communist state.[30] It was the social structure and wartime situation of rural North China that made all of these possible.[31] Under the Communist mobilization, the North China village was successfully transformed into the stronghold of the revolution and the building block of the edifice of the Communist state. We can say without exaggeration that the wartime North China bases were the real springboard from which the Chinese Communist revolution marched from victory to victory.

6　Social structure and local politics in the Yangzi delta

The Yangzi delta had been the most commercialized area of the country since the Ming (1368–1644). Long-term commercialization of the regional economy brought a series of profound social changes to this area which made the Yangzi delta a highly stratified society characterized by spatial segregation between urban absentee landlords and rural dwelling tenant-peasants. Due to this social structural change, rent collection became increasingly difficult and contentious. Conflicts between these two classes revolving around rent collection dominated the local political scene after the mid-Qing. Disputes and conflicts over rent continued and intensified during the Republican period, and the Yangzi delta became the site of the most intense forms of class struggle between landlords and tenant peasants in the country.

The development of absentee landlordism left the Yangzi delta countryside as a homogeneous society composed mainly of tenants and part-tenants. This change not only reduced state presence in the rural community to a minimum, it also reduced social conflicts within the community to a minimum. As a result, political life in the delta's rural communities became much simpler and less antagonistic. The intense strife over the allocation of *tankuan* levies and the management of village funds that characterized village politics on the North China plain had never been an issue here. The characteristics and qualifications of community leadership in the Yangzi delta therefore also differed substantially from that of its counterparts in rural North China.

The different socioeconomic structure in the Yangzi delta not only conditioned different local politics, it also shaped a different pattern of Rural Reconstruction. Social reformers here faced a set of issues quite different from those encountered by the reformers in rural North China. Rural Reconstruction in the Yangzi delta focused more on concrete social and economic issues and was less politically oriented. It thus contrasted sharply with the Rural Reconstruction conducted on the North China plain.

Commercialization and social stratification

Commercialization in the Yangzi delta benefited greatly from the delta's stable ecological system, fertile land, convenient water transportation, advanced agriculture, as well as a secure social and political order. As early as in the Song (960–1279), the Yangzi delta was one of the major commercial centers of the country. Since the Ming, it became the most commercialized area. The commercialization of the regional economy was accompanied by urbanization. The growth of cities and towns, increasingly attracted people to urban areas, most of whom were landlords, merchants or gentry. Commercialization and urbanization thus brought about not only social stratification but also spatial segregation between the rich and the poor, and between elites and peasants.

Commercialization and urbanization

Vigorous and accelerated commercialization in the Yangzi delta began in the early Ming. It was cotton and the cotton industry, as Philip Huang has argued, that "[lay] at the heart of the story of commercialization in the Ming-Qing Yangzi delta" (Huang 1990: 44). Besides cotton, silk was also a major product of the delta, though silk weaving, a specialized craft, was basically an urban industry separate from peasant family production. Mulberry cultivation, silkworm raising, and silk reeling were exclusively peasant household activities. The story of commercialization in the delta was thus the story of the commercialization of the peasant economy. Commercialization not only increasingly involved the delta's peasants in market activities outside their village communities, it also brought about profound social changes in the delta's rural society.

Except for a small portion which was consumed by the delta peasant producers themselves, most cotton products were produced for the market and were sold to different regions of the country. As early as in the Ming, it was said that the cotton cloth produced in Songjiang Prefecture, the country's leading cotton handicraft center, could clothe the whole country (*yibei tianxia*) (See *Hongzhi shanghai xian zhi*, Preface; and *Zhengde huating xian zhi*, vol. 3). According to Wu Chengming's estimate, on the eve of the Opium War, the delta exported perhaps 40,000,000 bolts of cotton cloth a year. This amount of cotton cloth required about 280,000,000 workdays per annum to produce, or about 117 workdays per delta household (Huang 1990: 45–46). Xu Xinwu tells us that in Songjiang prefecture, where virtually all peasant households wove, the average household produced 66.3 bolts of cloth a year, but kept only 8.4 bolts for its own consumption (ibid.: 46). This meant that more than 85 percent of the cotton cloth produced by the delta peasants eventually went to markets.

In the Yangzi delta, the cotton handicraft industry was basically concentrated in the area to the east of the Grand Canal, in Songjiang prefecture and Taicang department. The area lying to the west of both the Canal and the eastern and southern shores of Lake Tai was the country's leading silk handicraft center. This area generally included Hangzhou, Jiaxing, Huzhou, and Suzhou prefectures. In this area, sericulture and raw silk production very often overshadowed grain production, and in fact became the peasants' primary occupation.[1] According to a contemporary estimate, during the Qianlong period (1736–1795), about 300,000 *catties* of raw silk, valued at nearly one million taels of silver, were exported annually from the delta to foreign countries (Quan 1972: 2: 491). In comparison to cotton, silk was exclusively a market commodity and not consumed by peasant producers. All of the productive activities related to silk were market oriented. In the area where silk instead of cotton was the major sideline, mulberry cultivation, silkworm raising, and silk reeling accounted for more than half of a peasant's workdays per year. Moreover, these tasks absorbed almost all surplus labor of the peasant household beyond that needed for rice production (Huang 1990: 78–80).

Since land and manpower in the delta were increasingly devoted to cotton and silk, grain production decreased significantly during the Ming and Qing in this area. The rapid expansion of the urban population greatly increased the demand for grain. By the end of the Ming, instead of being a grain exporting area, the delta was a grain importing area. Every year about 15,000,000 shi of rice were shipped to the Yangzi delta, enough to feed a population of 4,000,000–5,000,000 (Wu Chengming, quoted in Huang, 1990: 48). Grain trade thus also contributed greatly to the delta's commercialization.

Commercialization triggered a great boom of urbanization in the Yangzi delta. The growth of market towns and cities, both in number and in size, during the Ming and the Qing was astonishing. According to Liu Shiji's study, from 1500 to 1900 the number of cities and towns in the six prefectures of the Yangzi delta increased almost four-fold. Table 6.1 demonstrates the quantitative growth of market towns and cities in the Yangzi delta during the Ming–Qing period.

Table 6.1 Market towns in the Yangzi delta during the Ming and Qing

Area	Date/Number	Date/Number
Suzhou	1506–1521/45	1875–1908/206
Songjiang	1506–1521/44	1909–1911/303
Changzhou	1465–1487/22	1909–1911/185
Hangzhou	1573–1619/44	1909–1911/145
Jiaxing	1573–1619/28	1909–1911/78
Huzhou	1621–1628/17	1875–1908/57
Total	*c.* 1500–1600/200	*c.* 1900/974

Source: Liu Shiji (1987: 141–156).

Moreover, Liu's study also shows that in the first three hundred years, from 1500 to 1800, urban growth was rather steady at less than 2.5 percent per annum. From the nineteenth century onward, especially around the mid-nineteenth century, urban growth experienced a real surge (Liu Shiji 1987: 156). By the turn of the twentieth century, the number of towns and cities finally reached 974, almost five times the number that had existed around the year 1500.

During the Ming and the Qing, the urban population in the Yangzi delta increased much more rapidly than that of the general population, making the Yangzi delta one of the nation's most urbanized areas. G. William Skinner estimates that by 1843 about 9.5 percent of the inhabitants of the lower Yangzi macro-region (of which the Yangzi delta forms the core) lived in towns with more than 2,000 people (Skinner 1977a: 229). If we consider the Yangzi delta alone, the proportion would be much higher. Liu's study rather convincingly shows that in Wujiang County, as early as the 1740s town dwellers constituted as much as 35 percent of the population (Liu Shiji 1987: 137). However, Wujiang's case might not be representative of the delta in general, since it was one of most prosperous counties in the delta. Another general estimate of urban population in Jiangsu and Zhejiang provinces made in the 1920s asserts that by that time 19 percent of the population in Jiangsu lived in towns and cities with populations of more than 10,000; while in Zhejiang the percentage was 14.4 percent (Zhu Kezhen, quoted in Liu Shiji 1987: 139).

Social stratification between urban and rural areas

With commercialization and urbanization, first of all, wealthy people (most of whom were landlords) moved from their countryside estates to towns and cities in pursuit of commercial opportunities and the amenities of urban life. This change began in the early Qing and by the nineteenth century absentee landownership had already become the dominant form of landownership in the delta. In many prefectures and counties, the percentage of land owned by absentee landlords was as high as 80–90 percent. A contemporary described the general situation of Yangzi delta's landownership in these words: "In Jiangnan area, many *yanhu* (lit. smoking households) own large amounts of land.[2] Of these, four- or five-tenths live in cities, three- or four-tenths inhabit towns, and one- or two-tenths reside in dispersed villages" (Zhao Xixiao, "On Labor Services," quoted in *Suzhou fu zhi* 1883: vol. 13, 29b).

The growth of absentee landlordism promoted the development of a system of two-tiered land ownership. Under this arrangement:

[L]and is divided into two layers: namely, the surface and the subsoil. The possessor of the subsoil is the title holder of the land. His name will be registered with the government because he pays the taxes on the land. But he may possess only the subsoil without the surface, that is, he has no right to use the land directly for cultivation. The person possessing both the surface and the subsoil is termed the full owner. The one possessing only the surface without the subsoil is termed tenant.

(Fei 1939: 177)

According to Pan Gaungdan and Quan Weitian's estimate, two-tiered land ownership was found in an area of southern Jiangsu containing 4,000,000 peasants, about 40 percent of the agricultural population. This area was concentrated in southeast and south-central Jiangsu, i.e. the Yangzi delta area of southern Jiangsu (Pan Guangdan and Quan Weitian 1952: 37–38). Tao Xu, a local scholar of the late Qing, revealed the connection between these two phenomena very clearly:

Nowadays the land tenure system in the Suzhou area [*wuzhong*] differs greatly from the past. That land cultivated by the owners themselves is called *qizhongtian*, or *zitian* (fully owned land), and it is not divided into the surface and the subsoil. However, this kind of land does not account for even one- or two-tenths of the total land cultivated. Apart from this, all land cultivated is rented land . . .

It is human nature that if one owns something he wants to own it exclusively, and not to share it with others. However, this does not apply to landownership. Today all of the urbanites call the land with surface and subsoil rights together *huatian* (slippery land and hence unreliable land). They disdain this kind of land, and only want to possess the subsoil of the land and let the tenants have the surface. Because if the tenant does not have the surface of the land, he will readily change his landlord when he is ill-treated by his lord. But if he owns the surface of the land, then even if his lord treats him very cruelly by asking a high rate of rent or of *zhejia* (commutation of rent to cash payment), and forcing a rigid deadline of payment, he will not leave the land because this is his property, upon which his descendants depend.

(Tao Xu [1884] 1977: 229–230)

This passage reveals a close relation between absentee landlordism and two-layered landownership. They were very often two aspects of the same system.[3] Highly developed absentee landlordism indicates a profound stratification between landed elites and land tillers. More importantly, this social stratification was *spatially* displayed, i.e. it was explicitly expressed in the differentiation between towns/cities and the countryside in the Yangzi delta. This same degree of social stratification was not present on the North China plain.

A direct consequence of this profound social and spatial stratification was that wealth, institutionalized power as well as symbolic capital were increasingly concentrated in towns and cities, leaving the delta's countryside an increasingly homogeneous society composed of tenant peasants. James Shih's study of the social background of *juren* degree holders in Tongxiang County

Table 6.2 Juren degree holders in Tongxiang county from rural and urban backgrounds

Date	Total (N)	Rural (%)	Urban (%)	Unknown (%)
1370–1643	70	76	20	4
1644–1795	132	17	61	22
1796–1889	70	1	89	10
1644–1889	202[a]	11	71	18

Source: Shih (1992: 86).

Note:
[a] In Shih's book this figure is 227. However, it does not match the total sum of the figures drawn from different periods at that time.

during the Ming and Qing outlines this structural change. He finds that in Ming times, the majority of the *juren* degree holders in this county were from the countryside; by the Qing, however, the situation had reversed with most *juren* degree holders coming from urban areas. Table 6.2 is based on his statistics.

These statistics not only show the change from the Ming to the Qing, they also demonstrate the accumulated result of the urbanization of local elites in nineteenth-century Yangzi delta. During this century, of the 70 *juren* degree holders in this county, only one was from the countryside. Though we cannot say that the degree holders were drawn exclusively from local elite, the situation discussed here was no doubt a significant indicator of the urbanization of local elite.

Tongxiang's case was by no means exceptional, but was, as Shih believed, representative of the region (Shih 1992: 85). The stratification of the elite and the peasantry between towns/cities and rural communities in the Yangzi delta, was also embodied in and characterized by the two-tiered kinship system revealed by Kathryn Bernhardt's study. In the delta, as Bernhardt's study convincingly demonstrates, "highly articulated and organized lineages among the elite in the cities and towns and more loosely organized descent groups among the peasantry in the villages" constituted the two-tiers of the local kinship system (Bernhardt 1992: 19).

These urban elite lineages differed greatly from the lineages in South China, especially in Guangdong and Fujian, where lineage ties bound elites and peasants, and landlords and tenants closely together, with elite lineage heads as village leaders, and peasant lineage members as tenants cultivating lineage corporate land (Freedman 1966). In the Yangzi delta, however, lineage corporate property generally took the form of charitable estates. Similar to private landownership, these lineage estates were also highly fragmented and characterized by absenteeism. Moreover, these lineage estates seldom rented to their own lineage members. Under these conditions, the lineage in the delta did not create strong personal links between elite and peasant, or landlord and tenant, and therefore hardly served the function of mitigating the tension between the two antagonistic classes as it did in South China (Freedman 1966: 19–21).

On the other hand, among the peasantry in the villages the descent group was normally very small and weak. The average size of a common descent group was, according to Fei Xiaotong's field study in Kaixiangong, about eight households. This kind of descent group actually played little part in organizing peasant collective activities. It was, as Fei observed, "no more than a cere-monial group which assembles periodically at wedding and funeral occasions, taking a common feast, offering sacrifices to the common ancestors together, and contributing a small sum barely enough to cover the food" (1939: 85).

Huang's field study in Huayangqiao tells the same story. In Huayangqiao, the descent group was the basic social circle for funeral and wedding gather-ings. People outside of this circle were seldom invited. This circle was kept very small; once the members of a descent group increased, further fragmentation took place. For example, the Lus in Xilihangbang were further divided into two groups and hamlets, namely Lujiada (with nine households) and Nanda (with ten). This fragmentation took place in the 1930s, by which time, most of the Lus no longer invited their kin from the other hamlet (Huang 1990: 148–149).

The emigration of local elite from the countryside left the delta's country-side as an increasingly egalitarian and homogeneous society composed mainly of tenants, part-tenants and small owner-cultivators. In his book, Huang studied eight Yangzi delta villages. In these eight villages there were only five resident landlord households, who amounted to only 0.5 percent of the total 966 households. Moreover, there were no managerial farmers. The majority of households were tenants and part-tenants, which constituted about 80 percent of the total households. This represented the general situ-ation of the social structure in the rural Yangzi delta (see Chapter 1). This social structure decisively shaped politics in local society.

Class formation and confrontation

Social stratification in the Yangzi delta was characterized by the spatial differentiation and physical separation between the two basic social strata or classes, i.e., the landed elite and the tenant-peasantry. This situation greatly benefited and promoted integration and solidarity within each class, and in turn fostered confrontations and conflicts between these two classes on a larger scale. Confrontations and conflicts were no longer confined to the rural community; rather, they took place in a larger arena involving both urban and rural areas. In rural China, full-fledged struggle between the two classes transcendent of parochialism was first seen and fully devel-oped only in this area. This class warfare dominated, to a great extent, local political scene. This development should, first of all, be attributed to the development of absentee landlordism.

Rent collection and the formation of the landlord class

Living away from the countryside, absentee landlords lost direct control over their landed properties and tenants. They were thus caught in an unfavorable position in rent collection. Originally, rent was collected by landlords in person. But this was not viable under conditions of absentee landlordism. As Fei observed:

> It takes time and pains for the landlord to visit each tenant in different villages . . . Moreover, direct and personal contact sometimes handicaps the process of collecting. The tenants may be poor and always ready to ask for exemptions or reductions. The landlord, on the other hand, is not infrequently inspired by humanitarian teachings, especially if he belongs to the old literati.
>
> (1939: 178)

Owing to free and frequent land (i.e. the subsoil) transactions among absentee landlords, the personal relations between owners and their properties, and between landlords and their tenants were reduced to a minimum. As a result, most absentee landlords did not know where their properties were located nor who their tenants were (ibid.: 178). Also, most tenants did not know who their landlords were (Pan Guangdan and Quan Weitian 1952: 21). Actually, only a small portion of landlords in the delta still collected rent in person in the twentieth century, most of whom were small landlords living in the countryside (Fei 1939: 187; see also He Menglei [1934] 1977: 33133).

Obviously the development of absentee landlordism demanded new institutional arrangements to ensure rent collection and at the same time to free absentee landlords from the process of actual rent collecting. The development of a special rent collection agency, i.e. the rent bursary, provided a good solution to this problem. The origin of the rent bursary can be traced back to the mid-Qing (see Chapter 2, note 31). Entering the twentieth century, the rent bursary had become a widely used institution for rent collection. It was known by different names in different localities of the Yangzi delta. For example, it was called *zuzhan* (rent storehouse or rent bursary) in Suzhou; *cangfang* (granary warehouse) in Changshu; and *cangting* (granary hall) in Wuxi (He Menglei [1934] 1977: 33125–33131); and *ju* in Wujiang County (Fei 1939: 187).

The rent bursary was a public agency for rent collection, delegated to and managed by professional accountants. The strength of this agency system was that it changed rent collection from a personal affair of individual landlords into a public service for the landlord class as a collectivity (Faure 1989). The following passage quoted from Fei's book gives us some general description about how this system worked:

Landlords of big estates establish their own rent collecting bureaux and petty landlords pool their claims with them. The bureau is called Chu [*ju*]. The tenants do not know and do not care who is their landlord, and know only to which bureau they belong.

Names of the tenants and the amount of land held by each are kept in the bureau records. At the end of October, the bureau will inform each tenant of the amount of rent that should be paid that year. The information is forwarded by special agents. These agents are employed by the bureau and have been entrusted with police power by the district government. The bureau is thus in fact a semi-political organ.

In the village, rent is paid into the hands of agents of the bureau. This is a peculiar practice different from that of other parts of the same district.[4]. . . If the tenant refuses to pay, the agent has power to arrest him and put him into the prison of the district government. But if the tenant is really unable to pay, he will be released at the end of the year. It is no use keeping him in prison and leaving the farms uncultivated.

(Fei 1939: 188–189)

According to Muramatsu's study, the amount of land managed by a rent bursary was usually very large, and the internal structure of a rent bursary was complicated. For example, the Yu-jing bursary of the Wu clan in Suzhou was entrusted by its patrons to collect rent from several thousand *mu* of land scattered across countries of Yuanhe, Changzhou, and Wuxian from 1893 to 1928 (Muramatsu Yuji 1970: 679–746).[5] The bursary did not deal with the individual landlords directly, rather it dealt with groups of landlords, which were called *hao* locally. The *hao* was, as Muramatsu suggested, a geographically organized unit of landlords who possessed plots in the same location. However, this did not mean that the bursary was a strictly organized hierarchy. On the contrary, the relations between landlords, the *hao* and bursaries were very complex and promiscuous. Since very often a landlord owned land in different locations, his properties might thus be organized into several different *hao*, and therefore delegated to several different bursaries.

The relationship between the *hao* and the bursary was also fairly free. For example, the Yu-jing bursary was entrusted with a total of 66 *hao* during the period from 1893 to 1928; but the actual number of *hao* it administered in each year of this period fluctuated from a high of 34 (1893) to a low of 17 (1916, 1917). This situation may suggest a certain degree of competition among different bursaries for winning over customers.

Detailed accounting records were kept by the bursary which revealed that it was managed in a very professional way by real experts. As Tao Xu tells us in his "Investigation of rents":

Today rent collection does not employ servants but specialists. He [the specialist] enjoys the prestige of a private tutor and guest [*shibin*], and is called Mr. *Zhisu* (i.e. Mr. Accountant). During the rent collection season, he is sitting there and supervising everything. He uses an abacus for calculating. The tenants cannot say a word before him.

([1884] 1977: 228)

The rent bursary system integrated the interests of individual landlords into a collectivity and a class. It served this class's interests in a way very similar to how a modern business company serves the interests of its stockholders. This institution was unique to the Yangzi delta. Facing a vast number of tenant-peasants, it represented landlords as a class in dealing with tenants, and changed what originally were person-to-person relations between land-lords and tenants into depersonalized and antagonistic relations. Indeed, ill-feelings between landlords and tenants were proportionately related to the development of absentee landlordism and the bursary system (Ash 1976: 43). This situation was exacerbated by the fact that rent bursaries always treated tenants badly and cruelly (Tao Xu 1977 [1884]: 231–233; Tao Zhicheng *et al.* 1951: 117–122).

Collective rent resistance from the tenant-peasantry

Profound social stratification in the Yangzi delta not only promoted integration among absentee landlords in towns and cities, it also benefited the solidarity of the tenant-peasantry in the countryside and strengthened their forces greatly in their struggle against landlords. Though the conflicts between tenants and landlords had always existed, the scale and intensity of these conflicts were determined, to a great extent, by the physical distance between landlords and tenants. Traditionally, landlords resided in villages. Tenant resistance, especially collective resistance, was plagued by the close supervision and direct control of their lords. Now, being remote from their lords and freed from their direct control, tenants could engage in concerted actions to resist much more easily. In areas with high tenancy rates, this kind of collective resistance very easily transcended the con-fines of both hamlets and compound villages and involved a much larger area. Of course, the village community was still the primary site for their resistance.

Composed mainly of tenant-farmers, now the rural community was a ready-made organization for tenant-villagers to pool their strength and to coord-inate their actions in the struggle against absentee landlords. For instance, when an absentee landlord wanted to evict his tenant, he would encounter a stubborn collective boycott from the fellow tenant-villagers of the evicted. As Fei tells us:

the practical difficulty of ejecting a tenant is to find a substitute. Absentee landlords do not cultivate the land themselves. Outsiders from the villages will not be welcomed into the community if they come at the expense of old members. Villagers are not willing to cut the throat of their fellow members who for any good reason cannot pay their rent.

(1939: 185)

Due to this practical resistance, tenant rights over topsoil actually became inalienable. This in turn consolidated the village community and strengthened the unity among tenant-villagers. The following is an example of collective resistance by tenant-villagers.

In 1771, there was a homicide case in Yixing County which was developed out of a collective rent strike. The dead person was a tenant who had lived in a village located in Jinxiao *xiang* (*xiang* was the sub-county district). Many of the villagers were the tenants of an absentee landlord named Jiang. Because of water-logging, the previous year's harvest had been poor. In many *xiang*, rent was reduced to between 70 percent and 80 percent of the normal rate. The tenants in this village who cultivated Jiang's land also asked for the same discount. But Xue Yulin, the servant-accountant of Jiang's family who was in charge of collecting rent from this village, still asked for a hundred percent of the normal rent payment. The reason was that the land in this village was located on higher ground and the harvest had not been affected. Li Yiqing, Jiang's *dianbao* (tenant-guarantor, the person who was responsible for helping the landlord in rent collection) in this village, said to Jiang's tenants: "All of Jiang's land in the village is purchased from us on conditional terms. Since Xue insists on collecting 100 percent of the rent, we can ask landlord Jiang to increase the price of land and use this to pay the rent. If he doesn't agree, we won't pay any rent." Under Li's leadership, the tenants resisted rent payment. After several fruitless trips, Xu went to the village again with several hired hands on the 15th day of the first month in 1771. This time Xu decided to bring some defaulting tenants to the county *yamen*, if he was still unable to collect the rent. As expected, no one was going to pay rent, and many of them, including Li, had gone into hiding. Enraged with this, Xu took Hu, a tenant he happened to catch, back to town. When Tang Dongqi, the murdered tenant, heard of this, he ran after them with several fellow villagers and tried to get Hu back. A fight followed and Tang was severely injured. He died several days later (QDTD 1988: 690–700).

As Kathryn Bernhardt points out, rent resistance was basically protective and reactive, aimed "not to gain something, but to keep from having to give something" (Bernhardt 1992: 37). This was especially true in times when harvests were poor. Poor harvests caused by bad weather could put tenants of the same locality into the same dire straits, and thus easily provoke them to adopt the same action to resist any landlord claim that would endanger their subsistence. Benefiting greatly from absentee landlordism, this kind of collective resistance was seldom confined to the boundaries of the rural community and usually covered quite a large area. In the Yangzi delta during the Qing, large-scale collective rent resistance was a remarkable local phenomenon which periodically burst out to stymie landlords as well as local governments. A contemporary commentator of the Kangxi period (1662–1722) remarked:

> Nowadays, the tenants of the countryside [*xiangqu dianmin*] are all collecting money for opera performances [*jujin yanxi*]. They [use this opportunity to] form alliances and swear to resist landlords [*zumeng shajie, yikang tianzhu*]. Although local governments have made announcements many times forbidding this kind of activity, the tenants are simply not afraid. If there are some good tenants who are willing to pay rent, others will attack them collectively, and sometimes even sink their boats, throw away their rice, and destroy their houses. It is very common. Moreover, recently we even hear that tenants insult and beat landlords . . . Now the tenants in Suzhou, Songjiang and Changzhou prefectures are all very furious and reckless . . . While those gentry-landlords are all afraid of incurring the public wrath (of tenants) and dare not say a word about this. What a terrible evil practice it is!
>
> (Huang Zhongjian: "On Rent Collection [*Zhengzuyi*]",
> quoted in Hong Huanchun 1988: 614)

In this passage, instead of using "of the village", the author uses "of the countryside" to define the tenant. This usage is worth noting and it conveys two meanings. On the one hand, it was used to exclude those who were not "of the countryside," i.e., town-dwelling absentee landlords, and thus highlights the division between the countryside and the town, and the landlord and the tenant. In Chinese, the word *xiangxia* or *xiangqu* (not the word *cunzhuang*, i.e., village) refers to the countryside, as opposed to the word *chengli* (in town). On the other hand, this usage tells us that collective rent resistance was conducted in a broader arena transcending the individual village community and embracing the whole countryside. Though the author might not be clearly aware of this, his wording unwittingly revealed this subtle but important difference. In his eyes, as well as in those of the absentee landlords, there was no difference between the countryside and the village. Interestingly enough, in the Yixing homicide case, all the confessions from the rent collector's side used the word *xiangxia* (the countryside) to talk about tenants and used the word *xiaxiang* (down to the countryside) to mention their rent-collecting activities. Only in the tenants' confessions was the word *cun* (hamlet or village) mentioned and specified to identify themselves (QDTD 1988: 690–700).

Similarly, for tenants, communal identity was no longer important in their collective struggle against landlords, and village boundaries also could no longer stifle the adoption of multi-village concerted actions. The struggle was now between town-dwelling landlords and country-dwelling tenants. In this case, both communal identity and boundaries blurred and became insignificant. The following case exemplified this very clearly.

In 1742, there was a large-scale rent strike in Chongming County. As usual, bad weather and a poor harvest were the chief reasons for the strike. Excessive rainfall that summer threatened the harvest and strained relations between landlords and tenants. According to local custom, each year in the eighth month landlords would go to the countryside to assess the harvest and then determine the rent rate. For town-dwelling landlords, on-the-spot assessments informed them of the real situation in the countryside and prevented them from being fooled by their tenants into an unnecessary rent reduction. On the other hand, for tenants in the countryside the bad weather was a good reason to ask for a universal rent reduction, though the actual harvest might not be universally poor. If the harvest was actually poor, tenants would not oppose the on-the-spot assessment by landlords. However, if the harvest was not as bad as predicted, tenants would not welcome landlord assessments. The 1743 rent strike in Chongming was aroused by the tenants' blockade of the landlord's on-the-spot assessment.

The story of the strike is long and complex, what is interesting here was the way the tenants organized themselves and the means they used in the strike. According to the plaintiff, Huang Ren (Huang was the servant of the absentee landlord Huang Shen), the tactic that the tenants used to prevent the landlords' rent assessment was that "the tenants of Landlord B expel Landlord A, and the tenants of Landlord A expel Landlord B" (QDTD 1988: 657). Huang Ren and his helpers were blocked, robbed and beaten by a group of strangers in Qixiao Town on their way to rent assessment. Armed with swords and sticks, the strangers told them that this year they were not allowed to assess the harvest. Old Shi the Second (*Lao Shier*), the leader of the strike, later said in his confession:

> In the seventh month of Qianlong 6 (1732), there were winds and rains in Chongming, but the cotton and rice were not hurt much. However, I was going to use the bad weather as a pretext to repudiate the rent anyway. On the twelfth day of the eighth month, I met five guys—Gu Qi, Zhang San, etc., in Qixiao Town, who were selling firewood there. I said to them: "Since there were winds and rains this year, we don't need to pay rent. But we must be of one heart. If someone pays rent secretly, we will go to destroy his house. If the big landlords come to the countryside to assess the rent, we will go to drive them away. Thus, those small landlords will not dare to assess the rent."
>
> (ibid.: 663)

The strike developed as Old Shi the Second had schemed. The tenants destroyed landlord Huang's house in Qixiao Town that was used for collecting rent. They also destroyed the house belonging to Li, the *baozhen* of Qixiao Town who helped *yamen* runners to identify the strangers who blocked Huang Ren in Qixiao Town at the very beginning. Believing in the principle of safety in numbers, the tenants finally forced the shopkeepers of three local towns to participate in the strike.[6]

This case clearly shows how the tenants of different landlords united to resist their common foe, the landlord class. In this struggle, village boundaries could no longer confine peasants and their collective resistance. Instead, their political maneuverings unfolded on a larger stage centered on the market town. It is obvious that the organizers of the strike, Old Shi the Second and five other people, were from different hamlets or villages. But they met and planned their strike in the town. These people mobilized their fellow tenants from different hamlets and villages and blockaded the absentee landlords in town, and even forced some shopkeepers in the town to participate in the strike. The struggle transcended rural communities and mobilized the tenant-peasantry into a united class front to confront landlords.

Conflicts between landlords and tenants in Republican Jiangnan

Entering the Republican period, due to a series of reasons, the conflicts between tenants and landlords over rent greatly intensified. According to Kathryn Bernhardt, these reasons included: "a succession of natural disasters, adverse economic conditions in the 1930s, the new context of greater landlord mobilization and state involvement in rent relations, and better peasant organization" (1992: 190). Bernhardt's study shows that between 1840 and 1859 and between 1873 and 1911 the frequency of collective tax resistance was slightly higher than that of collective rent resistance. However, during the Republican period, from 1912 to 1936, the situation was greatly reversed. Of a total of 144 collective actions recorded, 116 were rent resistance, 10 were resistance against both rents and taxes, and 6 were tax resistance (ibid.). Apparently, during this period, rent resistance became the overriding political issue in the Yangzi delta.

Intense and frequent rent resistance in the Yangzi delta dominated the local political setting and made the area the nation's haunt of struggle between landlords and tenants. From 1922 to 1936, collective rent resistance in the Yangzi delta accounted for three-quarters of the entire nation's total. Table 6.3 presents the statistics of annual rent resistance from 1922 to 1936 in the Yangzi delta and the whole country.

The collective rent resistance recorded in Table 6.3 is based on news coverage in major newspapers or statistics from an authoritative information agency. For example, Tanaka's statistics were drawn from news reports on *Shenbao* and *Xinwenbao* (Tanaka Tadao 1936: 307). The 1934 figures were based on statistics from the Economic Information Agency of China (Zhongguo jingji qingbaoshe) (Zhang Youyi 1957: 1019). And the 1936 figures were drawn from news reports published in 69 major newspapers (ibid.: 1021). Usually only rent resistance on a fairly large scale would be reported by major newspapers. According to Tanaka's statistics, the total number of people involved in 197 instances of rent resistance was 374,975. On average, therefore, 1,903 people were involved in each instance of rent resistance (Tanaka Tadao 1936: 307).[7] Similarly, the figures for people involved in rent resistance in 1934 and 1936 are also large. For example, in a

Table 6.3 Collective rent resistance in Jiangnan, 1922–1936

Year	Nationwide	Jiangnan[a]	(%)
1922	11	4	36
1923	11	5	45
1924	9	4	44
1925	17	13	76
1926	19	14	74
1927	18	14	78
1928	25	19	76
1929	46	33	72
1930	20	17	85
1931	21	16	76
(1922–31)	197	149	76
1934[b]	35	21	60
1936[c]	26	19	73

Sources: Tanaka Tadao (1936: 312–315), for 1922–1931; Zhang Youyi (1957: 1019, 1021–1023), for 1934 and 1936.

Note:
[a] The figures for the years from 1922 to 1931 in this table are based on Tanaka's statistics. Tanaka Tadao gives a geographical distribution of collective rent resistance detailed at the county level, which enables us to figure out the amount of rent resistance in the Yangzi delta area and its proportion on a nationwide scale. In this column the figures from 1922 to 1931 were drawn from 21 Jiangnan counties. They were: Songjiang, Suzhou, Changshu, Kunshan, Jiangying, Wuxi, Zhenjiang, Jiading, Baoshan, Chongming, Qingpu, Yixing, Nantong (the above 13 were from Jiangsu), Xiaoshan, Pinghu, Jiaxing, Huzhou, Jiashan, Ningpo, Shangyu, and Shaoxing (the above eight were from Zhejiang). Strictly speaking, Nantong, Ningpo, Shangyu and Shaoxing were not in the six Jiangnan prefectures of the Qing, but they were often considered to be Jiangnan counties. Even if we exclude these four counties, the figure for collective rent resistance in the remaining 17 Jiangnan counties during this period is 115, which still amounted to 58 percent of the whole nation's figure.
[b] Figures for this year include both rent and tax resistance, and the figure for Jiangnan actually included Jiangsu and Zhejiang provinces, thus was not specifically drawn from the Yangzi delta area.
[c] The nationwide figure for this year includes both rent and tax resistance, while the Jiangnan figure is for rent resistance only.

1934 incident, more than 4,000 Suzhou peasants took part. In 1936, there were 19 instances of rent resistance in the Yangzi delta, and the numbers of people involved in these actions ranged from 200 to more than 2,000 (Zhang Youyi 1957: 1019, 1021–1023).

Since the rent resistances recorded in Table 6.3 were all large in scale, it is understandable that they were concentrated in the Yangzi delta, the area with most developed absentee landlordism and the highest tenancy rate in the country. Only in areas like the Yangzi delta would collective rent resistance involve so many people and erupt with such high frequency to dominate local politics. During the same period, no other areas of the country ever witnessed the same intensity and scale of conflicts between landlords and tenants.

In his book on the Boxer Rebellion, Joseph Esherick reveals the close relationship between the weakness of landlordism, sparse orthodox Confucian gentry presence and local instability in northwest Shandong (1987: 36–37). This same logic can also apply to the Yangzi delta countryside. Why did the peasants in the Yangzi delta have a particular proclivity for collective rent resistance? One important reason was no doubt the sparseness of gentry-landlords in the countryside. To be sure, the delta was well known for its highly developed landlordism and strong scholar-gentry class. Nonetheless, gentry-landlords were concentrated in towns and cities; the delta's countryside was a homogeneous society composed mainly of tenant-peasantry. This greatly facilitated the ease with which peasants in the countryside could organize themselves to resist their common enemy in the town.

However, the intense and frequent conflicts between the landlord and tenant class in the Yangzi delta had never become a prairie fire out of control as the Boxer Rebellion had done in North China. Interestingly enough, in spite of these intense class conflicts, the Yangzi delta was always one of the most stable and secure regions. Class conflicts in the delta were well contained at the local level and never spilled over to become large-scale peasant rebellions engulfing the whole region. One important reason for this can also be attributed to the highly developed absentee landlordism in the area.[8] This development enabled the state, as we will see in the next chapter, to effectively mediate between landlords and tenant-peasants. As a result of this mediation, the conflicts between landlords and tenants were contained and confined to the local level. Both the state and local society actually benefited, to a certain extent, from this highly developed absentee landlordism.

Community politics and leadership

Long-term social structural change transformed the Yangzi delta countryside into a homogeneous world composed mainly of tenants and part-tenants. This change had a profound impact on political life within rural communities. First, a community composed mainly of tenants reduced the state presence to a minimum (Huang 1990). Because traditionally tenants had no tax obligations to the state, a community composed predominantly of tenants thus did not deal with the state in the realm of taxation, the most important area of state and rural society relations. More importantly, this situation prevented the state from imposing collective levies on the rural community as it had been doing in rural North China since the late Qing. Without the need to deal with the state collectively, communal politics naturally became much simpler.

Second, a tenant-composed community also greatly reduced intra-communal conflicts among its residents. This was due to the fact that the real political drama in this area was now characterized by class confrontation between town-dwelling landlords and country-residing tenant-peasants, in an arena which transcended both hamlets and compound villages. Within rural communities, there was no substantial political strife among tenant-peasants. Thus, the political life within the rural community differed greatly from that in North China villages, as did the characteristics and profiles of communal leadership.

Informal community leaders

In the rural Yangzi delta, no powerful and authoritative village government of the North China type could be found in either hamlets or compound villages. The community leadership here was *ad hoc* and informal. Instead of being responsible for organizing important communal activities, such as village self-defense, and *tankuan* allocation and collection, it was occupied by various trivial issues arising here and there. This was especially true in small hamlets. The following are some actual cases from Huayangqiao.

Huayangqiao was composed of six hamlets with 63 households altogether in 1940. Each hamlet was basically constituted by an agnatic group. Leadership there was

> strictly *ad hoc* and informal, and basically limited to the natural agnatic unit: when the need arose, the most respected member(s) of a descent group might be called on by others to settle disputes or extend a helping hand, but such authority was not formalized with a position or title.
>
> (Huang 1990: 150)

For example, in Xue Family Village, Xue Bingrong enjoyed the greatest prestige and was routinely called on to arbitrate disputes among his kinfolk. However, this status was not so much by force of seniority as by ability and character. In another hamlet, the Middle Hamlet of Xilihangbang, the *de facto* leader in the 1930s and 1940s was a woman, Lu Danan. Because of her forthright, capable, and generous personality, she had become the person everyone turned to in an emergency (Huang 1990: 150–151).

The informal leadership of the Huayangqiao type could be found everywhere in the Yangzi delta countryside. For example, Liuxiangcun was a compound village located in Wuxi County. The village was composed of four hamlets with fewer than two hundred households. During the Republican period, though the government imposed the *linlu* and *baojia* systems on the village, community affairs were, to a great extent, controlled by a group of informal leaders called *shuohuaren* (spokesmen). The main function of this group of informal leaders was to settle disputes among villagers. This function was, as a matter of fact, the major duty of community leadership in the Yangzi delta. Whenever there was a dispute among villagers, especially a dispute between people from different lineages, the judgment and arbitration of these informal leaders were sought by the concerned parties. There were two teahouses in the community and a teahouse in the nearby town run by a person from Liuxiangcun. These teahouses were the "court"

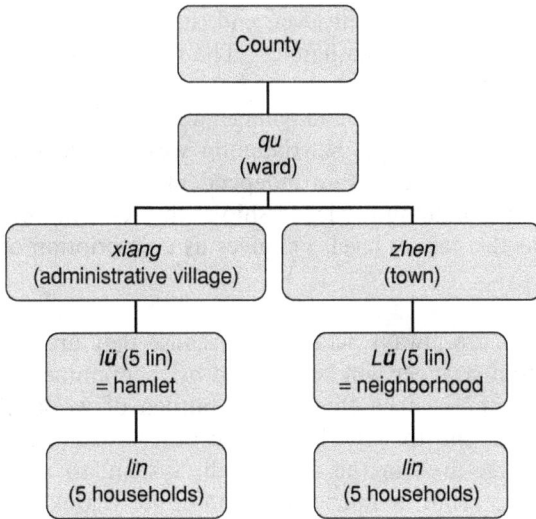

Figure 6.1 Sub-county administration in Jiangsu, 1929–1934

Sources: Wu Shuzi and Zhao Hanjun (1930: 173–174).

that those informal leaders used to settle disputes among villagers (Li Li 1988: 11–13).

The formal village administration

To be sure, there was formal administration established in the compound village during the Republican period, especially after the establishment of the Nanjing Government. During the Nanjing period, between 1929 and 1934, the sub-county administration system in Jiangsu was designed as shown in Figure 6.1.

According to this system, every five households constituted a *lin*, and five *lin* a *lü*. A rural community with more than one hundred households was organized into a *xiang* (the administrative village). A county was usually divided into five to fifteen *qu* (wards) according to its size and population (Wu Shuzi and Zhao Hanjun 1930: 173–174; *Jiangsusheng danxing fagui huibian* 1935: 2: 42).

In this system, the special structure of the Yangzi delta's rural community was taken into consideration. We have seen in the first chapter that the average size of hamlets in the Yangzi delta was around 20 households. The design of the *lü* was obviously used to organize these small hamlets. As the regulations for organizing administrative villages in Jiangsu emphasized: "Those people, who, due to residential reasons, live together with more than 25 households [but no more than 50 households] or fewer, were allowed to organize into one *lu*, and to install a *lü* head" (Wu Shuzi and Zhao Hanjun

1930: 173–174). However, in the whole sub-county administrative system, the *linlü* was the least important level, and the head of the *linlü* was by no means a powerful figure in the hamlet.[9] The real leaders at this level were those informal leaders discussed above.

Above the *linlü*, the compound village was usually organized into an administrative village (*xiang*). Kaixiangong was a good example of this. Before 1935, Kaixiangong was an independent administrative village with its own leaders. The community leadership at this level was of course different from that at the hamlet level. Fei gives us a description of these village heads:

> Village heads are always accessible, because they are known to every villager, and a stranger will be received by them immediately. The visitor will be impressed by their heavy burden of work. They help the people to read and to write letters and other documents, to make the calculations required in the local credit system, to manage marriage ceremonies, to arbitrate in social disputes and to look after public property. They are responsible for the system of self-defense, for the management of public funds, and for the transmission and execution of administrative orders from the higher government. They take an active part in introducing beneficial measures such as industrial reform into the village.
>
> (1939: 106)

From this passage we can hardly see any significant difference in village leadership between the Yangzi delta villages and North China villages. However, Fei's description was actually at a rather general nature, talking of something *de jure*, not *de facto*. For example, Fei mentions managing village public funds and organizing village self-defense systems as village heads' duties, but gives no further information about these matters. In Kaixiangong, there was no self-defense system, except for the railings constructed at the entrance of the stream which were closed during the night to prevent outsiders (ibid.: 175). Also, no village public funds were managed by the village government. These two institutions, as we know, were very common and essential to North China villages, which made village governments there authoritative. Besides, the village government here also seemed to take no responsibility for managing and financing the village school (in the passage quoted above, Fei did not include this as the village government's responsibility). As we know, this was also a very important duty of the village government in North China. Of course, no word has ever been mentioned about the village government being responsible for government taxation. What really occupied the village heads in Kaixiangong were therefore trivialities such as reading and writing letters and documents for villagers, making calculations for the local credit system, managing marriage ceremonies, and mediating disputes.

After 1934, the *xiangzhen linlü* system was replaced by the *xiangzhen baojia* system.[10] The *baojia* was a decimal system, requiring every ten households to be organized into a *jia*, ten *jia* a *bao*. But in practice, this decimal requirement compromised with the local situation in the Yangzi delta, and was never strictly followed, as many contemporary local gazetteers show. Above the *baojia*, the *xiang* was expanded significantly. It was no longer an administrative village, rather, a rural township which commanded around ten *bao* and a thousand households. For example, after this change Kaixiangong was still a *xiang* but now it incorporated 11 *bao* and had jurisdiction over more than one thousand households (Fei 1939: 114–115). The *baojia* system continued during wartime, and lasted until the Communists took over the Yangzi delta.

However, the change from the *linlu* to the *baojia* had no major impact on communal politics in the Yangzi delta. The *bao* was now often equivalent to the compound village. The *bao* head was thus the formal leader of the compound village but his power was quite limited, as was that of the previous *xiang* head. Most of them were ordinary peasants with no influential and wealthy family background. For example, in Zhuhui *xiang*, Haining, Zhejiang, from September 1945 to February 1947, a total of 18 people served as *bao* heads and deputy heads. Among them, one was a landlord, one a rich peasant, 12 were middle peasants, three were poor peasants, and the last person's background is unknown (Zhang Letian 1992). The same source also revealed that the position of *bao* head was usually filled by two kinds of people. The first kind was made up of greedy and lazy people, who wanted to exploit this position to gain petty advantages. The second kind was made up of honest people who liked to serve the community (ibid.).[11] People from Liuxiangcun used vivid descriptions to compare the *bao* head with the *xiang* head: "The *xiang* head eats fish and meat, the *bao* head is awfully busy [for running official errands], the household head weeps and wails [for their hardships] (*Xiangzhang chiyu chirou, baozhang touwu touliu, huzhang dati xiaoku*)" (Li Li 1988: 6).

The qualifications for and characteristics of community leadership

Because of significant differences in community politics, the qualifications for and characteristics of community leadership in Yangzi delta also differed greatly from North China villages. In North China villages, village leaders were usually from wealthy and powerful families and represented the major lineages in the village. Moreover, their status and positions were very often hereditary (Gamble 1963: 323; Huang 1985: 238–242). However, in the Yangzi delta, this was not the case. Fei stated explicitly that the headmanship in Kaixiangong was not hereditary and was also not connected with any privileged class (1939: 108–109).[12] Similarly, no evidence shows that lineage representation was an important qualification for village leadership. In Kaixiangong, for instance, the old village head was surnamed

Chen, though only four of 360 households in the community were surnamed Chen. Obviously he had no strong lineage background at any rate and was by no means the representative of the major descent group in the village.

The younger village head, Mr Zhou (Chou), was from the largest surname group in the village, but this was not the reason for his assumption of the position. There were a total of 98 households surnamed Zhou in the village, but they belonged to two entirely separate descent groups (Fei 1939: 92). Moreover, the kinship structure in this area differed greatly from that of rural North China. People with a common ancestor might not be recognized socially as kin due to clan organization (ibid.: 92). According to accepted principle, in this area, "all the patrilineal descendants and their wives that can be traced to a common ancestor within five kinship grades consider themselves as belonging to a kinship group called *zu (tsu)*" (ibid.: 84). Because of this, a *zu* might not include all the descendant members of a common ancestor. The average size of a *zu* was only about eight households. If there was an increase in members, people would exclude those distant kin in ceremonial gatherings (ibid.: 85). Due to these reasons, the lineage never played the same part in organizing the communal polity as it did in North China villages.

What was really important to enable people to qualify as community leaders was therefore their personal attributes and achievements such as personality, ability, command of knowledge and skills, social experiences and connections, willingness to serve their communities, and so forth. For example, in Kaixiangong, Mr. Chen and Mr. Zhou's assumption of village headship was largely because of their literacy, their willingness to serve the village, and the contribution they made in the reforms of the village's silk industry (Fei 1939: 197–198, 211).

Similarly, in Huayangqiao, Xue Bingrong and Lu Danan acted as informal community leaders and enjoyed their fellow villagers' respect because of their personality and ability. For instance, Lu Danan was well known and respected in the town. It was her, not her elder agnatic kin, who helped her cousin at his father's funeral, because she could purchase the coffin and the funeral clothes on credit in the town. Also, she later got him a job as a "little year-laborer." Her personality, ability and social connections had no doubt commanded her great respect in her community of Xilihangbang, where she was called affectionately "Big Elder Sister", whom everyone turned to in an emergency (Huang 1990: 150–151).

The informal leaders in Liuxiangcun, i.e. those spokesmen, were also people with various attributes or achievements. These people were teahouse owners, lineage hall managers, schoolmasters, tilers, hog dealers, boatmen, salt smugglers, etc. Some of them became spokesmen because of their virtuous actions and their willingness to serve the villagers. Some because of their command of some skills or resources which made the villagers look to them for help. Some simply because of their boldness and recklessness: they dared to do what the others dared not. All of them were able persons who had the "gift of gab" and were experienced and knowledgeable (Li Li 1988: 12).

Rural Reconstruction in the Yangzi delta

The significant differences in communal politics and leadership between the Yangzi delta and the North China plain fostered two entirely different patterns of political development within the rural communities in these two areas. Since political life within rural communities was much simpler and community leaders were less powerful, communal politics in the Yangzi delta was thus less eventful. The corruption of village leaders and deterioration of village politics that characterized political life in many North China villages in the first half of the twentieth century were rarely a burning issue in the Yangzi delta countryside.

When the social reformers came to the Yangzi delta countryside during the 1920s and 1930s, the issues that immediately attracted their attention were various concrete social and economic issues rather than political ones. Because of this, in the Yangzi delta, another major testing ground of the Rural Reconstruction, the reform progressed in a different fashion and focused on a different set of issues such as popular education, economic cooperation, public health, etc. The political issues that warranted the concern and consumed the energy of the reformers in North China—such as strengthening and reorganizing village community, reforming village administration, and improving village finance—were generally overlooked here. Therefore, Rural Reconstruction in the Yangzi Delta was mainly a social reform rather than a political campaign, as it was in North China.

In the Yangzi delta, the organizations most active in Rural Reconstruction during the late 1920s and 1930s were the Society for Chinese Vocational Education (the SCVE, *Zhonghua zhiye jiaoyu she*),[13] the Jiangsu Provincial College of Education (*Jiangsu shengli jiaoyu xueyuan*),[14] the College of Agriculture and Forestry, University of Nanjing (*Jinling daxue nongxueyuan*) and the Chinese YMCA. These organizations undertook and directed many reform projects in various locations. These projects displayed a different pattern in the Rural Reconstruction in the Yangzi delta.

The SCVE's Xugongqiao rural improvement experiment

Xugongqiao was a small town located in Kunshan County near the Nanjng-Shanghai Railway. The SCVE selected this town and the nearby countryside to be its first experiment district and called it *Xugongqiao xiangcun gaijing shiyan qu* (the Xugongqiao experiment district for rural improvement). The area covered 40 square *li* with 735 households and 3,597 people, of whom, 70 percent belonged to tenant households. The experiment began in October 1926. The reformers worked there for more than seven years until June 1934 (Xu Yinglian *et al.* 1936: 431). After that, the reforms were continued by the local people themselves (Zhang Yuanshan and Xu Shilian 1934: 243). The major achievements of the Xugongqiao rural improvement were as follows:

1. A census, conducted annually.
2. Achievements in civil construction: (a) improved the social environment of the market town, such as street cleaning, banning opium, reforming teahouses, encouraging proper entertainment, etc; and (b) rebuilt the major bridges and roads connecting the town with nearby villages.
3. Agriculture and economy: (a) introduced improved crop varieties and made great efforts to prevent of crop diseases and insect control; (b) introduced new farming tools and machines; (c) establish a weather broadcasting service; (d) holding a farming cattle race every Spring; (e) encouraged the peasants to engage in extra activities to earn cash, such as fishponds, chicken farms, forestry, fruit growing, embroidery, etc; (f) establish loan and credit cooperatives, and agricultural product sales cooperatives. By June 1934, there were 467 members with 225 shares and 1,780 *yuan* of total capital, and the total volume of business reached 35,000 *yuan*; and (g) built a public granary in the winter of 1931.
4. Education: (a) children's education: there were six schools in this district, four public and two private, enrollment among school-aged children exceeded 90 percent; and (b) social education: the Peasant Education House and People's Schools were established to eliminate illiteracy and improve rural cultural life.
5. Public health and security: (a) established a public clinic for prevention of epidemics, and daily and emergency treatment; (b) organized a fire-fighting association and a self-defense corps.

(Xu Yinglian et al. 1936: 429–442; Zhang Yuanshan and
Xu Shilian 1934: 243–245)

The achievements in Xugongqiao were explicitly concentrated in social and economic areas rather than on political ones. Though there was a self-defense corps organized during the reform, it had never played as important a role as the *Qingmiaohui* did in North China villages. Because of the generally peaceful environment in the Yangzi delta, this self-defense corps had no need to conduct a nightly watch of patrols, it also had no regular training and drills (Zhang Yuanshan and Xu Shilian 1934: 245). Besides this, there was no other reform project that was clearly politically oriented. Therefore, the rural reform in Xugongqiao presented an entirely different picture from what we saw in the Zouping experiment and the Zhaicheng village reform. Xugongqiao's case was not exceptional, it represented the general pattern of the Rural Reconstruction in the Yangzi delta. The following is another similar case.

The YMCA's Weitingshan Rural Service

Weitingshan was located in Wu County near Suzhou. It was a small rural community and also an administrative village (*xiang*) before the implementation of the *baojia* system. The community was composed of 19 hamlets with a small town, Weitingzhen, at its center. According to the 1933 census, there were 303 households and 1,444 people living in 19 hamlets in this *xiang*. The YMCA Suzhou Branch opened an office called "the Office for Rural Service in Weitinshan" and began its reform project after September 1928. Although there were usually one or two staff members from the YMCA working there with very modest funding, by the end of 1933 the project achieved some tangible successes.[15]

The reformers started with a very modest plan. Two staff members began their work in typically missionary fashion. They made friends among the peasants by playing chess with them, singing songs for them, and showing them audio recorders and slides. When curiosity was aroused among the peasants and many questions were raised, they lectured to the peasants about new developments on various topics. Also they provided some medical care for the peasants, and organized the peasants for visits to Suzhou and Shanghai. In this way, the YMCA staff established their credibility and commanded respect among the peasants. After this preliminary warm-up, the YMCA staff began their reform in the community.

The YMCA's Weitingshan reform was very similar to the SCVE's Xugongqiao experiment. The YMCA staff organized a Youth League and several study groups among the peasants, to encourage them, especially the young people, to eliminate illiteracy and to learn basic accounting skills and the use of the abacus. These organizations later were very active in various reform projects. With the help of the YMCA staff, a full-time public elementary school was opened in June 1931. The YMCA also initiated some projects to improve public health and environmental sanitation: such as building a public cemetery, introducing modern medical knowledge among the peasants, providing Western medicines and immunization, and eliminating witchcraft.

The YMCA members paid great attention to rural economic problems. They encouraged the peasants to adopt new varieties of wheat, rice, vegetables and fruits developed by the Jingling University, the Suzhou Agricultural College, or imported from abroad. Originally, silk weaving was a major rural industry in this area. However, this rural industry declined due to the rise of modern industry. The decline led to economic depression in the community. The YMCA members introduced some new opportunities to the peasants to relieve their economic hardship. One of these was making matchboxes for a Suzhou match factory. This business employed mainly women and children and added 130 *yuan* a month to the community as extra income. Another was encouraging peasants to market the chickens they raised. A club for selling chickens (*Mai ji hui*) was thus organized. It collected chickens raised by individual peasant households and sold them to restaurants in Suzhou and Shanghai. This also helped the peasants to increase their income.

With the help and encouragement of the YMCA, the *xiang* government and the *xiang* peasant association worked more actively and efficiently than before. For example, the *xiang* government was officially established in 1930. After its establishment, it successfully conducted three censuses and a land registration, and it also organized the peasants to widen the roads and dredge the rivers.

Social reform versus political reform: a comparison

The Xugongqiao and the Weitingshan reforms were only two of several dozens of various rural reform projects conducted in the Yangzi delta in the 1920s and 1930s.[16] They nevertheless are representative of the general pattern of rural reforms in this area. Comparing them with the rural reforms in the North China plain, for example, Liang Shuming's Zuoping experiment and Zhaicheng's village reform, we can find some conspicuous differences in Rural Reconstruction between the two areas. These differences characterized two distinct patterns of rural reform. While the reformers in the Yangzi delta preferred piecemeal social reforms, their comrades in North China advocated comprehensive reforms with political reform at the core.[17] The North China reform always employed the village community as an institutional means to carry out various reform projects, but no parallels were found in its Yangzi delta counterpart. Why were there such significant differences in Rural Reconstruction between these two macro-regions?

People may argue that these differences were attributable to the fact that people who conducted rural reforms in these two macro-regions happened to be people who embraced different political ideas. Those who conducted rural reforms on the North China plain were politically more radical, and those in the Yangzi Delta were more moderate. Obviously, Liang Shuming and the YMCA would not share the same vision of rural reform needed by twentieth-century China. As a Christian organization, the YMCA favored more gradual and peaceful social improvements in the countryside. A comprehensive reform involving the political dimension, as Liang and his comrades advocated, no matter how moderate it might be, was unlikely to be the YMCA's choice. Similarly, the SCVE was also politically less radical than Liang's SRRI. This ideological discrepancy would no doubt set the reformers in the Yangzi delta apart from their counterparts on the North China plain.

However, the coincidence of geographical distribution—radical reformers concentrated on the North China Plain and moderates in the Yangzi delta—can be examined from a different angle. Why were people of different political inclinations separated by these two macro-regions? To answer this question we need to find the concrete reasons that distinguished the Rural

Reconstruction of one area from the other, and also to explore the conditions that benefited as well as restricted reformers and their reforms in these two areas.

On the North China Plain, as we have seen, the natural village was a ready-made institutional means for political mobilization. The very nature of the North China village attracted and also convinced many reformers, as represented by Liang Shuming, into believing that the revitalization of the village was the cornerstone of the modernization of the whole nation. To revitalize the village, a comprehensive reform was preferable to piecemeal improvements. Moreover, to conduct a comprehensive reform, a strong and effective village political authority was indispensable. However, in the first half of the twentieth century, the village political situation deteriorated due to increasing state intrusion and overall rural socioeconomic change. In order to improve village politics and to reform village government, reformers had to pay great attention to rural political issues. This internal logic made the Rural Reconstruction in North China more politically oriented, focusing more on village political issues.

In the Yangzi delta, the rural community displayed a multi-layered structure and was loosely organized. This structural discrepancy made it impossible for the rural community to function in the same way as the North China village did. Moreover, the role of the rural community in organizing rural society was further weakened by highly commercialized rural economy. Because of commercialization, the peasants spent increasingly more time and energy in market activities outside their hamlets and compound villages. Commercialization thus greatly reduced the importance of the rural community in the peasants' social activities and intercourse, and gave increasingly more importance to markets and market towns.[18]

On the other hand, the rural populace here was overwhelmingly comprised of tenants and part-tenants who bore little tax responsibility to the state. The increase of the state's demands on rural resources since the late nineteenth century thus had seldom been imposed on rural communities in the form of *tankuan*. Within these homogeneous communities, social conflicts were also greatly reduced. Due to these reasons, community leadership was informal and wielded no real political power. Many of the political problems that troubled North China villagers were irrelevant here. For example, the management of village funds was a hotly disputed issue in every North China village, but it was never a problem in the Yangzi delta, for there were simply no standing village funds. Another important source of political conflicts and power abuse in North China villages, the allocation and collection of *tankuan* levies, was also an unknown story to the delta peasants.

When the reformers came down to the countryside, the first things that caught their eyes were social and economic issues, such as the decline of the traditional handicraft industry, the depression of the financial market, the illiteracy and ignorance of the peasantry, and poor sanitation. To be sure, these social and economic illnesses and crises were also very common in rural North China, but in the delta countryside, they seemed more striking and prominent since political issues were absent here at the communal level. Putting aside their political and ideological preferences, reformers in the Yangzi delta paid more attention to social rather than political issues because social issues were more urgent and relevant to the situation in the delta countryside. As some students from the Zhejiang Provincial Institute for Self-Government (*Zhejiangsheng difang zizhi zhuanxiu xuexiao*) who conducted local self-government programs in the delta countryside, remarked, "to pursue and promote local self-government, we should put the local people's needs first. Therefore, we should start by increasing their literacy and improving their economy" (Zhejiang, 1934: 361).

Conclusion

In many ways, the Yangzi delta was unique when compared to the rest of country (Ash 1976: 52).[19] Most significantly there was profound and spatially displayed social stratification between landlords and tenant-peasants. This profound social stratification fostered intense and frequent conflicts and struggles between the two antagonistic classes. As a matter of fact, in China, full-fledged class struggle between landlords and tenant-peasants in Qing and Republican Jiangnan found no parallel in the country. This struggle dominated local politics and also greatly shaped, as we will see in the next two chapters, the relationship between the state and rural society. Compared to this, rural communal politics, either in hamlets or in compound villages, were quite insignificant. Communal politics in this region was rather simple, and community leaders were less authoritative and oppressive. The abuse and corruption of village power that victimized many North China villages in the first half of the twentieth century and became a major local grievance exploited by the Communists for revolutionary mobilization was never a serious issue in the Yangzi delta.

The intense conflicts between landlords and tenants posed a serious challenge to the state. This situation, plus a countryside composed of homogeneous tenant-peasants, also seemed to favor the Communists in mobilizing and organizing successful class warfare to overthrow the existing social order and political rule. However, the following two chapters will show that the challenge actually turned out to be an advantage for the state, allowed it to mediate between landlords and tenants, and hence to gain a secure footing in local society. The seemingly favorable social structure and environment did not turn out to be conducive and hospitable to Communist mobilization and revolution. Instead, it stubbornly and faithfully channeled the Communist operation into the existing pattern of state–rural society relations and made their wartime operation in the Yangzi delta not significantly different from that of their predecessors and counterparts in this area.

7 State and society in the Yangzi delta countryside

The Republican period

During the Republican period, the Yangzi delta was ruled by several different state powers successively and sometimes even simultaneously. Although in this period, especially during the period of the Nationalist rule, the pace of state-making and modernization greatly accelerated, the relationship between the state and rural society generally followed the pattern set in the late Qing. Both the Nationalist state and the wartime Japanese Occupation authorities exploited absentee landlordism to ensure the collection of land taxes and to mediate between antagonistic classes. Even the Communists followed suit in their wartime operation in this area. This development stands in sharp contrast to the situation in rural North China. This chapter will discuss the state–society relations during the Nanjing period and the War of Resistance, and leave the Communist wartime operation to the next chapter.

State and society under the nationalist rule

The 1911 Revolution overthrew the imperial system, thus changed the overall polity of the country. However, the revolution had little impact on local society with regard to the existing social structure and order. What made things even worse was great chaos and the anarchy resulting from the collapse of central authority. From 1916 to 1927, China was torn and ruled by several warlord cliques who waged wars against each other constantly, turning many areas into battlefields.

Fortunately, the Yangzi delta generally remained untouched and therefore escaped the horrible ravages of the war. The warlords who ruled the Yangzi delta during this period were merely content to tap into the existing systems of revenue extraction, and had no intention of interfering with local society (Bernhardt 1992: 161). This situation continued until the Nationalists finally secured their rule over the area in 1927.

The establishment of the Nanjing Nationalist regime in 1927 ushered in a new stage of political development in the rural Yangzi delta. The Nationalists, inspired by Sun Yet-sen's Three People's Principles and in pursuit of modernization, were determined to reform and improve rural China. They were also eager to mobilize more resources from the countryside so as to finance various modernization projects. They therefore adopted a more interventionist stance towards rural society. This was especially true in the Yangzi delta, the political and economic core of the Nationalist regime.

However, crippled by their limited resources and weak control over rural society, the Nationalists could not bring their reforms to a quick success. Urgent and quickly expanding financial needs, on the other hand, forced the Nationalist Government at various levels to tolerate and continuously exploit existing means and practices in revenue extraction. The Nationalist rule thus brought about no substantial change to the existing pattern of state–society relations in rural Yangzi delta. Nevertheless, it did accelerate many historical changes beginning in the late Qing.

Finance and land taxation in Republican Jiangnan

During the Nanjing period, government expenditures in the Yangzi delta, as elsewhere in the country, increased rapidly. This ever growing government spending inevitably resulted in a rapid tax hike. For example, Bernhardt's study shows that land taxes in the six Jiangnan counties of Chuansha, Wu, Wuxi, Wujin, Changshu, and Wuxing, almost doubled in the two decades following the 1911 Revolution, "with the bulk of increase occurring from 1927, the year the KMT assumed rule of the region." For example, in Chuansha, land taxes more than doubled from 1912 to 1932, three-quarters of the total increase came in the final six years (Bernhardt 1992: 208–215). The same situation could actually be found in every Jiangnan county. Table 7.1 shows the increase in land tax in Jiangsu between 1927 and 1931.

Table 7.1 Land taxes in Jiangsu, 1927–1931

Year (%)	Statutory tax	Tributary grain	Rent	Misc. taxes	Surcharges	Total	Index
1927	234,490	5,419,172	561,121	9,831	527,331	6,751,945[a]	100
1928	2,550,512	4,438,354	130,676	651,892	399,500	8,170,934	121
1929	1,477,698	5,266,413	131,561	791,892	1,755,471	9,423,034[b]	140
1930	3,214,428	7,232,413	175,878	231,330	2,780,000	13,634,049[c]	202
1931	9,594,483[d]	–	–	200,000	2,332,000	12,126,483	180

Source: Zhao Ruheng (1935: 2: 574).

Notes: Unit = *yuan*.
[a] The original figure for the 1927 total given by the source is 8,316,938 which is larger than the sum of itemized figures. This figure is the actual sum of the itemized figures.
[b] The original figure is only 2,423,035 which is obviously wrong.
[c] The original figure is 13,734,049.
[d] In this year, statutory tax (*diding*) and tributary grain (*caoliang*) were amalgamated into one and called *dijiashui* (lit. land value taxes).

Table 7.1 shows us the actual land taxes collected in Jiangsu during this five-year period. During the first four years of Nationalist rule in Jiangsu, the government revenue from land tax increased at least 20 percent each year. However, this table does not include county surcharges (*xian daizheng fushui*) (Zhao Ruheng 1935: 2: 575). As a matter of fact, during this period, this portion of the land taxes increased even faster. Before we examine the increase in county surcharges and its impact on state–rural society relations, we should first discuss a very important evolution in the structure of government taxation in the beginning of this period.

In November 1928, the Nanjing Government issued a new tax law: the Standard Resolution for Dividing Central Revenue and Local Revenue (*Huafen guojia shouru difang shouru biaozhun'an*). This law divided all government taxes into central revenue (*guojia shouru*) and local revenue (*difang shouru*). It also stipulated the financial rights and regulations for both central and provincial governments (Wu Zhaoxin [1937] 1965: 2: 129–131). This change was of great significance for it granted the local government, both provincial government and county government, for the first time in history, separate and independent tax sources, and hence its own independent finance and budget.[1]

In imperial China, theoretically, all taxes belonged to the central government, and the local government had no independent source of revenue and hence no finance or budget of its own. This situation began to change in the late Qing when local governments were asked to undertake some modernization projects such as modern education and modern police reforms. To finance these projects, local governments were allowed to levy surcharges on land and collect some new taxes. However, these changes were not institutionalized and the central government ultimately reserved its claim on all taxes. Entering the Republican era, the Northern Warlord government had proclaimed twice, first in 1912 and then in 1923, a change in the old taxation structure by separating central taxation from local taxation. However, none of these laws had ever been implemented (ibid.: 2: 123–129).

According to the tax law of 1928, land taxes were yielded to the province and became a provincial source of revenue, together with the deed tax (*qishui*), brokerage tax (*yashui*), business tax (*yingyeshui*), etc., while the central government retained the salt tax, customs taxes, taxes on tobacco and liquor, *lijin*, income tax, inheritance tax, etc (ibid.).[2] Within a province the division of taxes between province and county or city was determined by the particular province itself. In Jiangsu, for example, the land tax was further divided into four main categories: (1) the provincial statutory tax (*sheng zhengshui*); (2) the provincial special taxes (*sheng zhuanshui*); (3) the county statutory tax (*xian zhengshui*); and (4) county surcharges (*xian fujia*). As their names indicate, the first two categories of land tax were provincial revenue, and the latter two were county income. Table 7.2 shows the composition and rate of land tax in Jiangsu after the 1928 taxation reform.

Table 7.2 Composition and rate of land taxation in Jiangsu

Category	Item	Rate (yuan)
1 Provincial statutory tax	Silver rate (*yin'e*)[a] Rice rate (*mi'e*)[b]	1.28/liang 2.60/shi
2 Provincial special taxes	Education fund[c] (*Jiaoyu zhuankuan*)	0.47/liang 1.40/shi
	Water control fund Road construction fund Agricultural Bank fund Grand Canal maintenance fund	vary by locations same as above same as above same as above
3 County statutory tax	Silver rate Rice rate	0.30/liang 1.00/shi[d]
4 County surcharges	varied by county	varied with time

Source: Zhao Ruheng (1935: 2:751–772).

Notes:
[a] This item originated from *diding* (statutory land tax). Usually, it was still called *diding*. And in 1931, it was amalgamated, together with *caoliang*, into *dijiashui* (see Table 7.1, Note d).
[b] This item originated from *caoliang* (tribute grain). Like *yin'e*, it was still called *caoliang*, and was later amalgamated into *dijiashui*.
[c] The education fund, like other provincial special taxes and county surcharges, was based on two items of the provincial and county statutory taxes, it was thus composed of two parts: the amount for each *liang* of *diding*, and for each *shi* of *caoliang*.
[d] Three items in the table had fixed rates, they were the silver rate and rice rate for both provincial and county statutory taxes (*shengxian zhengshui*) and the education fund. Together they amounted to 2.05 yuan per *liang* of *diding* and 5.00 *yuan* per *shi* of *caoliang*. In Jiangsu, these three items were considered to be regular land tax (*tianfu zhengshui*). The remaining items were considered irregular taxes or surcharges.

After the tax reform of 1928, land tax became the major source of provincial and, especially, county revenue. In Jiangsu and Zhejiang, for example, land tax constituted 40 percent or more of provincial revenue (ibid.: 141). In most Jiangnan counties, the land tax made up 70 percent or more of county revenue (Zhao Ruheng 1935: 2: 813–907). The different proportions of land tax in provincial and county revenue meant that for the province, land tax was one of several major sources of revenue, while for the county, land tax was the single most important source of revenue. Table 7.3 shows the proportion of land tax and the revenue structure in Jiangsu Province and Changshu County.

Table 7.3 gives us a general idea of the importance of the land tax in provincial and county budgets, and a basic picture of provincial and county revenue structure. It shows us that land tax, though very important for both provincial and county finance, was obviously more crucial to the latter. While the province had other sources such as business taxes and government loans to exploit, most counties could only depend on the land tax. Since the regular tax (*zhengshui*) had a fixed rate, any increase in land tax

Table 7.3 Composition of government revenue in Jiangsu and Changshu

Location	Category	Amount (yuan)	Budget share (%)
Jiangsu	Land tax	11,320,000	42.33[a]
(1934)	Business tax	4,116,000	15.39
	Loans	6,000,000	22.44
	Deed tax	1,042,000	3.90
	Income from gov't property	262,672	0.98
	Income from gov't business	291,396	1.09
	Administrative income	300,000	1.12
	Court income	473,472	1.77
	Subsidies	2,580,960	9.65
	Other income	355,522	1.33
	Total	26,742,022	100.00
Changshu	Land tax	1,027,128	85.56
(1933)	Deed tax	28,750	2.39
	Brokerage and slaughter taxes	17,001	1.41
	Miscellaneous tax	42,219	3.52
	Income from gov't property	35,010	2.91
	Income from gov't business	2,262	0.27
	Other income	36,963	3.10
	Administrative income	10,088	0.84
	Total	1,200,421[b]	100.00

Source: Zhao Ruheng (1935: 2: 735–36, 862–863).

Notes:
[a] Many of the figures in this column given by the original source for Jiangsu Province were miscalculated. The figures presented in this table were recalculated and corrected.
[b] The figure given by the original source differed from the sum of the itemized categories, which is 1,199,421.

as well as the county budget was thus mainly derived from irregular land surcharges (*tianfu fujia*), which quickly surpassed the regular tax and became the major source of county revenue.[3] In the Yangzi delta, for example, during 1933 and 1934, irregular land surcharges constituted 75–90 percent of county land tax, and 60 percent of the county budget on average (Zhao Reheng 1935: 2: 586–590; Zhongyang daxue 1935: 15–17; Bernhardt 1992: 212–213). Of all the land taxes collected, the amount retained by the county now equaled or very often greatly surpassed that remitted to the provincial government. Table 7.4 shows the distribution of land taxes between the county and the province.

The taxation reform of 1928 put the central government, the provincial government and the county government in entirely different situations relating to land tax. The central government freed itself from all of the troubles pertaining to land taxation, while the provincial government could also satisfy its financial needs with mainly statutory land taxes and other revenue sources. Only the county government had to bear the major responsibility for imposing heavy surcharges and to undertake all of the tedious work of

Table 7.4 Distribution of land taxes between the county and the province in eight Jiangnan counties (1934)

County	Retained by county	Remitted to province	Retained/Remitted (%)
Wuxi	711,790	555,181	128
Jiangyin	695,699	416,254	167
Wu	823,981	846,222	97
Changshu	988,774	657,313	150
Kunshan	494,752	491,552	100
Wujiang	675,400	630,401	107
Songjiang	501,332	512,371	98
Jiading	505,380	227,381	222

Source: Zhao Ruheng (1935: 2: 738–770).

Note: Unit = *yuan*.

tax collection. Though the county government was still dealing with local society on behalf of state interests, in the case of land taxation however, state interests were now divided into three different parts. This structural change in land taxation is the key to understanding, as we will see, the considerable disparities and constant conflicts between the Nationalist state policy and local practice.

To be sure, because of the agricultural richness and the high statutory quotas inherited from the Qing, the increase in land tax in the Yangzi delta was kept comparatively modest (Bernhardt 1992: 215). However, the absolute amount of land tax collected in any Jiangnan county was still much greater than the national average. To collect these land taxes was definitely an overriding concern of any Jiangnan county magistrate. In the Yangzi delta, these taxes were never imposed on the rural community collectively in the form of the *tanpai* as in North China. Since the tenancy rate here was very high and land taxes had long come out of rents, local governments followed the example of their Qing predecessors to exploit absentee land-lordism to ensure taxes. The deep concern over their revenue induced provincial and county governments, as we will see in the following sections, to act passively in radical rent reduction, but encouraged them to involve themselves enthusiastically in rent collection.

Rent reduction in the Yangzi delta

From 1927 to 1937, the Yangzi delta took the lead in agrarian reforms in the country. The Nationalists had implemented a series of reform programs in this area, which included rent reduction, land surveys and registration, land tax rectification, the cooperative movement, and the improvement of agricultural technology. These reforms served a dual purpose, i.e., to improve the rural economy and peasant livelihood, on the one hand, and to strengthen the state mobilization of rural resources, on the other. Though the reformers were very eager to achieve their goals, they carried out these reforms cautiously, moderately, and gradually. By the end of this period, most of these reforms were still in their initial stages, and had been implemented only in an experimental fashion in scattered localities. The outbreak of the Sino-Japanese War in 1937 brought these reforms to an end before they had achieved much success.

Among these reforms, the most radical and controversial was rent reduction in Zhejiang Province, of which part of the Yangzi delta was included. Though rent reduction was one of the major Nationalist reform goals in rural China, during the Nanjing period (1927–1937), only Zhejiang carried out this reform seriously on a province-wide scale. It is not my intention in this section to study this reform.[4] Instead, we will take this reform as a case to discuss the reasons for the unsuccessful and unsatisfactory performance of the Nationalist agrarian reforms in the Yangzi delta.

Rent reduction in Zhejiang commenced immediately after Nationalist forces had taken over the province in 1927 but it was vigorously carried out on a province-wide scale only in the following year. On July 26, 1928, the newly reorganized KMT provincial committee and the provincial government jointly promulgated the revised laws for rent reduction. According to these new laws, the rent ceiling on a main crop was to be 50 percent of the total annual production. All rents were then to be reduced additionally by 25 percent, leaving 37.5 percent as the highest annual rent.

This time, rent reduction was put into practice vigorously in the province, especially in the northern counties where the party was strong and enthusiastic, and tenancy rate was high (Miner 1980: 82). The implementation of rent reduction, however, immediately produced a great number of disputes between tenants and landlords and met with stubborn resistance from landlords. The instant and direct casualty of the landlords' resistance was, of course, government taxation. This immediately persuaded the government to back away from the reform. In April 1929, the provincial government issued a resolution on its own, declaring the cessation of rent reduction, and most county governments followed the order quickly. This action provoked a strong protest from the party. Party activists published many articles in party newspapers criticizing this decision and also lodged complaints with the central authority. The government, on the other hand, closed down the provincial party newspaper in Hangzhou and imprisoned the editor-in-chief.

The conflict forced the Nationalist central authority to step in promptly. As a result, the 1928 rent reduction laws were restored, but now the government rather than the party was to take the responsibility for their implementation. Though the central authority asked Zhejiang to continue the reform, after this serious clash, rent reduction lost its momentum. The reform was now at the mercy of the government, especially the county government, which was concerned more with its tax revenue than party ideology. Most party activists now lost their enthusiasm for the reform (Zheng Kangmo 1933: 33993–33994). Rent reduction was thus discontinued in many counties and was no longer a province-wide campaign.[5]

Though rent reduction in Zhejiang had not achieved the ultimate success desired by its initiators, it can help us understand the situation in which the Nationalist state was caught during the Nanjing period in the Yangzi delta.[6] The reasons for the unsatisfactory outcome of rent reduction in Zhejiang were complicated and multifaceted. Putting aside concrete technical considerations, there were some contradictions within the Nationalist state which were, more than other factors, responsible for the actual outcome of the reform.[7] Of them, one was the disparity between the Nationalists' political goals and their actual capacity for local mobilization, and the other was the conflict between the party's ideology and the government's financial needs.

According to Zheng Kangmo's recollections (Zheng had participated in rent reduction in Zhejiang and later wrote a research thesis on it), rent reduction before the 1929 party–government clash was mainly pushed forward by party activists at the county level. The government played quite a limited role. However, the party activists could only effectively direct the movement at *this* level. Below the county, at the *qu* and *xiang* levels, they did not have enough cadres to mobilize local society and enforce the reform. This was one of the major reasons for the failure of rent reduction (Zheng Kangmo 1933: 33972–33973). Ironically, the provincial government, upon deciding to stop rent reduction, justified its actions in these terms (ibid.: 33982).

The government, at both the provincial and county levels, on the other hand, had its own difficulties. Local government was dealing with daily administration rather than the party's concern for ideology. Rent reduction was crucial to local governments only in a negative sense, for it had a negative effect on government revenue. This was because in Zhejiang, especially in the northern and richest part of the province which included the southern Yangzi delta, rent was the major source of land tax, which was now in turn the major source of provincial as well as county revenue.[8] Numerous disputes generated by rent reduction immediately threatened land taxation. Landlords now had well-justified excuses to resist tax payment (Miner 1980: 80). This led to a drastic drop in government revenue from land tax (Bernhardt 1992: 186–187). At that time, the province was about to undertake ambitious railway and road development projects, and it needed funds desperately. In this situation, the support and cooperation of tax payers, i.e., landowners, were more important than the improvement of tenants' conditions. It was this financial pressure that forced the government to take action which ran against the party's ideology and policy of rent reduction.

Therefore, superficially, rent reduction in Zhejiang was ruined by the conflict between the party and the government.[9] In reality, it was a victim of the rapid expansion of both provincial and county governments' expenditures discussed in the last section. This financial pressure forced the local governments to compromise with landlords, the main body of the tax-payers, and to abandon the reform. This same reason can also explain why there was no government-sponsored rent reduction campaign in Jiangsu Province, where the major part of the Yangzi delta was located.[10]

State involvement in rent collection

In Chapters 5 and 6 of her book, *Rent, Taxes, and Peasant Resistance: The Lower Yangzi Region, 1840–1950*, Kathryn Bernhardt has provided an excellent study on how the state was involved in rent relations and how the relationship between the state and rural society developed in Republican Jiangnan. I have nothing new to contribute to this topic. However, a brief account of the development of state–rural society relations during this period is indispensable for us to understand their changes and continuity when the area came under the Japanese and Communist (guerrilla regime) rule during the war.

According to Bernhardt's study, absentee landlordism in the Yangzi delta was continuously increasing throughout the Republican era. More and more rent bursaries and various landlord associations were organized. They represented a collective effort of absentee landlords to put rent collection on a more stable and efficient footing. This development increased landlords' power to command state assistance in the collection of rents (Bernhardt 1992: 163–165).

During the Republican period, state involvement in rent collection developed along two lines started by late Qing local government in the 1870s. On the one hand, the state employed modern police forces to aid landlords in rent collection and to suppress tenant protest. On the other hand, the state employed specialized rent dunning agencies and rent dunning bureaus to enforce rent payment. Rent dunning bureaus were most common in the rice-growing areas since absentee landlordism was most developed here. Typically, a rent dunning bureau was organized and operated in this way:

> [It] was headed by a county magistrate or a specially appointed rent-prompting official and was located within the county administrative compound; clerks in the county complex, often those whose responsibilities encompassed land taxation, saw to the secretarial and book-keeping chores; and policemen or public rent dunners had the task of pressing peasant for back rent. In years when tenants proved especially intransigent, local military forces might accompany the dunners on their house-to-house dunning missions. Counties often also established branch bureaus in major market towns.
>
> (ibid.: 166)

A tenant debtor prison was always attached to the rent dunning bureau. Tenant prisoners were treated badly in the prison. For the state, using rent dunning bureaus and tenant prisons to help landlords collect rents was not an end in itself, but "a means to another end—successful tax collection" (ibid.: 162). Rent dunning bureaus were thus to serve this ultimate purpose. Therefore, these facilities were only available to the landlords who owed no taxes. Those who had not yet paid their taxes were usually denied dunning services (ibid.: 172).

Dunning bureaus and tenant prisons were prohibited by the Nationalist central government, after its settlement in Nanjing, for the reasons that they violated the laws of the Republic and were "tools of warlords oppression" (ibid.: 170–171). However, this prohibition was unsuccessful, especially in Jiangsu. Even in Zhejiang, after the provincial government abandoned the rent reduction campaign, rent dunning bureaus and prisons were established or restored in Jiaxing, Jiashan and several other delta counties (Zhang Youyi 1957: 3: 306–307).

The primary reason for the failure of the Nationalist prohibition against rent dunning agencies is not difficult to find. The county magistrate, who was directly responsible for the matter, was concerned more about tax revenue than about justice or righteousness as defined by Nationalist ideology. If these two conflicted, he would definitely look after the former and ignore the latter. Though the county magistrate certainly worked on behalf of state interests in dealing with local society, in the case of land taxation, however, state interests were now a tripartite entity composed of the interests of the central government, the provincial government and the county government rather than a monolithic bloc. While the central government had the smallest stake in the situation, the county government had the largest. As the head of the county government, the magistrate would no doubt give more consideration to the interests of his own county.[11]

By involving itself in rent collection, the government could also exert a much greater influence on landlords. In this respect, the Republican state departed further from earlier practices: during the Republican period, the government in many delta counties vigorously involved itself in determining rent ceilings. Landlords' compliance with county-approved rent ceilings usually constituted a prerequisite for receiving official assistance in rent dunning (Bernhardt 1992: 172).[12] For the local government, this move was more a pragmatic measure than an ideological commitment. It aimed to reduce rent resistance and hence to contain social conflict and maintain domestic peace. Moreover, it also aimed to reduce any friction in rent collection and hence to ensure tax revenue.

Interestingly, a more intrusive state presence in local society prompted "not an escalation in tax resistance, but an escalation in rent resistance" (ibid.: 189–190). In Republican Jiangnan, as Bernhardt demonstrates, rent resistance displaced organized protest against land taxation as the principal form of peasant collective action (ibid.). The escalation in rent resistance was due to growing landlord mobilization and increasing state involvement in setting and collecting rents, not raising rents. Though Jiangnan peasants toughened their resistance to rents, their struggle was spontaneous in nature, and it was not easily channeled into the anti-state political revolution advocated and expected by the Communists (ibid.: 196–202). To Jiangnan peasants, the state was generally perceived (as it actually was) as a mediator and arbitrator between themselves and landlords, rather than a mere oppressor.

Comparing state and rural society relations in the Yangzi delta with those on the North China plain during the same period, we can draw a sharp contrast between them. In North China, since the late Qing, the rapidly expanding fiscal burden of the state had been mainly imposed on village community collectively in the form of *tanpai*. This taxation arrangement inevitably strained the relationship between the state and village communities. In order to cope with the state's demands and to survive the situation, the villages there were greatly mobilized and strengthened. These developments engendered many conflicts between the state and villages. Paradoxically, the strengthening of village community also further facilitated the state's effort to mobilize and reorganize rural society. The Communist success in rural North China was achieved exactly along these lines.

However, in the Yangzi delta during this period, no government taxation had ever been imposed on rural communities as a collective responsibility. The state here, more precisely, the local government, mainly exploited the highly developed absentee landlordism to satisfy its increasing financial needs and at the same time to mediate between antagonistic social classes, and hence to pacify the local society. This situation can explain, in large measure, why there was no intense mobilization and strengthening of rural community in this area during this period. It was the social structure and political development in the Yangzi delta that gave the state great latitude to manipulate state–society relations and avoid direct and violent confrontations with rural society. As a result, much less anti-state collective resistance was witnessed in the Yangzi delta than on the North China plain during the Republican period before the war.

The Yangzi delta under the Japanese Occupation

The Japanese occupation of the Yangzi delta from 1938 to 1945 did not bring about any innovations in state–rural society relations, but it did create a new situation of great political complexity which had not been seen before or elsewhere. Even in this core area of Japanese occupation, Japanese control was never complete. Moreover, the Nationalists, in contrast to their policies in North China, did not totally abandon the area. Instead, the Nationalists conducted guerrilla warfare and maintained local governments and resistance forces in the delta. At the same time, the Communists also moved in to compete with the Japanese as well as the Nationalists. Several competing political forces and state powers, therefore, operated in this area and each established its own sphere of jurisdiction and influence. Of course, they also constantly fought each other. A war-torn society thus had to endure the tax appropriations of several competing states. This situation made tax collection a very difficult task for all political authorities, but definitely more difficult for the Japanese Occupation authority and its collaborationist government.

The financial plight of the collaborationist government

Confronting an antagonistic environment and an economy devastated by war, the ability of the Japanese Occupation authority and the collaborationist government to extract taxes was greatly handicapped. As the Financial Department of the puppet Jiangsu provincial government confessed in a working report, the two major sources of provincial revenue were land tax and business tax. Before the war, the annual income from land tax was 12,000,000 *yuan*; however, in 1939, it was only 760,000 *yuan*. The prewar income from business tax was between 3,000,000 to 4,000,000 *yuan*, but in 1939 it was only 190,000 *yuan* (MGSL 1981: 6: 4: 1267).

The decline in government revenue was also found at the county level. Changshu County, for example, experienced a dramatic decrease in government revenue. The land tax collected was 246,858 *yuan* in 1938, 231,891 *yuan* in 1939, and 271,659 *yuan* in 1940, while the prewar figure was between 1,200,000 to 1,300,000 *yuan* annually. In other words, the land tax collected annually from 1938 to 1940 was less than 20 percent of the prewar figure (Shen Lansheng 1943: 119–120).[13] This comparison does not take into consideration the extraordinary rate of inflation beginning with the war. With inflation, the difference was even greater. The same situation could be found in all Jiangnan counties (MT, Shanghai [Songjiang] 1941: 65; Shen Lansheng 1943: 91–95).

The general financial plight of the collaborationist government can be seen from a comparison of financial subsidies to provincial governments from the central government under the Nationalists (1935) and the collaborationists (1940) (Table 7.5).

Table 7.5 Financial subsidies to provinces during and before the war

Locality	1940, per month	1935, per month	Comparison
Jiangsu	792,738	430,670	+362,068
Zhejiang	394,624	138,435	+265,198
Anhui	387,316	334,945	+52,371
Shanghai	1,139,842	0	+1,139,842
Nanjing	116,820	174,983	−58,163
TOTAL	2,831,340	1,079,032	+1,752,307

Source: MGSL (1981: 6: 4: 1266–1267).

Note: Unit = *yuan*.

The great decrease in provincial revenues under the Japanese occupation resulted from the drop in land taxes which had been the major source of revenue of the province. This revenue decrease necessitated much larger central subsidies to the provinces during the Japanese occupation.

The joint collection of rent and tax in Changshu and Wu

In order to ensure the collection of land taxes, the Occupation authority and local collaborationist governments were very eager to exploit any available means. Some common measures they employed were: (1) recruiting former tax collectors; (2) enlisting the *baojia* system; (3) giving higher rewards and tougher punishments to tax collectors; and (4) organizing landlord associations and rent bursaries to collect the land tax (MGSL 1981: 6: 4: 1269). Here it was not surprising that the Occupation authority also employed absentee landlordism and followed the precedent of utilizing rent bursaries for taxation, since this was a ready-made infrastructural means that could serve taxation. More rent bursaries were established in many counties under the command of local puppet governments and they served the purpose of taxation more than they had in the past.

For example, in Changshu, at the urging of the Japanese military authority, a solution was drawn up in early 1939 at a joint meeting of county and ward governments. This solution asked landlords to organize rent bursaries (*zuzhan*) in the *xiang* they lived. This rent bursary was actually a rent dunning bureau jointly operated by the landlord and the government, not merely a landlord-operated rent bursary. It spelled out that there should be at least one rent bursary in each *xiang*. By the end of 1939, a total of 92 rent bursaries had been established in 25 *xiang*, which encompassed 60 percent of the landlords of the whole county. Only six *xiang* reportedly had not organized rent bursaries, and these six *xiang* were controlled by anti-Japanese guerrilla forces (MT, Shanghai 1939b: 17–18).

The wartime rent bursary was jointly operated by landlords and tax officials. The written regulations (the only such regulations I have seen) were entitled *The Provisional Regulations for the Operation of Rent Bursaries in Each Ward of Changshu County* (*Changshuxian gequ zuzhan zanxing guize*), and contained 15 articles stipulating in detail how rent bursaries were to operate. The general pattern of operation reflected in these regulations was similar to that of prewar rent dunning bureau. For example, the rent bursaries were used for collecting rents for landlords and taxes for the government. The rent commuting rate (*zhejia*) was unified and fixed and also written down in the regulations. This measure was intended to reduce and avoid disputes between landlords and tenants (Article 11; ibid.).

However, there were some differences worth noting. One was the compulsory nature of the rent bursary under the Occupation authority. The regulations spelled out that landlords should delegate all their land to the rent bursary and also provide all their rent records (*zuce*), such as tenants' names, amount of land rented out, rent rate, and location of land, to the rent bursary (Articles 5 and 13). Otherwise, the landlords would be punished by the county government (ibid.: 19–20). However, this measure was not unprecedented in Jiangnan history. Bernhardt's study shows that during the period of Taiping occupation and immediately after the Taiping War, the same method was adopted by both the Taipings and the Qing authority (Bernhardt 1992: 106–107, 126–129). This measure greatly expanded the state's power at the expense of landlords' interests, and was an unusual measure employed only in turbulent periods when landlords could do nothing except compromise part of their interests to ensure the interests of the rest.

The same rent-tax coalition could also be found in many other Jiangnan counties during the war. For example, in Wu County, Kunshan, Taicang, Songjiang, Jiading, Qingpu, Wuxing, and Jiaxing, this kind of organization and practice can be found. This rent-tax joint venture was then well known as *zufu bingzheng* (meaning: joint collection of rent and tax) (Shen Lansheng 1943; MT, Shanghai 1940; Hayashi 1943; MGSL 1981: 6: 4: 1269; Jiading xianzheng, Chapter 1, sec. 3, Appendix 4; Shanghai, 1986: 324). Once again, it was Wu County that took the lead in this venture (Shen Lansheng 1943: 113).

Hayashi Megumi's wartime field study gives us some detailed accounts of joint collection of rent and tax in Wu County. Hayashi notes that before the war, there were between 300–400 rent bursaries in the county. Each rent bursary took charge of at least 500–600 *mu* of land. The outbreak of war in 1937 brought about great chaos in the countryside, and absentee landlords collected almost no rent that year. In the following year, a general organ for the joint collection of rent and tax was established, called *zufu bingzheng weiyuanhui* (the Committee for Joint Collection of Rent and Tax). Alongside this committee was the *Wuxian shouzuchu* (the Wu County Bureau for Rent Dunning), and under the county bureau there were 15 sub-bureaus (*shouzu fenchu*) in different townships (Hayashi 1943: 188–189).[14] The structure of the joint collection of rent and tax in Wu County can be seen in Figure 7.1.

The committee was chaired by the county magistrate and the head of the county's financial department (*xian caizhengju*), and was composed of 12 members, most of whom were the representatives of landowners.[15] The main function of the committee was to assess the harvest (*qiukan chengse*) and to set the rent commuting rate (*zhejia*). In 1938, the rate was one *shi* of rent commuted at 6 *yuan*; in 1939, it was 11 *yuan*; and in 1940, 30 *yuan*.[16] Each sub-bureau would ask tenants to pay rent in cash at this rate. After the rent was collected, the rent dunning bureau would withhold taxes and other fees before handing it to landlords. However, the tax was not withheld according to a fixed tax rate; rather, it was based on a percentage of the rent actually collected. For each *yuan* of rent, 17 cents was withheld as tax, an additional 2 cents was taken as a peace-keeping fee (*zhi'anfei*), 5 cents went to the county bureau, and 7 cents went to the sub-bureau as a service charge. The other 70 percent of the rent was given to the landlords (Hayashi 1943: 188–191).[17]

```
                        The Magistrate
        ┌──────────────────────┴──────────────────┐
   Committee for Joint                    Wu County Bureau
  Collection of Rent and Tax              for Rent Dunning[a]
                              ┌──────────────────┴───────────────┐
                         Sub-bureau                              │
                                          ┌───────────────┼───────────────┐
                                     Accountant    General Affair    Rent Collection
                                                          │
                                                  Punishment Office
                                                          │
                                                   Detention House
```

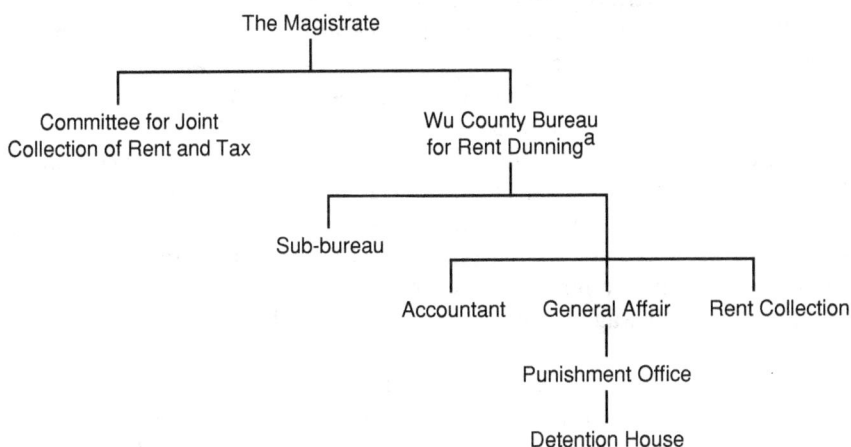

Figure 7.1 Structure of rent-tax collection in Wu county

Source: Hayashi (1943: 189).
[a] Another Source referred it as the *bingzheng zongchu* (the General Bureau for Joint Collection) (see Shen 1943: 119).

The general pattern of joint collection

Compared to the prewar practice of government-assisted rent collection, some noticeable changes in the wartime joint collection of rent and tax can be found in the Changshu and Wu cases. First, the joint collection was now more unified, more tightly controlled, and the government became more vigorously involved. Second, joint collection was now a compulsory measure which incorporated all landlords. Third, land tax was withheld not based on a fixed rate according to the acreage of land, but on the percentage of rent actually collected.

These new phenomena did not mean that the Occupation authority deviated from the prewar pattern of joint collection of rent and tax, it only showed how the Occupation authority pushed this pattern further to serve its urgent financial needs. Shen Lansheng, a financial expert and official in the collaborationist Nanjing Government, wrote many newspaper articles discussing these changes. These articles provide us with valuable information about the joint collection of rent and tax during wartime.

Shen confessed that the joint collection (of rent and tax) was a very common practice in Jiangnan area during the war. This phenomenon, Shen argued, should be attributed to the chaotic situation and strained governmental finances brought about by the war and an antagonistic environment. Under these circumstances, absentee landlords could hardly collect rent, and therefore local governments could not collect taxes either. Both parties felt it necessary to form a closer collaboration to ensure the collection of rent and tax (Shen Lansheng 1943: 7, 70–71, 113–115).

The general pattern of joint collection was the same as that in the Changshu and Wu cases, but Shen's discussion provides us with more details. From his discussion we gain a more comprehensive picture about wartime joint collection in Jiangnan (especially in the years 1938–1941). The following is a summary of the wartime joint collection based on Shen's discussion.

Unlike prewar practice, joint collection in many counties now combined biannual tax collection (each of the periods of tax collection usually lasted two to three months) into one. And the collection period now lasted the entire year, from the autumn harvest to the following autumn harvest. This situation was quite common before 1941. Shen described it as "an old ox pulling a wrecked wagon, which moves slowly and clumsily (*laoniu poche, tuoni daishui*)" (ibid.: 116).

The procedure of joint collection was made up of many steps. First, the conversion rate for rent commuted into currency was set, and was to be taken as the standard rent rate. Second, landlords were asked to register their rented land and the names of their tenants at the dunning bureau. If a landlord failed to do so, rent dunning policemen could still collect rent from his tenants, but part of his rent thus collected would be taken away by the bureau as a fine. Third was the actual collection of rent. This was done by armed rent dunning policemen in teams. According to regulations, landlords were forbidden to collect rent themselves. When these rent dunning policemen went down to the countryside, the peasants there suffered from extortion and abuse (ibid.: 117–118).

After rent was collected, the next step was to withhold taxes. However, unlike prewar practices, tax-withholding was not based on a fixed rate imposed by acreage, rather, it was based on a preset percentage of the rent. For example, in 1940, the percentage for land tax was 18 percent of the rent in Wu county, 15 percent in Changshu, and 12 percent in Wujiang (ibid.: 117, 199). This method of tax-withholding was called *jiuzu huafu* (withholding taxes according to the amount of rent collected). Besides the land tax, local surcharges (*quxiang zhenbao shiyefei*) as well as the operating expenses for joint collection (*bingzheng fei*) were also to be withheld before rent was released to landlords. These surcharges and fees usually doubled the land tax and raised the amount withheld to around 30 percent of the rent. Only after these withholdings could landlords get their rent, and in most cases, what they received was about 70 percent of the total rent collected (ibid.: 198; see also Table 7.3).

The joint collection of rent and tax enabled both absentee landlords and local collaborationist governments to ensure their revenue to a certain extent. But its results were far from satisfactory. In Changshu, as we have seen above, the actual income from land tax in 1938–1940 was less than 20 percent of that of the prewar level, and this figure also included those taxes collected from owner-cultivators. In Wu county, where the joint collection was most successful, the tax collected in 1940 was, according to one estimate, about 750,000 *yuan*, which was only around 60 percent of the prewar level (ibid.: 119–121).

Another serious problem of wartime joint collection was the high operating cost (*bingzheng fei*). The main cost was, of course, the salaries paid to the people engaged in rent collection. In Wu county, the monthly expense for joint collection was 47,500 *yuan*. Of this, 3,000 *yuan* went to the county bureau, 32,500 to the 13 sub-county bureaus (2,500 *yuan* each), and 12,000 *yuan* for hiring 200 rent dunning policemen. Since the collection period now lasted almost the entire year, and if we take this period as nine months, then the annual expenditures was 427,500 *yuan*. However, the actual funds allocated for operating costs were even higher. In Wu county, the rent collected in 1940 was about 6.7 million *yuan*. According to regulations, the operating costs were 7 percent of the collected rent, about 469,000 *yuan*. In Changshu, it was said, operating costs were 12.5 percent of the collected rent. Shen estimated that in 1941, the amount allocated as operating costs was around 1,000,000 *yuan*. Shen said this figure was only one-third of what it should have been, because some areas of Changshu were then under the control of anti-Japanese guerrilla forces. Even so, this amount was still astonishing (ibid.: 121–122). In many counties, this situation led to operating costs for joint collection being higher than the total expenditures of the county government (ibid.).

Landlords under the joint collection

Though joint collection was a cooperative effort of landlords and the government, landlords were apparently in the weaker position. Joint collection increasingly became a means by which the government ensured the allocation of land taxes and other local surcharges. It was also heavily exploited by those people who engaged in the business and were widely known as *bingzheng yezhe* (meaning: professionals of joint collection). As mentioned above, the rate at which tax was withheld was now based on a percentage of the rent rather than on a fixed rate based on acreage. When this percentage was converted to an acreage rate, the actual land tax paid by absentee landlords under wartime joint collection was actually much higher than that paid by owner-cultivators for land of the same acreage and quality. According to Shen's investigation, for example, in 1940, an absentee landlord in Wu county paid 5.40 *yuan* of land tax for one *mu* of land he rented out, while an owner-cultivator only paid 1.23 *yuan* for one *mu* of best quality land (Shen Lansheng 1943: 127, 199). Table 7.6 is a comparison of land taxes paid for owned land (*ziye*) and rented land (*zuye*) during 1938 to 1941.

Because of joint collection, landlords were not only subject to a much higher rate of land tax, they also had to bear, as we have seen above, the heavy burden of local surcharges and the high cost of operating expenses for joint collection. These two items usually doubled the land tax and increased the total amount withheld to up to 30 percent of the rent. Table 7.7 shows how rent was divided between the government and the landlords in five Jiangnan counties.

Table 7.6 Land tax rate in Wu county, 1938–1941

Year	Land tax for owned land/mu	Land tax for rented land/mu[a]
1938	1.01[b]	1.2
1939	1.01	2.50
1940	1.01	5.40
1941	2.02	9.00

Source: Shen Lansheng (1943: 199).

Notes: Unit = *yuan*.
[a] The rented land here referred to the land owned by landlords and administered through joint collection. The land tax rate listed here is converted from the percentage of the rent *zhejia*. For example, the rent *zhejia* for 1938 was 5 *yuan* for one *shi* per *mu*, land tax was 25% of the rent, so it was about 1.25 *yuan*. In 1939, the rent *zhejia* was 10 yuan, and tax rate was also 25%. In 1940 and 1941, the *zhejia* was 30 and 50 *yuan* respectively, and the tax rate was 18%.
[b] The land in Wu County was classified into four categories and 12 grades. The tax for the best quality land, i.e., the first grade of the first category, was 1.23 *yuan* per *mu*, and for the poorest land, the twelfth grade of the four category, was 0.12 *yuan* per *mu*. In Wu County, 80 percent of land fell into the first four grades. The tax range for these four grades was 0.89 to 1.23 *yuan* per *mu*, and the average was 1.01 *yuan*.

Table 7.7 Distribution of rent under the joint collection in five Jiangnan counties, 1941

County	Zhejia (yuan/shi)	Land tax (%)	Other withholding (%)	Actual rent (%)
Wu County	50	15 (18)[a]	12 (15)[b]	70
Kunshan	70 (35)[c]	18	14	68
Songjiang	65	15	?	?
Wujiang	60	12	?	?
Changshu	50	15	15	70

Source: Shen Lansheng (1943: 198).

Notes:
[a] Of these two figures, 15 percent was for *qingxiang* areas; 18 percent for non-*qingxiang* areas. *Qingxiang* was a political and military campaign conducted by Japanese authority and the collaborationist government in the Yangzi delta beginning in mid-1941 to pacify the countryside and to consolidate their control.
[b] Here, 12 percent was for non-*qingxiang* areas; 15 percent for *qingxiang* areas.
[c] Here, 70 *yuan* was the rent *zhejia* for rice land, and 35 *yuan* for cotton land.

However, the landlords' plight under wartime joint collection did not stop here; in addition, they were also subject to an additional loss of their rent. Under joint collection, the rent *zhejia* was regulated and unified by the government, and was usually set at a rate lower than the current market price. For example, in Wu county in 1941, the government dictated that rent *zhejia* was 50 *yuan* per *shi* of rice, while the current market price for one *shi* of rice was about 100 *yuan* (Shen Lansheng 1943: 159–161).[18] In 1938, 1939 and 1940, the rent *zhejia* was 5, 10 and 30 *yuan* for one *shi* of rice respectively (Table 7.2, note a), all of these figures were lower than the prevailing market prices. For example, the market price for one *shi* of rice in Nanjing was 6 *yuan* in mid-1938 and 23 *yuan* in December 1939 (MGSL 1981: 6: 4: 1123). In Songjiang, it was between 11 and 13 *yuan*, 16 and 20 *yuan* and 47 and 48 *yuan* in 1938, 1939 and 1940 respectively (MT, Shanghai 1940: 189). And in Jinshan, 12 *yuan*, 18 *yuan*, and 60 *yuan* in the autumns of 1938, 1939 and 1940 (Huang Wei and Xia Lingen 1984: 57).[19]

The purpose behind the enforcement of a lower *zhejia* by the Occupation authority and the collaborationist government was to ease social and political tensions in the countryside, and to win over the support of the rural populace. As Shen emphasized several times in his book, one of the advantages of the joint collection was that the unified and fixed lower *zhejia* could prevent disputes between landlords and tenants and also actually reduce rent, and so keep tenants in the countryside from the influence of Communist propaganda for rent resistance (Shen Lansheng 1943: 115, 127–128). Of course, this was accomplished at the expense of landlords.

Under this situation, it was no wonder that more and more landlords became resentful of joint collection and some of them withdrew from it and tried to collect rent themselves, even though this action was punishable (ibid.: 126, 132–133). Shen himself also strongly opposed joint collection and advocated abolishing this practice. Shen argued that though joint collection had some merits, such as ensuring land taxes, generating funds for local governmental expenses, and reducing rent (ibid.: 7, 72–73, 132–133), this system also had many drawbacks which definitely overshadowed its merits. These included, Shen argued: (1) an unfairness of tax burden between rented land and owned land; (2) high operating costs which resulted in serious corruption; (3) tax collection focused mainly on this endeavor, while tax collection on owned land was greatly neglected; (4) joint collection confused rent and tax, two different economic categories (one being private economy, the other public finance); and (5) armed force was used to press tenants and collect rents for landlords, threatening the government's neutral stance (ibid.: 8–9, 129–135). Therefore, Shen ardently advocated abolishing joint collection, and returning to the old way of collection (ibid.: 11, 101, 131).

Shen's opinion represented not only landlord interests, it also reflected the attitude of some higher level authorities toward joint collection. For instance, a discussion meeting held by the Committee for Economic Planning (*Jingji sheji weiyuanhui*) of the collaborationist Nanjing government concluded in August 1941 that:

> For the government, joint collection cannot increase revenue and reduce collection expenses; and for people, it makes the burden on the poor peasants heavier [*sic*],[20] and makes the land taxation very uneven among

people. In addition, collaboration between landlords and tax clerks generates corrupt practices. Therefore, this system should be abolished.

(Shen Lansheng 1943: 113)

However, those in local government argued that the old way of collection was not as convenient as joint collection and that by using joint collection, the government could at least get some tax revenues. Under the present circumstances, it was better to maintain the system of joint collection (ibid.: 84). Their stance prevailed.

Joint collection in the Qingxiang campaign

Beginning in mid-1941, the Occupation authority and the collaborationist government launched a political and military campaign called *qingxiang* (meaning: mopping up the countryside). This campaign aimed at pacifying the countryside, driving away anti-Japanese guerilla forces, especially the Communists, and strengthening rural control (Yu Zidao *et al.* 1985: 1, 124–129). Rectification of land taxation was one of the most urgent tasks on the *qingxiang* agenda (ibid.: 64; Shen Lansheng 1943: 84). The *qingxiang* campaign lasted more than three years, almost to the end of the war. It started in the Lake Tai basin, and gradually expanded to encompass the whole area controlled by the collaborationist Nanjing Government.

The areas chosen for the first three stages of the *qingxiang* campaign covered southeast Jiangsu, east of Lake Tai (Yu Zidao *et al.* 1985: 79). Absentee landlordism in these areas was, as we know, most developed, and so too, was the joint collection of rent and tax. During the first three stages of the campaign, the *qingxiang* authority asked county governments within the *qingxiang* area to abolish their county financial bureaus and establish a new office called *Fushui guanli chu* (the Department for Tax Management). Under this new arrangement, the joint collection of rent and tax, instead of being abolished, was continued and further enforced (ibid.: 64, 318, 320–321; Shen Lansheng 1943: 7). The results of joint collection in the *qingxiang* area were, according to official sources, quite satisfactory (Yu Zidao *et al.* 1985: 64, 321).

Though no direct evidence is available, it seems that the joint collection of rent and tax continued in the Yangzi delta throughout the war. An official document issued by the propaganda department of the collaborationist Jiangsu provincial government said that, in 1942, joint collection was abolished in the *qingxiang* area (ibid.: 340). However, this claim was contradicted by many other official sources from the administration. For example, the sources cited in the previous paragraph are all dated after July 1942. These sources tell us that after that date, the authority still worked hard to enforce the joint collection. Among these sources, one was a short document introducing the department of tax management in Taicang county, dating from July 2, 1942. This document urged people to inform against landlords who collected rent by themselves (*yange jianju sizi shouzu*), in order to combat tax evasion. On the other hand, the document discussed the situation of joint collection in the county (ibid.: 318–319).

In early 1943, the *qingxiang* committee of the collaborationist Nanjing Government decided to abolish the joint collection in the *qingxiang* areas (Zhongyang dang'anguan 1995: 238). But there was no evidence to confirm that this resolution had been carried out faithfully. The available sources suggest that in 1943 joint collection was still a common practice, but no longer seemed to be a compulsory measure. This can be seen from the March 1943 regulations for rent dunning bureaus promulgated by Jiangsu provincial government. According to the regulations, landlords were now allowed to collect rent by themselves. However, the regulations still asked the county government to set up a rent dunning bureau (*Zhuizuchu*) to help landlords in rent collection. The rent dunning bureau operated in the same way as the joint collection. Once landlords asked the bureau for help, the bureau would withhold taxes and charge 10–15 percent of collected rent as an operating fee. Since landlords were allowed to collect rent by themselves, they had to pay taxes regardless of whether or not they had received rent payments (Yu Zidao *et al.* 1985: 329). The regulations thus gave the local government more flexibility in handling rent and tax affairs.

The decline of the landlord class during the war

The wartime joint collection of rent and tax contributed greatly to the decline of the landlord class in the Yangzi delta. This decline can be seen from the continuous deterioration of landlords' economic situation. On the one hand, the decrease in rent income made absentee landlordism no longer a viable way of life.[21] According to Shen's estimate, in 1941, an absentee landlord should at least own 500 *mu* of land to maintain a moderate urban life for a family of six people (Shen Lansheng 1943: 177). In Qing times, by contrast, a Jiangnan landlord with about 100 *mu* of land could live a decent life in the urban area (Fang Xing 1983: 2: 90). Therefore, for most absentee landlords, if they were not engaged in other business at the same time, they would suffer a serious decline in their standard of living, and even could not make ends meet.[22]

On the other hand, the land owned by landlords was drastically devalued. We know that in the Yangzi delta, in the case of absentee landlordism, landownership was usually divided into subsoil and topsoil rights. The subsoil was owned by the absentee landlord which entitled him to the rights to collect rent from the tenant who cultivated that land. Cultivation of the topsoil was the tenant's rights. Normally, the value of the subsoil was higher than that of the topsoil. However, under wartime conditions, the rights to collect rent on the subsoil was greatly curtailed. Therefore, the price of subsoil rights also declined markedly. For example, in 1941, the price for subsoil rights was between 100 to 200 *yuan* per *mu*, while that for topsoil rights was between 200 to 500 *yuan* per *mu* (Shen Lansheng 1943: 145–146; see also Table 7.4).[23]

The decline of the landlord class was not only seen in the economic realm, it was also manifested in the political sphere. As we have seen, under wartime joint collection, landlords could wield less and less bargaining power to secure their interests. They could not collect rent by themselves, could not bargain with tenants directly over *zhejia* (commute rate in cash payment) and *chengse* (harvest assessment), could not determine the percentage of tax-withholding and operating costs, and could not withdraw from joint collection.

On the other hand, their power was also greatly curtailed by tenants in the countryside. War made rent resistance more intense in the Yangzi delta. In many localities, during the first several years of the war, landlords simply could not get a single grain of rent rice from tenants. For example, in Xietang *zhen* of Wu county, between 1937 and 1939, peasants paid no rent, because the landlords had run away. After 1940, peasants had to pay rent again. But most of them paid only 40–60 percent of their rent due. Some paid merely 10–20 percent. Only "cowards" would pay 80 percent (Huadong, 1952: 180). Similarly, in *Bao'an xiang*, it was said that from 1939 to 1949, 70 percent of tenants paid no rent or only part of their rent to absentee land-lords. Many tenants simply took their topsoil rights as full ownership. During harvest seasons, tenants organized themselves and asked their children to watch out for rent collectors. Once rent collectors appeared, all of the tenants would run and hide. Some tenants bribed rent collectors in order to avoid rent payment (ibid.: 168).

Under these circumstances, the rent rate dropped dramatically during the war. This also contributed greatly to the devaluation of subsoil rights. Table 7.8 shows the change of rent rates and decline of land prices in different localities of Jiangnan before, during and after the war.

In contrast to the decline of the landlord class, the economic conditions of Jiangnan peasants, both owner-cultivators and tenants, improved slightly because of low land taxes for owner-cultivators, the rise of prices and demand for agricultural products, and lowered rent or even non-payment of rent (Shen Lansheng 1943: 145, 161; Huadong, 1952: *passim*). This was especially true in the first three or four years of the war. Because of this, some tenants even managed to become owner-cultivators (Huadong, 1952: 73, 175). However, we have to be very cautious so as to avoid exaggerating the improvement of peasants' economic conditions during the war.

The decline of the landlord class in the Yangzi delta was not a new phenomenon. Kathryn Bernhardt's study has already demonstrated that this was a long-term trend resulting from the structural change of the delta society (1992: 221–225). However, her study did not cover the wartime development. This section shows that the wartime period was very crucial to this long-term historical development. To be sure, the war did not change the existing social structure in the Yangzi delta, but it did exert great pressure on this structure, and made the vulnerable part of this structure even

Table 7.8 The change of rent rate and land price in the Yangzi delta before, during and after the war

Localities[a]	Rent (mu)			Price of subsoil (mu)			Price of topsoil (mu)		
	Before	During	After	Before	During	After	Before	During	After
Changshu									
Dayi	1.1	0.6–0.7		5		1	5		6
Tang	1.2	0.5–1.2							
Songjiang				8–9	7–8	1–4	2–4	2–4	3–5
Wuxi	1	0.5–0.8	0.5–0.8	10	4				
Fangqian	1	0.6–0.8			3–4				
Yanqiao[b]	0.7–0.8	0.4–0.5	0.2–0.3						
Wuxian[c]									
Xietang *zhen*		0.7–1.1	0.3–0.8						
Yanli					3–4	3–4			6–8

Source: Huadong (1952: 57, 73, 123, 145, 174–175, 179, 250).

Notes: Unit = *shi.*
[a] Except when specifically noted, the localities listed under the county were *xiang.*
[b] The rent rate in this locality is quoted from the *Hushi yizhuang* (the charitable estate of the Hu clan). The *Hushi yizhuang* owned 1,560 *mu* of subsoil land, which was actually located in four different *xiang* of Wuxi. Some of the land was even in Jiangyin County. This land was rented out to more than one thousand tenants. The source tells us that besides the decline of rent rate, the method of rent payment also changed at the expense of landowners. Before the war, tenants had to deliver rent to the estate, while during the war, the estate had to collect rent from tenants (Huadong, 1952: 249–250).
[c] The source gives many narrative accounts about rent resistance in the county since the war, but few concrete figures about the decline of rent.

weaker. Therefore, it definitely accelerated the historical process of the decline of the landlord class.

Conclusion

During the Republican period, the relationship between the state and rural society in the Yangzi delta differed significantly from that on the North China Plain. On the North China plain the state always assumed a position in opposition to rural society, especially the village community, in terms of its being the extractor of taxes from rural society. In the Yangzi delta, the highly developed absentee landlordism provided the state with an alternative means to extract tax revenue. On the other hand, the profound social and spatial differentiation and intense confrontation between landlords and tenant-peasants required the state to play the role of a mediator and arbitrator between these two antagonistic classes.[24] State involvement in rent collection simultaneously served both purposes quite well. Under rapidly increasing financial pressure, state involvement in rent collection became deeper, wider and more institutionalized. This development in turn gave the state stronger leverage in mediating between landlords and tenant-peasants.

Paradoxically, increasing state involvement in rent collection, i.e. intervention into local society, did not provoke violent anti-state resistance.

Rather, it seemed to ease state–society relations. A conspicuous indicator of this situation was that during this period rent resistance had displaced tax resistance as "the principal form of peasant collective action" (Bernhardt 1992). To understand this, we should turn to the structure of the delta's rural society. In the Yangzi delta, the small tenant-composed communities bore no tax responsibilities to the state and therefore no violent confrontations between the state and rural communities over taxation occurred in this area. On the other hand, rent disputes, the major source of social disturbance in the region, were frequent and intense, both absentee landlords and tenants expected and welcomed state mediation to ensure their interests. Under normal circumstances, neither party wanted to antagonize the state. This gave the state great leverage to maneuver between the two parties and to ensure its own goal in rural society: tax extraction as well as peace maintenance. Of course, to achieve this goal, the state, i.e., the local government, has to be fair and impartial in handling rent disputes. In this threesome game, the rational choice for each party was, therefore, to restrain itself from going to the extreme. A delicate equilibrium was thus maintained and state–rural society relations in this area thus became much less contentious compared to those in rural North China.

However, under the dual pressures of state involvement in rent collection and tenant rent resistance, the absentee landlord class, as Kathryn Bernhardt has argued, was reduced to a weak position and fell into gradual decline. This long-term historical trend greatly accelerated during the war. Though the war did not change the existing social structure in the Yangzi delta, it did exert greater pressure on this structure and made the weak even weaker.

To be sure, all these developments were not new; they began in the late Qing and continued in the Republican times. Different state powers, no matter what different political ideologies they had, could not change the logic of these historical developments, they could only follow it and accelerate it. This situation was also true for the Communists. The following chapter will turn to the Communists' operations in the Yangzi delta.

8   The Communists and the Yangzi delta countryside

Since the Yangzi delta maintained the nation's highest tenancy rate as well as the nation's highest absentee landlord rate, and since intense conflicts between absentee landlords and tenant-peasants here found no parallel elsewhere in the country, we might expect that this area would be a fertile ground for the rural revolution advocated by the Chinese Communists. Paradoxically, this was not the case.

From 1927 to 1930, the Communists organized several unsuccessful peasant insurrections in the Yangzi delta. They quickly learned that it was easy to stir up rent resistance among the delta peasants, but very difficult to push them to go beyond this to engage in a revolution aimed at overthrowing the existing system. An equally serious challenge faced by the Communists, we shall see, was that they could not secure the sustained support of human and material resources from the countryside. They could not find recruits to organize armed forces since a highly commercialized economy made soldiering simply unattractive to the delta peasants. Nor could the Communists get grain provisions from the countryside since it would be unfair to take them from peasants; most were tenants who owed no tax obligation to the state. Landlords and surplus grain were concentrated in towns and cities, which were the strongholds of government control beyond the grasp of Communists' early maneuvers.

The War of Resistance against Japan changed the political and military situation of the Yangzi delta and enabled the Communists to establish their guerrilla regime in the region. Once they had established a competing state, the Communists also, like the Qing state, the Nationalists, and the Japanese, exploited absentee landlordism to mediate the disputes between landlords and peasants and to ensure taxes. However, the war did not change the socioeconomic structure of the delta countryside or make the delta peasants revolutionaries. The Communists still found it difficult to recruit local peasants into their armies and therefore could not expand their forces quickly. This factor, together with the political and military situation in the delta, persuaded the Communists to bypass the Yangzi delta and shift their main focus of wartime operation in Central China to northern Jiangsu.

Studies of the Chinese Communist revolution usually focus on the areas where the revolution was most dramatic or successful such as South China (e.g., Mao's Autumn Harvest Uprising in Hunan and his bases in Jiangxi and Fujian, as well as Peng Pai's Hailufeng in Guangdong) before the War of Resistance against Japan and North China during the War of Resistance and the civil war. Few serious studies have been done on the revolution in the Yangzi delta.[1] The reason for this is not difficult to discern. Although the Communists spared no effort and energy making revolution in this area before and during the war, their operations never scored a major success. The Yangzi delta thus did not play a significant role in the revolution.

However, the futility of the revolution in the area should not necessarily imply the futility of studying it. This chapter offers a preliminary study of the Communist revolution in the Yangzi delta. Contrary to our expectation, the study of the revolution in an infertile land can be fruitful, for it can shed new light on old issues and can help us better understand how and why the revolution succeeded in other areas—especially on the North China plain, where the revolution finally consolidated and then advanced to the 1949 triumph.

Communists and Jiangnan peasants during the Nanjing decade

Although the Chinese Communist Party (CCP) was founded in 1921 in Shanghai, the Communists did not pay serious attention to the peasant movement in the Yangzi delta until late 1925, the eve of the Northern Expedition. The Northern Expedition started as a joint effort of the Communists and the Nationalists to overthrow the Northern warlords and reunify the country. During 1925 and 1926, in order to secure support for their military campaigns, both parties worked vigorously to mobilize the peasants in the countryside. In August 1925, the CCP reorganized its Shanghai committee and transformed it from a local committee to a provincial committee that would take charge of both Jiangsu and Zhejiang provinces. Under this committee was the Department of Workers and Peasants (*Gongnong bu*), which was responsible for organizing peasant and labor movements. Meanwhile, the Nationalists also established their provincial committee in Jiangsu, under which there was also a department for directing peasant movements. The director of this department was, however, a CCP member. Immediately thereafter, the Nationalist Jiangsu committee sent ten people, the majority of whom were CCP members, to study at the Guangzhou Peasant Movement Training Institute (*Guangzhou nongmin yundong jiangxisuo*). In September 1926, the CCP Shanghai Committee again set up a special committee for organizing peasant movements (Jiangsusheng dang'an guan 1983: 430–437).

For a brief period during the Northern Expedition, the KMT and the CCP organized several peasant protests in the delta against landlords and warlord Sun Chuanfang (who controlled the Yangzi delta area before he was driven out the area by the Nationalist army in early 1927). These protests were targeted on the extra land levies charged by Sun's warlord government and also demanded rent reduction; in so doing, they echoed and supported the military campaigns of the Northern Expedition (Jiangsusheng dang'an guan 1983: 430–437). The Shanghai coup of April 12, 1927, however, ended the short period of the first united front between the Nationalists and the Communists. After the coup, the CCP became a rebellious political force: its ultimate political goal was to overthrow the governing Nationalists. The organization of armed peasant insurrections was believed to be indispensable to achieving this goal.

From September to December, 1927, the CCP Jiangsu provincial committee promulgated several programs for organizing peasant insurrections in Jiangsu. These programs counted on the eager willingness of Jiangsu peasants to participate in revolution. They called for immediate peasant insurrections all over the province, for guerrilla war in southern Jiangsu, and for the establishment of peasant regimes in northern Jiangsu (Jiangsusheng dang'an guan 1983: 439–442).[2] By the end of 1930, the Communists had organized a series of peasant uprisings in the Yangzi delta. They believed that peasant uprisings in this core area of Nationalist control would give a vital blow to the Nationalist regime and lead to the collapse of its rule. However, none of these uprisings proceeded as their organizers had expected. Some were called off before they had even began, while others were short-lived and had no substantial impact on either the Nationalist regime or the delta's rural society.

A typical insurrection usually involved between several hundred to several thousand peasants and lasted a couple of days. The initial targets of the insurrection were always landlords and especially their rent collectors. During these events, the rebels burned land deeds, debt contracts, and sometimes the houses of landlords and rent collectors. In some extreme cases, one or two landlords or their agents were killed. Government suppression immediately followed and the rebellion quickly collapsed. Although the Communists tried very hard to lead these insurrections further and to turn them into prolonged armed revolution, none of their efforts was successful. (Table 8.1 is a list of major peasant insurrections in the Yangzi delta led by the Communists during this period.)

The Communists obviously had overestimated the willingness of the delta peasants to participate in political revolution. Without a doubt, the peasants here would not hesitate to fight for their subsistence rights through collective struggle as they had done in the past. However, the evidence suggests that they did not favor radical mobilization and, more importantly, had no aspirations to turn their *ad hoc* struggle into a political revolution aimed at overthrowing the state. The Communists thus could easily stir up collective rent resistance among the delta peasants, but they were incapable of transcending the old pattern of collective action and pushing the peasants beyond the immediate goal of rent resistance. As Kathryn Bernhardt has argued, the Yangzi delta peasants had their own way of dealing with

Table 8.1 Major peasant uprisings in the Yangzi delta led by the Communists, 1927–1930

Date	Location	Scale*	Result
Nov. 1927	Yixing	4,000	Occupied the county seat for one day, executed several "local bullies and evil gentry," burned land deeds.
Nov. 1927	Danyang	Thousands	Apprehended several *xiangzhang* (township head), declared a cessation to payment of rent and tax. Lasted several hours.
Nov. 1927	Wuxi	Thousands	Attacked and occupied a dozen small towns (*cunzhen*), burned land deeds and debt contracts, executed one landlord.
Nov. 1927	Jiangyin	1,000	Attacked the local public security bureau and opium-prohibiting bureau, burned landlords' houses, deeds, and contracts.
Dec. 1927	Qingpu	One township	Attacked police, beat landlords, resisted rent payment.
Feb. 1928	Jiangyin	Three townships	Burned landlord houses, land deeds and contracts, and fought with the police.
Apr. 1928	Jiading	One township	Resisted rent and taxes, attacked local police, punished local bullies and distributed their properties.
Nov. 1928	Jintan	800	Attacked local police, burned landlords' and merchants' houses, land deeds, debt contracts, and confiscated their properties.
Jan. 1929	Fengxian	One township	Attacked local police bureau, burned the houses of big landlords and the heads of merchant corps, shops, and land deeds, and confiscated and distributed their properties.
Feb. 1929	Songjiang	One township	Attacked local militia, burned a landlord's house and account books, distributed his properties. Killed a local bully and a police officer.
Aug. 1930	Nanhui	1,000	Attacked local police, occupied the house of a big landlord, proclaimed the establishment of a local Soviet. Lasted for three days.

Sources: Jiangsusheng dang'an guan (1983: 429–163); *Jiangsu wenshi ziliao xuanji* (1981: 4: 9–30); *Jiading xian zhi* (1992: 18); *Nanhui xian zhi* (1992: 21); Guan Wenwei (1985: 70–71); *Zhang Donghui* et al. (1997: 68, 71, 78, 85, 116,159,183–184, 236, 240, 242, 365).

Note:
* Refers to the number of people involved.

landlords and resisting their demands. Their protests targeted the abuses of the existing system, rather than the system itself. The Communists' revolutionary programs therefore had little appeal to them. "Not just the goals, but the methods of the Communists as well, differed radically from those of typical peasant protest" (Bernhardt 1992: 202).

Guan Wenwei, a Communist activist who had organized several peasant insurrections in the Yangzi delta between 1927 and 1930, recounts his own experiences in his memoirs. In late 1927, when Guan was the Party Secretary of Danyang County, he organized a peasant uprising in Huqiao *qu* (ward) immediately after the Yixing Rebellion of November 1927 (see Table 8.1). The original plan for the uprising was based on the decision of the CCP's provincial committee: i.e. to order Communist activists to seize local power, organize a peasant army, confiscate landlords' land and properties, and distribute them to poor peasants (Guan Wenwei 1985: 70–71). By the day of the insurrection, the Communists had been able to mobilize between 2,000–3,000 peasants. However, the ward officers escaped beforehand, and only several lower level officials (*xiangzhang*) were apprehended. The rebels proclaimed the establishment of a local Soviet government, and declared a cessation of payment of rent and tax. However, the rebellion only lasted several hours. Hearing that government forces nearby were approaching, the participants were all dragged home by their wives and children and the rebellion quickly collapsed (Guan Wenwei 1985: 77).

Obviously, the Danyang insurrection turned out to be more a staged show than a serious rebellion. Though Guan attributed its failure to the peasants' lack of political education, organizational preparation, and military training, he later realized that the causes were more fundamental. After this failure, Guan was ordered to organize two more insurrections, one in Baita qu of Jintan (see Table 8.1), and one on the border of Danyang and Jintan counties.[3] Both, however, suffered a similar fate (Guan Wenwei 1985: 77, 104). This series of failures took a heavy toll on local Communist organizations, forcing local Communist activists like Guan to ask: "Should we consider [objective] conditions before organizing an insurrection (*baodong shi bushi yao jiang tiaojian*)?" (ibid.: 78). Guan began to doubt it was possible to organize a successful rebellion in core areas of Nationalist control such as the Yangzi delta.[4]

This doubt finally led to a very thoughtful exchange between Guan and Chen Yun, the provincial party leader at that time. In 1929, Guan was appointed the Party Secretary of Changzhou County, and was ordered to organize another peasant insurrection during the autumn harvest. When Guan passed on the order to local Communist activists, they questioned its wisdom, arguing that such a move would inevitably fail (ibid.: 109). Chen Yun, who was sent by the provincial party committee to inspect and direct preparation for the insurrection, asked Guan if the local Communist activists were confident of success. Rather than answering the question directly, Guan listed the unfavorable local conditions and lessons he had drawn from his own experiences. Among them are two points that deserve special attention.

First, Guan said, the Communists could not organize their own armed forces because they could not find recruits among local peasants. Without a core military organization, a rebellion would be easily crushed by government forces. Second, any military action faced serious problems of securing provisions. Because the majority of Jiangnan landlords lived in cities and towns, surplus grain was also stored there and thus out of the Communists' reach. And because tenant-peasants in the countryside had no tax obligations, it would be improper to collect grain from them. Without grain provisions, an insurrection could not be sustained for more than a couple of days. As Guan said: "Though there is much room in the countryside for us to maneuver, if we have no funds, no food, we still cannot have a foothold" (ibid.: 77, 123–124, 130).

Guan's opinion gives us very important information to help us discover the crucial reasons for the repeated setbacks of the Communist-led peasant insurrections in this area during this period. We have already seen that Jiangnan peasants did not lend ready support to Communist revolutionary programs and methods. Their reluctance can explain in part the repeated failures of Communist-led peasant uprising in this area, because nowhere could a spontaneous peasant collective action be automatically transformed into the political revolution expected by the Communists.[5] Jiangnan peasants might have been more indifferent toward Communist revolution, but this indifference should not have been an insurmountable barrier for revolutionaries attempting the game of revolution.[6] There must also have been other crucial, less subjective factors responsible for the miscarriage of the Communist revolution in Jiangnan.

The rural revolution as defined and pursued by the Chinese Communists was to be a protracted and arduous armed struggle. Making revolution therefore demanded more than a short-term commitment by its participants; more important, it needed long-term support in human and material resources. What Guan emphasized is exactly this crucial point. Armed revolution required an army, and organizing an army required both recruits and supplies, especially food.

However, in the Yangzi delta, the Communist activists found they lacked both. In this area, as Guan said, few peasants were willing to join the army. Soldiering did not appeal to Jiangnan peasants, as it did to peasants elsewhere, as an alternative way to earn a living.[7] The generally better economic conditions in the Yangzi delta and the various employment opportunities available for peasants made a soldier's life less attractive. In the past, army recruits in China were primarily landless peasants, who, after losing their regular means of living, did not hesitate to join the army for survival.[8] However, in the Yangzi delta, the more commercialized and diversified economy provided people with more opportunities for off-farm employment. Being landless did not necessarily mean being jobless and homeless.[9]

Furthermore, the majority of Jiangnan peasants were tenants, who for centuries had had no tax obligations. It was therefore inappropriate and illegitimate to collect grain from tenants, for this action was *de facto* taxation. On the other hand, most landlords lived in urban areas and were beyond the reach of the Communists in their early stage of maneuvering. Thus, the Communists faced the serious difficulties in provisioning their activities. The lack of reliable and sufficient human and material resources played a major role in dooming Communist efforts to achieve a sustained and successful revolution in the Yangzi delta during the Nanjing decade.[10]

Wartime operations

The War of Resistance against Japan dramatically changed the political situation in the Yangzi delta. After the formation of the Second United Front in early 1937, everyone, the Communists included, now had the political legitimacy to organize an army to fight against the Japanese invaders and their collaborators. The Communists wasted no time in seizing this opportunity. The Communist-led New Fourth Army (NFA),[11] quickly entered the Yangzi delta six months after the fall of Nanjing (June 1938) and established their first guerrilla base, the Maoshan base, in the delta (*Xinsijun huiyi shiliao* 1990: 217).[12] Meanwhile, those Communists who had previously worked underground in this area now openly and actively organized local resistance forces. This time, their enemies were the Japanese invaders and their collaborators, rather than the Nationalists and the landlord class. Their anti-Japanese resistance received widespread political support from local society yet encountered no effective suppression by the Japanese.[13] The war thus ushered Communist operations in the Yangzi delta into a new, potentially more successful period.

Although the Yangzi delta was the core area of the Japanese occupation, the Japanese control of the area was still incomplete. Their forces were mainly concentrated in cities along the major transportation routes, and the vast countryside was left to be struggled over by different forces: namely, the Nationalists, the Communists, collaborators, and other local forces, including bandits. The Communists usually referred to their rivals as *di wei fei wan* (lit. enemies, collaborators, bandits and diehards. Here "enemies" refer to the Japanese, "diehards" refer to the Nationalists). Agreements between the supreme commanders of the Nationalist Third War Zone and the NFA established distinct areas of operation for each,[14] but neither the Nationalists nor the Communists intended to honor these accords. The Communists actually benefited from this situation. They managed to establish and expand their guerrilla bases in different locations of the Yangzi delta. These bases were later subsumed under the Sunan Anti-Japanese base (*Sunan kangri genjudi*), one of the 19 Communist bases established during the war. It was located in southern Jiangsu (i.e. the area east of Nanjing, south of the Yangzi River), and also encompassed parts of northern Zhejiang, and

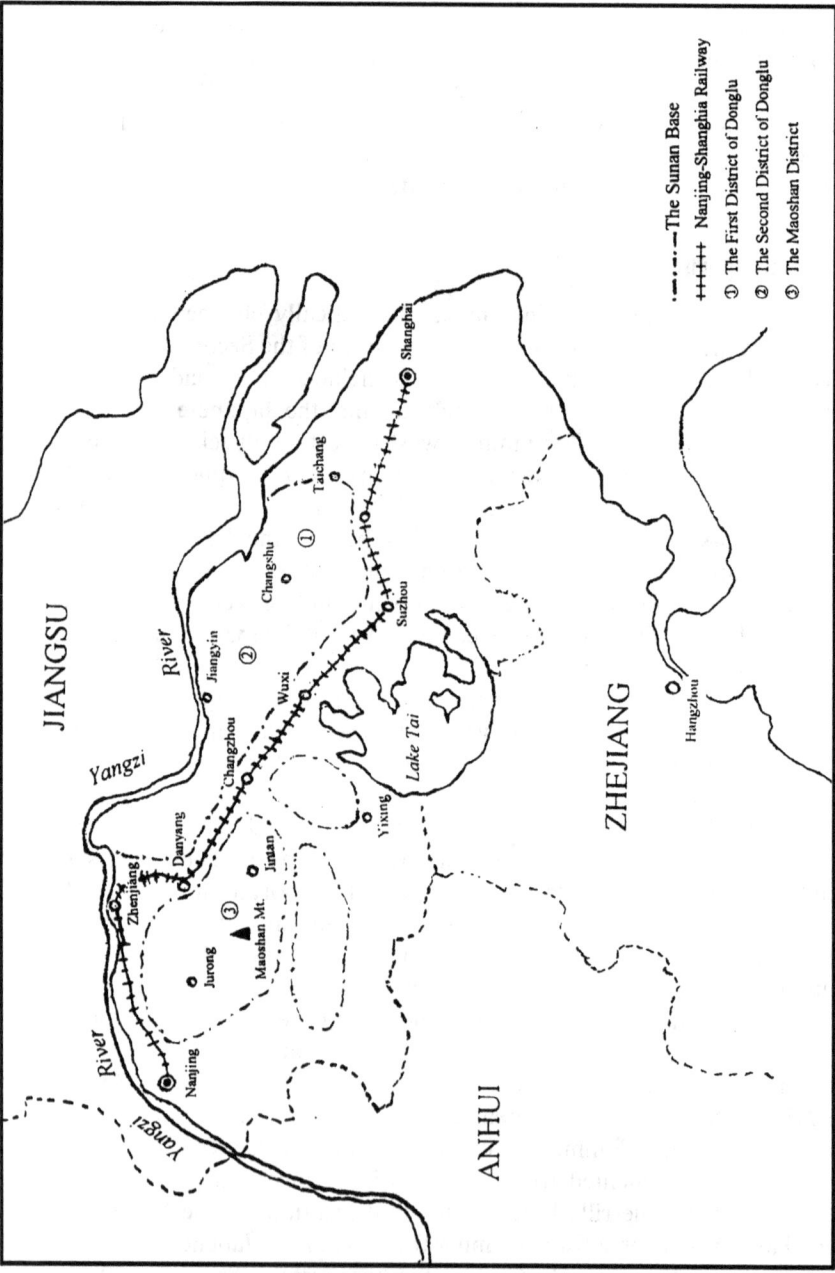

Map 8.1 The Sunan anti-Japanese base, c. 1942.

southeastern Anhui (Map 8.1). By the end of 1944 it controlled 2.7 million people and 15 counties (Fan Zhengfu 1983: 81).

Mediation between landlords and peasants

During the war the Communists functioned as a state or a local government in the Yangzi delta, in competition with both the Japanese and the Nationalists. The change in the overall situation as well as of their own political role induced the Communists to alter the radical policies they had practiced before the war. Once this transformation was realized, the Communists found that their position was not substantially different from those of the other state powers operating in the area. They were compelled to follow the historical logic that governed the relationship between the state and local society since the late Qing. They had to act as a mediator between landlords and tenants. And most interestingly and surprisingly, they, like their predecessors and competitors in the delta, also employed absentee landlordism to ensure tax collection.

In the Yangzi delta, absentee landlordism had long been the dominant social and economic reality, and rent disputes a very common issue. These disputes escalated in the wartime due to the destruction and chaos of the war and the alternation of political power caused by the war. Some landlords fled the area, but the majority remained in Japanese-occupied cities and towns. Generally, the bargaining power of the absentee landlords was weakened significantly by the wartime situation. Tenants in the countryside now had more excuses and reasons to refuse to pay their rent.[15] Absentee landlords thus often turned to the Japanese Occupation authorities for help. Apparently, if rent disputes could not be solved properly, they would weaken the anti-Japanese united front among different classes and thus benefit the Japanese. As Chen Yi, the chief commander of the NFA, said:

> If we have no proper solution for this crucial issue related to the Resistance and people's livelihood, or simply ignore it, then landlords and creditors would resort to the armed forces of the [Japanese] invaders, and tenants and debtors would also respond with arms. What a danger this civil strife would be!
>
> (Sunan 1987: 76)

To prevent this dangerous pitting of Chinese against Chinese, the Communists, now a competing state power, were determined to mediate rather than to aggravate the conflicts between the landlords and tenants. This dramatic change took place in the very beginning of their Sunan base building. Chen Yi states that during the first harvest (1938) after the NFA entered the delta, the Communists faced severe rent disputes in the Maoshan base. After careful consideration, the party stipulated several principles for handling such disputes: (1) collaborators were to be strictly forbidden from collecting rent and interest; (2) disputes over rent and interest were to be solved through negotiation and cooperation between landlords and tenants, and creditors and debtors; and (3) rent and interest concessions (*rangzu rangxi*) were to be advocated, while rent and interest resistance (*kangzu kangxi*) was to be opposed (Sunan 1987: 75–76).

These principles became the guidelines for handling rent and interest disputes in the Sunan base, and were clearly embodied in the party's policies and government regulations. For example, in 1940, the CCP committee of the Eastern Nanjing-Shanghai Railway Area promulgated *The Ten Program for Continuing Resistance in the Eastern Shanghai-Nanjing Railroad Area* (*Jianchi ludong kangri shida gangling*). This program sought to "implement rent and interest reduction, [and] protect the property rights of landlords, business owners, and merchants" (ibid.: 119). In March 1943, the CCP's Jiangsu and Anhui Regional Committee published *The Administrative Program for the Sunan Base* (*Sunan shizheng gangling*) to reiterate these principles.[16] This program called on Jiangnan people of all classes, all political parties and all resistance forces, to unite and drive out the Japanese invaders. For this purpose, the program stated that the Communists were willing to follow Sun Yet-sen's Three People's Principles and to promote class unity. Article Eight of the program dealt directly with the land issue and specifically emphasized the need to "adhere firmly to the CCP's land policies; protect landlords' ownership, creditors' rights, and tenants' tenure; implement rent and interest reduction; ensure rent and interest payment; and adjust rent relations and debt relations properly" (ibid.: 245).

To implement these general principles, more specific regulations were worked out. The provisional regulations on land issues promulgated by the Sunan base administration in March 1942 stated:

> In the case of runaway landlords, no matter where they may have fled, their land should not be confiscated. The government would find tenants to till the land if there is no one taking care of it, collect and deposit rents, pay taxes on the owner's behalf, and return the land and rents to the landowner when he returns home.
>
> (ibid.: 225)

This policy was to apply even to those landlords who were forced to be Japanese collaborators (ibid.).

The policy did not just remain on paper; though the evidence is very limited, the available sources do show clearly that the Communists followed this policy to collect rent for landlords (*daishouzu*). For example, Deng Zhenxun, the Deputy Secretary of the CCP's Jiangnan Committee, mentioned in his January 1942 work report that because the government in some areas of the Sunan base collected and kept rent for runaway landlords, relations between the CCP authorities and local peasantry were fairly tense (Sunan 1987: 183). In the first and second administrative districts of the

Sunan base,[17] tenants complained about the NFA asking them to pay rent. They claimed that before the coming of the NFA, they had in fact paid no rent because Chiang Kai-shek and the Nationalist government had promised that people in Japanese-occupied areas were to be exempted from tax and rent payments. Deng Zhenxun said that the Communists had to explain repeatedly to local people the reasons for rent payment.[18] The policy was troublesome, especially in the cases involving runaway landlords, as the government had to take care of their land and collect and deposit rent on their behalf (ibid.: 183). In the same report, Deng also criticized some cadres who committed petty corruption in handling financial affairs: they pocketed and spent the rent money they had collected for landlords (ibid.: 187–188).

By implementing the principles and regulations discussed above, the Communists claimed that they had successfully won the allegiance of the local people, including landlords. Deng Zhenxun reported that because the Communists allowed rent collection, some landlords who had originally opposed them became supporters (ibid.: 181). Chen Yi compared the Communist rent policy with that of the Japanese Occupation authorities and stated that Japanese invaders and their collaborators, in the name of returning to normal a process that they claimed had been ruined by the Communists, collected rent for landlords during their qingxiang campaigns. However, they either appropriated all the rent they collected or gave only a small portion to landlords. But the Communists still allowed landlords to collect rent, albeit at a reduced rate. The landlords therefore hated the Japanese and the collaborators but were willing to maintain good relations with the NFA (Sunan 1987: 213, 217).

Collection of taxes and rents

Acknowledging landlords' rights of rent collection was not only intended to win political legitimacy among the propertied classes, it was also aimed at gaining financial support from them. In the Yangzi delta, taxes had for centuries come out of rents. This revenue structure made rent collection the precondition of tax collection, a fact of which the Communists were fully aware. The source materials pertaining to this subject, though limited, make it clear that the methods Communists used for collecting land tax were not substantially different from those of their predecessors and competitors. They too exploited highly developed absentee landlordism to serve their taxation needs.

Because most landlords lived in enemy-occupied towns and cities, it was convenient for the Communists who controlled the countryside to ask tenants to pay land taxes on behalf of landlords. This method was employed by the *Minkang* (the abbreviation of *Changshu minzhong kangri ziweidui*, the People's Anti-Japanese Self-defense Corps of Changshu), a guerrilla force of the NFA, between 1938 and 1939 in Changshu county. After Changshu fell to the Japanese, the Nationalist county government fled inland. The tax rate set by the Communists was low and tenants who paid taxes would receive receipts that would enable them later to reduce their rent payments to landlords by the same amount (He Zhenqiu 1986: 134). This method of collecting land taxes was also adopted in other localities in the Eastern Area of the Sunan base (*Donglu*, the area east of Jiangyin, Wuxi and Lake Tai) in the first half of 1940 (Huazhong caijing 1984: 453). Tenant payment of taxes also took place in the Eastern Zhejiang base.[19] In August 1943, the Communist authorities in the Eastern Zhejiang base promulgated *The Provisional Regulations for Collecting Army Grain and Fees for Resistance and Self-Defense*.[20] Article 22 of this document states:

> The army grain and fees for resistance and self-defense should be paid by the actual cultivators. For rented land, the grain and fees should be shared by both the landowners and tenants. The landowners' due should be paid by the tenants [*you dianhu daiwei jiaona*]. This part should then be deducted from the tenants' rent. Tenants should not refuse payment for any reason, and landowners should also not raise any objection.
>
> (XSJ 1984: 6: 277)

Obviously, in the case of tenant payment of tax, what tenants paid served simultaneously as rent and tax. From the tenants' viewpoint, what they paid were rents, but the Communists saw what they collected were taxes, albeit taxes collected via rents. This expedient method of tax collection was not a Communist invention. The Taipings had used this method in the Jiangnan area 80 years earlier for the same purpose of ensuring tax collection (see Bernhardt 1992: 103–106). In the Yangzi delta, since the late Qing, the practice of exploiting absentee landlordism to ensure tax collection was commonly supported and adopted by local governments, which often relied on various rent collection agencies for tax collection. Although tenant payment of tax differed from collection of tax by rent collection agencies, it was in fact another version of tax collection based on absentee landlordism.

Tenant payment of tax was convenient and expedient but not efficient, because the tenants—who were not landowners and had no tax obligations —could not be pressed hard to pay taxes. Therefore, the specific collection method was to ask tenants to report the acreage of their rented land and pay taxes voluntarily (He Zhenqiu 1986: 135). In the Changshu area, once they had consolidated their local control and established a formal committee for financial affairs in mid-1939, the Communists changed their method and focused instead on landlords.[21] That year during the tax season, the committee on financial affairs met with local elites and persuaded them to take the lead in paying taxes, as well as assisting the government in collecting taxes. Reportedly, because of this new method and especially because of the assistance of local elites, tax collection proceeded quite smoothly (ibid.: 135).[22]

Focusing on and working with landlords, the Communists had to make sure that landlords had collected rents before collecting taxes from them. In the Donglu area, the disruption of the war had prevented landlords in many localities from collecting rent since 1938.[23] In the fall of 1940, the Japanese Occupation authorities moved to use military force to help landlords collect rent. The Communists, in competition with the Japanese in rent collection, announced their method of rent collection in a signed article in their official periodical, *Jiangnan*.[24] In a signed article, the Communists emphasized that they did not oppose rent collection. Instead, they were willing to solve rent disputes and promote cooperation and unity between landlords and peasants for the sake of resisting the Japanese. For this purpose, the author put forward several principles of rent collection which advocated making the people's economic burden reasonable (*heli fudan*) (Huazhong caijing 1984: 451–452). He then proposed an important institutional arrangement for implementing reasonable rent payment and guaranteeing rent collection:

> Because the rent paid should be even and reasonable, and also because of changes that have taken place in the last three years [of war], it is very difficult for landlords to collect rent by themselves. We have decided, therefore, to help landlords organize rent collection committees [*shouzu weiyuanhui*] to collect rent for the whole area. This method can be called "guaranteeing rent collection" [*baozheng shouzu*] . . . After all rent is collected, we will calculate the average rent for each *mu* of land, and return it to the landlords.
>
> (ibid.: 452)

He further emphasized that after rents were collected, landlords should pay taxes. Again, the Communists proposed a progressive tax rate to make the tax burdens of big and small landlords proportionate:

> According to the principle of tax coming out of rent, the Donglu Economic Committee should collect the land contribution for national salvation [*tianmu jiuguojuan*] from landlords, rather than from tenants as the committee had done in the first half of this year [1940]. Because landlords own varying amounts of land, their financial abilities are different; therefore, the contribution for national-salvation should be collected at a progressive rate. Big landlords should pay more (i.e., at a higher rate) and small landlords pay less.
>
> (ibid.: 453)

Following these principles, the article provided a formula for calculating rent and tax at a progressive rate based on rent and the tax payers' economic situation. All of the calculations were supposed to be done by the rent collection committee (ibid.: 454–455). Although the article did not make clear whether the committee withheld taxes from the rent it collected or the government later collected them from individual landlords, the fact that the rent committee handled the calculation and collection of rent strongly suggests that tax withholding was the more likely method. Research by He Zhenqiu shows that the adoption of this new way of collecting rents and taxes made the year's tax collection was very successful. By February 1941, a total of two million *yuan* of land tax had been collected, which amounted to 70 percent of the Sunan base government's annual expenditure in the Donglu area (He Zhenqiu 1986: 136).

It is quite surprising to see the Communists helping landlords to organize rent collection committees; such aid in ensuring rent collection was unique to the Sunan base. But various approaches to organizing rent collection, such as creating a rent bursary or rent dunning bureau, and joint collection of rent and tax, had been taken by the late Qing government, the Taipings, the Nationalists, and the Japanese in this area before and during the war. The Communists were different only in that they seemed more committed to make rent and tax payment equitable. By helping landlords collect rents, the Communists could have an edge in bargaining with landlords to reduce rents. In addition to this assistance, the Communists also often offered tax cuts to persuade landlords to reduce rents. For example, the Communists negotiated with a landlord in Shazhou County nicknamed the King of Shoal (*Sha dawang*), who owned a large amount of land that he rented out to peasants. In return for rent deduction on his part, the Communists agreed to cut his taxes between 20 percent and 30 percent. In his 1942 work report, Deng Zhenxun used this case to illustrate how the Communists used flexible tactics and compromised on rent and tax issues to win cooperation and support from powerful local elites (Sunan 1987: 173, 183).

There was precedent for this approach as well. As Bernhardt's (1992) study shows, in the Yangzi delta, the close link between rent and tax was widely recognized and exploited from the late Qing onward. The government used tax cuts to persuade landlords to reduce rent, tenants took tax cuts as an excuse to refuse to pay rent; and landlords even imposed levies on themselves to induce tenants to pay rent (Bernhardt 1992: 104n). In the Republican era, many Jiangnan counties required that landlords complied with government-approved rent ceilings to receive official assistance in dunning their renters (ibid.: 172).

The Communists shared the same primary concern as their competitors and predecessors—to collect taxes. In this regard, the Communists in the Yangzi delta were not innovative but practical, and they relied on the same methods as their adversaries. They also exploited absentee landlordism to ensure that they would receive tax revenue. They, therefore, had to make sure rents were collected, landlords were cooperative, and tenant resistance was contained. Their behavior thus differed significantly from that of their counterparts in the North China bases.

The Communists and the Delta rural communities

Unlike in wartime rural North China, where the village community played a vital role in Communist mobilization and organization, in the Yangzi delta, rural communities were not the principal target of Communist mobilization.[25] Consider taxation as an example: in the North China bases, the village was the basic unit for imposing and collecting taxes but in the Sunan base, there is no evidence that the village was ever asked to shoulder collective responsibility for taxation.

A significant factor in these contrasting approaches was the difference in social formation of the rural community in these two regions. In rural North China, the majority of taxpayers (i.e., landowners) lived in villages, the Communists made taxation the collective duty of the village. Moreover, the implementation of a new tax system—the unified progressive tax system—in the North China bases required the village government to rank villager households according to their wealth. All these arrangements depended on the willing compliance and vigorous cooperation of the village government. It was therefore extremely important for the Communists to mobilize and control villages and thus ensure their revenue base. In the Yangzi delta, however, the major taxpayers were landlords, most of whom lived in towns and cities; rural residents were mostly tenants who bore no tax obligations. The unified progressive tax system thus simply could not find its way into rural communities; to collect tax, the Communists had instead to focus on absentee landlordism. Consequently, there was no urgent need to mobilize and organize these rural communities, at least for the purpose of taxation.

To be sure, in some cases, taxes were collected directly from tenants in the Sunan base, as we saw from the last section, but the whole context of tenant payment of tax as well as social relations embodied in it differed from owner-cultivator payment of tax in North China villages. In the case of tenant payment of tax, what the Communists collected from tenants was in fact part of rents, but it was withheld as taxes. The Communists thus acted as rent collecting agents, and their relation with tenants was defined and dictated by the rent relations between tenants and absentee landlords; they could not change this relationship into one between the government and taxpayers, let alone ask tenants to be collectively responsible for taxation. Moreover, relying on tenants to pay taxes was not very successful. Since in the delta taxes came out of rents, working directly with landlords to collect tax was a more viable and efficient solution for any state, including one run by the Communists. No governments could afford to overlook this solution and opt for working with tenants in rural communities to ensure tax collection.

Taxation pressures in the Sunan base were further eased by the substantial commercial tax, which—unlike in most North China bases—contributed significantly to government revenue. Indeed, revenue from the commercial tax in many areas surpassed that from the land tax

(Nankai daxue 1986: 490–491), and it was much easier to collect. All that was required was simply for armed tax collectors to go to market towns and major transportation junctures, rather than deal with a multitude of individual taxpayers (He Zhenqiu 1986: 134, 136–137).[26]

Largely for these reasons, the Communists made little effort to mobilize and reorganize rural communities in their Sunan base. Their only attempt came in early 1941, when they sought to "abolish the *baojia* system and establish the village head system" (*feichu baojiazhi, jianli cunzhangzhi*) in the Jiangnan countryside (Sunan 1987: 131). In some localities, the *baojia* system was indeed abolished, but generally this effort of rural political reform was not widely implemented; it was even criticized by Deng Zhenxun, the Deputy Secretary of the CCP's Jiangnan Committee, as a "leftist tendency." Deng explained that local people recognized the *baojia* system as the legitimate system established by the Nationalists, and could not understand why the Communists wanted to abolish it and even resented the attempt (ibid.: 131, 186–187). Because of such local resistance, the existing *baojia* system generally remained unchanged in the countryside.

The top officials of the Communist Party and of the Sunan base government admitted freely that in the Sunan base the political power below the *qu* (ward) level was basically controlled by "feudal forces" (*fengjian shili*).[27] In mid-1941, Liu Shaoqi, the Secretary of the CCP's Central China Bureau and the political commissar of the NFA, criticized the mass movement in Jiangnan as unsatisfactory for its failure to mobilize the masses (Sunan 1987: 142–143). Fan Yulin, who represented the Sunan base government, reported at the joint conference of county magistrates of the Sunan base on 18 March 1943 that in many places, the local administration under the *qu* was still under feudal influence (ibid.: 259–260).[28]

The base leaders' disappointment was strongly expressed in an article written by Jiang Weiqing in late 1944, when Jiang was the Party Secretary of the CCP Jiangsu and Anhui Committee (*Suwanqu dangwei*) and the Committee Chair of the Sunan Base Administration (*Sunan xingzheng gongshu*):

> After several years of struggle, can we say that all of our tasks have been implemented very well? And that there are no shortcomings in our work? Surely not. There are still shortcomings in our work that made us incompetent to meet the challenges we are facing. To a certain extent, these shortcomings are very serious. For instance, right now our base is still not quite consolidated; general [political] construction is poor; the basic masses are still not fully and widely mobilized; production movement is limited only to some places; rent and interest reduction has not been implemented thoroughly and resolutely; and some places simply have not implemented it under the pretext of harsh conditions. Especially, the grassroots governments [*jiceng zhengquan*] have not yet been reformed. Many grassroots governments are still under the sway

of feudal forces, and some are even controlled by a handful of bad elements who exploit and oppress the people.

(ibid.: 370)

In the early stage of Communist base building, it was rather common to find communal power controlled by the old rural elite. For example, in the Jin-Cha-Ji (Shanxi-Chahar-Hebei) base, and in the Suzhong (Central Jiangsu) and Subei (Northern Jiangsu) bases, Communist control of rural communities was initially quite weak. Nevertheless, the Communists later made great efforts to mobilize the rural masses and reform village politics and finally achieved firm control of village communities (Gao Defu 1986: 258–268; Suzhong 1989: 11; Subei 1989: 12). In the Sunan base, however, the weak control of rural communities plagued the Communists almost throughout the entire history of the base. Jiang Weiqing attributed this failure to "objective difficulties" (*keguan kunnan*) in the Yangzi delta, particularly, strong enemies and frequent fighting. Because of these difficulties, Jiang explained, the Communists had to expend most of their energy in fighting the enemy, forcing them to neglect other tasks (Sunan 1987: 371).[29]

Deng Zhenxun, however, offered another explanation for the failure of mass mobilization in the Sunan base. In his report to a working conference on the mass movement (*minyun gongzuo huiyi*) in the Sunan base in August 1942, he instead pointed to subjective factors. He specifically criticized the base leaders for lacking a sound understanding of Jiangnan society, for they believed that Jiangnan people were rich and therefore in no need of rent and interest reduction, as well as difficult to mobilize. He also criticized the base leaders for trying to run the mass movement themselves, rather than encouraging the masses to take the initiative and act independently (ibid.: 231–233).

Both Jiang's and Deng's explanations were valid. It was true that the military situation in wartime Jiangnan was harsher and more complicated than that in other areas, but this was not the only reason for the Communists' failure to mobilize Jiangnan rural communities. It also is plausible that the subjective weaknesses of the base leaders handicapped mass mobilization. But another important reason, which both critics failed to acknowledge, lay in the taxation pattern of the Yangzi delta, which in turn was shaped by socioeconomic structure of the region. Since the Communists could exploit highly developed absentee landlordism and market relations to collect taxes while bypassing rural communities, there was no urgent pressure on them to mobilize and reorganize rural communities.

Army recruitment and military expansion

During the Nanjing decade, the Communists' effort to make a sustained revolution in the Yangzi delta failed largely because it lacked long-term supplies of human and material resources from local society. This situation was altered, to a certain extent, by the war, when the Communists were able to establish a guerrilla regime to collect taxes from landlords. But the war only changed local politics, not the social and economic structure or delta peasants' disdain for soldiering. The Communists still had a hard time finding army recruits among delta peasants. Lin Youyong, a Communist activist working in the Shanghai suburban counties, recalled that though they gave local peasant youths "patriotic education" to persuade them to join the army, few were persuaded. Lin did not give any convincing reasons for their reluctance to join the NFA, merely mentioning casually that some of them had to take care of their families (Shanghai 1986: 102). But I believe the explanation was the same as it had been in the prewar days: for the delta peasants, soldiering was neither a preferred nor necessary way of earning a living.

For this reason, in the early years of the Sunan base, Chen Yi emphasized mobilizing unemployed workers in urban areas to join the army (Sunan 1987: 75). According to the recollections of Ye Fei, Jiang Weiqing, and Gu Fusheng,[30] the NFA troops stationed and operating in Jiangnan were mainly composed of unemployed workers and students from Shanghai. In Shanghai, the Japanese occupation had resulted in serious social and economic dislocation, making it quite easy to find army recruits. The NFA even sent their representatives to Shanghai to recruit soldiers fairly openly and publicly (Huazhong huiyi 1984: 3: 90–91). Most recruits thus mobilized were sent to the NFA Sunan base by the Shanghai CCP organization (Sunan 1987: 413, 459, 480).[31] The recruitment in Shanghai continued at least to mid-1943. One army work report by a NFA regiment published in a party periodical, *Jiangnan Dangkan*, complained that some 20 newly recruited soldiers from Shanghai were sick and unqualified people and that most of them had to be sent back to Shanghai, thereby wasting several thousand *yuan* (XSJ 1984: 6: 552). According to an incomplete reckoning by the CCP's Shanghai Municipal Committee for Collecting Historical Materials, in wartime more than 21,000 Shanghai people were sent to the NFA, among them more than 8,000 went to the Yangzi delta area (*Shanghai remin yu xinsijun* 1989: 9, 16). Because of its large number of recruits from Shanghai, the NFA, as Benton maintained, had a greater proportion of workers, students and intellectuals, and women than any other Chinese army, including the Eighth Route Army, and it was hence China's best-educated army (Benton 1999: 723). Ironically, this situation also made it easy for the enemy to identify the NFA soldiers among local people simply by listening to their accent.[32]

In the North China bases, in contrast, soldiers were overwhelmingly recruited from local peasantry. In the early stage of the army and base building, army recruits were composed of mainly landless peasants. Once the base was consolidated and well established, the recruitment of soldiers, like tax collection, also became a collective responsibility of the village. A special organ, called *Kuojun weiyuanhui* (the Army Recruitment Committee), was set up in the village as well as in the higher levels of the government (XSJ 1984: 7: 423; Chen Yung-fa 1986: 392). Base governments would launch campaigns to recruit soldiers in winter and spring, assigning recruitment quotas to villages. Village officials often worked desperately to meet these quotas, resorting to any means available, including coercion (Chen Yung-fa 1986: 383–401). To support these campaigns and assure the recruits that their families would be well taken care of, base governments promised favorable treatment to servicemen's families, such as farming assistance, winter relief, and holiday gifts. To make sure the village officials would deliver on these promises, base governments worked out special regulations (JCJ 1984: 4: 567–584; JJLY 1985: 4: 87–101, 282–289, 368–375; Subei 1989: 425–433). In addition, a special committee called *Youkang weiyuanhui* (the abbreviation of *youdai kangri jiashu weiyuanhui*, the Committee for Special Treatment to Anti-Japanese Servicemen's Families) was set up in the village and in the higher levels of the government to take charge of this matter (JCJ 1984: 4: 575; Subei 1989: 206–207, 210; XSJ 1984: 7: 368). However, no such institutional arrangements were made in the Sunan base, simply because there was no such need.

It was very possible that the supposed "political backwardness" of Jiangnan peasants sometimes made the Communists very critical of them. In a work report presented before the joint conference (1943) of county magistrates in the Sunan base, Fan Yulin accused Jiangnan people of being tame and frail, sophisticated, rather cunning, superstitious, fond of gambling, corrupt, and lacking in fighting spirit (Sunan 1987: 249–250; see also Benton 1999: 26–27). It was quite unusual for a high-level Communist cadre to reproach local people in such scathing terms in a formal work report.

Interestingly enough, this accusation contradicted repeated Communist criticism of another prevalent phenomenon: namely, the "leftist tendency" (*zuoqing*) of local people in their response to rent reduction. As previously mentioned, in the early stages of the war, peasants in many localities took advantage of the chaos to avoid paying their rent. The Communists thus advocated rent and interest reduction (*jianzu jianxi*) and emphasized rent and interest payment (*jiaozu jiaoxi*) after that reduction.[33] A special committee for mediating rent and interest disputes (*zuxi tiaojie weiyuanhui*) was organized in many counties of the base (Sunan 1987: 96). In practice, however, peasants often resisted paying even the reduced amount. For example, Tan Zhenlin, the Secretary of the CCP Jiangnan Committee and the commander and political commissar of the Sixth Division of the NFA, said in late 1941 that because of "leftist tendencies" in dealing with rent issues, labor issues, and the organization of the democratic regime, many landlords and merchants remained neutral during the qingxiang campaigns. Some even helped the enemy (ibid.: 166–167). The same criticism can also be found in other Communist leaders' speeches (ibid.: 178–179, 186–187, 204, 230). But Deng Zhenxun argued that "it is normal for the masses to be 'too left' [*guozuo*, meaning too radical]. Our task is not to prevent the masses from being too left, but to prevent our cadres from being too left." Deng suggested that Communist cadres exploit the leftist tendency of the masses to force landlords to compromise (ibid.: 238).

That Jiangnan peasants, on the one hand, were very combative on rent issues and, on the other, were deficient in the "fighting spirit" that would make them eager to join the NFA and the revolution was hardly contradictory. Since the late Qing, Jiangnan peasants had shown that they did not lack the spirit to resist demands for rent. What they did lack was the enthusiasm to join the army and participate in political revolution. The war had neither changed the social and economic structure of the Jiangnan countryside nor the attitude of Jiangna peasants.

Although the Yangzi delta was economically rich, and the Sunan base had served as an important revenue source for the NFA,[34] the Communists seemed to feel uncomfortable there. Shortly after the NFA entered the Yangzi delta, they decided to move their main forces to Northern Jiangsu and establish their main base there. In November 1939, the main NFA Sunan forces crossed the Yangzi River and entered northern Jiangsu. At the same time, Liu Shaoqi, who was then the Secretary of the CCP's Central China Bureau (*Zhongyuan ju*, later renamed *Huazhong ju*), which had authority over the NFA, suggested that the CCP Central Committee shift the focus of its political and military operations in Central China to northern Jiangsu (i.e. the area north of the Yangzi River). Northern Jiangsu was, he argued, the strategically most important area of Central China. Liu's suggestion was adopted by the CCP Central Committee (Subei 1989: 4–5). This strategic movement led to serious clashes with the Nationalist forces stationed in northern Jiangsu, culminating in the Battle of Huangqiao (*Huangqiao juezhan*), the single most important battle in the NFA's history, in October 1940. In this battle, the greatly outnumbered NFA decisively defeated the Nationalist forces and expelled them from northern Jiangsu, thus gaining a firm foothold in the area.

Chen Pixian, who was then the Deputy Secretary of the CCP's Northern Jiangsu Committee, later recalled:

> During the Anti-Japanese War, the Sunan base could only be considered as a "military base" [*junshi genjudi*]. The political regime had not been completely established there . . . If we are talking about the real anti-Japanese democratic base [*kangri minzhu genjudi*], we should say that this base was established only after we entered northern Jiangsu. Since then, we began to collect grain and taxes regularly, to mobilize the masses.
>
> (Chen Pixian 1986: number 3)

Geographically as well as socially and economically, northern Jiangsu was a part of the North China plain. Compared to Jiangnan, northern Jiangsu was not only strategically safer, being far away from the major urban centers of Japanese occupation, it was also more responsive and hospitable to the Communist revolution (Chen Yung-fa 1986: 511–514). The Communists found a more favorable and supportive local society there. Though northern Jiangsu was much poorer than the Yangzi delta, the Communists encountered no serious difficulties in building their base and expanding their forces there because they had no difficulty finding army recruits among local peasants.[35] Establishment of its major base in northern Jiangsu was, therefore, a turning point in the Communist revolution and its wartime operations in Central China, after which the Communist forces in Central China grew quickly and steadily.[36] As Ye Fei remarked decades later, "Before we entered and established the bases in Northern Jiangsu, the whole NFA had less than one hundred thousand troops. After that it expanded to three hundred thousand" (1986: 8–9).

Conclusion

The revolutionary activities and wartime operations of the Communists in the Yangzi delta have been neglected for too long. This situation should be attributed primarily to the fact that the Yangzi delta was not the main focus of the Communist revolution and indeed played only a minor role in it. The political situation in the Yangzi delta—that the delta was always the core area of Nationalist and Japanese control—was of course a key impediment to the Communists' efforts. However, this study suggests that other factors also contributed to the revolution's lack of success in the Yangzi delta.

On its face, that failure seem surprising, for there were numerous local grievances in the Yangzi delta that might have encouraged revolutionary mobilization. For centuries, the local scene was dominated by rent disputes and resistance unparalleled elsewhere in the country. However, this struggle of tenant-peasants against landlords was not to be easily translated into a rural revolution advocated by the Communists. Aside from the apathy of Jiangnan peasants—they did not favor a political revolution—a more crucial reason for the Communists' continuous setbacks in Jiangnan was their inability to secure a sustained flow of human and material resources from the countryside. Without that support, their prewar revolution in the Yangzi delta was doomed to failure.

The war provided the Communists with an opportunity to establish a local regime and act as one of several competing governments in the Yangzi delta. In so doing, the Communist state did not function substantially differently from its predecessors and competitors. Like them, the Communists exploited absentee landlordism to mediate rent disputes and to ensure tax collection. So long as this was possible, the Communists had no pressing need to mobilize and reorganize rural communities in their Sunan base. Communist mobilization in rural North China took a very different approach: there the village community was always the primary focus of revolutionary mobilization, and the villages were reorganized and rebuilt into the stronghold and the long-term supporting base of the revolutionary cause.

In the Yangzi delta, however, the war only changed the political situation, not the region's socioeconomic structure. Although the Communists successfully established guerrilla bases in the Yangzi delta, the lack of long-term support, especially army recruits, still prevented them from expanding their forces quickly and effectively. The Communists, instead of choosing to change Jiangnan peasants, chose to change their own strategic focus. Therefore, their major base in Central China and the headquarters of the NFA were moved to northern Jiangsu, an area that, with regard to its geographical location, physical environment, and social and economic structure, was a part of rural North China.[37]

Conclusion

Rural political changes on the North China plain and in the Yangzi delta during the late Qing and the Republican period demonstrate two entirely different patterns. These patterns are the products of the two different social structures in the two macro-regions.[1] The key difference in social structure is that on the North China plain, the village composed of mainly owner-cultivators was the single most important institution in the organization of rural populace and mobilization of local resources. In the Yangzi delta, no rural community could assume this role; instead, rural society was torn and shaped by profound differentiation between absentee landlords and tenant-peasants. The different social and communal structures of these two regions nurtured different local politics and also molded different state–society relations.

During this period, political changes on the North China plain revolved around the village community, because it was the focal point of various types of political mobilization. Beginning in the late Qing, villages as collectivities were asked to undertake modernization projects such as opening schools. They were also increasingly burdened by *tanpai*, a notorious extra tax levied by different levels of government. In times of turmoil, villages also organized self-defense to guard against outside intrusion. Under the pressure of continuous political mobilization, the formal and secular village government was established and its power expanded rapidly without any effective check from its constituents; meanwhile, the village community was reorganized in order to strengthen its control over its resources. Continuous mobilization also resulted in intensified conflicts between the state and the village, especially over the issue of *tanpai*.

The conflicts between the state and the village and between power holders and ordinary villagers within the village led to the deterioration of local politics, and also jeopardized state control over rural society. This situation was exacerbated by socioeconomic changes. During this period, especially in the first half of the twentieth century, socioeconomic differentiation accelerated due to commercialization, population pressure, world-wide economic depression, and social and political turbulence. As a result, the stratum of owner-cultivators, who were the backbone of the community, declined in many villages. This change opened the door for the abuse of power within the village. Which in turn sharpened state–village conflicts, because it was the allocation of *tanpai* that gave those dishonest village heads the chance to abuse their power. Intensified struggles against corrupt village heads, against exorbitant taxes, and ultimately, against the oppressive state, became the major political drama on the North China plain before the War of Resistance against Japan. These struggles, either set in the village or based on the village, threatened the existing order and gave the Communists opportunities for revolutionary maneuvering.[2]

In the Yangzi delta, the picture is entirely different. Long-term commercialization since the Ming (1368–1644) had brought profound social changes to the area and had made it a highly stratified society characterized by spatial segregation between town-dwelling landlords and country-residing tenant-farmers. The development of absentee landlordism made rent collection increasingly difficult and contentious. To secure rent, landlords organized rent bursaries and changed rent collection from a small business of individual landlords to a joint venture of the landed class. Facing a united landlord class, tenants also mobilized in the countryside in order to confront their common enemy. Thus, full-fledged class struggle, revolving around rent collection and transcendent of parochialism, was well developed in the delta by the mid-Qing. It dominated the local political scene and necessitated state intervention.

The state was vigorously involved in mediation and arbitration of rent disputes because these disputes threatened not only local order but also government revenues. This was due to the fact that in this area taxes had long come out of rents. This move decisively changed the state's role from being a mere extractor of tax to also the one of mediator in a stratified society. The state's involvement in rent affairs also focused on rent bursaries. Since the late Qing, the local governments had energetically supported rent bursaries to collect rents from tenants and thus to ensure the collection of taxes from landlords. This method was adopted and gradually institutionalized by the various regimes which ruled the delta during the Republican era. On the other hand, the state also used this support to force landlords to comply with government regulations on rent relations, and therefore to reduce the tension between landlords and tenants. During the Republican period, as we have seen, landlords' compliance with government approved rent ceilings was a prerequisite for receiving official assistance in rent collection.

By exploiting absentee landlordism, the state could meet its tax needs without imposing collective levies on rural communities. Of course, small and scattered hamlets comprised mainly of tenants also prevented the state from doing so. Therefore, in the Yangzi delta unlike on the North China plain, intense conflict between state and rural community over the *tanpai* was a rare story. On the other hand, state involvement in rent collection also weakened the landlord class, because this move put the landlords' fortune under the sway of the state. On the whole, it is not surprising that increasing state involvement in rent relations, i.e., increasing state intrusion into local society, did not strain state–society relations, nor provoke intensified anti-state resistance.

Two distinct patterns can be identified by comparing political changes on the North China plain and in the Yangzi delta. On the North China plain, the village community was the gravitational center around which political changes unfolded. Various political forces all relied heavily on the village to organize rural society and enlist rural resources. As a result, the villages were highly mobilized. This in turn greatly strained state–village relations and dramatically escalated state–village conflicts.

In the Yangzi delta, however, the political drama evolved around rent and hence class relations. It was class rather than community that played the vital role in organizing and mobilizing different social and political forces; and it was the conflicts between landlords and tenant-peasants that dominated the local political scene. The state also exploited class relations to ensure the collection of tax revenue and to mediate between landlords and tenants. Paradoxically, intense struggle between tenants and absentee landlords significantly eased the tension between the state and rural society. Since the belligerent classes were all expecting the state to mediate in their favor, none of them were willing to antagonize the state. Therefore, throughout the Republican period, although the Yangzi delta witnessed intense conflicts between these two classes, the legitimacy of existing political order was not seriously challenged and threatened.

The long-term political changes on the North China plain and in the Yangzi delta set different stages for the Communist revolution. Though the Communists made revolution in both areas, the strategies they used to mobilize the rural society and the outcomes of their revolutionary efforts differed significantly.

On the North China plain, the Communists followed their predecessors' examples and employed the village community to organize peasants and mobilize resources during the War of Resistance against Japan. Two elements distinguished Communist mobilization from those of the late Qing state, the warlords and the Nationalists. On the one hand, the Communists exploited the strategy of enlisting the village as a collectivity to its full capacity and extreme limits. They organized everyone tightly into the village community and made all taxes (both material resources and manpower) the village's collective responsibility. They thus changed multi-layered state–society relations into a bilateral state–village relation. On the other hand, the Communists introduced a series of social and economic reforms into villages. These reforms, especially tax reforms, burdened landlords and rich peasants and relieved poor and middle peasants, thus narrowed the gap between the rich and the poor and revived the owner-cultivator stratum within the village. Under the Communist mobilization, the North China village was successfully restored to a homogeneous owner-cultivator community and transformed into the building block of the Communist state and the stronghold of the revolution. Supported by the human and material resources generated from the village, the Communist revolution finally succeeded in 1949.

In the Yangzi delta, the Communists' efforts focused on class structure. In the late 1920s, the Communists organized peasants to struggle against landlords. During the war, they also exploited absentee landlordism to mediate between landlords and tenants and to ensure the collection of taxes. However, the delta's class structure did not turn out to be a fertile ground for the revolution. Over the years the delta peasants, as Kathryn Bernhardt has argued, had "worked out their own strategies to cope with landlords and the state; the Communist programs thus had little appeal to them" (Bernhardt 1992: 202). Though the Communists could easily stir up rent resistance among the peasants, they could not push them to go beyond this immediate goal and engage in political insurrection. In the late 1920s they organized a series of peasant insurrections, but none of them lasted longer than a few days.

A more serious problem faced by the Communists was that they could not find army recruits and collect grain provisions from the delta peasants. Since the peasants here had many employment opportunities due to the highly commercialized and diversified rural economy, soldiering was rarely considered as an employment possibility. On the other hand, since most peasants were tenants who owed no tax obligation to the state, collecting grain from them would violate this time-honored tradition and illegitimize the Communists themselves. Without support in human and material resources the Communists simply could not organize, let alone sustain, armed struggles. This situation did not improve significantly during the war. The lack of army recruits still prevented the Communists from expanding their forces quickly. Because of this, they finally gave up the Yangzi delta as their main focus of wartime operation in Central China.

Furthermore, we need to distinguish between two stages of revolution building: the stage of initial building, and the stage of consolidated growth. In the first stage, the revolution started with a small group of activists operating in a local area, who needed volunteers to organize armed forces and easy targets to generate resources. At this stage the best strategy for the revolution to survive and sustain was to limit its operation to the countryside and carefully avoid direct confrontation with the strong government forces concentrated in cities and towns. Only after succeeding in the stage of initial building could the revolution go further to establish its base in this local area, and to mobilize and reorganize the local society in order to ensure long-term support in both human and material resources.

In the Yangzi delta, the Communists could not survive even the initial stage. They could not find volunteers to join their forces, nor could they extract resources from the countryside since most peasants were tenants, while the landlords and their wealth were concentrated in cities and towns. Though the Communists established guerilla bases during the war, they still lacked the effective institutional means to mobilize rural society, let alone obtain long-term support in resources, especially army recruits. On the North China plain, the initial stage of revolution building was much easier: the landless peasants were ready volunteers for revolutionary armies, and the resident landlords were easy targets for provisions. After this stage, the villages were a ready-made institution for organizing the populace and mobilizing resources.

Though both stages are important for making a revolution, the second stage is more crucial for a revolution to succeed. Therefore, the capacity of long-term support in resources is the most crucial factor that determines the fate of a revolution in a given area. Rural revolution pursued by the Chinese Communists was a protracted and arduous armed struggle. Making revolution therefore was not only an issue of short-term commitment by its participants; more importantly, it was an issue of securing long-term support in human and material resources from its constituency.[3] On the North China plain, the revolution took root deeply in the countryside and finally achieved success because it could secure a stable long-term support in resources by mobilizing and reorganizing the village. However, in the Yangzi delta, no such institution could be exploited to generate this long-term support. The North China village therefore is the key for us to understand the success of the revolution.

The important role of the North China village in the revolution has generally been overlooked in the existing literature.[4] The study of the wartime revolution focuses mainly on three issues: "the role of socioeconomic factors, the role of organization, and the impact of the war" (Hartford and Goldstein 1989: 15; see also Saich and van de Ven 1995: xiv). Thus, Mark Selden (1971) underscores the appeal of Communist socioeconomic reforms to the peasants, Tetsuya Kataoka (1974) and Yung-fa Chen (1986) stress the Communist leadership and the organizational weapons used by the Communists, while Chalmers Johnson (1962) emphasizes the impact of war and peasant nationalism.[5] These three issues reflect clearly the dichotomous attention among scholars in the field of the Chinese revolution (see Introduction). The war was, as a matter of fact, the historical setting, while the other two issues represent the structural approach (the role of socioeconomic factors) on the one hand and the agent approach (the role of organization) on the other.

No study has ever paid special attention to the North China village. The village is neither treated as a socioeconomic factor nor considered as an organization (since it was "natural" and not created by the revolution). However, no one can deny the fact that the socioeconomic reforms introduced into rural North China by the Communists targeted the village and aimed to strengthen the village. Also, all of the grassroots organizations set up by the Communists—such as local militias, peasant associations, and women's confederations—were built upon the village, defined by the village, and served to strengthen both the village itself as well as Communist control over the village. The village, both its communal structure and its social formation, were no doubt the product of long-term structural development. Meanwhile, it was the village that provided the Communists with an institutional means or organizational base, enabling them to maneuver. The North China village was thus the meeting point for interactions between structure and agents.

Scholars may overlook the North China village, but history will not forget: it was based on the North China villages and supported by the human and material resources generated from them, the Chinese Communists eventually grew into a formidable political and military force able to compete and finally defeat the Nationalists to win the revolution. Moreover, this North China experience, as a living heritage of the revolution, greatly shaped the patterns of Communist mobilization, organization, and control after 1949.

Appendix 1   The structure and
history of Kaixiangong

Kaixiangong (Kaihsienkung) is situated on the southeast bank of Lake Tai (Map A.1). In 1935, this community was composed of a total of 360 households. In Fei Hsiao-tung's opinion, it was a natural village. However, its inner structure was very similar to that of Huayangqiao: all the households in Kaixiangong were clustered in four separate *yu*, forming four distinct residential areas.[1] Moreover, these four residential areas were separated by waterways. One of the residential areas had its own name, Tanjiadun (Tan Family Mound). This multi-layered structure can be seen more clearly if we trace the history of Kaixiangong, and as a matter of fact, this history will tell us that originally the four clusters of Kaixiangong did not form a single village; rather, they were separate hamlets.

In the 1883 edition of the Suzhou prefectural gazetteer, both Kaiyuangong and Tanjiadun were listed in the *xiangdu tuyu cunzhen* section (the section of sub-county administrative units), but they belonged to different *du* and *tu*. Kaiyuangong belonged to the 13th *du* (*fu*) 7th *tu*, and Tanjiadun belonged to the 5th *du* 6th *tu* (*Suzhou fu zhi*, 965, 957).[2] The *du* and *tu* were artificial units for rural administration, especially for taxation.[3] In the Yangzi delta, the *tu* was a supra-village unit which usually contained several hamlets. For example, in the 13th *du* 7th *tu* to which Kaiyuangong belonged, there were altogether three hamlets, and the 5th *du* 6th *tu* had a total of five hamlets including Tanjiadun. The gazetteer quoted above records in the *xiangdu tuyu cunzhen* section that: "The *xiang*, *du*, *cun* and *zhen* (hamlets and towns) were used to organize the populace . . . [in this section] the names of *yu* and *cun* will be listed under the *du* and *tu* to which these *yu* and *cun* belonged" (720).[4] Clearly the *tu* was a supra-village unit which commanded the hamlets under it. Another source presents this more clearly: "The *xiang* commands the *du*, the *du* commands the *tu*, and what the *tu* commanded are *zhen* and *cun*" (*Wuxian zhi* 1934: 271). Under this administrative hierarchy, the *tu* usually contained several hamlets, but it rarely happened that one hamlet belonged to two or more *tu* at the same time. This principle is verified by the Suzhou prefectural gazetteer and many other local gazetteers. Because of this, we can confirm that at least in the 1880s, 50 years before Fei's field

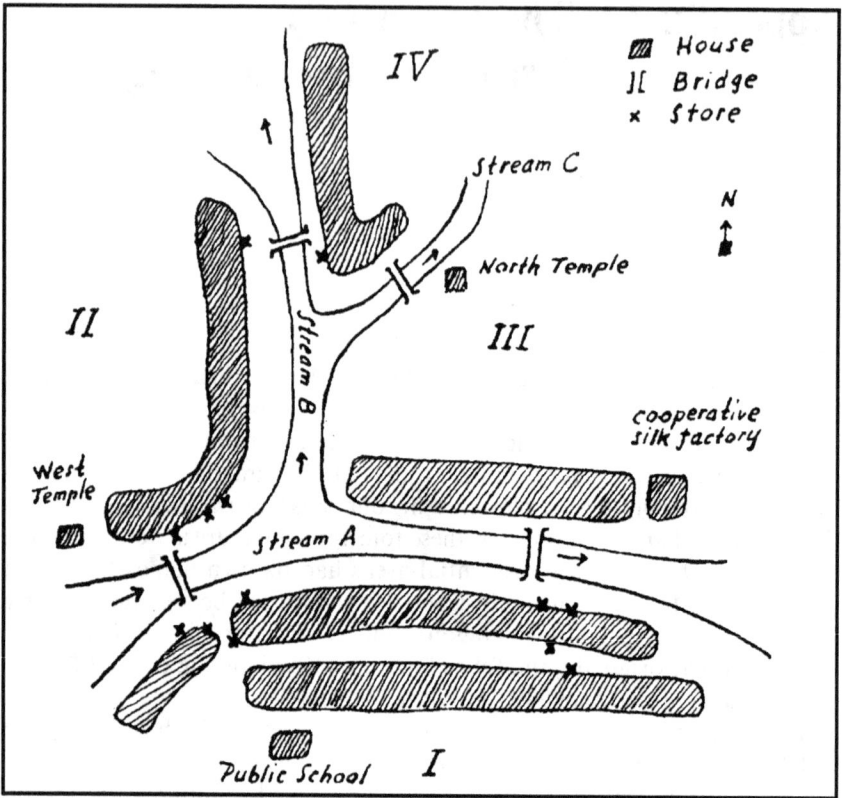

I	Ch'eng Kioh *yu* [Chengjiao *yu* 城角圩]	133 households
II	Liang Kioh *yu* [Liangjiao *yu* 凉角圩]	95 households
III	His Chang *yu* [Xichang *yu* 西长圩]	75 households
IV	T'an Chia Têng (Wu Tsŭ *yu*)	
	[Tanjiadun 淡家墩，Wuzi *yu* 無字圩]	57 households

Map A.1 Kaixiangong, 1930s

Sources: Fei, Hsiao-tung (1939: 18–20); Chinese edn. (1996: 13–15). Reproduced by permission of Taylor & Francis Books UK.

study, Kaiyuangong and Tanjiadun were two separate and distinct hamlets belonging to two different *tu* and *du*.

Since Kaixiangong was composed of four residential areas, the above discussion identified only one that was originally a separate hamlet: that was Tanjiadun in Wuzi *yu*. What about the other residential areas? Did they belong to a single village originally? Fei shows that the four *yu* in which the four residential areas were located were Chengjiao *yu*, Liangjiao *yu*, Xichang *yu*, and Wuzi *yu*, with 133, 95, 75, and 57 households living there respectively in 1936. Table A.1 shows 200 years of historical change in these four *yu*, and their *tu* affiliation.

Table A.1 Historical changes in Kaixiangong

Fei (1936) Name of yu	Suzhoufu zhi (1883) du/tu	Zhenzexian zhi (1746) du/tu
Chengjiao	13/9	10/9
Liangjiao	13/7	10/5
Xichang	13/7	10/5
Wu (Tanjiadun)	5/6[a]	5/15[a]

Sources: Fei (1939: Ch. 2); *Suzhou fu zhi* ([1883] 1970), vol. 2; *Zhenze xian zhi* ([1746] 1970), vol. 3.

[a] In the Chinese version of Fei's book (published in 1987), *wu* is written as a surname (吴), but in both prefecture and county gazetteers, a homophone is used, meaning "nothing" (無). Though the two words are different, I believe they refer to the same places. My reasons are: (1) There are another two *yu* in the 5th *du* 6th *tu* of the prefectural gazetteer, and in the 5th *du* and 15th *tu* of the county gazetteer that are also listed in the Wuzi *yu* of Fei's book: They are Xidou and Dou. In the Chinese version of Fei's book, however, these two *yu* are named Xiduo and Duo. The pronunciation of *dou* (斗) and *duo* (多) are very close, especially in the local dialect. (2) In the prefectural gazetteer, the 5th *du* 6th *tu* contained five villages, as mentioned above, one of which was Tanjiadun. Since in Fei's book Tanjiadun was located in the Wuzi *yu*, we can affirm that the *yu* named "wu" in the prefectural and county gazetteers was the Wuzi *yu* in Fei's book.

As we have seen already in the prefectural gazetteer, Kaiyuangong belonged to the 13th *du* 7th *tu*. From Table A.1 we know that Chengjiao *yu* and Liangjiao *yu* also belonged to the 13th *du* and 7th *tu*. This *tu* had a total of three hamlets and four *yu*. The three hamlets were Kaiyuangong, Taipingqiao (Peace Bridge), and Labakou (Trumpet Mouth). The four *yu* were Liangjiao, Xichang, Tian and Xintian. Except for Tian, the other three were later listed in Fei's book and belonged to Kaixiangong. From this we can determine that either one of the two hamlets located in these two *yu*, i.e. Liangjiao *yu* and Xichang *yu*, must have been Kaiyuangong in the 1880s. However, we cannot determine which it was, nor can we determine if both hamlets located in Liangjiao *yu* and Xichang *yu* belonged to Kaiyuangong at that time. One thing is clear, though: Chengjiao *yu*, the location of a hamlet with 133 households in 1935, belonged to another *tu* in 1883, the 13th *du* 9th *tu*. This *tu* had three hamlets and three *yu* (*Suzhou fu zhi* 1883: 966). As I mentioned before, the function of *tu* was for land registration and taxation. In the delta, every *tu* possessed one or more *yu*, and at the same time contained one or several hamlets. The hamlet or hamlets were of course located in this or these particular *yu*. It never happened that a *yu* belonged to one *tu* while the hamlet(s) located in it belonged to another *tu*.[5] So we can confirm that the hamlet located in Chengjiao *yu* could not belong to Kaiyuangong since the latter belonged to another *tu*.

Up to now, we can assert that 50 years before Fei did his field research, Kaixiangong was not a single village, but at least three separate and distinct hamlets. Moreover, they belonged to different *tu*, hence were organized into different supra-hamlet administrative units. Significantly, this situation can be traced back at least one hundred and thirty years before the 1880s. The 1746 edition of Zhenze county gazetteer states that these four *yu* belonged to three different *tu*. This situation remained unchanged in 1883 (see Table A.1). The only difference was the *tu* affiliation, though in the county gazetteer we cannot find the names of any of these three or four possible hamlets.[6] Obviously, the three hamlets became a single community, i.e. under the common community name of Kaixiangong only recently. Very possibly it was a development since the fall of the Qing Dynasty; a result of the collapse of the Qing rural administrative order.

Fei's book did not tell us if there was also a multi-layered sense of community identity in Kaixiangong similar to that found in Huayangqiao by Philip Huang. It also did not mention whether the residents of the four hamlets had their own communal or sub-communal identity. It is very clear that Fei did not refer to any of the local histories in his study, so he never realized that Kaixiangong originally and for a long time was not a single village as it was when Fei conducted his field study. Since Kaixiangong was composed of several originally distinct hamlets, it is reasonable for us to assume that the internal structure of Kaixiangong was similar to Huayangqiao. It was not a natural village, but was, to use Huang's term, "a cluster of villages (hamlets)," or, a compound village.

Appendix 2   Character list

Anhui	安徽
Anyang	安阳
Baita	白塔
Baixiang	柏乡
bao	保
Baoan xiang	保安乡
baodong shibushi yaojiang tiaojian	暴动是不是要讲条件
baojia	保甲
baolan	包揽
Baoshan	宝山
baoweituan	保卫团
baozheng	保正
baozheng shouzu	保证收租
Beixia	北夏
Beiyue qu	北岳区
benwei zhuyi	本位主义
biangong	变工
Bianqu canyihui	边区参议会
Bianzheng daobao	边政导报
bingfang	兵房
bingzheng fei	并征费
bingzheng yezhe	并征业者
bingzheng zongchu	并征总处
caizheng dongyuan	财政动员
cangfang	仓房
cangting	仓厅
Cangzhou	沧洲
caoliang	漕粮
caozhe	漕折
ceshu	册书
Changshu	常熟
Changshu minzhong kangri ziweidui	常熟民众抗日自卫队
Changzhou	常州

Chen Pixian	陈丕显
Chen Yi	陈毅
Chen Yun	陈云
Chengjiao	城角
chengli	城里
cheyao	车徭
Chongming	崇明
Chuansha	川沙
cuchahou	粗茶候
cuizuju	催租局
cun	村
cun wei benwei	村为本位
cundong	村董
cunfu	村副
cungongsuo	村公所
cunliu	存留
cunmin dahui	村民大会
cuntan jingkuan	村摊警款
cunzhang	村长
cunzheng	村正
cunzhi	村治
da	墷
Dabeiguan	大北关
Dadaohui	大刀会
dageng	打更
dahu	大户
daishouzu	代收租
Danyang	丹阳
Daoguang	道光
datao	搭套
dayan tanpai	大盐摊派
Dayandi	大眼滴
Deng Zhenxun	邓振询
Deye shijianhui	德业实践会
di wei fei wan	敌伪匪顽
dianbao	佃保
Dianfa xiang	殿发乡
dianli	典吏
dibao	地保
Didaozhan	地道战
diding	地丁
difang	地方
difang shouru	地方收入
dijiashui	地价税
Dileizhan	地雷战

Dingjia cun	丁家村
Dingxian	定县
Dong'a	东阿
dongcao	冬漕
Donglu	东路
dongshi	董事
Dongting qu	东亭区
Dongzhao cun	东召村
dou	斗
du	都
Du Fuxin	杜复新
duo	多
Enxian	恩县
Fan Yulin	樊玉琳
feichai	飞差
feichu baojiazhi, jianli cunzhangzhi	废除保甲制，建立村长制
Feixiang	肥乡
fengjian shili	封建势力
Fengrun	丰润
Fengxian	奉贤
Fu Zuoyi	傅作义
fuli	富力
fushu	夫束
Fushui guanli chu	赋税管理处
futou	夫头
Fuzi hui	父子会
Gailiang fengsuhui	改良风俗会
Gaojiada	高家埭
Gaoyingxiang	高英巷
Gongchaiju	公差局
gongguqu	巩固区
gongkan yipo	公看义坡
gongzhai tanpai	公债摊派
gongzhan	公栈
Gu Fusheng	顾复生
Guan Wenwei	管文蔚
Guangfu zhen	光福镇
Guangxu	光绪
Guangzong xian	广宗县
Guanxian	冠县
Guanyin hui	观音会
guanzu	官租
guishou	柜收
guojia shouru	国家收入

Guoqu (wangu zhengfu) nayang hen, zhuade nayang lihai, wo dou wei chuguofu, xianzai dou zuzhi haole, pao dou pao budiao.	过去(顽固政府)那样狠，抓得那样厉害，我都未出过伏，现在都组织好了，跑都跑不掉。
guozuo	过左
Haining	海宁
hao	号
Hao Guoliang	郝国梁
haocheng xiangcun yundong er xiangcun budong.	号称乡村运动而乡村不动
Hebei	河北
Hejiada	何家埭
Hejin cun	鹤金村
heli fudan	合理负担
Henan	河南
Hongqianghui	红枪会
Houxiazhai	後夏寨
huahu	花户
Huang Ang	黄卬
Huang Ren	黄仁
Huang Yanpei	黄炎培
Huangqiao juezhan	黄桥决战
Huangshahui	黄纱会
huanzu huanxi	还租还息
Huapaohui	花炮会
huatian	滑田
Huayangqiao	华阳桥
Huazhong ju	华中局
hufang	户房
hui	会
Huibei	惠北
huishou	会首
huohao	火耗
huoquan	活圈
Huqiao	胡桥
Hushi yizhuang	胡氏义庄
Huzhou	湖州
Jiading	嘉定
Jianbang xiang	戩浜乡
jiancha weiyuanhui	监察委员会
Jianchi ludong kangri shida gangling	坚持路东抗日十大纲领
Jiang Hengyuan	江恒源
Jiang Weiqing	江渭清
Jiangnan	江南
Jiangnan kangri ziwei zongtun	江南抗日自卫总团

Jiangsu	江苏
Jiangsu shengjian	江苏省鉴
Jiangsu shengli jiaoyu xueyuan	江苏省立教育学院
Jiangyin	江阴
jiaoyu zhuankuan	教育专款
Jiashan	嘉善
Jiaxing	嘉兴
jicen zhengquan	基层政权
Jimuhui	辑睦会
Jinchaji kangri genjudi	晋察冀抗日根据地
Jing Tingbing	景廷宾
Jingji sheji weiyuanhui	经济设计委员会
jingshu	经书
Jinling daxue nongxueyuan	金陵大学农学院
Jintan	金坛
Jinxiao xiang	旌孝乡
jiuguo gongliang	救国公粮
jiuguojuan	救国捐
jiuzu huafu	就租划赋
Jizhong qu	冀中区
ju	局
jujin yanxi	醵金演戏
juntian junyi	均田均役
juren	举人
Kaixiangong	开弦弓
Kaiyuangong	开元弓
kangjuan kangshui, fandui haoshen cunzhang	抗捐抗税，反对豪绅村长
kangri minzhu genjudi	抗日民主根据地
kangwei junliang he jingfei	抗卫军粮和经费
Kangxi	康熙
kangzu kangxi	抗租抗息
keguan kunnan	客观困难
kunbao	捆保
kundian	捆垫
Kunshan	昆山
kuojun weiyuanhui	扩军委员会
Labakou	喇叭口
Lao Shier	老施二
laoniu poche, tuoni daishui	老牛破车，拖泥带水
Laonong xueyuan	劳农学院
laoren	老人
Li Jianmo	李建模
Li Yiqing	李亦卿
liang cong zu chu	粮从租出

Liang Shuming	梁漱溟
liangbian xiang zhongjian ji	两边向中间挤
Liangjiao	凉角
liangmian fudan	两面负担
liangtou xiao, zhongjian da	两头小，中间大
Liangxiang	良乡
liangzhang	粮长
Lianzhuanghui	联庄会
lijia	里甲
lijin	厘金
Lin Youyong	林有用
Linqing	临清
linshi tanpai	临时摊派
lishou guanjie	吏收官解
lishu	吏书
Liu Lantao	刘澜涛
Liu Shaoqi	刘少奇
Liuxiangcun	刘巷村
lizhang	里长
Lu Danan	陆大囡
Luanzhou	滦州
Lujiadajun	陆家埭
Ma Wenhuan	马文焕
maidi bu maiquan	卖地不卖圈
Mahui	马会
maijihui	买鸡会
maimichi	买米吃
Maoshan gengjudi	茅山根据地
Mi Digang	米迪刚
Mi Jiansan	米鉴三
mi'e	米额
mingyun gongzuo huiyi	民运工作会议
Minkang	民抗
Minzhong jiaoyu yuan	民众教育院
nan kun yu fu, bei kun yu yi.	南困于赋，北困于役
Nanda	南埭
Nangong	南宫
Nanhui	南汇
Nantong	南通
Nashui zuhe	纳税组合
neili	内力
Ningbo	宁波
paijia	牌甲
Pan Nianzu	潘念祖
Peng Zhen	彭真

Pinggu	平古
Pinghu	平湖
Pingmin jiaoyu cujinghui	平民教育促进会
pingyu	平余
pingzu weiyuanhui	评租委员会
Qianlong	乾隆
qingchahou	清茶候
Qingmiaohui	青苗会
Qingmiaoshe	青苗社
Qingming hui	清明会
Qingpu	青浦
qingquan	青圈
qingxiang	清乡
qishui	契税
Qiubaoshe	秋保社
qiukan chengse	秋勘成色
Qixiao zhen	七溆镇
qizhongtian	起种田
quxiang zhenbao shiyefei	区乡镇保事业费
rangzu rangxi	让租让息
Rehe	热河
Ren Tianshi	任天石
renban dibuban	人搬地不搬
ri jiu sheng bi	日久生弊
Rusong	如松
sankan	散看
sanmian fudan	三面负担
Shajiabang	沙家浜
Shajing	沙井
Shandong	山东
Shandong xiangcun jianshe yanjiuyuan	山东乡村建设研究院
Shanggong hui	上供会
shangmang	上忙 (芒)
Shangyu	上虞
Shaoxing	绍兴
she	社
Shen Lansheng	申阑生
sheng zhengshui	省正税
sheng zhuanshui	省专税
Shenpengshe	神棚社
Shi Zhongyi	施中一
shibing	师宾
shoushi	首事
shouzu fenchu	收租分处

shouzu weiyuanhui	收租委员会
shouzu zongzhan	收租总栈
shouzuju	收租局
Shuangshi gangling	双十纲领
shudi zhuyi	属地主义
Shulu	束鹿
Shunde fu	顺德府
shunzhuang gongfu	顺庄供赋
shuohuaren	说话人
Sibeichai	寺北柴
siling sai niumao, zhuren bian tianxia	司令赛牛毛，主任遍天下
siquan	死圈
Song Shaowen	宋劭文
Songjiang	松江
Subei	苏北
Suiyuan	绥远
Sun Faxu	孙发绪
Sunan kangri gengjudi	苏南抗日根据地
Sunan shizheng gangling	苏南施政纲领
Sunan xingzheng gongshu	苏南行政公署
Sunjiaxiang	孙家巷
Suwanqu dangwei	苏皖区党委
Suxian	宿县
Suzhou	苏州
Taicang	太仓
Taiping xiang	太平乡
Taipingqiao	太平桥
Taishan she	泰山社
Taitou	台头
Tan Zhenlin	谭震林
tanding rudi	摊丁入地
Tang Dongqi	汤东其
tangzhang	塘长
Tanjiadun	谈家墩
tankun	摊款
tanpai	摊派
tanpai jiajuan, shangxia jiaokun	摊派加捐，上下交困
Tengxian	滕县
tewei	特委
tianfu fujia	田赋附加
Tianmenhui	天门会
tianye gonghui	田业公会
Tongxiang	桐乡
tongyi leijingshui	统一累进税
Touzongmiao	头总庙

tu	图
Tu Zhishen	屠之申
tuidong shehui, zuzhi xiangcun	推动社会，组织乡村
tuochan ganbu	脱产干部
Wang Qinglong	王庆龙
Weitingshan	唯亭山
wu	吴
wu	無
wu de qi gong	误得起工
Wujiang	吴江
Wujin	武进
Wuxi	无锡
Wuxian	吴县
Wuxing	吴兴
Wuzhong	吴中
Wuzi	無字
xiamang	下忙 (芒)
xian fujia	县附加
xian zhengshui	县正税
Xian zuzhi fa	县自治法
xiang	乡
xiangbao	乡保
xiangcun jianshe	乡村建设
xiangdi	乡地
Xianghuo hui	香火会
xianglao	乡老
Xiangnong xuexiao	乡农学校
xiangqu dianmin	乡曲佃民
xiangtou	香头
xiangxia	乡下
xiangxue cunxue	乡学村学
xiangyue	乡约
xiangzhang chiyu chirou, baozhang	乡长吃鱼吃肉，保长头五头六，
touwu touliu, huzhang dati xiaoku	户长大啼小哭
xiangzhen linlu	乡镇邻闾
xiannian	现年
Xiaodingxiang	小丁巷
xiaodonghui	校董会
xiaohu	小户
Xiaoshan	萧山
xiaxiang	下乡
xichang	西长
xidou	西斗
xiduo	西多
xiehui	谢会

Xietang zhen	斜塘镇
Xihui	戏会
Xilihangbang	西里行浜
Xingtai	邢台
xingzheng cun	行政村
Xintian	新天
xinzheng	新政
Xu Shen	徐申
Xu Shuren	徐树人
Xubushanqiao	许步山桥
Xue Bingrong	薛炳荣
Xue Yulin	薛玉林
Xuejiada	薛家埭
xuezhong	学众
Xugongqiao	徐公桥
Xujia	盱嘉
Yan Xishan	阎锡山
Yan Yangchu	晏阳初
Yang Shangkun	杨尚昆
Yang Yuan	杨源
yange jianju sizi shouzu	严格检举私自收租
Yangmuqiao	杨木桥
yanhu	烟户
Yanjiashang	严家上
Yanwang hui	阎王会
yanxi choushen	演戏酬神
Yaojing	姚泾
yaozhang shi lingdao	要帐式领导
yashui	牙税
Ye Fei	叶飞
yezhu	业主
yibei tianxia	衣被天下
yifa	役法
yin'e	银额
yingyeshui	营业税
Yinli xieshe	因利协社
Yipohui	义坡会
Yixing	宜兴
you dianhu daiwei jiaona	由佃户代为缴纳
Youdai kangri jiashu weiyuanhui	优待抗日家属委员会
youjiqu	游击区
Youkang weiyuanhui	优抗委员会
youqian chuqian, qiaoduo duochu, qianshao shaochu	有钱出钱，钱多多出，钱少少出
yu	圩

Yuan Shikai	袁世凯
yuye	圩业
zafan chaiyao	杂泛差徭
zafu	杂赋
Zeng Guofan	曾国藩
Zhaicheng	翟城
zhandi dongyuan weiyuanhui	战地动员委员会
Zhang Jie	张傑
Zhang Wentian	张闻天
Zhangjiatun	张家屯
Zhao Shuyu	赵叔愚
Zhao Xixiao	赵锡孝
zhejia	折价
Zhejiang	浙江
Zhejiangsheng difang zizhi zhuanxiu xuexiao	浙江省地方自治专修学校
zhen	镇
zhengshe heyi	政社合一
Zhengxiang	郑巷
Zhenjiang	镇江
Zhenze	震泽
zhi'anfei	治安费
Zhili	直隶
zhishu	知数
zhiying jiguan	支应机关
Zhonggong suwan quwei	中共苏皖区委
Zhonghua zhiye jiaoyushe	中华职业教育社
Zhongshan cun	中山村
zhongxin chayuan	中心茶园
zhongyao	重要
Zhongyuan ju	中原局
Zhou Enlai	周恩来
Zhou Hengqi	周恒祺
zhuangzhang	庄长
Zhuhui xiang	祝会乡
zhuizuchu	追租处
zhuyao	主要
zifeng tougui	自封投柜
zitian	自田
ziye	自业
zongjia	总甲
Zouping	邹平
zuce	租册
zufu bingzheng	租赋并征
zuke	租课

zumeng shajie, yikang tianzhu	诅盟歃结，以抗田主
zuogui shoutou	坐柜收头
zuoqing	左倾
Zuxi tiaojie weiyuanhui	租息调解委员会
zuye	租业
zuzhan	租栈
Zuzong she	祖宗社

Appendix 3   Conversion of Chinese measurements

1 mu = 1/6 acre = 1/15 hectare
1 catty = 1.1 pound = 0.5 kilogram
1 shi ≈ 160 catties
1 liang = 1/16 catty = 31.25 grams ≈ 1 ounce

Notes

Introduction

1 As a matter of fact, almost all important works on rural China in the modern period have focused on these two areas. For the North China plain, these are Sidney Gamble's *North China Villages: Social, Political, and Economic Activities Before 1933* (1963), Ramon Myers' *The Chinese Peasant Economy, Agricultural Development in Hopei and Shantung, 1890–1949* (1970), Elizabeth Perry's *Rebels and Revolutionaries in North China, 1845–1945* (1980), Philip Huang's *The Peasant Economy and Social Change in North China* (1985), Joseph Esherick's *The Origin of the Boxer Uprising* (1987), and Prasenjit Duara's *Culture, Power, and the State: Rural North China, 1900–1942* (1988). As for the Yangzi delta, these are Fei Hsiao-tung's *Peasant Life in China: A Field Study of Country Life in the Yangtze Valley* (1939), David Faure's *The Rural Economy of Pre-Liberation China: Trade Expansion and Peasant Livelihood in Jiangsu and Guangdong, 1870 to 1937* (1989), Philip Huang's *The Peasant Family and Rural Development in the Yangzi Delta, 1350–1988* (1990), and Kathryn Bernhardt's *Rents, Taxes, and Peasant Resistance: The Lower Yangzi Region, 1840–1950* (1992). However, the list here is by no means complete, it only names several important studies.
2 For example, both Philip Huang (1985) and Prasenjit Duara (1988) conclude that the deterioration of rural politics due to excessive state intrusion into and extraction of resources from North China villages in the first half of the twentieth century was a prerequisite for the success of Communist mobilization during the War of Resistance.
3 One of few exceptions is Elizabeth Perry's study of rural Huaibei (Northern Anhui Province). In this study, Perry explores the historical linkage between peasant rebellions and the Communist revolution (Perry 1980). In his study of the Yangzi delta, Philip Huang covers both the pre-revolution period and the post-revolution era. But his comparison is between these two periods, it does not deal with the revolution itself. More recently, Ralph Thaxton, Jr. also has discussed the connections between Communist mobilization and protracted community struggle for survival in rural North China (Thaxton 1997).
4 We have already mentioned past scholarship on rural political change in the two areas in note 1. For a brief synopsis of past scholarship on the revolution, see the Introduction ("Perspectives on the Chinese Communist Revolution") in Kathleen Hartford and Steve M. Goldstein (eds.) *Single Sparks: China's Rural Revolutions* (1989). The most important works on this topic are Chalmers Johnson's *Peasant Nationalism and Communist Power, the Emergence of Revolutionary China, 1937–1945* (1962), Mark Selden's *The Yenan Way in Revolutionary China* (1971), Tetsuya Kataoka's *Resistance and Revolution in China, the Communists and the Second United Front* (1974), and Chen Yung-fa's *Making Revolution: the Communist*

Movement in Eastern and Central China, 1937–1945 (1986). These works actually deal with the revolution during the war. There are also numerous studies on the revolution in the prewar period.

5 Prasenjit Duara, for example, emphasizes that state strengthening had greatly "transformed local society," and "changed the links between politics, culture, and society in rural North China" (Duara 1988: 1).

Chapter 1 Comparison of rural communities in the North China plain and the Yangzi delta

1 In this study, the late Qing period covers the last century of the dynasty, but the major political changes in rural China that will be discussed in the book all took place after the outbreak of the Taiping Rebellion in 1851.

2 The North China plain covers a very large area, including a major part of Hebei and Henan, the western part of Shandong, and the northern part of Anhui and Jiangsu.

3 Another set of data collected by Huang shows that between 1883 and 1948, population in 16 Hebei prefectures and districts increased 27 percent; and between 1820 and 1948, the population in four northwest Shandong prefectures and districts increased 17 percent (Huang 1985: 323). We should note that all population data discussed here are from the Qing registries and their accuracy is highly questionable.

4 Sidney Gamble, an American sociologist, who did extensive field studies in rural North China during the 1920s, also maintains this (see Gamble 1963: 109).

5 Several different surveys carried out in the 1930s had very similar results regarding the proportion of owner-cultivators in Hebei and Shandong. For example, surveys by the Central Agricultural Experimental Station in 1935, surveys performed in the 1930s by the research office of the Mantetsu (the South Manchurian Railway Company), and surveys by John Lossing Buck, show that the percentage of owner-cultivators in Hebei was 67 percent, 68 percent, and 79.8 percent respectively; and in Shandong, 74 percent, 72 percent, and 77.5 percent (cited in Myers 1970: 303).

6 During the 1920s and the 1930s, Chinese scholars made many field studies of various kinds of mutual aid groups in North China villages, such as Yao Yong's "*Yudong xiangcun zhuzhi zhi yanjiu* (A study of rural organizations in East Henan)"; Qiao Qiming's "*Anhui Suxian yuanyou xiangcun zuzhi zhi gaikuang* (A survey of traditional rural organizations in Su county, Anhui province)"; Wang Yaoyu's "*Shandong Changyixian nongcun de xiaomaozi hui* (The filial cap society in rural Changyi County, Shandong)". These field studies provide us with very detailed information about different forms of cooperation among villagers.

7 For example, in Shajing, there was *Shanggong hui* (Society of sacrifice); in Sibeichai, *Fuzi hui* (Father and sons society) and *Guanyin hui* (Society of Bodhisattva); in Houjiaying, *Qingming hui* (Pure brightness society) and *Xianghuo hui* (Incense society); in Wudian, *Shanggong hui* (Society of sacrifice); in Houxiazhai, *Zuzong she* (Ancestor society), *Taishan she* (Association of Mt. Tai), and *Yanwang hui* (Society of Yama), etc.

8 All these activities were of course not purely religious and spiritual ones, they often served definite secular and material purposes and interests simultaneously. However, they were first of all religious activities.

9 In 1914, the magistrate Sun Faxu launched a secularization movement in the county. He asked villagers to destroy idols and transform temples into schools. In this year alone, 200 temples were destroyed in Dongting *qu* (Li Jinghan 1933: 423).

10 This was a quite common situation in rural North China. Hsiao has discussed this in his book (Hsiao 1960: 276).

11 In Chinese, the single word *hui* has three meanings: meeting, gathering, association. Originally, *hui* meant meeting or gathering, its extended meaning is association. In rural North China *hui* is actually used in these two ways simultaneously. It sometimes refers to meetings or gatherings, sometimes associations. The meaning depends on context. Generally, during the gathering times, it means meeting; during the time of adjournment, it means association.

12 In nineteenth-century North China, this level of sub-county administration usually incorporated a group of 20-odd villages. The officer at this level was called *xiangbao* in many places (for the status and function of *xiangbao*, see Huang 1985: 224–231).

13 Though Smith uses the term "village headmen," he is actually referring to the types of village leaders discussed here; indeed, according to Smith, the "headmen" were called *xianglao* (hsiang lao) and *shoushiren* (shou shih jen) locally (1899: 227). These titles obviously refer to informal village councilors, not formal village officers. They should not be confused with the formal *cunzhang* and *cunfu* found in twentieth-century North China villages.

14 Generally, during the Qing, the Yangzi delta included the six prefectures of Suzhou, Songjiang, Changzhou, Hangzhou, Jiaxing, and Huzhou and Taicang District. This region is commonly referred as *Jiangnan liufu* (lit. the six prefectures south of the Yangzi River), or simply Jiangnan. In this study, "the Yangzi delta" and "Jiangnan" are used interchangeably.

15 In Chinese, there are no corresponding words to distinguish "village" from "hamlet." The word *cun* or *zhuang* is widely used to denote rural settlements regardless of their size. In the Yangzi delta, *zhuang* is rarely used; *cun* being the term generally employed in gazetteers. Nevertheless, the real meaning or actual definition of *cun* differs greatly between gazetteers.

16 Contemporary field studies also support this general picture of the Delta's hamlets. For example, Cao Jinqing, Zhang Letian and Chen Zhongya's recent study about rural Northern Zhejiang shows that in Haining County the average size of hamlets (*Zirancun*) is 33 households (Cao *et al.* 1995: 3). If we take into consideration the fact that China's population doubled during the People's Republic period, the actual size of a hamlet in this area should have been less than 20 households in the late nineteenth and early twentieth centuries.

17 *Da* (locally pronounced *dai*) is local parlance for a small settlement or hamlet. Originally, this word meant an earth bank. In this area, people used to build their hamlets on or near river banks for easy access to water. The word "*da*" was thus used very often to refer to these hamlets.

18 However, I do not maintain that all the delta's rural communities matched the type as seen in Huayangqiao. Rather, we will argue that it was a very common type of rural community in this area.

19 They were Touzongmiao in Nantong, Xiaodingxiang in Wuxi, Yanjiashang in Changshu, Yaojin in Taicang, Dingjiacun in Jiading, Sunjiaxiang in Wuxian, Kaixiangong in Wujiang, and Huayangqiao in Songjiang.

20 Of course, even if we agree that Kaixiangong was a compound community similar to Huayangqiao, it was still large by local standards. However, there is no further information that could help us to explain this.

21 For example, in Kaixiangong, the biggest *yu* enclosed 986.4 *mu* and the smallest was only 8.5 *mu* (Fei 1939: 18).

22 The 1746 edition of *Zhenze xian zhi* also mentioned this kind of organized water drainage. It said that in the event of a flood, peasants would gather *jigao* pumps to drain water. They beat drums and gongs to wake people and used a water-clock to assign the time for workshifts (*Zhenze xian zhi* 1970 [1746]: 932).

23 This was especially true in low-lying rice growing areas. For example, in the suburban area of Suzhou, where most *yu* housed more than one hamlet, water

control at the *yu* level was often a multi-hamlet endeavor (*Suzhou fu zhi* 1970 [1883]: vols 29–32).

24 Fei's book does not tell if there was a community-wide water control system in Kaixiangong. Since the community was located in several *yu*, it seems there was no such need. So the community-wide religious activity might have played a more important role in organizing this compound village.

25 We should note that the two circles of water control and collective religious activities were not necessarily coincidental, though they often overlapped. This situation made the structure of the rural community more complicated, but less coherent.

26 Under the Qing household registration system, the *yanhu* differed from the *huahu* (miscellaneous household), for it was used in the *baojia* registration, while the latter was in the *lijia* registration (Sun Haiquan 1990: 80). The reason for it being called *yanhu* (smoking household) is that every domestic group with its own stove was counted by the *baojia* as an independent household. For the Qing *baojia* and *lijia* system, see Sun Haiquan's research (Sun 1990, 1994).

27 As Philip Huang has forcefully argued, the delta's commercialization was driven by three different forces, and he therefore distinguished three different kinds of commercialization: extraction-driven, survival-driven, and enterprise-driven commercialization (Huang 1990: 102).

28 Cao thus argues that in the delta the market town was the center of rural economic and political lives, and the basic economic unit in the delta should be a market town-centered community (Cao Xingsui 1989: 151).

Chapter 2 State and rural society in the late Qing

1 Since the 1960s, more and more China historians in the United States have devoted themselves to local studies in order to advance Chinese studies. With few exceptions, most of these local studies have been focused on a particular area. This new trend of intellectual efforts has already yielded plentiful results. This approach of focusing on a single area seems to dominate the Chinese studies, especially in the field of socio-economic history. The few exceptions are David Faure (1989) and Philip Huang (1990). Faure compared rural economy between Jiangsu and Guangdong provinces while Huang compared socio-economic development between the North China Plain and the Yangzi delta. Their works provide a good start for comparative regional studies and inspired me (especially Huang's work which not only compared the socio-economic structure of the two regions but also explored different state–society relations in these two regions) in the study.

2 As a matter of fact, the tax reforms of the Yongzheng Reign were a synthesis of a series of tax reforms inaugurated in the late Ming and continued in the early Qing. The purpose of these reforms was to commute labor services into the land tax and to simplify the contents as well as the procedures of taxation.

3 The Qing land tax was divided into two categories after the tax reforms of early Qing. One was *diding* which reflected the amalgamation of the labor service tax and the land tax. The other was *caoliang* (the tribute grain). The *diding* was universal to all 18 provinces of China Proper, but the *caoliang* was only levied in eight provinces. These provinces were Henan, Shandong, Anhui, Jiangsu, Zhejiang, Jiangxi, Hunan, Hubei (HBZL 1968: vol. 19).

4 In practice, however, different kinds of tax farming still existed throughout the Qing in different localities (Wang 1973: 39–48; Cong Hanxiang 1995; Zhu Hanguo and Wang Yinhuan 2004; Zheng Qidong 2004). But the dominant and also officially sanctioned system of tax collection and delivery was the one we discussed here, i.e. the taxpayers paid their taxes directly to the government treasury (HBZL 1968: vol. 9).

5 The tax collection device during the Ming dynasty was called *lijia* and *liangzhang* (the *liangzhang* system was only practiced in the early Ming) which required landowners to take turns to collect taxes for his *li* or *jia* (i.e. his community or neighborhood) and deliver them to the government treasuries. The people who provided these services were responsible for any loss in the process of collection, and they were also asked to pay for tax arrears. Many people became bankrupt (*Mingshi*, vol. 78; see also Liang 1957). This notorious system was finally given up by the late Ming's Single Whip Reform. The principle of the reform was to combine all taxes and labor services and impose this single tax on land. However, this reform was not carried out thoroughly and universally. The remnants of the old system were still lingering on in many areas well into the early Qing.

6 In Qing times, the two tax seasons were called *shangmang* (the first busy season) and *xiamang* (the second busy season). In some areas, especially areas where tributary grain was collected, there were three tax seasons. For example, in Wujing, Jiangsu, besides the above mentioned two, another one was called *dongcao* (the Winter tribute grain) (Wan *et al.* 1934: 62).

7 According to Qing regulations, only the revenue department (*hufang*, in charge of taxation) and military affairs department (*binfang*) under the county magistrate could hire three chief clerks (called *dianli* or *lishu*), all other departments such as civil office (*li*), rites (*li*), punishment (*xin*), and public works (*gong*), could hire only one or two chief clerks. Later, the number of chief clerks of the military affairs was reduced to only one (Li Rongzhong 1989: 1: 97). The chief clerks in each department then hired clerks (*jingshu*) to handle the department's business. The number of clerks in each department was determined by the workload of the department, and of course with the approval of the magistrate. In late Qing Baxian County (Sichuan), for example, the revenue department always maintained the largest workforce, ranging from 60 to more than 80 clerks, and this does not include the large number of assistants hired by clerks (Li Rongzhong 1989: 1: 96–97). According to one estimate, on average, the salaried staff in the revenue department was between several dozen to a hundred in a county, but there were many unsalaried people whose number could run to as high as a thousand (Zheng Qidong 2004: 226). There are quite a few case studies on land taxation made by the Rural Reconstruction Committee of the Executive Yuan (Xingzhengyuan nongcun fuxing weiyuanhui) during the 1930s. From these we can find many descriptions about the actual tax collection procedures. All these studies are now published as a large series edited by Xiao Zheng, under the general title: *Materials on Land Problems in Mainland China during the 1930s*.

8 The capacity of the regular taxation system to increase tax revenue was quite limited. In particular, it had little room to generate extra revenue to meet the government's irregular financial needs.

9 Since all of the labor services were commuted into the land tax during the Qing, there should have been no labor service at all. But in reality, various temporary and extra, hence irregular, labor services were sometimes still required. Many of these irregular tax needs may not have been sanctioned by the central government, but they were often found in different localities.

10 One reason for the existence of irregular taxes was that very often the government funds for various projects were not enough to cover the expenses, so the local government was asked for assistance. Of course, finally it was the local people who had to submit themselves to this kind of extortion (for further information, see Chen Zhenghan *et al.* 1989, vol. 3, pt. 1, pp. 53–61; *Qingshigao* 1976: vol. 121).

11 Actually, this policy of compensation of heavy labor service with light land tax was applied to the whole of North China, not just Zhili alone. As one Qing

source puts it: "The government policy for [balancing] land tax and labor service is constant. Generally, in the Southeastern provinces, the land tax is heavy but the labor service is light; while in Northwestern provinces, the land tax is light but the labor service is heavy" (*Qingshigao* 1976: vol. 121, p. 3548; see also JSXB 1972: vol. 38).

12 *She* was a common supra-village administrative unit found in Qing North China. The number of villages in each *she* varied in different localities. In Luanzhou, the average number of villages in each *she* was about 20 (*Luanzhou zhi* [1898] 1969: 323).

13 Luanzhou's case was not an isolated one, it was rather common in North China. For example, in Luancheng County, Zhili, all extra labor services were allocated equally among villages. Since villages differed greatly in their size and wealth, the actual burden on each village was very uneven. Some villages paid 70 to 80 cash (*qian*) per *mu* a year, while some other villages paid up to 200 to 300 cash per *mu*. Though local people asked many times for this situation to be changed, no magistrate had made any attempt to do so (Beiyang 6: 12a).

In Liangxiang County, there was also a stone tablet erected in 1885 (Guangxu 11). It was to commemorate a reform of cart service identical to the one conducted in Luozhou District. Though the gazetteer does not clearly tell us whether the cart service was imposed on a village collectively or on villagers individually, we can infer that the same methods were employed here (*Liangxiang xian zhi* [1924] 1968: 481–483).

14 In Chinese, *tan* means to allocate, and *pai* means to assign. Both words suggest the coercive nature of these irregular taxes. *Kuan* means money or fund. In Qing sources, *tan* and *pai* very often were used separately in various governmental documents and personal writings. Their appearance together as a common term and a special category in taxation was ostensibly a late Qing phenomenon. A brief preface to *Shihuozhi* (the treatise on economy) of *Qingshigao* (Qing history) states:

> From the Daoguang and Xianfeng periods (1820–61) on, the country was opened to foreign trade, and many troubles came out of this situation. The governmental expenditures expanded dramatically, but its income was shrinking. The people in power did not know the general trend of the world; they launched wars and incurred disasters. The government treasury was squandered by indemnities which amounted to more than 400 million [*taels*] . . . [therefore the government] imposed levies [on people and asked them] to contribute more taxes. Both the government and the society were beset with financial crises [*tanpai jiajuan, neiwai jiaokun*].

However, I do not know exactly when *tankuan* as a term first appeared. Very possibly this term became popular during the New Policy period.

15 These subjects will be discussed further in Chapter 3.

16 The final accomplishment of this process had to wait until the Communists established their regime in rural North China during the period of the War of Resistance against Japan. The Communist mobilization in North China will be discussed in Chapter 5.

17 The same appreciation can be found in many local gazetteers (*Songjiang fu xuzhi* [1883] 1975: 1487; *Changshu xian zhi* [1904] 1979: 107). The one from the Jiading gazetteer is most cheerful:

> During the Shunzhi and Kangxi periods (1644–1722), the collection and delivery of tax was changed from using local people to a system in which the government undertook those tasks by itself. The labor services that

previously had been imposed on male adults were commuted into silver and the government used this money to hire people. The local people were no longer disturbed (by labor services) since. Compared to the situation in the Ming times, this was like freeing people from water and fire and letting them rest on a cool mat.

(*Jiading xian xuzhi* [1930] 1970: 219)

18 The actual method of *juntian junyi* was to take the total land of a county as a whole and divide it into certain number of *tu*, each of which was further divided into ten *jia*. Then the labor services were imposed equally on the land of each *jia* (*Suzhou fu zhi*, [1883] 1970: 360; see also Jiang 1991; Sun 1994). The principle of this reform was to impose the burden of labor services on owned land.

19 The *juntian junyi* became the law for all of Jiangsu in 1674, and was later implemented in the whole Yangzi delta area, while the *lijia* system of collecting taxes became illegal (Dennerline 1975: 119).

20 People may well doubt the authenticity of the picture depicted above. Since we do not have sufficient evidence to either confirm or deny whether this system worked exactly as designed, we should be cautious to avoid exaggeration. But judging from many Qing local gazetteers, we can find the reality was not far from this picture. The following is a very interesting example which told us how the new system worked and even changed local people's character.

Huang Ang, an erudite and rigorous scholar from the eighteenth century, wrote of an interesting change of local customs in Wuxi and Jingui counties brought about by this tax reform. According to Huang, originally the local people in these two counties were pure, simple and unsophisticated. They were afraid of dealing with the government and its functionaries. All the taxes were thus handled by middlemen. However, during the Yongzheng reign, tax farming (*baolan*) was strictly prohibited. All taxes had to be paid to the government chest directly by landowners themselves. From then on, even those who lived in distant and mountainous areas had to go to the county seat twice a year. Some of them would stay overnight at the homes of *yamen* functionaries. They became familiar with legal procedures (from these *yamen* functionaries) and thought there was nothing to be afraid of. These people gradually became clever and cunning, no longer afraid of the severity of the law. They themselves would become involved in lawsuits. Nowadays, Huang sighed, these distant country fellows were becoming even more litigious than town dwellers (Huang, Ang [1896] 1970: 76).

21 For example, as we saw in Chapter 1, Table 1.5, Jiading County had a total of 2,964 hamlets with an average of 16 households in each village.

22 For example, in Wuxian, Changzhou, Yuanhe, Kunshan, and Zhenze, the average number of hamlets in each *tu* was 5.26 (*Suzhou fu zhi* [1883] 1970: vols 29–30).

23 For example, it was called *xiannian* and *difang* in Suzhou, *zongjia* in Changzhou (*Suzhou fu zhi* [1883] 1970: 350).

24 We should not confuse the labor services discussed in this passage with the labor services discussed in the North China section. Though they were often referred to by the same word, *yi*, their content and nature were clearly different. The former was a kind of government service, while the latter was actual corvée labor. As Zhao Xixiao, a Qing scholar, emphasized when he was talking about these public services in the delta area: "Right now the so-called *yi* in this area is nothing but extra government services [*feichai*]" (*Suzhou fu zhi* [1883] 1970: 360).

25 For example, in Qianmentang xiang, Jiading, most people were tenants of absentee landlords and were illiterate. They spent a lot of money to hire outsiders to take the position of *baozheng* (Tong [1921] 1962: 35–36).

26 As Zhao Xixiao said:

> While on duty, he was responsible for all public affairs of the *tu*, such as
> dealing with the crimes of theft, robbery, fighting, homicide, harboring rebels
> and escaped criminals; questioning salt smugglers; examining cases of tax
> evasion; river dredging and dike building; constructing beacon towers, bar-
> racks, bridges, roads, city walls, official residences, railings and so on; as
> well as household registration; and providing coffins for unidentified floating
> corpses and murder victims.
>
> (*Suzhou fu zhi* [1883] 1970: 360)

27 The term *kunbao* refers to the same type of malpractice as *kundian*. Here *bao*
denotes *baozheng*, the term means to tie *baozheng* up together with (the taxes of)
his *tu*.

28 In order to combat the *kundian* malpractice, in some localities, for instance,
in Wujin County, people organized *yitu* to handle tax collection by themselves.
The *yitu* arrangement was aimed at protecting taxpayers from the extortion of
yamen functionaries. For detailed discussions of *yitu*, see Wan Guoding *et al.*
(1934) *Jiangsu wujin nantong tianfu diaocha baogao*, and David Faure (1976)
"Land Tax Collection in Kiangsu Province in the Late Ch'ing Period."

29 As a matter of fact, *shunzhuang* was a Qing local taxation system which replaced
juntian junyi and was adopted in many localities during Yongzheng (1723–1735)
and Qianlong (1736–1795) periods. It changed the concrete methods of land
registration and tax prompting, i.e. to register the land under the landowner's
name, rather than under the *tu* where the land was located; also sending tax
notices directly to the real landowner rather than to the *tu* where his land was
located (*Zhenzhe xian zhi* [1746] 1970: 1089–1094; Sun 1994: 62–64). Zhao's
discussion here is intended to oppose adopting this method in Jiangnan area.

30 Though in most cases, this quota would be allocated among villagers according
to the amount of land they owned, in some cases, it was imposed evenly on each
household, or on the amount of land people cultivated. These cases would become,
as we will see later, more and more common in the twentieth century.

31 Kawakatsu Mamoru's study shows that some of the delta's rent bursaries' records
date from the mid-Jiaqing period (1796–1820) (Kawakatsu 1992: 376–377).
Some archives I have come across suggest an even earlier date (DYDA 1985:
690–700).

32 A detailed discussion on the Yangzi delta's rent relations and rent bursary is
given in Chapter 6.

33 Of course, not all the villages were strengthened under the pressure of state
intrusion. There were many forces that worked in different directions in village
society. I will discuss these in Chapters 3 and 4.

34 Bernhardt's study shows that during Republican times, collective tax resistance
in the Yangzi delta decreased drastically. From 1911 to 1936, there were only
16 incidents of collective tax or tax-rent combined resistance (Bernhardt 1992:
242–243).

35 The *lijin* tax originated in several market towns near Yangzhou in 1853. Literally, *lijin* means 1 percent of the value of commercial goods. This was the
rate that the *lijin* tax was supposed to be when it was first introduced. However,
the actual rate later greatly exceeded this original designation, and reached to 5,
even 10 percent (Luo 1936: 61).

36 Susan Mann maintained that the *lijin* tax, together with other late nineteenth-
century reforms and changes, heralded the process of modern state-building
(Mann, S. 1987: 2).

Chapter 3 Mobilization and reorganization of village communities in North China

1 This is the classic definition of mobilization advanced by Charles Tilly (1975a: 503).
2 Philip Kuhn argued that mobilization means using new techniques to generate and discipline the higher intensities of local political energy required for modernization of the nation (1975: 269). This notion, however, cannot cover the mobilization discussed here that was aimed at maintaining the existing social order. Mobilization for this purpose certainly did not accommodate a dimension of modernization.
3 For example, in his study of political change in rural North China, Presanjit Duara focuses on modern state building and its impact on rural North China. He asserts that rural political change in North China was brought about "both by the conscious design of state policies and by state-involutionary forces that accompanied the implementation of these policies" (Duara 1988: 194). Sidney Gamble and Ramon Myers held similar assumptions about the motion of village political change (Gamble 1963: 3, 39; Myers 1970: 258, 262–263).
4 For example, in Shandong, a total of 170 primary schools were established between 1901 to 1905. Between 1906 and 1910, 945 more schools were established (Chang Yu-fa 1982: 403). In Jiangsu, the number of modern schools founded in 1906 alone was 1,182, whereas the total number of schools built between 1902 and 1905 was 997. Of these, 562 were founded in 1905, the year when the Qing government announced the abolition of the examination system (Wang Shu-hwai 1984: 244).
5 There were other factors contributing to political change in North China villages, in particular, state intrusion and socio-economic differentiation. These factors will be discussed in the next chapter.
6 A detailed description of the operation of *Qingmiaohui* can be found in Chapter 5 of Gamble's book.
7 Actually, many villages graded tuition fees according to the amount of land owned by the student's family (Li Jinghan 1933: 207). For example, in 1910, Village I (located in Shulu County, Hebei) charged $1.20 for families with less than 15 *mu* of land; $1.60 for families with 15 to 50 *mu*; and $2.0 for those with more than 50 *mu* (Gamble 1963: 107). The tuition for non-resident students was usually much higher than resident students (Huang Di 1936: 402). However, in some villages, no tuition was charged. For example, in Dongting *qu* of Dingxian, out of 62 villages, 19 charged no tuition (Li Jinghan 1933: 207).
8 For example, in 1913 in Shandong, there were 10,056 primary schools with a total of 239,827 students; the average size of each school was 24 students (Chang Yu-fa 1982: 404). In Shunyi, a Hebei county, there were 203 village schools with 6,441 students in the 1930s; the average number of students per school was 31 (*Shunyi xian zhi* 1933: vol. 8).
9 In 1906, the Qing Court published a decree of Preparatory Schedule for Constitutional Government which emphasized that local self-government was to be the basis of constitutionalism (XTZJ 1964: 5: 35). In 1909, it promulgated the Regulations for the Local Self-Government of Municipalities, Towns and Country Townships. The regulations asked that the officers of local self-government be elected by local residents (LXDA 1979: 2: 724–741).
10 Later, these addresses were changed to the *cunzhang* and the *fu cunzhang*. In Qing times, the *difang* and the *dibao* were intermediaries between the county government and villages. For the functions and social status of the *difang* and the *dibao*, see Hsiao Kung-ch'uan (1960: 64–66) and Chü T'ung-tsu (1962: 3–4).
11 Under the *xiang*, villagers were asked to organize the *linlü* (neighborhoods) system which required that every five households be organized into a *lin*, and every five *lin* a *lü*. Compared with the *xiang*, in North China, the design of the *linlü* was insignificant in the sub-county administrative hierarchy.

12 This can be verified by contemporary county gazetteers. For example, in Xushui, Hebei, after implementation of the County Organization Act, a total of 273 *cunzhen* (natural villages and towns) were organized into 200 *xiang*. These *xiang* were of two types: independent *xiang* (*dulixiang*) and joint *xiang* (*lianhexiang*). The independent *xiang* was a natural village with more than 100 households, whereas the joint *xiang* was composed of two or more natural villages (*Xushuixian xinzhi* 1976 [1932]: 315–316). Other county gazetteers compiled during this period describe the same situation (*Baixiang xian [Hebei] zhi* [1932] 1976; *Nangong xian [Hebei] zhi* [1936] 1976: 140; *Dong'a xian [Shandong] zhi* [1934] 1976: 178–179).

13 In 1932, the Nationalist Government issued a new decree requiring rural areas to organize the *baojia* system. This system was originally applied to the areas in which military operations for the punitive campaign against the Communists took place. In 1935, it was ordered to be applied to the whole country and to replace the *linlü* system. However, this decree was not implemented fully in many North China areas (Yang 1945: 242, 244–245; Shen Songqiao 1989; Zhu Dexin 1994: 27–28).

14 Social groups can be divided into two categories based on their principles of affiliation: ascriptive and voluntary. An ascriptive group is one where people are automatically its members if they meet its qualifications and cannot withdraw from it at their will. Voluntary groups are based on people's voluntary participation, and there is no restriction on joining and exiting. Emphasizing ascriptive or compulsory affiliation is crucial to political mobilization because this is the most effective way to maximize the strength and benefits of a social organization.

15 As Mancur Olson has argued in his classic work: *The Logic of Collective Action: Public Goods and the Theory of Groups*, without coercion or incentives other than common interests, members of a large group would not voluntarily act to achieve group interests (Olson 1965: 2). I thank my long-time friend, Dr. Jin Zhongren, for first introducing Olson's important work to me.

16 Douglass North argued exactly along these same lines when he discusses the case of military defense and protection (see North and Thomas 1973: 6–7).

17 Myers (1970) argues that before the twentieth century the village had no clear boundaries. Fixed village boundaries were a new phenomenon which resulted from increasing *tankuan* levies on the village.

18 As discussed in Chapter 2, *tankuan* was a collective levy imposed on the village rather than directly on land owned by individuals. The allocation of *tankuan* quotas among villages usually did not take into consideration land transactions between villages afterwards. A village might lose or get land in a fluid land market, but the *tankuan* quota, once it was worked out, was not likely to change accordingly (Amano 1936: 48–50; Beiyang 1966: 6: 12).

19 A similar situation was called *"renban dibuban"* (lit. though a person may relocate, the land remains behind) (KC 1:181), which refers to the case in which a landowner might move out of a village, but the village retained the right to assess his land within its territory.

20 This marked a significant departure from the Qing's policy on rural administration and jurisdiction. During the Qing, since the village bore no collective responsibility for land taxation, the state had little interest in village territoriality. The major concern of the state was to keep track of land ownership by individual taxpayers and land transactions between them. Similarly, local police also targeted people rather than territory. The *baojia* system, for instance, organized villages via groups of households and had little to do with village territories. The definition of village territory therefore reflected a dramatic change in the relationship between state and rural society resulting from continuous political mobilization.

21 Hebei's regulations for the definition of village territory were actually copied from Shanxi's regulations word for word (for Shanxi's regulations, see Wu Shuzi

and Zhao Hanjun 1930: 188–189). Shanxi was a model province in practicing village self-government (*cunzhi*), which was followed by many provinces.

22 Though Zhaicheng Village was located in Dingxian, its reform started much earlier than James Yan's high profile reform in Dingxian. James Yan and his colleagues chose Dingxian to be their experimental county partly because of the influence that Zhaicheng had in the county.

23 It is not easy to find an equivalent word or phrase in English for this Chinese term. Literally, it means village governance, but reformers meant more when they used it. A more proper translation may be "village reform and reorganization." In North China, this term became the alias of Rural Reconstruction and the title of the bimonthly journal of the SRRI.

24 For cart services (*cheyao*), see Chapter 2. In North China, many villages set up a special organ and fund to deal with this sort of labor service and to subsidize the people who provided cart service. There were many different names for this organ, such as *Gongchaiju, Chaiyaoju, Chemaju*, etc. (see Li Jinghan, 1933: 95, 97; Shen Songqiao, 1989: 199).

25 A very similar case of village reform were the reforms in Zhongshan Village, Anyang, Henan. For Zhongshan's reforms please see Sun Jiyuan & Sun Jiayou's (1933) *Yige xinnongcun* (A New Village).

26 Zhaicheng's reform was considered a pioneer of Rural Reconstruction and also inspired reformers of Rural Reconstruction.

27 In his book, Alitto translated them as lower level village school-centers (*cunxue*) and rural district school centers (*xiangxue*) (1979: 247).

28 Liang's theory of rural reconstruction originated from his philosophy of cultural conservatism (Alitto 1979; Hayford 1990). The core of his philosophy and his rural reconstruction theory was that China's Confucian cultural tradition was morally superior to Western culture and civilization. China's modernization must be realized through a revival of Confucian tradition and at same time it must incorporate and apply advanced Western science and technology. Liang believed that this tradition was still alive in the Chinese countryside, therefore China's modernization should start from the countryside and villages. The representative work of Liang's rural reconstruction theory was *Xiangcun jianshe lilun, zhongguo minzu zhi qiantu* (Theory of Rural Reconstruction: The Future of the Chinese Nation) (1937); the representative work of his philosophy was *Dongxifang wenhua jiqi zhexue* (Cultures and Philosophies in the East and the West [1922]). For western scholarship on Liang's thoughts and career, see Guy S. Alitto, *The Last Confucian: Liang Shu-ming and the Chinese Dilemma of Modernity* (1979).

29 A very similar reform, also conducted at the county level, was the Dingxian experiment led by the Association for Mass Education Movement (MEM). The preeminent leader of the Dingxian experiment was James Yen (Yan Yangchu), a Yale graduate and a western-style liberal intellectual. Though his philosophical assumptions for rural reconstruction differed significantly from those of Liang, the experiment he led in Dingxian shared similar features to Zouping's. For the Dingxian experiment, see Li Jinghan (1933); Xu Yinglian *et al.* (1936); Gamble (1963); and Hayford (1990).

30 The criticisms that best reflected left-wing intellectual and Communist opinions about Rural Reconstruction can be found in the Qian-Jiaju and Li-Zixiang edited *Zhongguo xiangcun jianshe pipan* (The Criticism of Rural Reconstruction in China) (1935). For left-wing intellectuals and the Communists, the fundamental causes of rural crises were imperialism and feudalism. The solution was to mobilize peasants to overthrow the existing social, political and economic order. The way to mobilize peasants, they believed, was to wage class struggle in the countryside.

Chapter 4 The state and North China villages in a changing world

1 Martin Yang gives us a very detailed description of this in Taitou (Yang 1945: 175–177). The same situation could also be found in Shajing (KC 1952: 1: 97, 123).

2 For example, in Sibeichai, before 1931, there was no village assembly, and the villagers had no chance to express their opinions about public management. Everything was determined by the village leaders (KC 1952: 3: 47). In Shajing, there was simply no village assembly; village affairs were determined by the village officers without listening to villagers' opinions (KC 1952: 1: 125, 127).

3 The same regulations could be found in many other counties. For example, in Shunyi County, similar regulations were worked out by the county government (KC 1952: 1: 148; *Shunyi xian zhi*, vol. 5).

4 In six KC villages, the only case indicating the existence of a supervisory committee was found in Shajing. However, this committee is not the one discussed here. The former village head, Zhou Shutang, said that it was established in 1914 or 1915, and disbanded in 1927 or 1928. This assembly had been composed of all villagers (KC 1952: 1: 101).

5 The 1929 regulations for the election of village and neighborhood heads in Hebei even provided that village assemblies should double the number of candidates so that the county government could make the final selection of village heads and other officers (HBFG).

6 The most notorious case of this practice is that in some areas local governments imposed the quota of opium cultivation on villages so as to generate higher tax revenue (see Perry 1980: 181).

7 In some places, *tanpai* and *tankuan* were also called *tanhua* and *tanqian* (both mean to allocate levies).

8 Philip Huang's study shows that ward and village heads played the crucial role in the collection of *tankuan* levies. The county government assigned quotas to the ward heads, who allocated these quotas among the village heads under their jurisdiction. The village heads were responsible for meeting the quotas assigned to their communities. After collection, village heads delivered the taxes to ward heads, who in turn delivered them to the county treasury (Huang 1985: 288).

9 Suiyuan was a province located in north of Hebei, but was abrogated in 1954.

10 A novel, *Guxiang Tianxia Huanghua* (Chrysanthemums of my homeland), which talks about the generations of power struggles in a North China village during this century, provides us with a very vivid story of this kind of competition, though the story exaggerates sometimes (Liu Zhenyun 1990, No. 2).

11 The unfair allocation of *tanpai* was not limited to the village. It was also found in the allocation of the *tanpai* quota by county and ward governments. The *tankuan* allocation at this level was usually based on the number of households of each village, not on the acreage of land owned by the village (Li Jinghan 1933: 565; Amano Motonosuke 1936: 48–50). Since the number of households was not proportionate to acreage in villages, this method of allocation was unfair to certain villages. For example, in a ward of Zhuoxian (Hebei), four villages had approximately the same amount of land. But two of them were categorized as first grade villages with assessments of ten points of *tankuan* quota. Another two were categorized as seventh grade with only four points of quota (Amano Motonosuke 1936: 48–49). The problem here was that the land actually owned by the village was usually much greater than what was registered with the government. The government knew this malpractice, but it could not solve it. Allocating *tankuan* by the number of households in each village was the only alternative.

12 This new type of network is voluntary in nature as opposed to the ascriptive network discussed previously. The voluntary network differs from the ascriptive

one in several aspects: first, people affiliate with it freely; second, because of this, its boundaries are open and unfixed, and hence it can penetrate and transcend those ascriptive networks such as kinship ties and territorial bonds; third, they are usually socially differentiated. These characteristics make the voluntary network a very significant source of power in village society. The development of voluntary networks in villages constitutes a very important aspect of rural political change in twentieth-century North China.

13 Generally, every 100 households constituted one *bao*. Since the three descent groups were concentrated in three separate residential sections of the village, and the *baojia* system was organized according to the residential-decimal principle, it is little wonder that the *bao* heads in the village came from different descent groups.

14 According to the statement of Yang Yuan, the village head of Shajing, this kind of decision was made at the joint meetings of village heads, assistant heads and village councilors (KC 1952: 2: 344).

15 As we see above, in the other three *KC* villages, levying *tankuan* on the land owned was firmly adhered to.

16 Though there were wage laborers in the village whose social status was even lower than poor peasants, they were not regarded as qualified villagers. They could not afford to have a family, they paid no levies to the village, and no taxes to the state and were excluded from most of the public activities (Huang 1985: 255–256).

17 Since the village levy was imposed on cultivated land in Shajing, it seems unreasonable that thanksgiving dinner was served according to the amount of land owned. It may have been that the various labor services continued to be allocated on land owned (see KC 1952: 2: 346).

18 In contrast, Xu Sen, a county clerk of Shunyi, said that the poor people liked to go to court and engage in lawsuits (KC 1952: 1: 147). This fact might suggest that poor people lacked effective means to protect their interests within the village.

19 As Tönnies pointed out, public opinion "brings the morality of *Gesellschaft* [community] into rules and formulas," it can thus urge the political authority to force everyone to do what is useful and undo what is damaging ([1887] 1957: 230).

20 Li Jinghan's investigation of 515 rural households in Ding County, Hebei, provides statistics that show a close relationship between the education rate and household landholding (Li Jinghan 1931).

Chapter 5 The Communists and North China villages

1 The Communists were by no means the newcomers in wartime rural North China. As a matter of fact, they had tried hard during the late 1920s and early 1930s to mobilize the peasants. They organized dozens of armed uprisings in Hebei, Henan, Shandong, northern Anhui and northern Jiangsu, but none of these uprisings achieved major success. A similar fate was also met by the Communist-led peasant uprisings in the Yangzi delta during this period. However, the reasons for their failure in North China differed significantly from those in the Yagnzi delta. As many people have argued, the chief reason for their failure in North China, besides political and military situation, was their wrong strategy (Hartfort 1995; Tiedemann 1997). While in the Yangzi delta, in addition to those factors, social and economic factors were also responsible to their repeated failure. I will discuss the Communist-led peasant uprisings in the Yangzi delta in Chapter 8. For prewar Communist mobilization in rural North China, see Elizabeth Perry (1980), Odoric Y.K. Wou (1994), Kathleen Hartford (1995), Ralph A. Thaxton, Jr. (1997), and R.G. Tiedemann (1997).

2 However, I have no intention here of claiming that the CCP was the only anti-Japanese resistance force operating in North China, but it was undoubtedly the major resistance force there.

3 As a matter of fact, state exactions from local society should include both collecting revenue and enlisting manpower, especially, military drafting. But my discussion here will focus mainly on collecting revenue. As a matter of fact, enlisting manpower is a part of taxation, it generally followed the same rules that governed taxation and was handled in the same manner as in taxation. Thus the discussion on taxation can help us understand the relationship between the Communist state and North China villages in their wartime base areas.

4 As a study showed, more than 30 items of taxes and levies had been abolished after the implementation of the reasonable burden tax (Guo Zhenshou and Li Shifang 1985: 237).

5 During this time, the land tax in the base area was temporarily resumed, which was, as it had long been, collected by the government taxation apparatus directly from individual taxpayers. The village government did have some responsibilities for land tax, for example, to investigate concealed land. But on the whole, the two parties involved in this tax were the state and individual landowners (JCJ 1984: 4: 54–55, 145–146).

6 See also *Jizhong cun heli fudan banfa* (The Regulations for the Village Reasonable Burden Tax in Central Hebei District), Article 2 (JCJ 1984 4: 157), and *Jin-Cha-Ji bianqu pingshanxian cun heli fudan banfa* (The Regulations for the Reasonable Village Burden Tax of Pingshan County, the Jin-Cha-Ji Border Area), Article 1 (ibid.: 4: 160).

7 For example, unregistered (acreage) and under-registered (under-assessment) land could be found in almost any village in North China, but outsiders could hardly know the exact amount in a given village (Feng Huade 1938; Cong Hanxiang 1995: 475–476; Zheng Qidong 2004: 233–234). Without this knowledge, it was impossible for the Communists to make tax burden equal to different villages.

8 Only after the land reform and collectivization, was the Communist regime able to, through mass mobilization, bring the highest percentage of arable land under registration, also carry out a thorough land survey and careful reassessment, an achievement never even imagined by any previous regime in Chinese history.

9 As a matter of fact, the Communists' advocacy of the unified progressive tax can be traced back to a very early period. In 1928, the CCP announced for the first time in its Sixth Congress that it would abolish all the taxes imposed by the Nationalist Government and institute unified, progressive taxes (see *The Program of the Chinese Revolution at the Present Stage*, in Brandt *et al.* 1952: 132). But they had never had chance to practice it until they established the anti-Japanese bases in the North China countryside. I believe that the intention of their early policy also differed substantially from their later practice.

10 According to this stipulation as well as the Temporary Regulations for Implementation of the Unified Progressive Tax in the Jin-Cha-Ji Border Region, the unified tax was simultaneously a property tax and an income tax. It merged the land tax, commercial tax and all other direct taxes into one and was applied to all of the people living in the base area. After the institution of the unified progressive tax, all old taxes except the import-export tax and deed tax were abolished in the base area (JCJ 1984: 4: 354–355).

11 Since no regimes could undertake this task effectively in a pre-modern agrarian society, why did they not adopt the method the Communists used? The main reason is that if this method was adopted without mobilizing rural society from the bottom up in the fashion of the Communists, taxation would fall into the hands of local elites. In choosing between central control and local domination of taxation, the state would of course prefer the former to the latter.

12 During the war, the tax grain and fodder were usually stored in villages; this was especially true in those guerrilla war zones. The villagers, instead of delivering tax grain or fodder to government granaries, were asked to preserve the tax grain and fodder in their own stores. The government and army later would use coupons to redeem grain or fodder from the villagers. Of course, the village government was responsible for the whole process and especially for the accuracy of collection and for the supervision of the villagers in storing and preserving the tax grain and fodder (JCJ 1984: 4: 333–341).

13 The system of unified progressive tax was adopted by the Jin-Ji-Lu-Yu base in 1943 (JJLY 1985: 1: 4–16, 300–304, 382–399, 4: 18–32; CZYJ 1987: 101–102). In the Shandong base, the major tax collected was *jiuguo gongliang* (the national salvation grain), which was imposed on rural areas following the same principle embodied in the unified progressive tax. The village was also the basic unit for the allocation and collection of this tax. However, in the Shandong base, the land tax had not yet been abolished during the anti-Japanese war (Baba 1984: 46–48; CZYJ 1985: 221–235; 1987: 233–246; Wei Hongyun and Zuo Zhiyuan 1990: 217–219). Nevertheless, the unified progressive tax never found its way into the Communist-led base areas in the Yangzi delta. The reason for this lay again in different local conditions. The wartime Communist mobilization in the Yangzi delta will be discussed in Chapter 8.

14 Ten Mile Inn was located in another Communist-led resistance base area, the Shanxi-Hebei-Henan-Shandong Border Area (*Jin-Ji-Lu-Yu bianqu*).

15 In Communist jargon, the middle and poor peasant economy was very often referred as the peasant petty commodity economy.

16 The revival of the middle peasant stratum during the War of Resistance in Communist North China bases was ubiquitous as more and more studies on Communist-led wartime base areas have told us. For example, David Goodman's study of the Taihang Base (the core area of the Communist-led Shanxi-Hebei-Shandong-Henan Border Region) shows that the social structure changed dramatically during the war. Both the number and landholdings of middle peasants swelled from one-third on the eve of the war to two-thirds at the end of the war, while other strata in the village shrank (Goodman 2000: 27–33).

17 Another reason given by the base government was that this change was in line with the united front policy pursued by the Communists for the sake of the resistance war.

18 For example, according to a survey of six villages in central Hebei, after the institution of the unified progressive tax, the proportion of household income taxed for landlords, rich peasants, middle peasants and poor peasants was 21.77 percent, 29.65 percent, 9.76 percent and 3.81 percent respectively (JCJ 1984: 4: 504). The Border Region government spelled out the burden ceilings for different classes. For poor peasants it was 7 percent, middle peasants 15 percent, rich peasants 25 percent, and landlords 70 percent (Guo Zhenshou and Li Shifang 1985: 248).

19 Both Wei and Zuo's and Zhao's books divided wartime rent and interest reduction into four periods, and agreed that the reduction campaign had not been implemented fully and thoroughly in the North China bases until 1942.

20 To be sure, tax reform, like the rent and interest reduction, targeted the propertied classes. However, in the case of tax reform, the propertied classes had to pay more taxes to the Communist state, rather than yield their interests to their poor fellow villagers, therefore it would not provoke intense conflicts between villagers. Besides, the reform was in the name of national salvation and the resistance war, it was not easy for the propertied classes to resist. Due to these reasons tax reform was less provocative and offensive to the propertied classes and also less harmful to the anti-Japanese united front than was rent and interest reduction.

21 Both villages belonged to the Jin-Ji-Lu-Yu Border Region. Long Bow was located in Changzhi, southern Shanxi. We are familiar with Ten Mile Inn already. For Long Bow, see Hinton's *Fanshen* (1966).

22 This can be found in Goodman's (2000) study of the Taihang Base, especially Chapters 5–7.

23 The other punishments included barring objects of class struggle from the mutual-aid groups, forcing them to wear a humiliating cloth patch to indicate their status as class enemies. In addition, the children of class enemies were not allowed to attend the village school (Crook and Crook 1959: 148).

24 One item of source materials I have come across is very illustrative. A villager from the central and northern Jiangsu base complained about Communist control and organization in these words:

> In the past, even though [the Nationalist Government] was so ruthless, and it pressed people so terribly, still, I managed to evade labor services and have never done any. Now [everything] is well organized, so you can't evade [labor services] (*guoqu [wangu zhengfu] naiyang hen, zhuade naiyang lihai, wo dou wei chuguofu, xianzai dou zuzhi haole, pao dou pao budiao*).
>
> (XSJ 1984: 7: 368–369)

25 Besides taxation, army recruitment was actually a more difficult task imposed on the village as a collective responsibility in the base area. However, taxation was a daily routine, while army recruitment was seasonal. I will discuss this issue and compare it in the North China bases with that in the Yangzi delta in Chapter 8.

26 An illustrative case can be found in Crooks' (1979) book, *Ten Mile Inn: Mass Movement in a Chinese Village*. The Crooks tell us that at the first, the village government tried to measure every plot of village land in order to correct the old record. However, facing villagers' resistance, they compromised to measure only those "fat" land (under-assessed land) and "thin" land (over-assessed land). And the result of measurement turned out that there was little difference from the former records (ibid.: 175–184). This result even contradicted the villagers' common belief.

27 In other base areas, for example, in the Jin-Ji-Lu-Yu base area, the village head was finally allowed to be a full-time cadre who was entitled to receive monthly provisions (JJLY 1985: 4: 503). This was unprecedented, which evidenced the further bureaucratization of village government under the Communist regime.

28 Excessive village expenditures was not the only wrongdoing by village cadres. With their increasingly unrestricted power within the community, village cadres would easily slip into the behavior pattern of their predecessors. Thus, some village cadres exploited their offices to evade taxes or to help their relatives to do so. Others imposed fines on villagers arbitrarily and forced them to make "contributions" (*juankuan*) (JCJ 1984: 1: 529–530).

29 It is worth noting that Chinese scholars have seldom paid attention to this important aspect. The studies by Chinese scholars of the CCP's wartime finance and taxation cited in this chapter have all ignored the role the village community played in Communist taxation. Some Western scholars, by contrast, have noticed this fact. For example, Michael Lindsay has briefly discussed in his article on the taxation system of the Jin-Cha-Ji base the village's role in this regard (Lindsay 1970). However, his emphasis is different from mine. His main concern is taxation procedure and method rather than the state-society relations embodied in taxation.

30 From the period of the anti-Japanese war through the 1980s, the basic measure of the Communist control was to bind everyone under its rule tightly into his or her village community, work unit, or urban neighborhood. These ascriptive

organizations were simultaneously local communities and the lowest level of administrative units. Under this arrangement, most state and society intercourse was limited to the realm between state and community, the state only dealt with these ascriptive organizations rather than individual citizens. This method is no doubt shaped by Communist wartime experiences in their North China bases.

31 Before the anti-Japanese war, the Communist revolution mainly focused on South China. The social situation there differed substantially from that of North China, as did the Communists' strategy for mobilizing the rural populace. In the realm of taxation, for example, the Communists continued the land tax, and imposed taxes mainly on individuals. No evidence shows that the village shouldered the collective responsibility for taxation (XGCJ 1986: 486–497; CZYJ 1985: 1–14).

Chapter 6 Social structure and local politics in the Yangzi delta

1 For example, the Tongxiang county gazetteer recorded: "In several southeast prefectures such as Jiaxing and Huzhou, the land is good for mulberry, so most people engage in sericulture. Sericulture has thus become more important than grain cultivation" (quoted in Liu Shiji 1987: 32).

2 Under the Qing household registration system, the *yanhu* differed from the *huahu* (miscellaneous household); the former was a category used in the *baojia* registration, the latter in the *lijia* registration (Sun Haiquan 1990: 5: 80).

3 The origin of two-layered land tenure system is very complicated, the absentee landlordism is not the only reason for this land tenure system. For a brief discussion of this land system, see *Huadong junzheng weiyuanhui tudi gaige weiyuanhui* (1952: 195–196) and Pan Guangdan and Quan Weitian (1952: 39).

4 As Table 4.2 revealed, tenant delivery of rent was the most common practice of rent collection in the delta. Fei's words here verified the county level survey data.

5 These three Suzhou suburban counties were amalgamated into Wu County after the founding of the Republic.

6 Bernhardt has discussed this principle in her book. This principle is: "the larger the number of protesters, the greater the likelihood that most would escape the economic and legal consequences of their actions" (1992: 36) This was just the principle the tenant-protesters of Chongming believed in. After several rounds of conflict with landlords, the protesters, being afraid of government punishment, decided to mobilize more people to join their action. That was why they forced the shopkeepers in nearby towns to strike (QDTD 1988: 665).

7 Tanaka's statistics also contain the number of people injured, killed and arrested every year from 1922 to 1931 in each rent resistance (Tanaka Tadao 1936: 307).

8 Of course, since a strong gentry-landlord class still existed in the towns and cities,—the strategic spots of rural society—and actually exerted a dominant influence in rural society, the tenants' collective resistance could hardly go very far. The typical scale of rent resistance, as we have seen, involved between hundreds to 2,000 or 3,000 participants; a scale that went well beyond a small rural community, but was still confined within a rural township.

9 From source materials I have read, no one had ever mentioned a *linlü* head. This apparently suggests that in reality, the head of *linlü* was very unimportant or simply did not exist.

10 The regulations for the organization of the *baojia* were published in Jiangsu in February 1934.

11 A lawsuit filed against a *bao* head for embezzling public funds that was brought to the Jiading county court in 1946 may help us to see the scope of power abuse by the *bao* head. Pan Nianzhu was the head of the Eighth Bao in Jinbang xiang, Jiading. Pan was a 38-year-old peasant. When at court, he could not even tell the number of the *baojia* he lived in and took charge of. Pan had recently collected

money from 170 households in his *bao* to pay for door plates. A total of 170,000 *yuan* was collected, but only 140,000 *yuan* was handed to the *xiang*. And Pan could not answer where the remaining 30,000 *yuan* were (*Jiading minbao*, 1947–12–8).

12 A survey of about 235 *xiangzhen* heads in six wards of Wuxi made by Li Heng in 1935 shows that more than 90 percent of these *xiangzhen* heads were landlords and rich peasants, whose landholdings were between 63 to 147 *mu*. However, these *xiangzhen* heads were not like those we saw in the villages, like Mr. Chen and Zhou in Kaixiangong, most of whom were absentee landlords living in towns and at the same time engaging in occupations other than farming (Li Heng 1935: 7: 412–415). Besides, after the establishment of the *baojia* system in 1934, the size of *xiangzhen* expanded greatly, and they were no longer equivalent to administrative villages. Therefore we should not confuse these *xiangzhen* heads with the rural community leaders that we have discussed here.

13 The SCVE was founded by Huang Yenpei, Jiang Hengyuan, Zhao Shuyu and several others in the early years of the Republic. It began to pay attention to rural education in 1919, when it established an Agricultural Education Institute to study rural education. In 1928, it started its first rural reform program in Xugongqiao, located in Kunshan, Jiangsu. By 1934, there were a total of 15 reform programs conducted in different localities of the Yangzi Delta under its direction (Xu Yinglian *et al.* 1936: 426–427).

14 Located in Wuxi, growing out of the Popular Education College (*Minzong jiaoyu yuan*, founded in 1928) and the Working Peasant Academy (*Laonong xueyuan*, founded in 1929), the JPEI was an institute devoted to popular education and agricultural improvement. Its tasks were to train cadres for popular education and agricultural improvement (Xu Yinglian *et al.* 1935: 375).

15 According to Shi Zhongyi, the YMCA staff working in Weitinshan, the initial fund was only 200 *yuan*, and the average yearly fund during 1928 to 1933 was about 1,100 *yuan*, of which 70 percent was paid as salary for the staff, 20 percent for office expense, and only 10 percent for real operating expenses (Shi Zhongyi 1933: 106).

16 For other rural reform projects in the Yangzi delta, see *Xiangcun jianshe shiyan* (1933–1935, 3 vols); Kong Xuexiong, *Zhongguo jinri zhi nongcun yundong* (1934) and Xu Yinglian *et al.*, *Quanguo xiangcun jianshe yundong gaikuang* (1935).

17 The distinction between social and political reforms has already been noted by some contemporary observers, though they might not have been clearly aware of the geographical differentiation of the distinction. For example, Ma Wenhuan, a renowned professor and social reformer at the Nanjing University (*Jinling daxue*), wrote in a preface to Shi Zhongyi's book that he believed that rural reforms should employ political forces and methods, but the YMCA's Weitingshan reform originated from social issues, which different from his position (Shi Zhongyi 1933: 1).

18 A story told by Shi Zhongyi, a YMCA member who worked in Weitingshan, was very illustrative. Shi told us that every day the peasants of Weitingshan traveled three *li* (approximately 1 mile) to Weitingzhen, the market town, to have a cup of tea. Thinking that this was a great waste of time and energy, Shi and several reformers opened a teahouse, called *zhongxing chayuan* (lit: the teahouse center), in the community in the hope of changing this habit. In order to attract villagers, the reformers equipped the teahouse with everything that market-town teahouses offered. The teahouse accommodated a sales section selling daily necessities, and it also gave talks on social news, local affairs, and market information. The community leaders and elders were invited to settle disputes and story-tellers were invited to tell stories. Also musical instruments, popular magazines, newspapers, and chess games were also provided.

However, the results were very disappointing. After a short period of prosperity, people satisfied their curiosity and stopped coming. The reformers made several attempts and finally learned that people went to the market-town teahouse every day not just to entertain themselves, but more importantly, this was their way of maintaining good credit in the market. Anyone who failed to present himself for a couple of days in the market-town teahouse would immediately become the object of rumors and his financial credit would become suspect to everybody in the whole market-town community. The market-town stores would refuse to delay the payment of debts or deny any extension of credit. Their friends would avoid them or greet them coldly. Ultimately, they would be in danger of bankruptcy. No one could afford this kind of loss (Shi Zhongyi 1936; also Yang 1945: 195–197).

This story may have exaggerated the importance of the market in the daily life of the delta peasants but it could not be a sheer fabrication. What interests us here is that this story shows how commercialization reduced the importance of the rural community in peasants' social life and precluded this community from being an effective institutional means of organizing and mobilizing the delta peasants.

19 Ash points out that Republican Jiangnan was unique in its highly-developed urban and industrial sectors, the existence of permanent tenancy and the growth of the bursary system, the changing patterns of landlords' investment behavior, as well as the evidence of tenant riots (Ash 1976: 52–53).

Chapter 7   State and society in the Yangzi delta countryside

1 Before this reform, revenue granted to the local government (both provincial and county governments) was usually a small portion of the central tax revenue retained locally. This retained central revenue was called *cunliu* (retaining funds) during the Qing. Though on average the *cunliu* accounted for 21 percent of statutory taxes, the real fund available for local expenses was very limited (Zelin 1984: 26–37). For example, in the late seventeenth century, the fund used for local expenses in Suzhou Prefecture was only about 5 percent of *diding* taxes (ibid.: 34). This amount definitely fell short of the real expenditures of the local government. To keep local governments operating, the Qing central government had to tolerate their imposing various surcharges along with statutory taxes. Several major surcharges collected by local governments during the Qing were *huohao* (the meltage fee), *pingyu* (balance surplus) and *caozhe* (commuting surplus) (Wu Zhaoxin [1937] 1965: 2: 38–39). Obviously, all these funds were not the independent revenue of the local government.

2 Business tax, income tax and inheritance tax were the new taxes created by this tax law to be collected in near future. *Lijin* was to be abolished and it was finally terminated in the beginning of 1931 (Wu Zhaoxin [1937] 1965: 2: 130–131; *Beijing jingji xueyuan* 1988: 73).

3 In Jiangsu, the regular land tax allocated to the county was *xian zhengshui* (county statutory tax). Its rate was, as showed in Table 7.2, 0.30 *yuan* per *liang* of *diding* and 1.00 *yuan* per *shi* of *caoliang*. This amount obviously fell far short of the rapidly expanding financial needs of any county in the Yangzi delta.

4 Several important studies have already been made on this topic. They are: Zheng Kangmo (1933), *Zhejiang erwu jianzu zhi yanjiu*; Hong Ruijian (1935), *Zhejiang zhi erwu jianzu*; Noel Miner (1980), "Agrarian Reform in Nationalist China: The Case of Rent Reduction in Chekiang, 1927–1937," and Kathryn Bernhardt (1992) *Rents, Taxes, and Peasant Resistance, Lower Yangzi Region, 1840–1950*, Chapter 5.

5 Not all counties abandoned rent reduction. In certain localities, rent reduction was continuously enforced, and disputes over rent reduction were thus constantly

brought to the authorities and reported by newspapers (see Feng Zigang 1936: 45–46; Zhang Youyi 1957: 305–306; Zhu Huisheng 1988: 110–127).

6 However, the reform could not be taken as a total failure. In fact, it had a definite impact on the Zhejiang countryside. As Kathryn Bernhardt observed:

> [The rent reduction in Zhejiang], while falling far short of its architects' intent, left its mark on the northern Zhejiang countryside. Rents in certain locales were reduced and remained at their reform levels even after the provincial government abandoned its efforts to enforce the new law. More generally, the campaign created a climate that made it all the more difficult for landlords to raise rents. To that degree, it strengthened the state's hand in the matter of setting rents and helped to restrain increases in the tenantry's burden in the Republican period.
>
> (1992: 188)

7 For example, both Zheng and Miner have emphasized that the imperfections of the rent reduction laws, such as the laws being too simple to cope with diversified and complex local conditions, and too vague (like the term "main crop") to be strictly followed, and so forth, were greatly responsible for the disputes that ensued from rent reduction. These technical problems also, they believed, were responsible to a great extent for the failure of rent reduction (Zheng Kangmo 1933; 33972–33973; Miner 1980: 78).

8 As discussed above, the new tax law of November 1928 was promulgated at the very crucial moment of rent reduction in Zhejiang. This taxation reform no doubt weighed very heavily on Zhejiang government's decision to abolish rent reduction in the following year.

9 In this conflict, the party activists were more in line with the ideology and central policy of the Nationalist Party, whereas the provincial and county governments were more concerned with their own interests which were, in this case, clearly differentiated from those of the central government.

10 In Jiangsu, though provincial government had also issued a decree for rent reduction in December 1927 stipulating that rent should be no higher than one-third of the yield of the main crop, this law had not been enforced (Zhang Youyi 1957: 302).

11 Bernhardt gives an excellent analysis of the dilemma of three unpalatable options which a county magistrate had to choose from. However, her analysis focuses on how the county magistrate dealt with three parties—the state, the landlords and the tenants—in matters of tax and rent. My discussion in this paragraph concerns more about different interests within the state, i.e. between the central, provincial and county governments.

12 As a matter of fact, the same method was adopted by the Qing government in post-Taiping period to a lesser degree and on a smaller scale (see Bernhardt 1992: 126–129).

13 Actually, the prewar figure was much larger than this. According to *Jiangsu shengjian* (The Jiangsu gazetteer), in 1933, the statutory land tax (*shengxian zhengshui*) collected from Changshu was 678,193 *yuan*, while the land surcharge (*shengxian fushui*) was 1,299,146 *yuan*. The total was 1,977,339 *yuan*. In 1934, the total land tax collected was 1,646,087 *yuan* (*Zhao Ruheng* 1935: 2: 588, 739, 757–758). If we compare these figures with the wartime figures, the percentage would be even smaller.

14 According to another source, this move was initiated by Suzhou landlords. In 1938, landlords in Guangfu zhen united their rent bursaries into one organ, called *gongzhan* (lit. the public bursary), to enforce rent collection. However, the *gongzhan* was destroyed immediately thereafter by peasants. The Occupation

authority then stepped in to support rent collection and organize joint collection (Tao Zhicheng *et al.* 1951).

15 Theoretically, there should have been tenant representatives on the committee, but actually there were none (Shen Lansheng 1943: 198).

16 The source does not tell what was the rent rate set by the committee. So we do not know whether one *shi* here was the fixed rent rate or not. However, in the Yangzi delta, generally, the rent rate was one *shi* per *mu*.

17 Again, the same measures were used by the Qing authority in post-Taiping period (Bernhardt 1992: 126–129).

18 In another place, Shen also said that in 1940 the rice price in the market was about 100 *yuan* per *shi* (1943: 127). This was contradicted by other sources. For example, in Wuxi it was between 34 to 44 *yuan* (MT, Shanghai 1941: 198), and in Songjiang it was between 47 to 48 *yuan* (MT, Shanghai 1940: 189).

19 In 1941, the committee for joint collection in Changshu set the *zhejia* rate of 30 *yuan* for one *shi* of rent, but the market price then was 100 *yuan* per *shi*. This meant that the *zhjia* rate was only 30 percent of market price. No wonder landlords there petitioned the puppet Nanjing authority for help (Zhongyang dang'anguan 1995: 577).

20 Shen also said that since joint collection put tenants at the mercy of armed dunning policemen, their situation under joint collection thus also deteriorated (Shen Lansheng 1943: 128). However, the biggest losers under joint collection were absentee landlords, while tenants benefited somewhat from the chaotic war situation. Shen's articles also implied this (ibid.: 145, 161). It can also be verified by other sources (Huadong 1952).

21 The decline of rent income was not only due to wartime joint collection, it was also due to rent resistance from tenants. This will be discussed later in this section.

22 In the Yangzi delta most absentee landlords were small landlords. This had been especially true since the late nineteenth century when modern industry and commerce provided more profitable and more secure investment opportunities for the propertied class, which led to the dispersion of landownership among absentee landlords (Ash 1976: 19; Cao Xingsui 1989: 36–45).

23 According an investigation of land tenure in Wu county, during the Northern Expedition period, topsoil rights were to be protected by law and could be bought and sold freely. Originally, the price ratio for subsoil and topsoil rights was 5 to 1. But subsoil price gradually declined relative to topsoil price due to overall socioeconomic change during the Republican era. By the end of the period, it was said that no one even wanted to buy the subsoil (Huadong 1952: 196).

24 Here, I do not mean that the state did not play this role in society before and elsewhere. On the contrary, it always did. However, in the Yangzi delta, mediation and arbitration between absentee landlords and tenants became a daily routine of the local government, and consumed a great deal of the local magistrates' energy. This was in sharp contrast to the situation on the North China plain, where heavy *tanpai* always pitted the village against the state and the local government was very often the target of peasant collective action.

Chapter 8 The Communists and the Yangzi delta countryside

1 There are several short articles published by Chinese scholars on Communist activities in the Yangze delta countryside. I have cited some of them in this chapter. The only serious study by Western scholars to date about the Communist wartime operations in this area is Gregor Benton's (1999) *New Fourth Army: Communist Resistance Along the Yangtze and the Huai, 1938–1941*. He argues that the New Fourth Army in Central China played a role in the War of Resistance

and in the Communist revolution no less significant than that of the Eighth Route Army in North China. However, his work deals with the New Fourth Army and their resistance in Central China as a whole, and his argument does not hold completely true for its operations in the Yangzi delta.

2 The sources do not explain why guerrilla war was to be pursued in southern Jiangsu and peasant regimes established in northern Jiangsu. This dual strategy was, as I see it, based on CCP activists' analysis of local social and political conditions in these two areas.

3 Other sources, such as those used in creating Table 8.1, do not mention this insurrection, probably because of its insignificance.

4 Other local Communist activists shared Guan's doubts about the party leadership's insurrection policy (see Gao Guanglin 1983).

5 As Joel Migdal has forcefully argued, "peasants' dissatisfaction is with very specific aspects of their immediate environment, and they usually do not have a vision of the overthrow of the entire system with which they are still relatively unfamiliar" (1974: 248).

6 As Roy Hofheinz has argued, the game of revolution can be played anywhere as long as there is a group of people who wants to try (1977: 304–305). However, I believe that he overemphasizes revolutionary leaders' "wits, flexibility, and strength of will" in determining the success of a revolution and downplays objective factors such as socioeconomic conditions.

7 Because becoming a soldier had no inherent appeal, Guan wrote, the Communist activists had to force peasants to join their guerrilla war (Guan Wenwei 1985: 89–90, 127). Obviously, such conscription could help little because it only alienated people from the Communists and their revolution.

8 For example, Elizabeth Perry's study about Huai-pei shows that soldiering was one of the major survival strategies for poor and landless peasants (1980: 58).

9 For example, Cao Xingsui's study of 12 Yangzi delta villages shows that of the 433 households, 51 were landless. Most of the latter had various off-farm employment and could earn an average living by local standards. Only three of them could not make ends meet, and the old people of these families eventually became beggars (Cao Xingshui 1989: 133–136). Similarly, Philip Huang provides examples of how the more commercially developed and diversified Yangzi delta economy offered opportunities for peasants to make ends meet and to help them move upward the ladder of employment from being landless laborers (1990: 160–161).

10 The phrase "sustained and successful revolution" here is used only in a relative sense. In other areas during this period, the Communists could establish their bases and sustain them for a while, but that was never the case in the Yangzi delta. The most famous successes were found in South China, such as Mao's base in Jiangxi and other bases in Hunan, Hubei, Sichuan, and Anhui. And in North China as well, the Communists had organized dozens of peasant uprisings during the late 1920s and early 1930s. Though none of them succeeded, these insurrections were of greater scale, intensity, and duration than those in the Yangzi delta (for Communist-led peasant uprisings in North China during the Nanjing decade, see Zhang Donghui et al. 1997; Kathleen Hartford's study [1995] on Communist mobilization in rural Hebei during 1921 to 1936 also details some cases). The peasants of Feixiang county (Hebei), led by the Communists, even occupied and controlled the county government for two years (JLY 1984: 160–162).

11 The New Fourth Army (Xinsijun), one of the two full-fledged Communist armies organized during the war (the other was the Eighth Route Army), was originally composed of the Communist forces that remained in South China after the Long March.

12 The base was located in the Mount Maoshan area southeast of Nanjing, between Jintan and Jurong counties.

13 Guan Wenwei's experience is a good example of the shift in the Communists' position. After spending seven years in Nationalist jails, Guan was released on the eve of the outbreak of the war (July 1937). He returned to his hometown in Jintan County and organized a resistance force immediately after the fall of Nanjing. This time, Guan's operation won the support not only of peasants but also of local elites, many of whom—gentry, landlords, and merchants—joined his efforts. They provided weapons and funds, and some even merged their own armed forces with his. When Guan proclaimed the establishment of the General Regiment of Jiangnan Resistance and Self-Defense Forces (*Jiangnan kangri ziwei zongtuan*) in February 1938, he commanded the vast countryside of three counties, Danyang, Zhenjiang and Wujin. In September 1938, Guan's force was absorbed into the NFA as a brigade with more than 2,000 soldiers (Guan Wenwei 1985: 255–288).

14 There were six war zones established by the Nationalist Government during the war, the Third War Zone covered mainly Jiangsu and Zhejiang provinces (Liang Hanbing and Wei Hongyun 1984: 168).

15 As a matter of fact, the Nationalist Government, while retreating to China's interior, granted tax and rent exemption to people under Japanese occupation. This was of course just a strategy aimed at undermining the social and economic order of the Japanese occupation, but it did give local people an excuse to resist, when possible, rent payment.

16 The CCP's Jiangsu and Anhui Regional Committee (*Zhonggong Suwan quwei*) was established in December 1939, and it commanded three sub-regional committees: the Special Southern Jiangsu Committee (*Sunan tewei*), the Special Jiangsu-Anhui Committee (*Suwan tewei*), and the Special Northern Jiangsu Committee (*Subei tewei*) (Sunan 1987: 5).

17 The first and second administrative districts included Suzhou, Changzhou, Taicang, Wuxi, Jiangyin, and Shazhou counties (Sunan 1987: 171).

18 Deng did not recount the specific reasons they gave to defend the continuation of rent collection. Very likely, the Communists preached national unity in the War of Resistance against Japan. We can imagine the Communists added some doses of coercion in addition to persuasion.

19 The Eastern Zhejiang base (*Zhedong kangri genjudi*) was established in late 1941. Although it was an independent base not belonging to the Sunan base, it covered part of the Yangzi delta, i.e. the suburban counties of Shanghai (except Chongming) (Zhedong 1987: 3–22). The social structure of rural eastern Zhejiang was as same as that of the Yangzi delta (CZYJ 1985: 147–150), and the Communists there adopted identical economic and financial policies as those practiced in the Sunan base.

20 These grain levies and fees (called *kangwei junliang he jingfei*) were mainly imposed on landowners and were actually land taxes collected by the Communists (XSJ: 6: 273–275).

21 Throughout the war, most Jiangnan absentee landlords lived in towns and cities occupied by the Japanese and the collaborators, sometimes by the Nationalists, while the Communists in their Sunan base controlled the countryside. Yet the Communists had relatively little difficulty in collecting taxes from those absentee landlords. Since rents flowed from the countryside to town, the Communists had a powerful leverage to strike a deal with landlords and force them to pay tax. Of course, under such circumstances, landlords often had to pay taxes to two even three rival governments. As a 1943 CCP document revealed, in the Sunan base, 90 percent of people were paying tax to two governments (*liangmian fudan*), and 40 percent to three governments (*sanmian fudan*) (Sunan 1987: 279). But rather than paying double or triple their prewar rate, people paid the same amount, which was shared by two or three governments as each government

acknowledged this situation and acted accordingly. (XSJ 6: 255; this source shows how the Communists applied different tax rates to people under different situations.)

22 In other cases, the Communists also asked the *xiang* and *bao* heads of the collaborationist government, the heads of local chambers of commerce, and big landlords to collect taxes for them and severely punished those who refused to cooperate (Shanghai 1986: 406). Many *xiang* and *bao* heads were actually double, even triple agents.

23 These localities included eastern Changshu, the border area of Suzhou, Changshu and Kunshan, and part of Taicang (Huazhong caijing 1984: 457).

24 The article was written by Li Jianmo, the chair of the Political Department of the Minkang and later the head of financial department of the Sunan base government (Fan Zhengfu 1983:2: 79, 86; He Zhenqiu 1986: 135).

25 For example, the archival materials documenting economics of the Jin-Cha-Ji base and the Jin-Ji-Lu-Yu base (such as JCJ and JJLY) contain plenty of information about Communist mobilization of villages, but source materials of the Sunan base such as the book *Sunan kangri genjudi* (1987), do not provide even a single document on organizing and mobilizing village communities. Interestingly enough, this comparison is also clearly reflected in literary works about the Communist-led resistance against Japan. For example, while many movies about the resistance war in North China, such as the *Tunnel Warfare* (*Didaozhan*) and the *Mine Warfare* (*Dileizhan*), take place in villages, a well-known Beijing opera, *The Sha Family River* (*Shajiabang*), which told the story of the New Fourth Army's operation in Jiangnan area, was set in a small teahouse located not in a village, but probably in a marketplace.

26 Because the commercial tax was paid in cash, and rent and land tax in Jiangnan also had long been commuted into cash payment, the government's income was mostly in cash. The Sunan base therefore witnessed a unique phenomenon: the army there could and had to buy grain from the market using tax money. This practice was severely criticized by Liu Shaoqi, the political commissar of the NFA (Sunan 1987: 142), who said that purchasing rice to eat (*maimichi*) was too wasteful and should be given up. He instead advised the troops in the Sunan base to eat tax grain (*gongliang*). However, two years after Liu's criticism, most troops in the Sunan area, as a July 1943 party document from the CCP Suwan Committee showed, were still eating purchased rice (Sunan 1987: 279); converting tax cash to tax grain probably would have greatly increased the Communists' workload.

27 The term "fengjian" has a very vague meaning in Communist political jargon. Generally, it refers to things that were old, traditional, out-of-date, and decadent; although common, the translation *feudal* is certainly misleading. The Communists called the sub-ward administrations feudal, mainly because they had undergone little change and remained in the hands of old local elite.

28 In wartime Jiangnan, the administrative system under the county was the *qu*, *xiang* (*zhen*), *bao* and *jia* (Yu Zidao *et al.* 1985: 437, 521). This system was inherited from the Nanjing period. In this system, the heads of *bao* and *jia* were only functionaries without substantial power. The heads of *xiang* and *zhen* were usually assumed by members of the local elite living in market towns, and the heads of *qu* were *de facto* government appointees, though by law they were supposed to be elected by local people. When the Communists talked about the political power under the *qu*, they were mainly referring to the *xiang* heads.

29 Benton's recent study confirms the difficulties reported by Jiang Weiqing. He tells us that in Sunan, the Japanese controlled most highways and feeder roads and built 400 fortified points in an area of 17,000 square kilometers. This situation made it impossible for the Communists to establish a consolidated base (Benton 1999: 715).

30 Ye Fei was the commander of the NFA eastern expedition of 1938–1939. Gu Fusheng was one of the CCP and NFA leaders operating in the Shanghai suburbs.

31 Many Communists who worked in Shanghai during the war also recalled that one of their major tasks was recruiting workers and students to join the NFA in the Sunan base. Rong Jiansheng recalled that from April 1939 to November 1940, when he was the liaison between the CCP Shanghai organization and the Sunan base, about 1,000 people were recruited from Shanghai and sent to join the NFA (Huazhong huiyi 1984: 3: 89–93. There are many such reminiscences in histories of the NFA.) Wang Yaoshan, at that time the director of the Organizational Department of the CCP's Jiangsu Provincial Committee, said that because of this, the CCP Central Committee highly praised the Shanghai party organization (Huazhong huiyi 1984: 3: 158–161).

32 For example, during their qingxiang campaigns, the Japanese would surround a village, then gather all people and ask them to speak; those without the local accent would be immediately arrested and tortured. To avoid betraying themselves, the NFA soldiers were advised to pretend to be mute if approached. Unfortunately, many tailors and barbers living in villages were arrested and tortured by Japanese who took them to be NFA soldiers, for most of them were not native villagers (Sunan 1987: 159, 199).

33 This approach differed from that in North China bases, where the Communists focused on taxation reform in the early stage of base construction. Only after their bases were consolidated, did they carry out rent and interest reduction. This issue thus did not assume as important a role in mobilizing rural populace in North China as it did in the Sunan base. Suzanne Pepper's study tells us how limited an impact of rent and interest reduction had on the North China bases (1978: 260–276).

34 Each year since 1940 the Sunan base turned over a large amount of their revenue to the NFA's headquarters located in northern Jiangsu (Sunan 1987: 9, 363; He Zhenqiu 1986). The surplus was mainly from the First, Second, and Third District of the Sunan base—that is, the *Donglu* area east of Jiangying, Wuxi, and Lake Tai, the richest area of Jiangnan. The large amount of surplus from these three districts was usually converted into gold in the Nanjing market to keep its value, despite the skyrocketing inflation rate in wartime Jiangnan, and then remitted to the NFA's headquarters (Sunan 1987: 363).

35 The Communist success in recruiting in northern Jiangsu can be verified by village-level information from the Subei base. For example, in Dianfa xiang, Xujia County, a 1943 investigation tells us that in this xiang, which had a total of 1,069 adults, there were 69 people serving in the NFA. This number did not include those who had no family members left in the village and thus had no contact with their villages since they joined the NFA. Among them, 37 previously were wage laborers, 9 were poor peasants, 8 middle peasants, one rich peasant, 4 handicraft workers, one peddler, one beggar, and one whose background was unknown (XSJ 7: 422–425, 445). It is evident that landless peasants constituted the majority of army recruits. This was especially true in the early stage of the Communist army- and base-building. Once the base was consolidated and well established, as we have seen, the recruitment of soldiers became a collective responsibility of the village.

36 During the war, the expansion of military forces was an overriding strategic task for the Communists, because they were not only engaging in the resistance against Japan, but also anticipating an all-out domestic fight against the Nationalists after the war. Therefore, the strategic importance of a base area was determined, to a great extent, by the potential for military expansion in that area.

37 The NFA's headquarters were originally in Southern Anhui. It was attacked and destroyed by the Nationalist forces in January 1941 while it was in the process of relocating to northern Jiangsu. Immediately afterwards, the CCP's central committee ordered it be reestablished in Northern Jiangsu under the leadership of Liu Shaoqi and Chen Yi.

Conclusion

1 As some scholars have argued, these two patterns represented two distinct types of peasant rebellions and hence of local politics in North and South China from the late Ming through the early twentieth century. Whereas northern rebellions were usually directed against the tax-levying state, in the South, rebellions tended to pit tenants against landlords in a class struggle to redefine the terms of rent (see Perry 1980: 260).

2 As a matter of fact, the Communists were active players in this political drama who organized and led quite a few collective resistance against those targets in prewar North China.

3 This is true not only for China, but also for peasant revolution in general. As Joel S. Migdal argues in his discussion of peasant revolution in general: "revolutionaries cannot depend upon a short-lived, cataclysmic uprising of frustrated peasants but must build organizations capable of executing complex tasks over time" (1974: 262).

4 Philip Huang has reminded us repeatedly of the crucial importance of village community in the Chinese revolution and the construction of the Communist society (Huang 1985, 1990, 1991). But he tends to talk of village in general, not the North China village in particular.

5 Though they both emphasize the role of organization in the revolution, Chen differs from Kataoka by arguing the importance of class struggle in mobilizing peasants (Chen Yung-fa 1986: 6–15).

Appendix 1 The structure and history of Kaixiangong

1 In the Yangzi delta, most farm land was surrounded by waterways. This kind of land was called *yutian*, simplified to *yu*. In Chinese, the character *yu* means embankment and enclosure. In the former meaning this word is pronounced *yu*, in the later meaning, it is actually pronounced *wei*. Both of these pronunciations and meanings were used in the delta (*Wuxian zhi* 1934: 733–734).

2 Though Kaiyuangong (开元弓) is a little different from Kaixiangong (开弦弓), I believe they refer to the same village because the pronunciations of *yuan* (元) and *xian* (弦) are very close, and in the local dialect, they are simply pronounced the same. Also because three of the four *yu* which belonged to this *tu*, i.e. the 13th *du* 7th *tu* in which Kaiyuangong was located, are also found in Fei's book, and they belonged to Kaixiangong at the time that Fei did his field research. These three *yu* were Liangjiao *yu*, Xichang *yu*, and Xintian *yu*. Two of Kaixiangong's residential areas were located in two of these three *yu*, Liangjiao *yu* and Xichang *yu*.

3 Formally, *tu* was called *li*, which was from the Ming *lijia* system. The Qing government adopted this system to organize the rural populace for the purpose of taxation. Theoretically, each *li* was composed of ten *jia*, and each *jia* ten households; one *li* thus contained about 100 households (strictly speaking, according to official regulation, it should be 110 households, i.e. ten *jia* plus ten *jia* heads, see Hsiao 1960: 32). In the Yangzi Delta area, *li* was usually called *tu*. Literally, *tu* means map. *Zhenze xian zhi* (1746) says: "Tu is li. It is not called li but tu, because the first page of the li registration book is always a map [about the land of this li]. Li is designed for household registration, . . . tu is for yu management and land registration." (140)

4 *Xiang, du* and *tu* were artificial sub-county administrative units used in the Yangzi delta, *yu* was the layout of land, *cun* (hamlet) and *zhen* (town) were natural rural settlements. *Xiang, du* and *tu* were used by local government to organize and manage *yu, cun* and *zhen*.

5 The simple reason for this is that people built their hamlet on the land they owned or cultivated. The *tu* arrangement could not change this situation but had to follow it. It commanded the *yu* and the villages located in these *yu*. Since the *tu* was originally designed for taxation and household registration, it would only enhance this *yu* and hamlet combination and affiliation.

6 The 1746 edition of the county gazetteer recorded a total of 97 *cun* (the equivalent Chinese word for village) in the county in Yongzheng 4 (1726). The 101 names of these *cun* were listed. However, neither Kaiyuangong (Kaixiangong) nor Tanjiadun is in the list. In 1731, the county had a total of 53,688 households and in 1744, there were 75,022 households (*Zhenze xian zhi*, [1746] 1970: 183, 186–190, 199–200). At that time Zhenze had five towns. Even we deduct those who lived in the five towns, taking 5,000 households for each town, the average household number of each *cun* would still be more than 500 in 1744. This is extraordinarily large. The possible explanation is that the *cun* counted in the gazetteer were not hamlets, but groups of hamlets. That is why we cannot find Kaiyuangong and Tanjiadun. While the 1883 edition of the prefectural gazetteer tells us that there were 907 *cun* in Zhenze County, obviously, the county gazetteer and the prefecture gazetteer had quite different criteria for *cun*. Otherwise we cannot imagine the number of *cun* would increase so rapidly during these 150 years.

Bibliography

Alitto, Guy S. (1979) *The Last Confucian: Liang Shu-ming and the Chinese Dilemma of Modernity*, Berkeley, CA: University of California Press.

Amano Motonosuke (1936) *Kaen zatsuseika no kahoku noson* (Rural Hebei under extortionate levies and miscellaneous taxes). *Mantetsu chosa geppo*, 16, no.4/5, Dalian: Minami Manshu tetsudo kabushiki kaisha.

Ash, Robert (1976) *Land Tenure in Pre-Revolutionary China: Kiangsu Province in the 1920s and 1930s*, Research Notes and Studies No. 1. London: Contemporary China Institute, School of Oriental and African Studies.

Baba Takeshi (1984) "Santo konichi konkyochi ni okeru zaisei mondai" (Problems in financial adminstration in the Shandong anti-Japanese base areas), *Shikan*, no.110, pp. 43–60.

Baixiang xian zhi (Gazetteer of Baixiang County) ([1932] 1976) Taibei: Chengwen chubanshe.

Beijing jingji xueyuan caizheng jiaoyanshi (Department of Finance, Beijing College of Economics), (ed.) (1988) *Zhongguo jindai shuizhishi gaishu* (A brief history of modern Chinese taxation system), Beijing: Beijing jingji xueyuan chubanshe.

Beiyang *Beiyang gongdu leizuan* (Collections of official documents of the northern warlord government) (1966) Taibei: Wenhai chubanshe.

Benton, Gregor (1999) *New Fourth Army, Communist Resistance along the Yangtze and the Huai, 1938–1941*, Berkeley, CA: University of California Press.

Bernhardt, Kathryn (1992) *Rents, Taxes, and Peasant Resistance, the Lower Yangzi Region, 1840–1950*, Stanford, CA: Stanford University Press.

Brandt, Conard, Schwartz, Benjamin and Fairbank, John K. *et al.* (1952) *A Documentary History of Chinese Communism*, London: George Allen and Unwin Ltd.

Buck, John Lossing ([1937] 1968) *Land Utilization in China*, originally published by the University of Nanking (Shanghai), reprinted by the Paragon Book Reprint Corp (New York).

Cao Jinqing, Zhang Letian and Chen Zhongya (1995) *Dangdai zhebei xiangcun de shehui wenhua bianqian* (Contemporary social and cultural changes in the northern Zhejiang countryside), Shanghai: Shanghai yuandong chubanshe.

Cao Xingsui (1989) *Shangping jingji yu xiaonong shengchan: jiu zhongguo sunan nongcun nongjia jingji yanjiu* (Commodity economy and small-scale farming production: research on farmers' economy in jiangsu in old China), PhD dissertation. Nanjing Agricultural University.

Chan, F. Gilbert (ed.) (1980) *China at the Crossroads: Nationalists and Communists, 1927–1949*, Boulder, CO: Westview Press.

Chang Yu-fa (1982) *Modernization in China, 1860–1916: A Regional Study of Social, Political and Economic Change in Shantung Province*, Taibei: Academia Sinica.

Changshu xian zhi [Gazetteer of Changshu County] ([1904] 1979) Taibei: The Association of Changshuness in Taiwan.

Chen Hanshen (1936) "Xiandai zhongguo de tudi wenti (Land issues in China today)," in Feng Hefa, ed. *Zhongguo nongcun jingji lun* (On China's agrarian economy), pp. 207–241.

Chen Pixian (1986) "Guanyu bianxie suzhong kangzhanshi de jige wenti (On several issues in writing the history of anti-Japanese war in Central Jiangsu)," *Dajiang nanbei*, 1986, No. 3.

Chen Tisi (1936) "*Xiangju riji* (Country diaries)," in Zhougguo nongcun jingji yanjiuhui (Research Association for Chinese Rural Economy) (ed.) *Zhongguo nongcun miaoxie*, pp. 89–95.

Chen, Yung-fa (1986) *Making Revolution: The Communist Movement in Eastern and Central China, 1937–1945*, Berkeley, CA: University of California Press.

Chen Zhenghan, Xiong Zhengwen and Yin Hanzhang ed. (1989) *Qingshilu jingji shiliao* (Economic materials from the veritable records of Qing), Beijing: Beijing University Press.

Chü, T'ung-tsu (1962) *Local Government in China under the Ch'ing*, Stanford, CA: Stanford University Press.

Cong Hanxiang (1995) *Jindai Ji-Lu-Yu xiangcun* (Modern rural Hebei, Shandong, and Henan), Beijing: Zhongguo shehui kexue chubanshe.

Crook, David and Crook, Isabel (1959) *Revolution in a Chinese Village: Ten Mile Inn*, London: Routledge and Kegan Paul.

Crook, David and Crook, Isabel (1979) *Ten Mile Inn: Mass Movement in a Chinese Village*, New York: Pantheon Books.

Cunzhi (Village governance) Bimonthly. N.p.

CZYJ (Caizheng kexue yanjiusuo [Institute of Financial Research]) (1985) *Geming genjudi de caizheng jingji* (The finance and economy in revolutionary base areas), Beijing: Zhongguo caizheng jingji chubanshe.

CZYJ (Caizheng kexue yanjiusuo [Institute of Financial Research]) (1987) *Kangri gengjudi de caizheng jingji* (Finance and economy in anti-Japanese base areas), Beijing: Zhongguo caizheng jingji chubanshe.

Dai Xuanzhi (1973) *Hongqianghui* (The Red Spears), Taibei: Shihuo chubanshe.

Dennerline, Jerry (1975) "Fiscal Reform and Local Control: the Gentry-Bureaucratic Alliance, Survives the Conquest," in Frederic Wakeman Jr. and Carolyn Grant (eds) *Conflict and Control in Imperial China*, Berkeley, CA: University of California Press, pp. 86–120.

Dong'a xian zhi (Gazetteer of Dong'a County) (1976 [1934]) Taibei: Chengwen chubanshe.

Dorris, Carl E. (1976) "Peasant Mobilization in North China and the Origins of Yenan Communism," *The China Quarterly*, 68: 697–719.

Duara, Prasenjit (1988) *Culture, Power, and the State, Rural North China, 1900–1942*. Stanford, CA: Stanford University Press.

DYDA (Zhongguo diyi lishi dangan guan [The first historical archives of China] and History Department of Beijing Normal University) (1985) *Xinhai gemin shinianjian minbian dang'an shiliao* (Archival materials about social disturbances during ten years before the 1911 Revolution), Beijing: Zhonghua shuju.

Engxian zhi (Gazetteer of Enxian County) ([1909] 1968) Taibei: Changwen chubanshe.

Esherick, Joseph W. (1987) *The Origin of the Boxer Uprising*, Berkeley, CA: University of California Press.

Fan Zhengfu (1983) "Sunan kangri minzhu zhengquan de fazhan" (The development of the anti-Japanese democratic regime in the Sunan base), in Huazhong huiyi, vol. 2. pp. 69–90.

Fang Xianting (1938) *Zhongguo jingji yanjiu* (A study of the Chinese economy), Shanghai: Commercial Press.

Fang Xing (1983) "Lun Qingdai qianqi dizhuzhi jingji de fazhan (On the development of landlord economy in the early Qing)," *Zhongguo shi yanjiu* (Chinese historical studies), 1983: 2: 87–99.

Faure, David (1976) "Land Tax Collection in Kiangsu Province in the Late Ch'ing Period," *Ch'ing-shih Went-t'i*, vol. 3, no.6, pp. 49–75.

Faure, David (1989) *The Rural Economy of Pre-Liberation China, Trade Expansion and Peasant Livelihood in Jiangsu and Guangdong, 1870 to 1937*, Hong Kong: Oxford University Press.

Fei, Hsiao-tung (1939) *Peasant Life in China, a Field Study of Country Life in the Yangtze Valley*, London: Routledge and Kegan Paul Ltd (Chinese edition of this book translated by Dai Kejing, and published in 1996 by Jiangsu remin chubanshe).

Feng Hefa (ed.) (1935) *Zhongguo nongcun jingji ziliao* (Materials on the Chinese rural economy), Shanghai: Liming shuju.

Feng Huade (1938) "Nongmin tianfu fudan de yige shili (A case of land tax burden on peasants)", in Fang Xianting (ed.) *Zhongguo jingji yanjiu*, Shanghai: Commercial Press.

Feng Tianfu (1987) "Yiqie weile kangri de Jin-Cha-Ji bianqu caizheng (All for the anti-Japanese war: finance in the Jin-Cha-Ji Border region)," in CZYJ, pp. 170–186.

Feng Zigang (1936) *Jiaxingxian nongcun diaocha* (Investigation in rural Jiaxing County), n.p.: Guoli Zhejiang daxue and Jiaxingxian zhengfu.

Fengren xian zhi (Gazetteer of Fengren County) ([1892] 1968) Taibei: Chengwen chubanshe.

FGDQ (*Zhonghua minguo fagui daquan* [The complete collection of laws and regulations of the Republic of China]) (1936) Shanghai: Shangwu yinshuguan.

Freedman, Maurice (1966) *Chinese Lineage and Society: Fukien and Kwangtugn*, London: The Athlone Press.

Friedman, Edward, Pickowicz, Paul G. and Selden, Mark (1991) *Chinese Village, Socialist State*, New Haven, CT: Yale University Press.

Fukutake Tadashi (1976 [1950]) *Social Structure of Rural China*, vol. 9 of *Complete Works of Fukutake Tadashi*, Tokyo: Tokyo University Press.

Gamble, Sidney (1963) *North China Villages: Social, Political, and Economic Activities Before 1933*, Berkeley, CA: University of California Press.

Gao Defu (1986) "Lun Jinchaji bianqu zhengquan jianshe zhong de minzhu zhengzhi (On democracy in political reconstruction of the Jin-Cha-Ji Border Region)," in Nankai daxue, pp. 258–268.

Gao Guanglin (1983) "Shilun tudi geming chuqi de jiangsu nongmin yundong (On the peasant movement in Jiangsu during the early period of Land Revolution)," *Shanghai shifan daxue xuebao*, 1983, no.3.

Goodman, David S.G. (2000) *Social and Political Change in Revolutionary China: The Taihang Base Area in the War of Resistance to Japan, 1937–1945*, Lanham, MD: Rowan and Littlefield Publishers, Inc.

Guan Wenwei (1985) *Guan Wenwei huiyi lu* (Guan Wenwei's reminiscences), Beijing: Renmin chubanshe.

Guangzong xian zhi (Gazetteer of Guangzong County) ([1933] 1969) Taibei: Chengwen chubanshe.

Guanxian xian zhi (Gazetteer of Guanxian County) ([1843] 1968) Taibei: Chengwen chubanshe.

Guo Zhenshou and Li Shifang (1985) "*Jin-Cha-Ji bianqu de heli fudan he tongyi leijingshui* (The reasonable burden and the unified progressive tax in the Jin-Cha-Ji Border region)," in CZYJ (1985), pp. 236–249.

Hartford, Kathleen (1995) "Fits and Starts: The Communist Party in Rural Hebei, 1921–1936," in Tony Saich and Hans van de Ven (eds) *New Perspectives on the Chinese Communist Revolution*, Armonk, NY: M.E. Sharpe, Inc., pp. 144–173.

Hartford, Kathleen and Goldstein, Steve M. (eds) (1989) *Single Sparks: China's Rural Revolutions*, Armonk, NY: M.E. Sharpe.

Hayashi Megumi (1943) *Chushi Konan noson shakai seido kenkyu* (Study of the social system of rural Jiangnan in Central China), Tokyo: Yuhikaku.

Hayford, Charles W. (1990) *To the People: James Yen and Village China*, New York: Columbia University Press.

HBFG (*Hebeisheng zhengfu fagui leibian* [The collection of laws and regulations of Hebei provincial government]) (1929) Ed. Hebei shengzhengfu mishuchu (Secretariat of Hebei Provincial Government, N.p.

HBGM (*Hebei geming huiyilu*, [Reminiscences of making revolution in Hebei]) (1980) vol. 1, Shijiazhuang: Hebei renmin chubanshe.

HBZL (*Qinding hubu zeli* [The regulations of the Board of Revenue]) (1968) Taibei: Chengwen chubanshe.

He Lie (1972) *Lijing zhidu xintan* (A new study of the Lijin system), Taibei: Dongwu University Press.

He Menglei (1934) *Suzhou, Wuxi, Changshu sanxian zudian zhidu diaocha* (An investigation into the tenancy system of the three counties of Suzhou, Wuxi and Changshu), in Xiao Zheng, vol. 63.

He Zhenqiu (1986) "*Su-Chang-Tai kangri youji genjudi de caijing gongzuo* (Finance and taxation in the anti-Japanese guerilla base of Suzhou, Changshu and Taicang)," *Suzhou daxue xuebao*, 4: 134–138.

Hebei (Institute of History, Hebei Social Sciences Academy) (ed.) (1983) *Jin-Cha-Ji kangri genjudi shiliao xuanbian* (Selected materials of the Jin-Cha-Ji anti-Japanese base area), 2 vols, Shijiazhuang: Hebei renmin chubanshe.

Hinton, William (1966) *Fanshen: A Documentary of Revolution in a Chinese Village*, New York: Vintage Books.

Hofheinz Jr., Roy (1977) *The Broken Wave: the Chinese Communist Peasant Movement, 1922–1928*, Cambridge, MA: Harvard University Press.

Hong Huanchun (ed.) (1988) *Mingqing suzhou nongcun jingji ziliao* (Source materials on rural economy of Suzhou), Nanjing: Jiangsu guji chubanshe.

Hong Ruijian (1935) *Zhejiang erwu jianzu* (The 25 percent rent reduction in Zhejiang), Nanjing: School of Land Economics, Central Political Institute

Hongzhi shanghai xian zhi (Gazetteer of Shanghai of Hongzhi reign) ([1504] 1990) Shanghai: Shanghai shudian.

Hsiao, Kung-ch'uan (1960) *Rural China, Imperial Control in the Nineteenth Century*, Seattle, WA: University of Washington Press.

Huadong (Huadong junzheng weiyuanhui tudi gaige weiyuanhui) (ed.) (1952) *Jiangsusheng nongcun diaocha* (Survey of rural society in Jiangsu Province), N.p.

Huang Ang (1970 [1896]) *Xijin shixiao lu* (Wuxi and Jingui gazetteer, miscellaneous items), Taibei: Chengwen chubanshe.

Huang Di (1936) "Qinghe cunzhen shequ, yige chubu yanjiu baogao (Qinghe rural community, a preliminary study)," *Shehuixuejie*, 10: 359–422.

Huang, Philip C.C. (1985) *The Peasant Economy and Social Change in North China*, Stanford, CA: Stanford University Press.

Huang, Philip C.C. (1990) *The Peasant Family and Rural Development in the Yangzi Delta, 1350–1988*, Stanford, CA: Stanford University Press.

Huang, Philip C.C. (1991) "The Paradigmatic Crisis in Chinese Studies: Paradoxes in Social and Economic History," *Modern China*, vol. 17, no.3, pp. 299–341.

Huang Wei and Xia Lingen (ed.) (1984) *Jindai Shanghai diqu fangzhi jingji shiliao xuanqi* (Selected materials of modern Shanghai economy collected from local gazetteers), Shanghai: Shanghai renmin chubanshe.

Huazhong caijing (*Huazhong kangri genjudi caizheng jingji shiliao xuanbian, Jiangsu bufen* [Selected materials on the financial and economic history of the anti-Japanese base in Central China]) (1984) Ed. Jiangsusheng caizhengting, Jiangsusheng dang'anguan, Caizheng jingjishi bianxiezu (Research group for financial and economic history, Financial Department of Jiangsu Provincial Government and Jiangsu Archives), vol. 1, Beijing: Dang'an chubanshe.

Huazhong huiyi (*Huazhong kangri douzheng huiyi* [Recollections of the anti-Japanese struggle in Central China]) (1982–1987) Ed. Shanghaishi xinsijun he huazhong kangri genjudi yanjiuhui Shanghai fenhui (Research Association for the New Fourth Army and CCP's Central China Bases for Resistance against Japan, Shanghai Branch), 7 vols, Shanghai: Shanghai Shelian.

JCJ (*Jin-Cha-Ji bianqu caizheng jingjishi ziliao xuanbian*, [Selected materials of the financial and economic history of the Jin-Cha-Ji Border region]) (1984) Ed. Wei Hongyun, Xing Guang, and Fu Shangwen, 4 vols, Tianjing: Nankai University Press.

Jiading minbao (Jiading people's daily) (1947) Jiading.

Jiading xianzheng gaikuang (The survey of Jiading County administration) (1939) N.p.

Jiading xian zhi (Gazetteer of Jiading County) (1992) Shanghai: Shanghai renmin chubanshe.

Jiading xian zhi (Gazetteer of Jiading County) (1880) N.p.

Jiading xian xuzhi (A continuation of the gazetteer of Jiading County) ([1930] 1970) Taibei: Chengwen chubanshe.

Jiang Zhaocheng (1991) "The Reforms of Local Labor services in Hangzhou, Jiaxing, and Huzhou during the Late Ming and the Early Qing," *Zhongguo shehui jingjishi yanjiu*, 1: 72–108.

Jiangsusheng dang'anguan (Jiangsu Archives) (ed.) (1983) *Jiangsusheng nongmin yundong shiliao xuanbian* (Selected materials of peasant movement in Jiangsu), Beijing: Dang'an chubanshe.

Jiangsu wenshi ziliao xuanji (Selected materials of Jiangsu history and culture) (1981) Ed. Zhongguo renmin zhengzhi xieshang huiyi jiangsusheng ji nanjingshi weiyuanhui and Wenshi ziliao yanjiuhui (Jiangsu and Nanjing Subcommittees, People's Political Consultation Committee of China, and the Research Association for Culture and History), vol. 1, Nanjing: jiangsu renming chubanshe.

Jiangsusheng danxing fagui huibian (The collection of separate laws and regulations of Jiangsu Province) (1935) Zhenjiang: Jiangsusheng zhengfu mishuchu shuwugu, N.p.

JJLY (*Jin-Ji-Lu-Yu kangri genjudi caijing shiliao xuanbian, Henan bufen*, [Selected materials of the financial and economic history of the Jin-Ji-Lu-Yu anti-Japanese base area, Henan]) (1985) Ed. Henansheng caizhengting and Henansheng dang'an guan (Financial Department of Henan Provincial Government and Henan Archives), 4 vols, Beijing: Dang'an chubanshe.

JLY (*Zhonggong Ji-Lu-Yu bianqu dangshi ziliao xuanbian* [Selected materials of the CCP history in Hebei-Shandong-Henan border region]) (1985) Ed. Zhonggong jiluyu bianqu dangshi ziliao xuanbian bianjizu (The group for compiling materials of the CCP history in Hebei-Shandong-Henan board region), Part 1, 2 vols, Jinan: Shandong Daxue chubanshe.

Johnson, Chalmers A. (1962) *Peasant Nationalism and Communist Power: The Emergence of Revolutionary China, 1937–1945*, Stanford, CA: Stanford University Press.

Johnson, Kay Ann (1983) *Women, the Family and Peasant Revolution in China*, Chicago: University of Chicago Press.

JSTB (1980) (*Huangchao jingshi wen tongbian* [Complete collection of essays of the Qing period on practical political and economic issues]), Taibei: Wenhai chubanshe.

JSWB (1972) (*Huangchao jingshi wen bian* [Collection of essays of the Qing period on practical political and economic issues]), Taibei: Wenhai chubanshe.

JSXB (1972) (*Huangchao jingshiwen xubian* [Sequel to collection of essays of the Qing period on practical political and economic issues]), Taibei: Wenhai chubanshe.

Kataoka, Tetsuya (1974) *Resistance and Revolution in China: The Communists and the Second United Front*, Berkeley, CA: University of California Press.

Kawakatsu, Mamoru (1992) *Studies on the Agricultural Economy of the Lower Yangtze, 1368–1911*, Tokyo: Tokyo University Press.

KC (*Chugoku noson kanko shosa* [Investigation of customary practices in rural China]) (1952) Ed. Niida Noboru, 6 vols, Tokyo: Iwanami.

Kong Xuexiong (1934) *Zhongguo jinrizhi nongcun yundong* (Rural Movement in China Today), Shanghai: Zhongshan wenhua jiaoyuguan.

Kuhn, Philip A. (1970) *Rebellion and Its Enemies in Late Imperial China: Militarization and Social Structure, 1796–1864*, Cambridge, MA: Harvard University Press.

Kuhn, Philip A. (1975) "Local Self-Government under the Republic, Problems of Control, Autonomy, and Mobilization," in F. Wakeman and C. Grant (eds) *Conflict and Control in Late Imperial China*, Berkeley, CA: University of California Press.

Liang Fangzhong (1957) *Mingdai de liangzhang zhidu* (The liangzhang system of the Ming), Shanghai: Shanghai renmin chubanshe.

Liang Hanbing and Wei Hongyun (eds) (1984) *Zhongguo xiandaishi dashiji* (Chronicle of major events in modern China), Ha'erbin: Heilongjiang renmin chubanshe.

Liang Shuming (1989–1990) *Liang Shuming quanji* (The complete works of Liang Shuming), 2 vols, Jinan: Shandong renmin chubanshe.

Liangxiang xian zhi (Gazetteer of Liangxiang County) ([1924] 1968) Taibei: Chengwen chubanshe.

Li Heng (1935) "*Zhongguo nongcun zhengzhi jiegou de yanjiu* (A study of the political structure in the Chinese countryside)," *Zhongguo nongcun*, July 409–420.

Li Hongyi (1934) *Hebei tianfu zhi yenjiu* (A study of land taxation in Hebei). Taibei: Chengwen chubanshe.

Li Jinghan (1931) "A Study of 515 Rural Households," *Shehuixuejie* (Sociological studies), vol. 5.

Li Jinghan (1933) *Dingxian shehui gaikuang diaocha* (Dingxian: a social survey), Beiping [Beijing]: National Association of the Mass Education Movement.

Li Li (1988) "Ge'an: jiangnan nongcun jiceng zuzhi bianqian, Wuxi Liuxiangcun diaocha (A case study: evolution of grassroots organization in rural Jiangnan, the investigation of Liuxiang cun, Wuxi county)," unpublished paper, Beijing: Fazhan yanjiusuo (Research Institute for Rural Development) and Jingji yanjiusuo (Institute of Economics).

Li Rongzhong (1989) "Qingdai baxian yamen shuli yu chayi (Clerks and runners in Baxian county during the Qing)," *Lishi dang'an*, 1989: 1: 95–102.

Li Zuozhou (1936) "*Juanshui zhongfu xia de fengyang nongmin* (Fengyang peasants under the heavy burden of taxes and levies)," in Zhongguo nongcun jingji yanjiuhui (ed.) *Zhongguo nongcun miaoxie*, pp. 69–74.

Lindsay, Michael (1970) "The Taxation System of the Shansi-Chahar-Hopei Border Region, 1938–45," *China Quarterly*, no. 42, pp. 1–15.

Liu Shiji (1987) *Mingqing shidai jiangnan shizhen yanjiu* (A study on towns and cities in Ming and Qing Jiangnan) Beijing: Zhougguo shehui kexue chubanshe.

Liu Zhenyun (1990) "*Guxian Tianxia Huanghua* (Chrysanthemums of my homeland)," *Zhongshan*, 1990, no.2.

Luanzhou zhi (Gazetteer of Luanzhou) (1969 [1898]) Taibei: Chengwen chubanshe.

Luo Yudong (1936) *Zhongguo lijin shi* (A history of *lijin* in China), Shanghai: Shangwu yinshuguan.

LXDA (*Qingmo choubei lixian dangan shiliao* [Archival materials of the preparatory constitutionalism in the late Qing]) (1979) Beijing: Zhonghua shuju.

Mackinnon, Stephen R. (1980) *Power and Politics in Late Imperial China: Yuan Shi-kai in Beijing and Tianjin, 1901–1908*, Berkeley, CA: University of California Press.

Mann, Michael (1984) "The Autonomous Power of the State: Its Origins, Mechanisms and Results," *Archives européennes de sociologie*, 25: 185–213.

Mann, Michael (1986) *The Sources of Social Power*, vol. 1: *A History of Power from the Beginning*, New York: Cambridge University Press.

Mann, Susan (1987) *Local Merchants and the Chinese Bureaucracy, 1750–1950*, Stanford, CA: Stanford University Press.

Mao Dun (ed.) (1936) *Zhongguo de yiri* (One day in China), Shanghai: Shenghuo shudian.

Mao Lirui and Shen Guanqun (1988) *Zhongguo jiaoyu tongshi* (A general history of Chinese education), Jinan: Shandong jiaoyu chubanshe.

Mao Zedong (1936) "Zhongguo geming zhanzheng de zhanlue wenti (On the strategy of revolutionary war in China)," in *Selected Works of Mao Zedong* (1964) Beijing: Renmin chubanshe, pp. 163–236.

MGSL (Zhongguo Guomindang zhongyang weiyuanhui dangshi weiyuanhui [Committee for the history of GMD, the Central Committee of Chinese Nationalist Party]) (1981) *Zhonghua minguo zhongyao shiliao chubian, duiri kangzhan shiqi* (The first compilation of the important historical materials of the Republic of China, the period of the War of Resistance), vol. 6: *Kuilei zuzhi* (Puppet regimes). Taibei.

Migdal, Joel S. (1974) *Peasants, Politics and Revolution: Pressures toward Political and Social Change in the Third World*, Princeton, NJ: Princeton University.

Miner, Noel R. (1980) "Agrarian Reform in Nationalist China: The Case of Rent Reduction in Chekiang, 1927–1937," in F. Gilbert Chan (ed.) *China at the Crossroads: Nationalists and Communists, 1927–1949*, Boulder, CO: Westview Press, pp. 69–89.

Mingshi (Ming History) (1974) Beijing: Zhonghua shuju.

Ministry of Industry (1933) *China Industrial Handbook: Jiangsu*, Shanghai.

MT, Shanghai (Minami Manshu tetsudo kabushiki kaisha, Shanhai jimusho) (1939a) *Shanhai tokubetsushi Kateilu noson jittai chosa hokokusho* (Report on the investigation of actual conditions in the countryside of Jiading district in the special municipality of Shanghai).

MT, Shanghai (Minami Manshu tetsudo kabushiki kaisha, Shanhai jimusho) (1939b) *Koso-sho Jojuku ken noson jittai chosa hokokusho* (Report on the investigation of actual conditions in the countryside of Changshu county, Jiangsu province).

MT, Shanghai (Minami Manshu tetsudo kabushiki kaisha, Shanhai jimusho) (1939c) *Kosho Taisoken noson jittai chosa hokokusho* (Report on the investigation of actual conditions in the countryside of Taicang county, Jiangsu province).

MT, Shanghai (Minami Manshu tetsudo kabushiki kaisha, Shanhai jimusho) (1940) *Koso-sho Shoko ken noson jittai chosa hokokusho* (Report on the investigation of actual conditions in the countryside of Songjiang county, Jiangsu province).

MT, Shanghai (Minami Manshu tetsudo kabushiki kaisha, Shanhai jimusho) (1941) *Koso-sho Mushaku ken noson jittai chosa hokokusho* (Report on the investigation of actual conditions in the countryside of Wuxi county, Jiangsu province).

Muramatsu Yuji (1970) *Kindai Konan no sosan: Chugoku chishu seido no kenkyu* (The rent bursary of modern Jiangnan: a study of the landlord system of China), Tokyo: Tokyo University Press.

Myers, Ramon H. (1970) *The Chinese Peasant Economy: Agricultural Development in Hopei and Shantung, 1890–1949*, Cambridge, MA: Harvard University Press.

Nagamura Jehee (1951) "Kahoku noson no sonhi: Gendai Chugoku no chiho zaisei no kenkyu (Village expenditures in North China, a study of local finance in contemporary China)," in Niida Noboru (ed.) *Kindai Chugoku no shakai to keizai* (Modern China's society and economy), Tokyo: Toko Shoin, pp. 83–111.

Nangong xian zhi (Gazetteer of Nangong County) ([1936] 1976) Taibei: Chengwen chubanshe.

Nanhui xian zhi (Gazetteer of Nanhui County) (1992) Shanghai: Shanghai renmin chubanshe.

Nankai daxue (Nankai daxue lishixi) (ed.) (1986) *Zhongguo kangri genjudi shi guoji xuesu taolunhui lunwenji* (Collected papers from the international symposium on the history of Chinese anti-Japanese bases), Beijing: Dang'an chubanshe.

NFH (*Nongcun fuxing weiyuanhui huibao* [Reports of the Committee of Rural Reconstruction]) (1934) Ed. Xingzhengyuan noncun fuxing weiyuanhui (Committee of Rural Reconstruction, the Executive Yuan), Nanjing.

Nongfuhui (Xingzhengyuan nongcun fuxing weiyuanhui [Committee of Rural Reconstruction, the Executive Yuan]) (1934a) *Jiangsu sheng nongcun diaocha* (Investigation in rural Jiangsu), Shanghai: Shangwu yinshuguan.

Nongfuhui (Xingzhengyuan nongcun fuxing weiyuanhui [Committee of Rural Reconstruction, the Executive Yuan]) (1934b) *Henansheng nongcun diaocha* (Investigation in rural Henan), Shanghai:Shangwu yinshuguan.

North, Douglass and Thomas, Robert Paul (1973) *The Rise of Western World: A New Economic History*, Cambridge: Cambridge University Press.

Olson, Mancur (1965) *The Logic of Collective Action: Public Goods and the Theory of Groups*, Cambridge, MA: Harvard University Press.

Pan Guangdan and Quan Weitian (1952) *Sunan tudi gaige fangwen ji* (Record of an inquiry into land reform in southern Jiangsu), Bejing: Shanlian shudian.

Pepper, Suzanne (1978) *Civil War in China: The Political Struggle, 1945–1949*, Berkeley, CA: University of California Press.

Perry, Elizabeth J. (1980) *Rebels and Revolutionaries in North China, 1845–1945*, Stanford, CA: Stanford University Press.

QDTD (*Qingdai tudi zhanyou guanxi yu diannong kangzu douzheng* [Land tenure and tenant rent resistances during the Qing]) (1988) Ed. Zhongguo diyi lishi dang'an guan, Zhongguo shehui kexueyuan lishi yanjiusuo (The First Historical Archives of China, Institute of Historical Research, Chinese Academy of Social Sciences), Beijing: Zhonghua shuju.

Qian Jiaju (1936) *Zhongguo nongcun jingji lunwenji* (A collection of essays on China's rural economy), Shanghai: Shijie shuju.

Qian Jiaju and Li Zixiang (1935) *Zhongguo xiangcun jianshe pipan* (Criticisms of Rural Reconstruction in China), Shanghai: Xinzhi shudian.

Qiao Qiming and Yao Yong (1934) "Anhui suxian yuanyou xiangcun zuzhi zhi gaikuang" (A survey of traditional rural organizations in Suxian county, Anhui Province)," unpublished paper from "E-Yu-Wan-Gan sisheng nongcun jingji diaocha chubu baogao di shiqi hao (The preliminary report on the investigation of rural economy in Hubei, Henan, Anhui and Jiangxi, no.17)." E-Yu-Wan-Gan sisheng nongmin yinhang weitou, Jinling daxue nongxueyuan nongye jingjixi diaocha ji bianzhi, n.p.

Qingshigao (Qing History) (1976) edn, Beijing: Zhonghua shuju.

Quan Hansheng (1972) "Meizhou baiyin yu shiba shiji zhongguo wujia geming de guanxi (The relation between American silver and the price revolution in eighteenth-century China)," in Quan Hansheng (ed.) *Zhongguo jingjishi luncong* (Essays on Chinese economic history), vol. 2, Hong Kong: Xinya yanjiuysuo, Hong Kong Chinese University, pp. 475–508.

Renmin chubanshe bianjibu (ed.) (1951) *Xinqu tudi gaige qian de nongcun* (The newly liberated area before land reform), Beijing: Renmin chubanshe.

Saich, Tony and Van de Ven, Hans (eds) (1995) *New Perspective on the Chinese Communist Revolution*, New York: An East Gate Book, M. E. Sharpe.

Selden, Mark (1971) *The Yenan Way in Revolutionary China*, Cambridge, MA: Harvard University Press.

Shanghai (*Shanghai jiaoxian kangri wuzhuang douzheng shiliao* [The historical materials about the resistance war against Japan in Shanghai suburban counties]) (1986) Ed. Zhonggong shanghai shiwei dangshi ziliao zhengji weiyuanhui (Committee for Collecting Historical Materials, CCP Shanghai Municipal Committee), Shanghai: Shanghai shehui kexue chubanshe.

Shanghai renmin yu xinsijun (Shanghai people and the New Fourth Army) (1989) Ed. Zhonggong shanghai shiwei dangshi ziliao zhengji weiyuanhui, Shanghai: Zhishi chubanshe.

Shen Lansheng (1943) *Jiangnan caizheng luncong* (On the finance and economy of Jiangnan), Shanghai: Jinglun chubanshe.

Shen Songqiao (1989) *"Cong zizhi dao baojia: jindai henan difang jiceng zhengzhi de bianqian, 1908–935* (From self-government to *baojia*: local political change in Henan, 1908–1935)," *Zhongyang yanjiuyuan jindaishisuo jikan*, no. 18, pp. 189–219.

Shi Zhongyi (1933) *Jiu nongcun de xin qixiang* (New atmosphere in an old village), Suzhou: Zhongguo jidujiao qingnianhui suzhou fenhui (Suzhou Branch, YMCA of China).

Shi Zhongyi (1936) "Village life in my rural service," in Xu Baoqian (ed.) *Nongcun gongzhuo jingyan* (Experiences in rural work), pp. 40–45. Shanghai: YMCA Press.

Shih, James C. (1992) *Chinese Rural Society in Transition: A Case Study of the Lake Tai Area, 1368–1800*, Berkeley, CA: University of California Press.

Shunyi xian zhi (Gazetteer of Shunyi County) (1933) Taibei: Chengwen chubanshe.

Skinner, G. William (1971) "Chinese Peasants and the Closed Community: An Open and Shut Case," *Comparative Studies in Society and History*, 13.3: 270–281.

Skinner, G. William (1977a) "Regional Urbanization in Nineteenth-century China," in G. William Skinner (ed.) *The City in Late Imperial China*, pp. 211–252.

Skinner, G. William (1977b) *The City in Late Imperial China*, Stanford, CA: Stanford University Press.

Smith, Arthur H. (1899) *Village Life in China: A Study in Sociology*, New York: Fleming H. Revell Company.

Songjiang fu xuzhi (Continuation of gazetteer of Songjiang Prefecture) (1975 [1883]) Taibei: Chengwen chubanshe.

Spence, Jonathan D. (1978) *The Death of Women Wang*, Harmondsworth: Penguin Books.

Subei (*Subei kangri genjudi* [The Northern Jiangsu Anti-Japanese Base]) (1989) Ed. Zhonggong Jiangsusheng dangshi gongzuo weiyuanhui, Jiangsusheng dang'an guan (the CCP History Committee of the CCP Jiangsu Provincial Committee and the Jiangsu Archives), Beijing: Zhonggong dangshi ziliao chubanshe.

Sun Haiquan (1990) *"Qingdai qianqi de lijia he baojia* (The *lijia* and *baojia* system in the early Qing)," in *Zhongguo shehui kexueyuan yanjiushengyuan xuebao* (Journal of Graduate School, Chinese Social Science Academy), no.5, pp. 77–80.

Sun Haiquan (1994) *"Lun qingdai cong lijia dao baojia de yanbian* (On the evolution of the lijia system to the *baojia* system during the Qing)," in *Lishi yenjiu*, 2: 59–68.

Sun Jiyuan and Sun Jiayou (1933) *Yige xinnongcun* (A new village), Kaifeng: Zhonghua nongcun cujingshe.

Sun Xiaocun (1934) *"Feichu kejuan zashui baogao* (A report on the abolition of extra taxes and levies)," *Nongcun fuxing weiyuanhui huibao*, no.12, Nanjing.

Sunan (*Sunan kangri genjudi* [The Southern Jiangsu anti-Japanese base]) (1987) Ed. the CCP History Committee of the CCP Jiangsu Provincial Committee and the Jiangsu Archives. 1987. Beijing: Zhonggong dangshi ziliao chubanshe.

Suzhong (*Suzhong kangri genjudi* [The Central Jiangsu Anti-Japanese Base]) (1989) Ed. the CCP History Committee of the CCP Jiangsu Provincial Committee and the Jiangsu Archives, Beijing: Zhonggong dangshi ziliao chubanshe.

Suzhou fu zhi (Gazetteer of Suzhou Prefecture) ([1883] 1970) Taibei: Chengwen chubanshe.

Tanaka Tadao (1930) *Kakumei shina noson no jissho-teki kenkyo* (A concrete factual study of the Chinese village in revolution), Tokyo: Shujinsha.

Tanaka Tadao (1936) *Kindai Shina noson no hokai to nomin toso* (The collapse of the countryside and peasant resistances in modern China), Tokyo: Taizanbo.

Tang Chenglie "*Guochao fuyi zhizhi xu* (Preface of the taxation system of the Qing)," in JSXB, vol. 34

Tao Xu (1884). *Zuhe* (Investigation of rents), in Suzuki Tomoo (1977) *Kindai Chugoku noson shakaishi kenkyu* (Study of modern China's rural social history), 195–268, Tokyo: Kyuko shoin.

Tao Zhicheng, Yang Leshui and Mei Rukai (1951) "*Zuzhan, xuexing de shouzu jiqi* (The rent bursary, a bloody machine for rent collection)," in Renmin chubanshe bianjibu (ed.) *Xinqu tudi gaige qian de nongcun* (The newly liberated area before land reform), 177–22.

Tengxian xuzhigao (A draft continuation of the gazetteer of Tengxian County) (1968 [1911]) Taibei: Chengwen chubanshe.

Thaxton, Ralph A. Jr. (1997) *Salt of the Earth: The Political Origins of Peasant Protest and Communist Revolution in China*, Berkeley, CA: University of California Press.

Tiedemann, R.G. (1997) "Communist Revolution and Peasant Mobilisation in the Hinterland of North China: The Early Years," *Modern Asian Studies*, vol. 31, pp. 132–152.

Tilly, Charles (ed.) (1975a) *The Formation of National States in Western Europe*, Princeton, NJ: Princeton University Press.

Tilly, Charles (1975b) "Revolution and Collective Violence," *Handbook of Political Science*, 3: 483–555.

Tong Shigao (1962 [1921]) *Qianmentang xiang zhi* (Gazetteer of Qianmentang township), Shanghai: Shanghai wenguanhui.

Tönnies, Ferdinand ([1887] 1957) *Community and Society*, East Lansing, MI: Michigan State University Press.

Tudi weiyuanhui (The land committee) (1937) *Quanguo tudi diaocha baogao gangyao* (Abstract of the report on the nationwide investigation of land), Nanjing.

Wakeman, Frederic Jr. and Grant, Carolyn (eds) (1975) *Conflict and Control in Imperial China*, Berkeley, CA: University of California Press.

Wan Guoding, Zhuang Qianghua and Wu Yongming (1971 [1934]) *Jiangsu wujin nantong tianfu diaocha baogao* (Report of survey on the land tax of Wujin and Nantong in Jiangsu), Taibei: Zhuanji wenxue chubanshe.

Wang Shu-hwai (1984) *Modernization in China, 1860–1916: A Regional Study of Social, Political and Economic Change in Kiangsu Province*, Taibei: Academia Sinica.

Wang, Yeh-chien (1973) *Land Taxation in Imperial China, 1750–1911*, Cambridge, MA: Harvard University Press.

Wei Hongyun and Zuo Zhiyuan (1990) *Huabei kangri genjudi shi* (The history of North China anti-Japanese base areas), Beijing: Dang'an chubanshe.

Wou, Odoric Y.K. (1994) *Mobilizing the Masses: Building Revolution in Henan*, Stanford, CA: Stanford University Press.

Wu Shuzi and Zhao Hanjun (eds) (1930) *Xianzheng daquan* (A comprehensive book of county administration), Puyi shuju.

Wu Zhaoxin ([1937] 1965) *Zhongguo shuizhi shi* (A history of Chinese taxation), Taibei: Shangwu yinshuguan.

Wuxian zhi (Gazetteer of Wuxian county) ([1934] 1970) Taibei: Chengwen chubanshe.

XGCJ (*Xiang-Gan geming genjudi caizheng jingji shiliao zhaibian* [Selected materials of financial and economic history of the Hunan-Jiangxi revolutionary base areas]) (1986) Ed. Hunansheng caizhengting (Financial Department of Hunan Provincial Government), Changsha: Hunan remin chubanshe.

Xiangcun jianshe shiyan (Experiments in Rural Reconstruction) (1933–35, 3 vols) ed. Zhang Yuanshan and Xu Shilian, Shanghai: Zhonghua shuju

Xiao Zheng (ed.) (1977) *Minguo ershi niandai Zhongguo dalu tudi wenti ziliao* (Materials on the land problem in mainland China during the 1930s), 200 vols. Taibei: Taibei chengwen chuban youxian gongsi.

Xinsijun huiyi shiliao (The recollections on the New Fourth Army) (ed.) (1990) Ed. Zhongguo renmin jiefangjun lishi ziliao congshu bianshen weiyuanhui (Committee for Compiling Historical Materials of Chinese People's Liberation Army), vol. 1. Beijing: Jiefangjun chubanshe.

XSJ (*Xinsijun he huazhong kangri genjudi shiliao xuan* [Selected historical materials on the New Fourth Army and the central China anti-Japanese bases]) (1982–1984) Ed. Ma Hongwu *et al.*, 7 vols, Shanghai: Shanghai renmin chubanshe.

XTZJ (*Daqing xuantong zhengji shilu* [The true records of the Xuantong period of the Qing]) (1964) Taibei: Hualian chubanshe.

Xu Shuren (1934) "*Banli difang zhizhi de kunnan yu ganxiang* (Difficulties and reflections in the implementation of local self-government)," *Cunzhi*, vol. 3, no.4.

Xu Yinglian, Li Jingxi and Duan Jili (eds) (1935) *Quanguo xiangcun jianshe yundong gaikuang* (A survey of the Rural Reconstruction movement in China), Wuchang: Zhongguo shuju.

Xushuixian xinzhi (A new gazetteer of Xushui County) ([1932] 1976) Taibei: Chengwen chubanshe.

Yan Zhongping (1955) *Zhongguo jindai jingjishi tongji ziliao xuanji* (Selected statistical materials on modern Chinese economic history), Beijing: Kexue chubanshe.

Yang, Martin C. (1945) *A Chinese Village: Taitou, Shantung Province*, New York: Columbia University Press.

Yao Yong (1935) "Yudong xiangcun zuzhi zhi yanjiu (A study on rural organizations in east Henan), unpublished paper from "E-Yu-Wan-Gan sisheng nongcun jingji diaocha chubu baogao di shijiu hao (The preliminary report on the investigation of rural economy in Hubei, Henan, Anhui, and Jiangxi, no.19)." E-Yu-Wan-Gan sisheng nongmin yinhang weituo, Jinling daxue nongxueyuan nongye jingjixi diaocha ji bianzhi, n.p.

Ye Fei (1986) "*Xinsijun douzheng lishi de tedian—zhai xinsijun shiliao congshu bianzhuan gongzhuo huibao huishang de jianghua*, (On the characteristics of the history of the NFA, a speech on the report-back meeting about compilation of source materials of the NFA's history)," *Junshi ziliao*, no.4, pp. 8–9.

Ye Xian'en (ed.) (1992) *Qingdai quyu shehui jingji yanjiu* (Research on regional society and the economy of the Qing), Beijing: Zhonghua shuju.

Yin Zhongcai and Mi Digang (1925) *Zhaichengcun zhi* (The gazetteer of Zhaicheng village), Beijing: Xinzhonghua shuju.

Young, Arthur N. (1971) *China's Nation-Building Effort, 1927–1937: The Financial and Economic Record*, Stanford, CA: Hoover Institution Press.

Yu Zidao, Liu Qikui and Cao Zhenwei (eds) (1985) *Wang Jingwei guomin zhengfu qingxiang yundong* (The campaign of cleaning up the countryside under Wang Jingwei's government), Shanghai: Shanghai renmin chubanshe.

Zelin, Madeleine (1984) *The Magistrate's Tale: Rationalizing Fiscal Reform in Eighteenth-Century Ch'ing China*, Berkeley, CA: University of California Press.

Zeng Guofan (1967) *Zhengwenzhenggong quanji* (The complete works of Zeng Guofan), Taibei: Wenhai chubanshe.

Zhang Donghui *et al.* (1977) Zhongguo gemin giyi quanlu (A complete record of revolutionary uprisings in China) Beijing: Jiefangjun chubanshe.

Zhang Letian (1992) A letter to Chang Liu, 25 December.

Zhang Wentian (1986) *Shenfuxian xingxian nongcun diaocha* (Rural investigation in Shenfu County and Xing County), Beijing: Remin chubanshe.

Zhang Yan, (1992) "Qingdai shouzu jigou jianlun (A brief discussion on rent collection agencies during the Qing)," in Ye Xian'en (ed.) *Qingdai quyu shehui jingji yanjiu*, pp. 975–986.

Zhang Yuanshan and Xu Shilian (eds) (1934) *Xiangcun jianshe shiyan, xiangcun gongzhuo taolunhui minguo ershisan nian shiyue Dingxian jihui gefang gongzuo baogao huibian* (Experiments in Rural Reconstruction: the collection of work reports presented at the conference of rural works in October 1934, Dingxian), Shanghai: Zhonghua shuju.

Zhang Youyi (ed.) (1957) *Zhongguo jindai nongyeshi ziliao, 1927–1937* (Materials on modern Chinese agricultural history, 1927–1937), vol. 3, Beijing: Sanlian shudian.

Zhang Zhongtang (1932) "Yige cunzhuang jizhong zuzhi de yanjiu (A study of several organizations in a village)," *Shehui xuejie*, 6: 229–260.

Zhao Ruheng (1935) (ed.) *Jiangsu sheng jian* (Yearbook of Jiangsu Province), 4 vols, Reprint. Taibei: Chengwen chubanshe, 1983.

Zhao Xiaomin (1990) *Zhongguo tudi gaige shi, 1921–1949* (The history of land reform in China, 1921–1949), Beijing: Renmin chubanshe.

Zhedong (*Zhedong kangri genjudi* [The Eastern Zhejiang anti-Japanese base]) (1987) Ed Zhonggong Zhejiang shengwei dangshi ziliao zhengji yanjiu weiyuanhui, zhejiangsheng dang'anguan (Committee for Collecting Historical Materials, CCP Zhejiang Provincial Committee and the Zhejiang Archives, Beijing: Zhonggong dangshi ziliao chubanshe.

Zhejiang (Zhengjiangsheng difang zizhi zhuanxiu xuexiao) (ed.) (1934) *Difang zizhi ziliao* (Materials on local self-government), n.p.

Zheng Kangmo (1977 [1933]) *Zhejiang erwu jianzu zhi yanjiu* (Study of the 25 percent rent reduction in Zhejiang), in Xiao Zheng (ed.) vol. 65, Taibei: Chengwen chubanshe.

Zheng Qidong (2004) *Zhuanxingqi de Huabei nongcun shehui* (Rural North China in transition), Shanghai: Shanghai shudian chubanshe.

Zheng Shijun (1977) *Sishui tianfu yanjiu* (A study of land taxation in Sishui county), in Xiao Zheng (ed.) vol. 13, Taibei: Chengwen chubanshe.

Zhengde huating xian zhi (Gazetteer of Shanghai of Zhengde reign) (1521) n.p.

Zhenze xian zhi (Gazetteer of Zhenzhe County) ([1746] 1970) Taibei: Chengwen chubanshe.

Zhongguo nongcun jingji yanjiuhui (Research Association for Chinese Rural Economy) (ed.) (1936) *Zhongguo nongcun miaoxie* (Sketches of the Chinese countryside), Shanghai: Xinzhi shudian.

Zhongyang dang'anguan, Zhongguo di'er lishi dang'anguan, and Jilin Academy of Social Sciences (eds) (1995) *Ri wang de qingxiang* (The mopping up the countryside by Japanese and Wang [Jingwei's puppet government]), Beijin: Zhonghua shuju.

Zhongyang daxue jingji ziliaoshi (ed.) (1935) *Tianfu fujiashui diaocha* (Investigation of land surcharges). Shanghai: Shangwu yinshuguan.

Zhou Qiren (1992) "Tenant game: an economic-demographic behavior pattern, a case study of Dabeiguan village in the 1930s," unpublished paper, University of California at Los Angeles.

Zhu Dexin (1994) *Ershi shiji sansishi niandai Henan jidong baojia zhidu yanjiu* (A study of the *baojia* system in Henan and Eastern Hebei during the 1930s and 1940s), Beijing: Zhongguo shehui kexue chubanshe.

Zhu Hanguo and Wang Yinhuan (2004) *Huabei nongcun de shehui wenti, 1928 zhi1937* (Social problems in rural North China, 1928–1937), Beijing: Beijing Normal University Press.

Zhu Huisheng (ed.) (1988) *Zhonghua minguo nongye shiliao* (Materials on the agrarian history of Republican China), vol. 1, *Tudi gaige shiliao* (Historical materials of land reform), Taibei: Guoshiguan.

Zhu Xiaolong ([1936] 1966) *Pinghu tianzhi gaige went* (On the reform of the land system in Pinghu county), in Xiao Zheng, vol. 73, Taibei: Chengwen chubanshe.

Index

For Product Safety Concerns and Information please contact our EU
representative GPSR@taylorandfrancis.com
Taylor & Francis Verlag GmbH, Kaufingerstraße 24, 80331 München, Germany

www.ingramcontent.com/pod-product-compliance
Lightning Source LLC
Chambersburg PA
CBHW050411280326
41932CB00013BA/1822